W9-ABH-625

Shakespeare's Tragedies

Blackwell Guides to Criticism
Editor Michael O'Neill

The aim of this new series is to provide undergraduates pursuing literary studies with collections of key critical work from an historical perspective. At the same time emphasis is placed upon recent and current work. In general, historic responses of importance are described and represented by short excerpts in an introductory narrative chapter. Thereafter landmark pieces and cutting edge contemporary work are extracted or provided in their entirety according to their potential value to the student. Each volume seeks to enhance enjoyment of literature and to widen the individual student's critical repertoire. Critical approaches are treated as 'tools', rather than articles of faith, to enhance the pursuit of reading and study. At a time when critical bibliographies seem to swell by the hour and library holdings to wither year by year, Blackwell's *Guides to Criticism* series offers students privileged access to and careful guidance through those writings that have most conditioned the historic current of discussion and debate as it now informs contemporary scholarship.

Published volumes

Shakespeare's Tragedies

Edited by Emma Smith

Blackwell
Publishing

Copyright © Blackwell Publishing Ltd 2004
Editorial material, selection and arrangement © Emma Smith 2004

350 Main Street, Malden, MA 02148-5018, USA
108 Cowley Road, Oxford OX4 1JF, UK
550 Swanston Street, Carlton South, Melbourne, Victoria 3053, Australia
Kurfürstendamm 57, 10707 Berlin, Germany

The right of Emma Smith to be identified as the Author of the Editorial
Material in this Work has been asserted in accordance with the UK Copyright,
Designs, and Patents Act 1988.

All rights reserved. No part of this publication may be reproduced, stored in a
retrieval system, or transmitted, in any form or by any means, electronic,
mechanical, photocopying, recording or otherwise, except as permitted by the
UK Copyright, Designs, and Patents Act 1988, without the prior permission
of the publisher.

First published 2004 by Blackwell Publishing Ltd

Library of Congress Cataloging-in-Publication Data

Shakespeare's tragedies / edited by Emma Smith.
     p.   cm. – (Blackwell guides to criticism)
   Includes bibliographical references and index.
   ISBN 0-631-22009-7 (alk. paper) – ISBN 0-631-22010-0 (pbk. : alk. paper)
   1. Shakespeare, William, 1564–1616 – Tragedies.   2. Tragedy.   I. Smith,
Emma, 1970–   II. Series.

PR2983 .S4499 2003
822.3'3 – dc21   2002038280

A catalogue record for this title is available from the British Library.

Set in 10 on 12.5 pt Caslon
by SNP Best-set Typesetter Ltd., Hong Kong
Printed and bound in the United Kingdom
by MPG Books Ltd, Bodmin, Cornwall

For further information on
Blackwell Publishing, visit our website:
http://www.blackwellpublishing.com

Contents

Acknowledgements

The editor and publisher gratefully acknowledge the following for permission to reproduce copyright material:

Cavell, Stanley, '*Coriolanus* and Interpretations of Politics', pp. 143–78, in *Disowning Knowledge in Six Plays of Shakespeare* copyright © 1987 Cambridge University Press; Cox, Brian, '*Titus Andronicus*', pp. 174–88, from Russell Jackson and Robert Smallwood, *Players of Shakespeare 3* copyright © 1993 Cambridge University Press; Dollimore, Jonathan, 'Radical Tragedy: Religion, Ideology and Power in the Drama of Shakespeare and his Contemporaries', 2nd edn, chapter 12: *King Lear*, pp. 189–203, Harvester Wheatsheaf (1984), reprinted by kind permission of the author; Evans, Malcolm, *Signifying Nothing*, pp. 113–41, copyright © 1989 Malcolm Evans, reprinted by permission of Pearson Education Ltd; Holland, Peter, 'The Resources of Characterization in *Othello*', from *Shakespeare Survey 41*, pp. 119–32 copyright © 1982 Cambridge University Press, reprinted by permission of Cambridge University Press and the author; Kahn, Coppélia, 'The Daughter's Seduction in *Titus Andronicus*', in *Roman Shakespeare*, pp. 47–76 (1997), Routledge; Kastan, David Scott, '*Macbeth* and the "Name of King"': copyright 1999 from *Shakespeare after Theory* by David Scott Kastan. Reproduced by permission of Routledge, Inc., part of The Taylor and Francis Group; Kermode, Frank: Excerpt from SHAKESPEARE'S LANGUAGE 2000 by Frank Kermode. Copyright © 2000 by Frank Kermode. Reprinted by permission of Farrar, Straus and Giroux, LLC. Reproduced by permission of Penguin Books Ltd; Leverenz, David, 'The Woman in Hamlet: An Interpersonal View', from *Signs: Journal of Women in Culture and Society* 4: 2, pp. 110–28, 1978, University of Chicago Press; Loehlin, James N., '"These Violent Delights Have Violent Ends": Baz Luhrmann's Millennial Shakespeare', from *Shakespeare, Film, Fin de Siècle* (eds Mark Thornton Burnett and Ramona Wray), pp. 89–101, copyright © 2000 Macmillan Press Ltd, reproduced with permission of Palgrave; Marcus, Leah S., 'Bad Taste and Bad *Hamlet*', from *Unediting the Renaissance*, pp. 132–52, Routledge (1996), used by kind permission of the author; Newman, Karen, 'Fashioning Femininity and English Renaissance Drama', copyright © 1991 the University of Chicago; Warren, Michael J., 'Quarto and Folio *King Lear* and the Interpretation of Albany and Edgar', pp. 95–107, from *Shakespeare, Pattern of Excelling Nature* (ed. David Bevington and Jay L. Halio), 1978, reprinted by permission of Associated University Presses, Inc; Wilson, Richard: 'Is This a Holiday from Shakespeare's Roman Carnival?' *English Literary History* 54 (1987), pp. 110–128. © The Johns Hopkins University Press. Reprinted by permission of the Johns Hopkins University Press; Q1 'To be or not to be' (1603), reproduced by permission of the Henry E. Huntington Library, San Marino, California.

The publishers apologize for any errors or omissions in the above list and would be grateful to be notified of any corrections that should be incorporated in the next edition or reprint of this book.

Introduction

This Guide to Criticism has two purposes. First, it offers a narrative overview of pre-twentieth-century responses to Shakespeare's tragedies, including generous extracts from major commentators. Part I ends with the influential contribution of A. C. Bradley's *Shakespearean Tragedy*, first published in 1904. In Part II twentieth-century criticism is divided into thematic sections: 'Genre', 'Character', 'Language', 'Gender and Sexuality', 'History and Politics', 'Texts' and 'Performance'. Each of these sections includes a short overview of criticism in the area, and then reprints in full two significant recent articles or chapters. Thus the Guide stands in itself as a substantial critical history and collection of recent criticism, reprinted in a single volume for ease of reference. Second, through the overview introductions to each section, and through the extensive Further Reading sections, the Guide also offers those readers who have access to further critical reading some suggestions about how to navigate the great sea of secondary literature on Shakespeare, by indicating key debates or interventions in the critical history. It is not, nor could it be, definitive or exhaustive, nor is it intended to canonize those authors and arguments included; rather it is intended to be indicative of the range and vitality of Shakespearean criticism over 400 years, from the earliest sixteenth-century responses to the new playwright up to the end of the twentieth century.

Emma Smith
Hertford College, Oxford

Part I

Criticism 1590–1904

1

Before Bradley: Criticism 1590–1904

1590–1660: Early Assessments

Contemporary mentions of Shakespeare are thin on the ground. It's striking – and salutary – for an historical account of early Shakespearean criticism to have its originating point in Robert Greene's disparaging remark about the young playwright as 'an upstart Crow, beautified with our feathers' (1592), but perhaps Greene's animosity was prompted by emerging jealousy of the newcomer's literary powers. By the time Shakespeare's narrative poems *Venus and Adonis* (1593) and *The Rape of Lucrece* (1594) had been published, however, their author was routinely included in lists of eminent Elizabethan authors. Francis Meres' commonplace book *Palladis Tamia* (1598) praises Shakespeare's generic versatility:

> As *Plautus* and *Seneca* are accounted the best for Comedy and Tragedy among the Latins so Shakespeare among the English is the most excellent in both kinds for the stage; for comedy witness his *Gentlemen of Verona*, his *Errors*, his *Loves Labours Lost*, his *Loves Labours Won*, his *Midsummer Night's Dream* and his *Merchant of Venice*: for tragedy his *Richard the 2. Richard the 3. Henry the 4, King John, Titus Andronicus* and his *Romeo and Juliet*. (Meres, 1598, p. 282)

In a jesting preface to his poem *Diaphantus* (1604), Anthony Scolokar identifies the characteristics of good writing:

> It should be like the never-too-well read *Arcadia* where the prose and verse, matter and words, are like his Mistress's eyes one still excelling another and without corival: or to come home to the vulgar's element, like friendly Shakespeare's tragedies, where the comedian rides when the tragedian stands on tiptoe: faith, it should please all, like Prince Hamlet. (Scolokar, 1604, sig. A2)

Scolokar's enjoyment of the play's generic mixture identifies and valorizes an aspect which was to be so offensive to neoclassical critics later in the century.

Other scattered references in the period exist, but the first substantial act of memorializing and of shaping Shakespeare's critical reputation was the publication in 1623 of a substantial folio volume collecting together thirty-six plays as *Mr William Shakespeares Comedies, Histories and Tragedies* (often known as the First Folio, or abbreviated to F). The title of the work reveals one of its most significant critical legacies: in dividing the plays into three genres in its catalogue, the First Folio established the critical categories still in use today: 'comedies', 'histories' and 'tragedies'. Thus the plays listed as tragedies in 1623 are, in their order, *The Tragedy of Coriolanus, Titus Andronicus, Romeo and Juliet, Timon of Athens, The Life and Death of Julius Caesar, The Tragedy of Macbeth, The Tragedy of Hamlet, King Lear, Othello, The Moore of Venice, Antony and Cleopatra, Cymbeline, King of Britain*. *Troilus and Cressida* is not listed in the catalogue, although the play does appear in the volume between the last history play, *Henry VIII*, and the first tragedy, *Coriolanus*.

John Heminges and Henry Condell, Shakespeare's fellow-actors and the men responsible for the publishing of his collected plays, addressed their prefatory epistle 'To the Great Variety of Readers':

> It had been a thing, we confess, worthy to have been wished, that the Author himself had lived to have set forth, and overseen his own writings; But since it hath been ordained otherwise, and he by death departed from that right, we pray you do not envy his Friends, the office of their care, and pain, to have collected and published them; and so to have published them, as where (before) you were abused with diverse stolen, and surreptitious copies, maimed, and deformed by the frauds and stealths of injurious impostors, that exposed them: even those, are now offered to your view cured, and perfect of their limbs; and all the rest, absolute in their numbers, as he conceived them. Who, as he was a happy imitator of Nature, was a most gentle expresser of it. His mind and hand went together: And what he thought, he uttered with that easiness, that we have scarce received from him a blot in his papers. But it is not our province, who only gather his works, and give them you, to praise him. It is yours that read him. And there we hope, to your diverse capacities, you will find enough, both to draw, and hold you: for his wit can no more lie hid, than it could be lost. Read him, therefore; and again, and again: And if then you do not like him, surely you are in some manifest danger, not to understand him. And so we leave you to other of his Friends, whom if you need, can be your guides: if you need them not, you can lead yourselves, and others. And such Readers we wish him. (Shakespeare, 1623)

The playwright Ben Jonson contributed an elegy:

Thou art a monument, without a tomb,
And art alive still, while thy book doth live,
And we have wits to read, and praise to give.
That I not mix thee so, my brain excuses;
I mean with great, but disproportioned Muses:
For, if I thought my judgement were of years,
I should commit thee surely with thy peers,
And tell, how far thou didst our Lyly out-shine,
Or sporting Kyd, or Marlowe's mighty line.
And though thou hadst small Latin, and less Greek,
From thence to honour thee, I would not seek
For names; but call forth thundering Æschylus,
Euripides, and Sophocles to us,
Paccuvius, Accius, him of Cordova dead,
To life again, to hear thy buskin tread,
And shake a stage: Or, when thy socks were on,
Leave thee alone, for the comparison
Of all, that insolent Greece, or haughty Rome
Sent forth, or since did from their ashes come.
Triumph, my Britain, thou hast one to show,
To whom all Scenes of Europe homage owe.
He was not of an age, but for all time!
And all the Muses still were in their prime,
When like Apollo he came forth to warm
Our ears, or like a Mercury to charm!
Nature herself was proud of his designs,
And joyed to wear the dressing of his lines!

In his *Timber, or Discoveries*, first published in 1640, Jonson again addressed Shakespeare's reputation, referring back to Heminge and Condell's 'To the Great Variety of Readers':

I remember the players have often mentioned it as an honour to Shakespeare, that in his writing, whatsoever to be penned, he never blotted out line. My answer hath been, 'Would he had blotted a thousand'; which they thought a malevolent speech. I had not told posterity this but for their ignorance, who choose that circumstance to commend their friend by wherein he most faulted; and to justify mine own candour: for I loved the man, and do honour his memory, on this side idolatry, as much as any. He was, indeed, honest, and of an open and free nature; had an excellent fantasy, brave notions, and gentle expressions; wherein he flowed with that facility that sometime it was necessary he should be stopped. '*sufflaminandus erat*' ['Sometimes he needed the brake'], as Augustus said of Haterius. His wit was in his own power, would the rule of it had been so too. Many times he fell into those things, could not escape laughter: as when he said in the person of Caesar, one speaking to him, 'Caesar, thou dost me wrong'; he replied 'Caesar did never wrong, but with just cause'; and such like: which were ridiculous. But he redeemed his vices with his virtues. There was ever more in him to be praised than to be pardoned. (Donaldson, 1985, pp. 539–40)

1660–1720: Texts in Print and on Stage

It is to post-Restoration culture that we need to look to see the establishment of many now-familiar preoccupations and approaches to Shakespeare. As Michael Dobson notes, in his study of the 'extensive cultural work that went into the installation of Shakespeare as England's National Poet' between 1660 and 1769:

> so many of the conceptions of Shakespeare we inherit date not from the Renaissance but from the Enlightenment. It was this period, after all, which initiated many of the practices which modern spectators and readers of Shakespeare would generally regard as normal or even natural: the performance of his female roles by women instead of men (instigated at a revival of *Othello* in 1660); the reproduction of his works in scholarly editions, with critical apparatus (pioneered by Rowe's edition of 1709 and the volume of commentary appended to it by Charles Gildon the following year); the publication of critical monographs devoted entirely to the analysis of his works (an industry founded by John Dennis's *An Essay upon the Writings and Genius of Shakespeare*, 1712); the promulgation of the plays in secondary education (the earliest known instance of which is the production of *Julius Caesar* mounted in 1728 'by the young Noblemen of the Westminster School'), and in higher education (first carried out in the lectures on Shakespeare given by William Hawkins at Oxford in the early 1750s); the erection of monuments to Shakespeare in nationally symbolic public places (initiated by Peter Sheemaker's statue in Poets' Corner, Westminster Abbey, unveiled in 1741); and the promotion of Stratford-upon-Avon as a site of secular pilgrimage (ratified at Garrick's jubilee in 1769). (Dobson, 1992, p. 3)

Ben Jonson's half-praise, half-sneer in his epitaph about Shakespeare's classical knowledge – 'small latin and less greek' – was an early suggestion of one of the obstacles to Shakespeare appreciation in post-Restoration culture. The Restoration aesthetics of neoclassicism favoured poetry as imitation of Classical, especially Roman, authors, and the idea of the writer as educated craftsman following ancient generic rules. Thus Thomas Fuller identifies Shakespeare among *The Worthies of England* in 1662, but is preoccupied with his subject's education, or lack of it:

> *Plautus*, who was an exact Comædian, yet never any Scholar, as our Shakespeare (if alive) would confess himselfe. Adde to all these, that though his Genius gen-

erally was *jocular*, and inclining him to *festivity*, yet he could, (when so disposed), be *solemn* and *serious*, as appears by his Tragedies, so that *Heraclitus* himself (I mean if secret and unseen) might afford to smile at his Comedies, they were so *merry*, and *Democritus* scarce forbear to sigh at his Tragedies they were so *mournfull*. He was an eminent instance of the truth of that Rule, *Poeta no fit, sed nascitur*, one is not *made* but *born* a Poet. Indeed his Learning was very little, so that as *Cornish diamonds* are not polished by any Lapidary, but are pointed and smoothed even as they are taken out of the Earth, so *nature* it self was all the *art* that was used upon him. (Fuller, 1662, p. 126)

The introduction of nature as a term of cultural valorization to balance against art is key to the recuperation of Shakespeare in this period. When, for example, Margaret Cavendish defends Shakespeare in one of her *Sociable Letters* of 1664, she argues that it is the vitality of his characters that is crucial to his success:

> So well he hath expressed in his plays all sorts of persons, as one would think he had been transformed into every one of those persons he hath described; and as sometimes one would think he was really himself the clown or jester he feigns, so one would think, he was also the King and Privy Counsellor [. . .] nay, one would think he had been metamorphosed from a man to a woman, for who could describe Cleopatra better than he hath done? (Thompson and Roberts, 1997, pp. 12–13)

Early in this process of recuperating Shakespeare is John Dryden's important statement of neoclassical aesthetics, *An Essay Of Dramatic Poesie* of 1668. Dryden's essay takes the form of a discussion between four interlocutors: Eugenius, Crites, Lisedeius and Neander, generally believed to represent Dryden himself. While others of the conversationalists praise Ben Jonson as 'the greatest man of the last age' because of his adherence to classical rules, particularly the unities of time, place and action (p. 14), Neander favours Shakespeare for his untutored but instinctive, intuitive expression. Shakespeare is to be praised for his natural learning, despite his flaws:

> he was the man who of all Modern, and perhaps Ancient Poets, had the largest and most comprehensive soul. All the Images of Nature were still present to him, and he drew them not laboriously but luckily: when he describes anything, you more than see it, you feel it too. Those who accuse him to have wanted learning, give him the greater commendation: he was naturally learn'd; he needed not the spectacles of Books to read Nature; he look'd inwards, and found her there. (Dryden, 1969, pp. 47–8)

In the comparison with Ben Jonson which was to be the touchstone for the nascent literary criticism of Shakespeare in the Restoration period, Neander's emotional loyalties were clear: 'If I would compare [Jonson] with *Shakespeare*, I must acknowledge him the more correct Poet, but *Shakespeare* the greater wit. *Shakespeare* was the *Homer*, or Father of our Dramatick Poets; *Johnson* was the *Virgil*, the pattern of elaborate writing; I admire him, but I love *Shakespeare*.' (p. 50)

Whereas Dryden's Neander can forgive Shakespeare his perceived failings and acknowledge his appeal to feeling, Thomas Rymer was much more intransigent. Rymer, an archaeologist and literary scholar, was convinced of the aesthetic value of the classical unities and, indeed, wrote his own unperformed rhyming play, *Edgar, or the English Monarch: an Heroick Tragedy*, which observed these rules precisely. Rymer's *A Short View of Tragedy; It's Original, Excellency, and corruption. With Some Reflections on Shakespear, and other Practitioners for the Stage* (1693) is remarkable for its devastating account of Shakespeare's *Othello*: 'So much ado, so much stress, so much passion and repetition about an Handkerchief! Why was not this call'd the *Tragedy of the Handkerchief?*' (Rymer, 1970, p. 139).

For Rymer, the play violates decorum in several ways. For one thing, Rymer argues, Othello's race makes it preposterous that he would be in so powerful a position in the state, and that Desdemona would ever have consented to marry him:

> The Character of that State [Shakespeare's Venice] is to employ strangers in their Wars. But shall a Poet thence fancy that they will set a Negro to be their General; or trust a *Moor* to defend them against the *Turk*? With us a Black-a-moor might rise to be a Trumpeter; but *Shakespear* would not have him less than a Lieutenant-General. With us, a *Moor* might marry some little drab, or Small-coal Wench; *Shakespear*, would provide him with the Daughter and Heir of some great Lord or Privy-Councellor: And all the Town should reckon it a very suitable match [. . . .] Nothing is more odious in Nature than an improbable lye; And, certainly, never was any play fraught, like this of *Othello*, with improbabilities. (pp. 91–2)

Rymer finds Othello's character insufficiently noble to carry the tragedy: '*Othello* shows nothing of the Souldier's Mettle: but like a tedious, drawling, tame goose, is gaping after any paultrey insinuation, labouring to be jealous; And catching at every blown surmise' (p. 120). He finds fault with the play's failure to observe the unities of place, and with Shakespeare's language. He also criticizes the moral temper of the play by extracting from it ludicrous maxims:

> First, This may be a caution to all Maidens of Quality how, without their Parents consent, they run away with Blackamoors. [. . .]

Secondly, This may be a warning to all good Wives, that they look well to their Linnen.

Thirdly, This may be a lesson to husbands, that before their jealousie be Tragical, the proofs may be Mathematical. (p. 89)

Rather than providing a moral framework for the instruction of its audiences, the play calls morality into question. Whereas for twentieth-century critics this troubling interrogation of received ideas would become one of Shakespeare's most significant qualities, for Rymer it is to be deplored:

What can remain with the Audience to carry home with them from this sort of Poetry, for their use and edification? how can it work, unless (instead of settling the mind, and purging our passions) to delude our senses, disorder our thoughts, addle our brain, pervert our affections, hair our imaginations, corrupt our appetite, and fill our head with vanity, confusion, *Tintamarre* and jingle-jangle. (p. 146)

Rymer concludes that the play is 'none other, than a Bloody Farce' (p. 146), and that '*Shakepears* genius lay for Comedy and Humour. In Tragedy he appears quite out of his element' (p. 156).

In his preface to the first scholarly edition of Shakespeare's works (1709–10), the poet laureate and tragedian Nicholas Rowe advocates a more historically informed appreciation of Shakespeare's apparent divergence from Classical precepts:

If one undertook to examine the greatest part of these [Shakespeare's tragedies] by those rules which are established by Aristotle, and taken from the model of the Grecian stage, it would be no very hard task to find a great many faults: but as Shakespear lived under a kind of mere light of nature, and had never been made acquainted with the regularity of those written precepts, so it would be hard to judge him by a law he knew nothing of. We are to consider him as a man that lived in a state of almost universal license and ignorance: there was no established judge, but every one took the liberty to write according to the dictates of his own fancy. (p. xxvi)

Rowe argues that writing outside the constraints of literary tradition allows Shakespeare's imagination free rein:

I believe we are better pleased with those thoughts, altogether new and uncommon, which his own imagination supplied him so abundantly with, than if he had given us the most beautiful passages out of the Greek and Latin poets, and that in the most agreeable manner that it was possible for a master of the English language to deliver them. (p. iv)

He also recognizes the generic hybridity of many, even the majority, of Shakespeare's plays:

> His plays are properly to be distinguished only into comedies and tragedies. Those which are called histories, and even some of his comedies, are really tragedies, with a run or mixture of comedy amongst them. That way of tragi-Comedy was the common mistake of that age, and is indeed become so agreeable to the English Taste, that though the severer critics among us cannot bear it, yet the generality of our audiences seem to be better pleased with it than with an exact tragedy. (p. xvii)

A final seventh volume appended to the series in 1710 added a more extensive critique of the dramatic qualities of the plays, in 'An Essay on the Art, Rise and Progress of the Stage in Greece, Rome and England' by Charles Gildon. Through his evaluation of Shakespeare, Gildon attempts the twin task of educating his readers' literary tastes more generally, proposing a definition of tragedy which draws extensively on Aristotelian ideas, but disagreeing with Rymer's conclusions:

> in spite of his known and visible errors, when I read Shakespear, even in some of his most irregular plays, I am surprised into a pleasure so great, that my judgment is no longer free to see the faults, though they are never so gross and evident. There is such a witchery in him, that all the rules of art, which he does not observe, though built on an equally solid and infallible reason, vanish away in the transports of those, that he does observe, so entirely, as if I had never known any thing of the matter. (p. iv)

Gildon suggests that Shakespeare's women were less satisfactory than his male characters – an early intervention into the debate about Shakespeare and gender representation (see chapter 2: Gender).

> It must be owned that Shakespear drew men better, than women; to whom indeed he has seldom given any considerable place in his plays; here and in Romeo and Juliet he has done most in this matter, but here he has not given any graceful touches to Desdemona in many places of her part. (p. 411)

Like Rymer he is disturbed at the apparent amorality of the conclusions of Shakespeare's tragedies, particularly *King Lear*:

> The King and Cordelia ought by no means to have died, and therefore Mr Tate has very justly altered that particular, which must disgust the reader and audience to have virtue and piety meet so unjust a reward. So that this plot, though of so celebrated a play, has none of the ends of tragedy moving neither fear nor

pity. We rejoice at the death of the Bastard and the two sisters, as of monsters in nature under whom the very earth must groan. And we see with horror and indignation the death of the King, Cordelia and Kent; though of the three the King only could move pity if that were not lost in the indignation and horror the death of the other two produces, for he is a truly tragic character not supremely virtuous nor scandalously vicious, he is made up of choler, and obstinacy, frailties pardonable enough in an old man, and yet what drew on him all the misfortunes of his life. (p. 406)

In the end, Gildon's view of Shakespeare is mixed:

Shakespear is indeed stor'd with a great many Beauties, but they are in a heap of Rubbish; and as in the Ruines of a magnificent Pile we are pleas'd with the Capitals of Pillars, the Basso-relievos and the like as we meet with them, yet how infinitely more beautiful, and charming must it be to behold them in their proper Places in the standing Building, where every thing answers the other, and one Harmony of all the Parts heightens the Excellence even of those Parts. (p. 425)

Gildon expanded this view in his book *The Complete Art of Poetry* (1718), in which the final chapter offers 'Shakespeariana: or Select Moral Reflections, topicks, Similies and Descriptions from Shakespear' – the first book of Shakespearean quotations.

It's easy to see how this idea of a Shakespeare good in parts also reflects contemporary stage practice. What Gildon is attempting critically – the sifting of worthy from unworthy elements of the plays – scores of stage-plays attempted dramatically, in adapting, rewriting and recombining Shakespeare's works to suit the tastes of new audiences. These adaptations are themselves works of criticism, often, in prefatory material and epilogues, explicitly so. John Dryden's preface to his reworking of *Antony and Cleopatra* as *All for Love* (1677) claims that his play 'imitate[s] the Divine Shakespeare' but does not copy 'servilely.: Words and Phrases must of necessity receive a change in succeeding Ages: but 'tis almost a Miracle that much of his Language remains so pure' (Vickers, 1974, I, p. 164). Edward Ravenscroft's *Titus Andronicus, Or the Rape of Lavinia . . . A Tragedy* (1687) condemned Shakespeare's play as 'the most incorrect and indigested piece in all his Works; It seems rather a heap of Rubbish than a Structure'(Vickers, 1974, I, p. 239), despite making relatively few changes until the final scene. Such adaptations also reveal many of the same critical judgements and preoccupations as the emerging literary scholarship on Shakespeare. Thus John Dryden adapts *Troilus and Cressida* in 1679 in order to 'correct' a tragedy Dryden sees as one of Shakespeare's earlier and less accomplished works (it is now generally dated to the period 1602–3). Dryden notes that the play fails on moral and aesthetic grounds: 'the later part of the Tragedy is nothing but a confusion of Drums and Trumpets, Excursions and Alarms. The chief persons, who give name to the Tragedy, are left alive: *Cressida* is false, and is not punish'd' (Vickers, 1974, I, p. 251). In order to rectify these perceived errors, Dryden announces 'the whole Fifth Act, both the Plot and the Writing, are my own Additions' (p. 251). The seal of approval on his changes is implied by the scripting of a patriotic prologue spoken by Shakespeare's ghost. Nahum Tate's version of *King Lear*, his *The History of King Lear* (1681), opens with a sententious Prologue warning 'Morals were alwaies proper for the Stage, / But are ev'n necessary in this Age' (Vickers, 1974, I, p. 346), thus implicitly endorsing Gildon's criticism about the cruel ending of Shakespeare's play. Tate rewrites a play rather closer to Shakespeare's source *The True Chronicle History of King Leir and his three Daughters* (1605), which ends with Lear retiring with Kent to 'pass our short reserves of Time / In calm Reflections on our Fortunes past, / Cheer'd with relation of the prosperous Reign / Of this celestial Pair' (p. 385) – the newly-wed sovereigns of ancient Britain, Cordelia and Edgar. In part this adaptation counters the questions about Shakespeare's aesthetics, but it also adapts this play of a king restored to his throne to the specific political tenor of the 1680s, as Nancy Klein Maguire's article in Marsden (1991) demonstrates. Similar political motives can be seen at work in Thomas Otway's rewriting of the plot of *Romeo and Juliet* crossed with the politics of *Coriolanus*, *Carius Marius* (first performed 1680) in which the fated lovers, Marius and Lavinia, are separated by political differences between their fathers in republican Rome.

John Dennis, who adapted *Coriolanus* as *The Invader of his Country, or the Fatal Resentment* (1705), also wrote an extensive criticism of Shakespeare in his *An Essay on the Genius and Writings of Shakespear*, published in 1712. Following previous commentators, Dennis counters the obstacle of Shakespeare's lack of scholarship with an appeal to nature, and makes a particular feature of Shakespeare's characterization and his emotional draw:

> He had so fine a Talent for touching the Passions, and they are so lively in him, and so truly in Nature, that they often touch is more without their due Preparations, than those of other Tragick Poets, who have all the Beauty of Design and all the Advantage of Incidents. His Master-Passion was Terror, which he has often mov'd so powerfully and so wonderfully, that we may justly conclude, that if he had had the Advantage of Art and Learning, he wou'd have surpass'd the very best and strongest of the Ancients. (Dennis, 1712, p. 2)

Dennis suggests that we can only begin to imagine what Shakespeare's plays might have been had their author 'join'd to so happy a Genius Learning' (p. 3). But the absence of this knowledge has led him into aesthetic error:

Shakespear has been wanting in the exact Distribution of Poetical Justice not only in his *Coriolanus*, but in most of his best Tragedies, in which the Guilty and the Innocent perish promiscuously; as *Duncan* and *Banquo* in *Mackbeth*, as likewise Lady *Macduffe* and her Children; *Desdemona* in *Othello*; *Cordelia*, *Kent*, and King *Lear*, in the Tragedy that bears his Name; *Brutus* and *Porcia* in *Julius Caesar*, and young *Hamlet* in the Tragedy of *Hamlet*. (p. 9)

Despite these lapses, Dennis reverses Rymer's view that Shakespeare was a better comic than tragic writer, arguing: 'Tho' *Shakespear* succeeded very well in Comedy, yet his principal Talent and his chief Delight was Tragedy' (p. 27).

By the second decade of the eighteenth century, therefore, both Shakespearean textual scholarship in the form of Rowe's edition of 1709–10, and literary criticism in the contributions of Rymer, Gildon and Dennis, were both established and contested fields. Divergent impulses towards the canonizing and concretizing of the Shakespearean text on the one hand, and towards disintegration on the other, are key to eighteenth-century approaches.

1720–1765: Editions and Editors

Alexander Pope's edition of 1725 described itself on its title page as 'Collated and Corrected by the former Editions'. Pope's 'Preface of the Editor' evades the task of the critic in favour of that of the new, humanist textual scholar, the editor. Rather than entering 'into a Criticism upon this Author', Pope sets out to 'give an account of the fate of his Works, and the disadvantages under which they have been transmitted to us. We shall hereby extenuate many faults which are his, and clear him from the imputation of many which are not' (Pope, 1725, I, pp. i–ii). Pope acquits Shakespeare of the charges neoclassical critics had laid at his door: 'To judge therefore of Shakespear by Aristotle's rules, is like trying a man by the Laws of one Country, who acted under those of another' (p. vi). Rather, Pope repeats the critical orthodoxy that Shakespeare 'is not so much an Imitator, as an Instrument, of Nature; and 'tis not so just to say that he speaks from her, as that she speaks thro' him' (p. ii), and makes a particular feature of Shakespeare's characterization:

His Characters are so much Nature her self, that 'tis a sort of injury to call them by so distant a name as Copies of her [. . .] Every single character in Shakespear is as much an Individual, as those in Life itself; it is as impossible to find any two alike; and such as from their relation or affinity in any respect appear most to be Twins, will upon comparison be found remarkably distinct. To this life and variety of Character, we must add the wonderful Preservation of it; which is such throughout his plays, that had all the Speeches been printed without the very names of the Persons, I believe one might have apply'd them with certainty to every speaker. (pp. ii–iii)

Pope praises Shakespeare's 'Power over our Passions' (p. iii), and also his intellectual control of 'the coolness of Reflection and Reasoning' (p. iv).

Many of Shakespeare's perceived faults are in fact, Pope proposes, errors of the printing and publication process. He surmises that Shakespeare did not authorize or check those of the plays published in quarto editions during his lifetime, and that therefore:

> how many low and vicious parts and passages might no longer reflect upon this great Genius, but appear unworthily charged upon him? And even in those which are really his, how many faults may have been unjustly laid to his account from arbitrary Additions, Expunctions, Transpositions of scenes and lines, confusion of Characters and Persons, wrong application of Speeches, corruptions of innumerable Passages by the Ignorance, and wrong Corrections of 'em again by the Impertinence, of his first Editors? (p. xxi)

In 1726, a volume appeared with the descriptive title *Shakespeare Restored, or a Specimen of the many errors as well Committed as Unamended by Mr. Pope in his late edition of this poet: designed not only to correct the said Edition, but to restore the true Reading of Shakespeare in all the Editions ever published. By Mr. Theobald.* Its author, Lewis Theobald, proposed numerous new readings and emendations, particularly of *Hamlet*, many of which were plagiarized by Pope for his second edition which appeared in 1728. (A 1971 edition of this title is available.) Pope pilloried Theobald in the first edition of his mock-epic poem the *Dunciad* published a few months later, mocking his pedantry in footnotes wondering whether 'Dunciad' should be spelt 'Dunceiad' and pitying 'hapless Shakespear, yet of Tibbald sore, / Wish'd he had blotted for himself before'. Theobald's riposte was his own Shakespeare edition of 1733, *The works of Shakespeare: in seven volumes. Collated with the Oldest Copies, and Corrected; With notes, Explanatory and Critical.*

Theobald's style is effusive:

> No Age, perhaps, can produce an Author more various from himself, than Shakespeare has been universally acknowledg'd to be. The Diversity in Stile, and other Parts of Composition, so obvious in him, is as variously to be accounted for. His Education, we find, was at best but begun: and he started early into a Science from the Force of Genius, unequally equally assisted by acquir'd Improvements. His Fire, Spirit, and Exuberance of Imagination gave an Impetuosity to his Pen: His Ideas flow'd from him in a Stream rapid, but not turbulent; copious, but not ever overbearing its Shores. The Ease and Sweetness of his Temper might not a little contribute to his Facility in Writing: as his Employ-

ment, as a Player, gave him an Advantage and Habit of fancying himself the very Character he meant to delineate. (Theobald, 1733, I, p. xv)

His view of his predecessor and literary rival Pope is clear; Shakespeare studies has its first real personality clash:

> He has acted with regard to our Author, as an Editor, whom Lipsius mentions, did with regard to Martial; Inventus est nescio quis Popa, qui non vitia ejus, sed ipsum, excîdit. He has attack'd him like an unhandy Slaughterman; and not lopp'd off the Errors, but the Poet.
>
> Praise sometimes an Injury. When this is found to be the Fact, how absurd must appear the Praises of such an Editor? It seems a moot Point, whether Mr. Pope has done most Injury to Shakespeare as his Editor and Encomiast; or Mr. Rymer done him Service as his Rival and Censurer. Were it every where the true Text, which That Editor in his late pompous Edition gave us, the Poet deserv'd not the large Encomiums bestow'd by him: nor, in that Case, is Rymer's Censure of the Barbarity of his Thoughts, and the Impropriety of his Expressions, groundless. They have Both shewn themselves in an equal Impuissance of suspecting or amending the corrupted Passages: and tho' it be neither Prudence to censure, or commend, what one does not understand; yet if a Man must do one when he plays the Critick, the latter is the more ridiculous Office. And by That Shakespeare suffers most. (pp. xxxv–xxxvi)

Theobald's is not, however, the last word in this particular bibliographic and personal spat. In 1747 Pope, together with his collaborator William Warburton, brought out an edition to trump Theobald: *The works of Shakespear in eight volumes. The Genuine Text (collated with all the former Editions, and then corrected and emended) is here settled: Being restored from the Blunders of the first Editors, and the Interpolations of the two Last: with A Comment and Notes, Critical and Explanatory.*

Theobald's edition establishes and promulgates his own theory of the editor's task. This covers three activities: 'the Emendation of corrupt Passages; the Explanation of obscure and difficult ones; and an Inquiry into the Beauties and Defects of Composition' (p. xl). He elaborates on his editorial principles:

> Where-ever the Author's Sense is clear and discoverable, (tho', perchance, low and trivial;) I have not by any Innovation tamper'd with his Text; out of an Ostentation of endeavouring to make him speak better than the old Copies have done.
>
> Where, thro' all the former Editions, a Passage has labour'd under flat Nonsense and invincible Darkness, if, by the Addition or Alteration of a Letter or two, I have restored to Him both Sense and Sentiment, such Corrections, I am persuaded, will need no Indulgence.

And whenever I have taken a greater Latitude and Liberty in amending, I have constantly endeavoured to support my Corrections and Conjectures by parallel Passages and Authorities from himself, the surest Means of expounding any Author whatsoever [. . .] Some Remarks are spent in explaining Passages, where the Wit or Satire depends on an obscure Point of History: Others, where Allusions are to Divinity, Philosophy, or other Branches of Science. Some are added to shew, where there is a Suspicion of our Author having borrow'd from the Antients: Others, to shew where he is rallying his Contemporaries; or where He himself is rallied by them. And some are necessarily thrown in, to explain an obscure and obsolete Term, Phrase, or Idea. (p. xliii–xliv)

Further editions, including those by Hamner and Capell, appeared throughout the eighteenth century as each editor claimed to be improving on the text of his predecessors (see chapter 12: Texts).

Shakespeare's most significant and influential eighteenth-century mediator was editor and critic Samuel Johnson, whose annotated edition appeared in 1765. Johnson sets out 'to inquire, by what peculiarities of excellence *Shakespeare* has gained and kept the favour of his countrymen' (Johnson, 1765, I, p. viii). The answer, for Johnson is that:

Shakespeare is above all writers [. . .] the poet of nature; the poet that holds up to his readers a faithful mirrour of manners and of life. His characters are not modified by the customs of particular places, unpractised by the rest of the world, by the peculiarities of studies or professions, which can operate but on small numbers; or by the accidents of transient fashions or temporary opinions; they are the genuine progeny of common humanity, such as the work will always supply, and observation will always find. His persons act and speak by the influence of those general passions, and the whole system of life is continued in motion. (pp. viii–ix)

For Johnson, Shakespeare is a philosopher and teacher, filled with 'practical axioms and domestick wisdom', but he argues strongly against the recent tendency to find Shakespeare's greatness in particular passages: 'he that tries to recommend him by select quotations, will succeed like the pedant in *Hierocles*, who, when he offered his house to sale, carried a brick in his pocket as a specimen' (p. ix). Verisimilitude, the quality of creating recognizable individuals, dialogue and scenarios, is key to Johnson's appraisal of Shakespeare's work. Thus '*Shakespeare* has no heroes; his scenes are occupied only by men, who act and speak as the reader thinks that he should himself have spoken or acted on the same occasion', he 'approximates the remote, and familiarizes the wonderful', and his reader can benefit from 'reading human sentiments in human language' (pp. xi–xii).

Johnson's approach to Shakespeare's genres is radical:

Shakespeare's plays are not in the rigorous or critical sense either tragedies or comedies, but compositions of a distinct kind, exhibiting the real state of sub-lunary nature, which partakes of good and evil, joy and sorrow, mingled with endless variety of proportion and innumerable modes of combination; and expressing the course of the world, in which the loss of one is the gain of another; in which, at the same time, the reveller is hasting to his wine and the mourner burying his friend; in which the malignity of one is sometimes defeated by the frolick of another; and many mischiefs and benefits are done and hindered without design. (p. xiii)

While this, Johnson admits, is 'a practice contrary to the rules of criticism', 'there is always an appeal open from criticism to nature'. Unlike the classical authors set as exemplars by neoclassical critics, '*Shakespeare* has united the powers of exciting laughter and sorrow not only in one mind but in one com-position' (p. xiv). Johnson exonerates him from the charge of neglecting the classical unities, arguing that spectators are not so literal-minded as to require the stage to represent a single place or continuous time:

the truth is, that spectators are always in their senses, and know, from the first act to the last, that the stage is only a stage and that the players are only players. [. . .] Where is the absurdity of allowing that space to represent first *Athens*, and then *Sicily*, which was always known to be neither *Sicily* not *Athens* but a modern theatre. (p. xxvii)

Shakespeare is close to nature, not nature itself: the consciousness of artifice is a necessary condition of the theatre:

The reflection that strikes the heart is not, that the evils before us are real evils, but that they are evils to which we ourselves may be exposed. If there be any fallacy, it is not that we fancy the players, but that we fancy ourselves unhappy for a moment; but we rather lament the possibility than suppose the pretence of misery, as a mother weeps over her babe, when she remembers that death may take it from her. The delight of tragedy proceeds from our consciousness of fiction; if we thought murders and treasons real, they would please no more. (p. xxvii)

Johnson's awareness of Shakespeare's 'excellencies' makes him equally clear about his failings. The moral objections to Shakespeare's tragic plots recur: writing of *King Lear*, Johnson notes that 'Shakespeare has suffered the virtue of Cordelia to perish in a just cause, contrary to the natural ideas of justice, to the hope of the reader, and, what is yet more strange, to the faith of Chronicles' (Johnson, 1765, IV, p. 160):

A play in which the wicked prosper, and the virtuous miscarry, may doubtless be good, because it is a just representation of the common events of human life: but since all reasonable beings naturally love justice, I cannot easily be persuaded, that the observation of justice makes a play worse; or, that if other excellencies are equal, the audience will not always rise better pleased from the final triumph of persecuted virtue.

In the present case the publick has decided. Cordelia, from the time of Tate, has always retired with victory and felicity. And, if my sensations could add any thing to the general suffrage, I might relate, that I was many years ago so shocked by Cordelia's death, that I know not whether I ever endured to read again the last scenes of the play till I undertook to revise them as an editor. (VI, p. 160)

He also criticizes Shakespeare for loose and sometimes careless plotting, and for a tendency to tail off in the latter part of his plays, so that 'his catastrophe is improbably produced or imperfectly represented' (I, p. xx) – *Hamlet* serves as an example. Shakespeare is rebuked for the violation of chronology and his use of anachronisms, and for occasionally strained or wearisome rhetoric, but Johnson reserves his most lengthy, and famous, censure for Shakespeare's wordplay:

A quibble is to *Shakespeare*, what luminous vapours are to the traveller; he follows it at all adventures, it is sure to lead him out of his way, and sure to engulf him in the more. It has some malignant power over his mind, and its fascinations are irresistible. Whatever be the dignity or profundity of his disqualification, whether he be enlarging knowledge or exalting affection, whether he be amusing attention with incidents, or enchaining it in suspense, let but a quibble spring up before him, and he leaves his work unfinished. A quibble is the golden apple for which he will always turn aside from his career, or stoop from his elevation. A quibble poor and barren as it is, gave him such delight, that he was content to purchase it, by the sacrifice of reason, propriety and truth. A quibble was to him the fatal *Cleopatra* for which he lost the world, and was content to lose it. (I, pp. xxiii–xxiv)

Like previous commentators, Johnson allows for a mixture of good and bad qualities in Shakespeare's work: 'he has scenes of undoubted and perpetual excellence, but perhaps not one play which, if it were now exhibited as the work of a contemporary writer, would be heard to its conclusion.' Rather, Johnson argues, 'it must be at last confessed, that as we owe everything to him, he owes something to us; that, if much of his praise is paid by perception and judgement, much is likewise given by custom and veneration' (I, p. xlvi).

1765–1800: Texts on Page and Stage

Johnson's interest in the texts of the plays did not extend to an interest in their theatrical performance. Sandra Clark describes the eighteenth century's preference for adapted Shakespeare on the stage as a 'paradox whereby Shakespeare's works achieved the status of "classics" in the study while for a long period on the stage the divine Bard (as he came to be called) was often represented by plays only a small proportion of which he actually wrote' (Clark, 1997, p. xliii). Shakespeare's position in the theatre during the eighteenth century was largely dependent on his tragedies (see Hogan, 1952, vol. II). Bell's Acting Edition of 1774, dedicated to David Garrick – 'the best illustrator of, and the best living comment on, Shakespeare' (Bell, 1969, I, p. 3) – presents itself as a 'a companion to the theatre' (p. 8) rather than a critical edition. It prints the texts with the standard performance cuts and emendations, proposing that these changes allow 'the noble monuments he has left us, of unrivalled ability, [to] be restored to due proportion and natural lustre, by sweeping off those cobwebs, and that dust of depraved opinion, which Shakespeare was unfortunately forced to throw on them' (p. 6). Bell's edition also presents itself as an alternative to the increasingly scholarly and specialized writing on Shakespeare, as a forerunner to self-consciously pedagogic or introductory volumes popular in the twentieth century:

> it has been our peculiar endeavour to render what we call the essence of Shakespeare, more instructive and intelligible; especially to the ladies and to youth; glaring indecencies being removed, and intricate passages explained; and lastly, we have striven to supply plainer ideas of criticism, both in public and private, than we have hitherto met with.
>
> A general view of each play is given, by way of introduction.
>
> Though this is not an edition meant for the profoundly learned, nor the deeply studious, who love to find out, and chace their own critical game; yet we flatter ourselves both parties may perceive fresh ideas started for speculation and reflection. (pp. 9–10)

The edition's particular stress on theatrical representation is often cited as an alternative locus of aesthetic success to critical appreciation. Thus *Macbeth* 'even amidst the fine sentiments it contains, would shrink before criticism, did not Macbeth and his Lady afford such uncommon scope for acting-merit: upon the whole, it is a fine dramatic structure, with some gross blemishes' (p. 3), and the end of *Hamlet* is criticized: 'The fifth Act of this play is by no means so good as we could wish; yet it engages attention in public, by having a good deal of bustle, and, what English audiences love, many deaths' (p. 84).

While Shakespeare criticism looks to be a male preserve, women were also increasingly involved. Elizabeth Montagu's *An Essay on the Writings and Genius of Shakespear, compared with the Greek and French Dramatic Poets* (1769) was extensively reprinted and translated. Montagu scorned as narrow-minded critics who criticized Shakespeare's learning:

> For copying nature he found it in the busy walks of human life, he drew from an original, with which the literati are seldom well acquainted. They perceive his portraits are not of the Grecian or of the Roman school: after finding them unlike to the celebrated forms preserved in learned museums they do not deign to enquire whether they resemble the living persons they were intended to represent. (Montagu, [1769] 1970, p. 17)

It is Shakespeare's facility with drawing recognizable characters which Montagu most admires: he 'seems to have had the art of the Dervise, in the Arabian tales, who could throw his soul into the body of another man, and be at once possessed of his sentiments, adopt his passions, and rise to all the functions and feelings of his situation' (p. 37). Writing of *Macbeth*, Montagu praises it for exciting 'a species of terror that cannot be effected by the operation of human agency, or by any form or disposition of human things' – constructing the play as a kind of Gothic story rather like Ann Radcliffe's *The Mysteries of Udolpho* (1794) which uses quotations from *Macbeth* for several of its chapter epigraphs.

Elizabeth Griffith, in her *The Morality of Shakespeare's Drama Illustrated* (1775), described Shakespeare as a 'Philosopher' whose 'anatomy of the human heart is delineated from *nature*, not from *metaphysics*; referring immediately to our intuitive sense and not wandering with the schoolmen' (Griffith, 1971, p. ix), and thus, perhaps, uniquely accessible and applicable to contemporary women largely denied a classical education. Like Montagu, Griffith is able to claim authority to write on Shakespeare by wresting him from the enervating grasp of the scholar and reinstating him as the poet of everyday life. At times in her extensive commentary, Griffith speaks consciously as a female reader of Shakespeare, as when she discusses Lady Macbeth's line 'That which hath made them drunk, hath made me bold' (2.2.1):

> Our sex is obliged to Shakespeare, for this passage. He seems to think that a woman could not be rendered completely wicked, without some degree of intoxication. It required two vices in her; one to intend, and another to perpetrate the crime. He does not give *wine* and *wassail* to Macbeth; leaving him in his natural state, to be actuated by the temptation of ambition alone. (pp. 412–13)

In this she echoes Elizabeth Montagu: 'The difference between a mind naturally prone to evil, and a frail one warped by force of temptations, is delicately

distinguished in Macbeth and his wife' (Montagu, 1970, p. 200), and anticipates the great female defender of Lady Macbeth, Mrs Jameson in her *Characteristics of Women* (1832).

Character study was to be the dominant theme of Romantic criticism of
Shakespeare. There were, however, other strands emerging. In 1794 Walter
Whiter published *A Specimen of a Commentary on Shakspeare. Containing I.
Notes on As You Like It. II. An Attempt to Explain and Illustrate various passages
on a new principle of criticism, derived from Mr. Locke's doctrine of The Association of Ideas*. Whiter explained John Locke's idea of 'association' as 'the combination of those ideas, which have no natural alliance or relation to each other'
(Whiter, 1972, p. 65). Whiter argued that critics had hitherto been preoccupied by discovering

> the *direct*, though sometimes perhaps obscure allusions, which the poet has *inten-
> tionally* made to the customs of his own age, and to the various vices, follies, pas-
> sions and prejudices, which are the pointed objects of his satire or his praise. But
> the commentators have not marked those *indirect* and *tacit* references, which are
> produced by the writer with *no* intentional allusion; or rather they have not
> unfolded those trains of thought, alike pregnant with the materials *peculiar* to
> his age, which often prompt the combinations of the poet in the wildest exer-
> tions of his fancy, and which conduct him, unconscious of the effect, to the
> various *peculiarities* of his imagery or his language. (pp. 71–2)

Whiter's commentary on Lady Macbeth's 'Come, thick Night, / And PALL me
in the dunnest smoke of Hell! / That my keen KNIFE see not the wound it
makes; / Nor HEAVEN PEEP thro' the BLANKET of the dark, / To cry, *Hold, hold*'
(1.5.49–53) is a model of his method to disinter connections between the
words highlighted. First, Whiter cites previous authorities: Steevens and
Warburton discuss 'pall' as a robe of state or funeral cloth; Malone has objected
to knife 'as being connected with the most sordid offices; and therefore unsuit-
able to the great occasion on which it is employed' (p. 153); the anonymous
play *A Warning to Fair Women* shows that it is in fact synonymous with 'dagger';
Malone suggests blanket was 'suggested to him by the coarse *woollen* curtain
of his own Theatre' (p. 154):

> Let not the reader smile at this specimen of conjectural criticism, nor imagine
> that it should be regarded only as a quaint and whimsical conceit. Nothing is
> more certain, than that all the images in this celebrated passage are borrowed
> from the stage [. . . .] the peculiar and appropriate dress of TRAGEDY personified
> is a PALL with a KNIFE. [. . .] With respect to the passage before us, I imagine
> that the whole of this image was suggested to our Poet from the appearance of
> the Stage, as it was furnished at those times when Tragedies were represented:
> it was then hung with *black* [. . .] supported with reference to Malone, and
> parallel to Marston's Insatiate Countess. (p. 154)

Whiter's careful exposition of linguistic details marks an early example of something twentieth-century critics as diverse as William Empson and Patricia Parker (see chapter 6: Language) have developed.

1800–1840: Romantic Criticism by Schlegel, Coleridge and Hazlitt

For many early nineteenth-century readers of Shakespeare the stage was inadequate to the plays. Charles Lamb's essay 'On the tragedies of Shakspeare, considered with reference to their fitness for stage representation' (1811) codified one of Romanticism's major feelings about Shakespeare: that his works were better read and studied than performed, indeed, that 'the plays of Shakspeare are less calculated for performance on a stage, than those of almost any other dramatist whatever' (Lamb, 1903, p. 115). Lamb's objection to performance was partly because of the difficulty of separating the character from the actor, thus displacing contemplation of the author with contemplation of the actor in a confusion 'from which persons otherwise not meanly lettered, find it almost impossible to extricate themselves' (p. 114). It is a relief to escape into plays which have remained unperformed and therefore unspoilt, Lamb suggests:

> I confess myself utterly unable to appreciate that celebrate soliloquy in Hamlet, beginning 'To be or not to be,' or to tell whether it be good, bad or indifferent, it has been so handled and pawed about by declamatory boys and men, and torn so inhumanly from its living place and principle of continuity in the play, till it is become to me a perfect dead member. (p. 115)

Hamlet is essentially an interior character:

> nine parts in ten of what Hamlet does, are transactions between himself and his moral sense, they are the effusions of his solitary musings, which he retires to holes and corners and the most sequestered parts of the palace to pour forth; or rather, they are the silent meditations with which his bosom is bursting, reduced to *words* for the sake of the reader, whom must else remain ignorant of what is passing there. These profound sorrows, these light-and-noise-abhorring ruminations, which the tongue scarce dares utter to deaf walls and chambers, how can they be represented by a gesticulation actor, who comes and mouths them out before an audience, making four hundred people his confidants at once? (pp. 116–17)

Watching an actor 'personating a passion' is true only to 'that symbol of the emotion which passes current at the theatre for it' (p. 119) – a derivative and enervated experience. Thus:

To see Lear acted – to see an old man tottering about the stage with a walking-stick, turned out of doors by his daughters in a rainy night, has nothing in it but what is painful and disgusting [. . .] The greatness of Lear is not in corporal dimension, but in intellectual: the explosions of his passion are terrible as a volcano: they are storms turning up and disclosing to the bottom that sea, his mind, with all its vast riches. It is his mind which is laid bare. This case of flesh and blood seems too significant to be thought on; even as he himself neglects it. On the stage we see nothing but corporal infirmities and weakness, the impotence of rage; while we read it, we see not Lear, but we are Lear – we are in his mind, we are sustained by a grandeur which baffles the malice of daughters and storms. (p. 124)

Lamb's final assessment, that 'the Lear of Shakspere cannot be acted' (p. 124) is consonant with contemporary stage practice, as adaptations such as that by Tate continued to hold the stage in place of Shakespeare's text.

Lamb's conclusions are elaborated elsewhere. In his 'Shakespeare und kein Ende' (translated as 'Shakespeare ad Infinitum') of 1815, Johann Wolfgang von Goethe claimed Shakespeare as a poet whose works are 'not for the physical vision':

Shakespeare speaks always to our inner sense [. . .] if we study the works of Shakespeare enough, we find that they contain much more of spiritual truth than of spectacular action. He makes happen what can easily be conceived by the imagination, indeed what can be better imagined than seen. Hamlet's ghost, Macbeth's witches, many fearful incidents, get their value only through the power of the imagination, and many of the minor scenes get their force from the same source. In reading, all these things pass easily through our minds, and seem quite appropriate, whereas in representation on the stage they would strike us unfavourably and appear not only unpleasant but even disgusting. (LeWinter, 1970, p. 58)

For Goethe, Shakespeare's power is in the language: 'there is no higher of purer pleasure than to sit with closed eyes and hear a naturally expressive voice recite, not declaim, a play of Shakespeare's' (p. 58). For Goethe, as for many critics of the period, Shakespeare is a Romantic thinker, 'a decidedly modern poet' (p. 60), and one whose work, particularly in his tragedies, is animated by the connection between 'Will and Necessity' (p. 62):

The person, considered as a character, is under a certain necessity; he is constrained, appointed to a certain particular line of action; but as a human being he has a will, which is unconfined and universal in its demands. Thus arises an inner conflict, and Shakespeare is superior to all other writers in the significance with which he endows this. But now an outer conflict may arise, and the individual through it may become so aroused that an insufficient will is raised through circumstance to the level of irremissible necessity. These motives [can be seen] in the case of Hamlet; but the motive is repeated constantly in Shakespeare – Hamlet through the agency of the ghost; Macbeth through the witches, Hecate and his wife; Brutus through his friends gets into a dilemma and situation to which they were not equal; even in Coriolanus the same motive is found. This Will, which reaches beyond the power of the individual, is decidedly modern. But since in Shakespeare it does not spring from within, but is developed through external circumstance, it becomes a sort of Necessity. (LeWinter, pp. 62–3)

Macbeth was a particular nineteenth-century favourite. Thomas De Quincey's essay, 'On the Knocking at the Gate in Macbeth' (1823), locates the play's tragic interest in its creation of sympathy not for the victim of murder but its perpetrator:

Murder in ordinary cases, when the sympathy is wholly directed to the case of the murdered person, is an incident of coarse and vulgar horror; and for this reason – that it flings the interest exclusively upon the natural but ignoble instinct by which we cleave to life [. . .] exhibits human nature in its most abject and humiliating attitude. Such an attitude would little suit the purposes of the poet. What then must he do? He must throw the interest on the murderer: our sympathy must be with *him*; (of course I mean a sympathy of comprehension, a sympathy by which we enter into his feelings, and are made to understand them, – not a sympathy of pity or approbation:) [. . .] In Macbeth, for the sake of gratifying his own enormous and teeming faculty of creation, Shakspeare has introduced two murderers: and, as usual in his hands, they are remarkably discriminated: but though in Macbeth the strife of mind is greater than in his wife, the tiger spirit not so awake, and his feelings caught chiefly by contagion from her, – yet, as both were finally involved in the guilt of murder, the murderous mind of necessity is finally to be presumed in both. (De Quincey, 2000, III, p. 152)

De Quincey, most famous for his account of opium addiction in his *Confessions of an English Opium-Eater* (1822), imagines the Macbeths cut off from humanity in a kind of trance of their own wickedness, broken only by the knocking at the gate:

Here, [in Macbeth] the retiring of the human heart and the entrance of the fiendish heart was to be expressed and made sensible. Another world has stepped in; and the murderers are taken out of the region of human beings, human purposes, human desires. [. . .] In order that a new world may step in, this world must for a time disappear. The murderers, and the murder, must be insulated – cut off by an immeasurable gulph from the ordinary tide and succession of human affairs – locked up and sequestered in some deep recess: we must be made sensible that the world of ordinary life is suddenly arrested – laid asleep – tranced – racked into a dread armistice: time must be annihilated; relation to things without abolished; and all must pass self-withdrawn into a deep syncope and suspension of earthly passion. Hence it is that when the deed is done – when the work of darkness is perfect, then the world of darkness passes away like a pageantry in the clouds: the knocking at the gate is heard; and it makes known audibly that the reaction has commenced; the human has made its reflux upon the fiendish: the pulses of life are beginning to beat again: and the re-establishment of the goings-on of the world in which we live, first makes us profoundly sensible of the awful parenthesis that has suspended them. (p. 153)

It was a frequent turn of eighteenth-century criticism to compare Shakespeare's tragedies with those of ancient Greece. In his *The Philosophy of Fine Art*, based on lectures delivered in the 1820s and published posthumously a decade later, G. W. F. Hegel used *Hamlet* to illustrate the difference between ancient and modern tragedy. The main difference is the role and inscription of individuality, or character:

The heroes of ancient classical tragedy discover circumstances under which they, so long as they irrefragably adhere to the *one* ethical state of pathos which alone corresponds to their own already formed personality, must infallibly come into conflict with an ethical Power which opposes theme and possesses an equal ethical claim to recognition. Romantic characters, on the contrary, are from the first placed within a wide expanse of contingent relations and conditions, within which every sort of action is possible; so that the conflict, to which no doubt the external conditions presupposed supply the occasion, essentially abides within the *character* itself, to which the individuals concerned in their passion give effect, not, however, in the interests of the ethical vindication of the truly substantive claims, but for the simple reason that they are the kind of men they are. [. . .] In a modern tragedy it is the individual character (and for such a character it is a matter of accident whether he chooses that which on its own account is right, or whether he is led into wrong and crime) who makes his decisions, either following his personal desires and needs or responding to purely external influences. (LeWinter, 1970, p. 81)

Hegel develops his idea of dialectical tragedy, arguing that:

It is precisely Shakespeare who, as a contrast to that exposition of vacillating and essentially self-divided characters, supplies us with the finest examples of essentially stable and consequential characters, who go to their doom precisely in virtue of this tenacious hold upon themselves and their ends. Unsupported by the sanction of the moral law, but rather carried onward by the formal necessity of their personality, they suffer themselves to be involved in their acts by the coil of external circumstances, or they plunge blindly therein and maintain

themselves there by sheer force of will, even where all that they do is merely
done because they are impelled to assert themselves against others, or because
they have simply come to the particular point they have reached. (pp. 85–6)

There are two possible responses to such tragedies, Hegel argues. One is to
see a kind of justice implied in its operations, along with the demand that the
characters

> should of necessity appear themselves to acknowledge the justice of their fate.
> Such a state of acceptance may either be of a religious nature, in which case
> the soul becomes conscious of a more exalted and indestructible condition of
> blessedness with which to confront the collapse of its mundane personality; or
> it may be of a more formal, albeit more worldly type [. . . which] preserves with
> unimpaired energy all its personal freedom [. . . or] the recognition that the lot
> which the individual receives is the one, however bitter it may be, which his
> action merits. (p. 87)

The other point of view sees the tragedy as a matter 'of the effect of unhappy
circumstances and external accidents':

> From such a point of view we have merely left us the conception that the modern
> idea of individuality, with its searching definition of character, circumstances,
> and developments, is handed over essentially to the contingency of the earthly
> state, and must carry the fateful issues of such finitude. Pure commiseration of
> this sort is, however, destitute of meaning; and it is nothing less than a fright-
> ful kind of external necessity in the particular case where we see the downfall of
> essentially noble natures in their conflict thus assumed with the mischance of
> purely external accidents. Such a course of events can insistently arrest our atten-
> tion; but in the result it can only be horrible, and the demand is direct and irre-
> sistible that the external accidents ought to accord with that which is identical
> with the spiritual nature of such noble characters. Only as thus regarded can we
> feel ourselves reconciled with the grievous end of Hamlet and Juliet. (pp. 87–8)

Whereas one major current in eighteenth-century Shakespeare criticism
was to sift the plays for their beauties and point out their weaknesses, Romantic critics such as Schlegel argued for their 'organic unity', a structural organization intrinsic to the literary work which 'unfolds itself from within' and
not imposed by a framework of rigid classical aesthetics. As Bate argues, the
ongoing influence of this method, taken up by I. A. Richards as 'practical criticism', can still be seen in the many educational contexts in which close reading
aimed at uncovering organic form is taught and examined (Bate, 1992, p. 5).
In his lectures, translated into English in 1864, Schlegel identifies characterization as one of Shakespeare's most dominant qualities:

Never, perhaps, was there so comprehensive a talent for characterization as Shakspeare. It [. . ;] grasps every diversity of range, age and sex, down to the lispings of infancy; [. . .] the king and the beggar, the hero and the pickpocket, the sage and the idiot, speak and act with equal truthfulness; not only does he transport himself to distant ages and foreign nations, [. . .] He gives us the history of minds; he lays open to us, in a single word, a whole series of their anterior states. (Schlegel, 1846, pp. 363–4)

His characterization is ironic:

Shakspeare makes each of his principal characters the glass in which the others are reflected, and by like means enables us to discover what could not be immediately revealed in us. [. . .] Nobody ever painted so truthfully as he has done the facility of self-deception, the half self-conscious hypocrisy towards ourselves, with which even noble minds attempt to disguise the almost inevitable influence of selfish motives in human nature. This secret irony of the characterization commands admiration as the profound abyss of acuteness and sagacity; but it is the grave of enthusiasm. (p. 369)

Schlegel's muscular Shakespeare is sometimes out of step with the tastes of an age of 'tragedies of which the catastrophe consists in the swoon of an enamoured princess: if Shakspeare falls occasionally into the opposite extreme, it is a noble error, originating in the fulness of a gigantic strength' (p. 368):

The objection that Shakspeare wounds our feelings by the open display of the most disgusting moral odiousness, unmercifully harrows up the mind and tortures even our eyes by the exhibition of the most insupportable and hateful spectacles, is one of greater and graver importance. He has, in fact, never varnished over wild and blood-thirsty passions with a pleasing exterior – never cloaked crime and want of principle with a false show of greatness of soul; and in that respect he is every way deserving of praise [. . .] I allow that the reading, and still more the sight, of some of his pieces, is not advisable to weak nerves, any more than was the *Eumenides* of Aeschylus; but is the poet, who can only reach an important object by a bold and hazardous daring, to be checked by considerations for such persons? If the effeminacy of the present day is to serve as a general standard of what tragical composition may properly exhibit to human nature, we shall be forced to set very narrow limits indeed to art, and the hope of anything like powerful effect must at once and for ever be renounced. (pp. 367–8)

Lecture XXXV concerns 'Criticisms on Shakspeare's tragedies'. Schlegel discusses *Hamlet*, which he judges infinitely mysterious:

Hamlet is singular in its kind: a tragedy of thought inspired by continual and never-satisfied meditation on human destiny and the dark perplexity of the events of this world, and calculated to call forth the very same meditation in the minds of the spectators. This enigmatical work resembles one of those irrational equations in which a fraction of unknown magnitude always remains, that will in no way admit of solution. (p. 404)

Although Hamlet's character was a favourite with Romantic critics, Schlegel's impression is not entirely favourable: 'He is not solely compelled by necessity to artifice and dissimulation, he has a natural inclination for crooked ways; he is a hypocrite towards himself; his far-fetched scruples are often mere pretexts to cover his want of determination' (p. 405). Ultimately, the play's message is a fearful one:

A voice from another world, commissioned it would appear, by heaven, demands vengeance for a monstrous enormity, and the demand remains without effect; the criminals are at last punished, but, as it were, by an accidental blow and not in the solemn way requisite to convey to the world a warning example of justice; irresolute foresight, cunning treachery, and impetuous rage, hurry on to a common destruction; the less guilty and the innocent are equally involved in the general ruin. The destiny of humanity is there exhibited as a gigantic Sphinx, which threatens to precipitate into the abyss of scepticism all who are unable to solve her dreadful enigmas. (p. 406)

There is a similar edge of apprehension and terror in Schlegel's account of *King Lear*, a play in which 'the scene of compassion is exhausted. The principal characters here are not those who act, but those who suffer' (p. 411). The ending of the play has little comfort: 'According to Shakspeare's plan the guilty, it is true, are all punished, for wickedness destroys itself; but the virtues that would bring help and succour are everywhere too late, or overmatched by the cunning activity of malice' (p. 413).

Schlegel's highest praise is reserved for *Macbeth*, a 'sublime work' showing 'an ambitious but noble hero, yielding to a deep-laid hellish temptation' (p. 407):

We might believe that we witness in this tragedy the over-ruling destiny of the ancients represented in perfect accordance with their ideas: the whole originates in a supernatural influence, to which the subsequent events seem inevitably linked. Moreover, we even find here the same ambiguous oracles which, by their literal fulfillment, deceive those who confide in them. Yet it may be easily shown that the poet has, in his work, displayed more enlightened views. He wishes to show that the conflict of good and evil in this world can only take place by the permission of Providence, which converts the curse that individual mortals draw down on their heads into a blessing to others. (p. 409)

Samuel Taylor Coleridge's important observations on Shakespeare are scattered through his papers and the extant accounts of his lectures. In his 'Notes on the Tragedies of Shakespeare', Coleridge argued that the unities of time and place are unnecesary inconveniences which can be dispensed with, and that 'Shakespeare stood pre-eminent' in the unity of action, which Coleridge described as 'homogeneity, proportionateness, and totality of interest' (Coleridge, 1987, I, p. 4):

> A *unity of feeling* pervades the whole of his plays. In *Romeo and Juliet* all is youth and spring – it is youth with its follies, its virtues, its precipitancies; it is spring with its odours, flowers, and transiency: the same feeling commences, goes through, and ends the play. (II, p. 265)

Coleridge argues that:

> With Shakespeare his comic constantly re-acted on his tragic characters. Lear, wandering amidst the tempest, had all his feelings of distress increased by the overflowings of the wild wit of the Fool, as vinegar poured upon wounds exacerbate[s] their pain; thus even his comic humour tends to the development of tragic passion. (II, p. 266)

Shakespeare's strength is seen in his verisimilitude: 'His dramas do not arise absolutely out of some extraordinary circumstance; the scenes may stand independently of any such one connecting incident, as faithful reflections of men and manners' (II, p. 266). For Coleridge, Shakespeare is also a moralist:

> The objection that Shakespeare wounds the moral sense by the unsubdued, undisguised description of the most hateful atrocity, that he rends the feelings without mercy, and even outrages the eye itself by scenes of insupportable atrocity. Now *Titus Andronicus* is admitted not to have been Shakespeare, I dare, with the one exception of the trampling out of Gloster's eyes in *Lear*, answer boldly in the name of Shakespeare, not guilty. (I, p. 78)

The account of Coleridge's lecture on *Macbeth* in Bristol in 1813 begins with a discussion of the witches as 'awful beings, blend[ing] in themselves the Fates and Furies of the ancients with the sorceresses of Gothic and popular superstition' (I, p. 269). Coleridge also draws a topical parallel, 'a comparison between the characters of Macbeth and Bonaparte – both tyrants, both indifferent to means, however barbarous, to attain their ends; and he hoped the fate of the latter would be like the former, in failing amidst a host of foes, which his cruelty and injustice had roused against him' (I, p. 275). Lady Macbeth gets more sympathetic treatment than the 'prejudiced idea of [her] as a monster's usually allowed. Coleridge sees her as 'a woman of a visionary and day-dreaming turn of mind' with her 'conscience, so far from being seared, [. . .] continually smarting within her' (I, p. 271).

Coleridge's lecture on *Hamlet* argued that 'the intricacies of Hamlet's character may be traced to Shakespeare's deep and accurate science in mental philosophy' (II, p. 272).

> Shakespeare seems to have conceived a mind in the highest degree of excitement, with this overpowering activity of intellect, and to have placed him in circumstances where he was obliged to act on the spur of the moment. Hamlet, though brave and careless of death, had contracted a morbid sensibility from this overbalance in the mind, producing the lingering and vacillating delays of procrastination, and wasting in the energy of resolving the energy of acting [. . .] The effect of this overbalance of imagination is beautifully illustrated in the inward brooking of Hamlet – the effect of a superfluous activity of thought. His mind, unseated from its healthy balance, is forever occupied with the world within him, and abstracted from external things; his words give substance to shadows, and he is dissatisfied with commonplace realities. It is the nature of thought to be indefinite, while definiteness belongs to reality. The sense of sublimity arises, not from the sight of an outward object but from the reflection upon it; not from the impression, but from the idea. Few have seen a celebrated waterfall without feeling something of disappointment: it is only subsequently, by reflection, that the idea of the waterfall comes full into the mind, and brings with it a train of sublime associations. Hamlet felt this: in him we see a mind that keeps itself in a state of abstraction, and beholds external objects as hieroglyphics. (II, pp. 272–3)

Coleridge identifies Hamlet's 'disposition to escape from his own feeling of the overwhelming and supernatural by a wild transition to the ludicrous, – a sort of cunning bravado, bordering on the flights of delirium' (II, p. 274). As Jonathan Bate has argued, the Romantics' 'reinvention of Hamlet as a paralysed Romantic was their single most influential critical act', epitomized in Coleridge's own claim to 'have a smack of Hamlet myself, if I may say so' (Bate, 1992, p. 2).

On *King Lear*, Coleridge began with a close account of its opening lines:

> It was [not] without forethought, and it is not without its due significance, that the triple division is stated here as already determined, and all its particulars, previously to the trial of professions, as the relative rewards of which the daughters were to be made to consider their several portions. The strange, yet by no means unnatural, mixture of selfishness, sensibility, and habit of feeling derived from and fostered by the particular rank and usages of the individual: the intense desire to be intensely beloved, selfish, and yet characteristic of the selfishness of a loving and kindly nature – a feeble selfishness, self-supportless and leaning for all pleasure on another's breast; the selfish craving after a sympathy with a prodigal disinterestedness, contradicted by its own ostentation and the mode and nature of its claims; the anxiety, the distrust, the jealousy, which more or less

accompany all selfish affections, and are among the surest contradistinctions of mere fondness from love, and which originate Lear's eager wish to enjoy his daughter's violent professions, while the inveterate habits of sovereignty convert the wish into claim and positive right, and the incompliance with it into crime and treason; – these facts, these passions, these moral verities, on which the whole tragedy is founded, are all prepared for, and will to the retrospect be found implied in, the first four or five lines of the play. (I, pp. 54–5)

Although character-study was an important part of Coleridge's Shakespearean criticism, he was also interested in generic questions. His lecture on *Richard II* began with a definition of tragedy absent from his lectures on the tragedy:

Fully to comprehend the nature of the Historic Drama, the difference should be understood between the epic and tragic muse. The latter recognises and is grounded upon the free-will of man; the former is under the control of destiny, or, among Christians, an overruling Providence. [. . .] In the tragic, the free-will of man is the first cause, and accidents are never introduced; if they are, it is considered a great fault. To cause the death of a hero by accident, such as slipping off a plank into the sea, would be beneath the tragic muse, as it would arise from no mental action. (I, pp. 277–8)

William Hazlitt's *Characters on Shakespear's Plays* published in 1817 sets out to extend Schlegel's analysis and to illustrate Pope's remarks on Shakespeare's distinctive characterization: 'every single character in Shakespear, is as much an individual as those in life itself' (Hazlitt, 1998, I, p. 85). On the tragedies, Hazlitt argues:

Lear stands first for the profound intensity of the passion; *Macbeth* for the wildness of the imagination and the rapidity of the action; *Othello* for the progressive interest and powerful alternations of feeling; *Hamlet* for the refined developement of thought and sentiment. If the force of genius is shown in each of these works is astonishing, their variety is not less so. They are like different creations of the same mind, not one of which has the slightest reference to the rest. (p. 99)

He prefaces his chapter on *Othello* by arguing that it illustrates the general remarks on tragedy to an 'extraordinary degree':

It has been said that tragedy purifies the affections by terror and pity. That is, it substitutes imaginary sympathy for mere selfishness. It gives us a high and permanent interest, beyond ourselves, in humanity as such. It raises the great, the remote, and the possible to an equality with the real, the little and the near. It makes man a partaker with his kind [. . .] Tragedy creates a balance of the affections. It makes us thoughtful spectators in the lists of life. It is the refiner of the species, a discipline of humanity. (p. 112)

Hazlitt praises the opening of *Macbeth* but his main interest is its central character:

> Macbeth himself appears driven along by the violence of his fate like a vessel drifting before a storm: he reels to and fro like a drunken man; he staggers under the weight of his own purposes and the suggestions of others; he stands at bay with his situation; and from the superstitious awe and breathless suspense into which the communications of the Weïrd Sisters throw him, is hurried on with daring impatience to verify their predictions, and with impious and bloody hand to tear aside the veil which hides the uncertainty of the future. (p. 100)

Unlike Richard III, Macbeth becomes wicked from 'accidental circumstances', 'tempted to the commission of guilt by golden opportunities' (p. 104). Lady Macbeth is 'a great bad woman, whom we hate, but whom we fear more than we hate', and her 'solid, substantial, flesh and blood display of passion exhibit[s] a striking contrast to the cold, abstracted, gratuitous malignity of the witches' (pp. 100–1). Many of Hazlitt's most realized conceptions of Shakespearean characters draw from his experiences in the theatre, and here he mentions Sarah Siddons' portrayal of Lady Macbeth in the sleepwalking scene (5.1): 'Power was seated on her brow, passion emanated from her breast as from a shrine; she was tragedy personified' (p. 102), although he argues, in common with many contemporary critics who preferred plays in the study to those on the stage, that 'we can conceive of no-one to play Macbeth properly, or to look like a man that had encountered the Weïrd Sisters' (p. 106).

On *Othello* Hazlitt takes time to consider Iago and to engage with Coleridge's assessment. Iago is

> an amateur of tragedy in real life; and instead of employing his invention on imaginary characters, or long-forgotten incidents, he takes the bolder and more desperate course of getting up his plot at home, casts the principal parts among his nearest friends and connections, and rehearses it in downright earnest, with steady nerves and unabated resolution. (p. 118)

Hazlitt's essay on *Hamlet* argues that 'we have been so used to this tragedy that we hardly know how to criticise it any more than we should know how to describe our own faces' (p. 143):

> It is the one of Shakespear's plays that we think of the oftenest, because it abounds most in striking reflections on human life, and because the distresses of Hamlet are transferred, by the turn of his mind, to the general account of

humanity. Whatever happens to him we apply to ourselves, because he applies it so himself as a means of general reasoning. (p. 144)

It is not a play for the stage:

> We do not like to see our author's plays acted, and least of all, *Hamlet*. There is no play that suffers so much in being transferred to the stage. Hamlet himself seems hardly capable of being acted [. . . Edmund Kean] throws a severity, approaching to virulence, into the common observations and answers. There is nothing of this in Hamlet. He is, as it were, wrapped up in his own reflections, and only *thinks aloud*. There should therefore be no attempt to impress what he says upon others by a studied exaggeration of emphasis or manner; no *talking at* his hearers. There should be as much of the gentleman and scholar as possible infused into the part and as little of the actor. A pensive air of sadness should sit reluctantly on his brow, but no appearance of fixed and sullen gloom. He is full of weakness and melancholy, but there is no harshness in his nature. He is the most amiable of misanthropes. (p. 148)

Hazlitt compares *Romeo and Juliet* with Wordsworth's 'Ode on the Progress of Life' – both are about the vividness of early attachments and the strength of youthful feeling. Hazlitt praises Juliet's speech, 'Gallop apace, you fiery-footed steeds' (3.2) as 'bolder in virgin innocence', and reclaims it as 'pure effusion of nature' from those who would expunge such passages (pp. 162–3). 'Romeo is Hamlet in love,' writes Hazlitt, 'there is the same rich exuberance of passion and sentiment in the one, that there is of thought and sentiment in the other. Both are absent and self-involved, both live out of themselves in a world of imagination' (p. 164). But it is for *King Lear* that Hazlitt reserves his strongest praise:

> It is then the best of Shakespear's plays, for it is the one in which he was the most in earnest. He was here fairly caught in the web of his own imagination. The passion which he has taken as his subject is that which strikes its root deepest into the human heart; of which the bond is the hardest to be unloosed; and the cancelling and tearing to pieces of which gives the greatest revulsion to the frame. This depth of nature, this force of passion, this tug and war of the elements of our being, this firm faith in filial piety, and the giddy anarchy and whirling tumult of the thoughts at finding this prop failing it, the contrast between the fixed, immovable basis of natural affection, and the rapid, irregular starts of imagination, suddenly wrenched from all its accustomed holds and resting-places in the soul, this is what Shakespear has given, and what nobody else but he could give. So we believe. (p. 167)

It is significant that Hazlitt calls the play *Lear* rather than *King Lear*: this is not a political play but a human one, a family drama rather than a national one.

Hazlitt's dramatic criticism also influenced his writing. While the general tenor of Romantic criticism was disdainful of the plays, particularly tragedies, in performance, there was also a significant strand of theatre reviewing as practised by Leigh Hunt and Hazlitt. In his collected dramatic criticism published as *A View of the English Stage* (1818; reprinted 1998), Hazlitt develops the interest in character evinced in his Shakespeare monograph, praising Kean's Iago as 'a gay, light-hearted monster, a careless, cordial, comfortable villain' (p. 20), and noting his portrayal of Macbeth in the scene after the murder of Duncan:

> as a lesson of common humanity, it was heart-rending. The hesitation, the bewildered look, the coming to himself when he sees his hands bloody; the manner in which his voice clung to his throat, and choked his utterance; his agony and tears, the force of nature overcome by passion – beggared description. It was a scene, which no one who saw it can ever efface from his recollection. (p. 37)

In *Romeo and Juliet* he finds Kean 'cold, tame and unimpressive': 'we never saw anything less ardent or less voluptuous' (p. 39), and he takes issue with Eliza O'Neill's scream, as Juliet seeing the ghost of Tybalt, since 'there is a distinction to be kept up between physical and intellectual horror (for the latter becomes more general, internal, and absorbed, in proportion as it becomes more intense)' (p. 30).

Also concerned with characterization is Anna Jameson's *Characteristics of Woman, Moral, Poetical, and Historical* (1832) – although as the title of her book suggests, its aims extend beyond Shakespeare criticism. Jameson's account of Shakespeare' heroines is often emotional. Of Juliet she suggests that 'All Shakespeare's women, being essentially women, either love, or have loved, or are capable of loving; but Juliet is love itself. The passion is her state of being, and out of it she has no existence' (I, p. 91). Desdemona she identifies as 'abstract goodness [. . .] a victim consecrated from the first, – "an offering without blemish," alone worthy of the grand final sacrifice; all harmony, all grace, all purity, all tenderness, all truth' (II, p. 49); Cordelia, 'governed by the purest and holiest impulses and motives, the most refined from all dross of selfishness and passion, approaches near to perfection' (II, p. 89). Writing sympathetically of Cleopatra, Jameson admires her 'impression [. . .] of perpetual and irreconcileable contrast' (II, p. 123), in Volumnia 'her lofty patriotism, her patrician haughtiness, her maternal pride, her eloquence, and her towering spirit, are exhibited with the utmost power of effect, yet the truth of female nature is beautifully preserved, and the portrait, with all its vigour, is without harshness' (II, p. 175). Lady Macbeth is the subject of Jameson's final chapter, and here, too, she is sympathetic:

She is a terrible impersonation of evil passions and mighty powers, not so far removed from our own nature, as to be cast beyond the pale of our sympathies; for the woman herself remains a woman to the last, – still linked with her sex and with humanity. (II, 304–5)

1840–1904: Bardolatry and Biography

The worship of Shakespeare's powers which George Bernard Shaw would later dub 'Bardolatry' had its most famous mid-century expression in Thomas Carlyle's 'The Hero as Poet', a chapter in his influential *On Heroes, Hero-Worship, & the Heroic in History* (1840), 'here, I say, is an English King, whom no time or chance, Parliament or combination of Parliaments, can dethrone! That King Shakspeare, does not he shine, in crowned sovereignty, over us all, as the noblest, gentlest, yet strongest of rallying-signs; indestructible' (Carlyle, 1993, p. 97). Like his Romantic predecessors, Carlyle stresses Shakespearean characterization:

it is in what I called Portrait-painting, delineating of men and things, especially of men, that Shakspeare is great. All the greatness of the man comes out decisively here. It is unexampled, I think, that calm creative perspicacity of Shakspeare. The thing he looks at reveals not this or that face of it, but its inmost heart and generic secret: it dissolves itself as in light before him, so that he discerns the perfect structure of it. Creative, we said: poetic creation, what is this too but *seeing* the thing sufficiently? The *word* that will describe the thing follows, of itself, from such clear intense sight of the thing. And is not Shakspeare's *morality*, his valour, candour, tolerance, truthfulness; his whole victorious strength and greatness, which can triumph over such obstructions, visible there too? Great as the world! No *twisted*, poor convex-concave mirror, reflecting all objects with its own convexities and concavities; a perfectly *level* mirror. (p. 89)

Shakespeare's tragedies were, according to Carlyle, the product of his own felt experience:

It seems to me a heedless notion, our common one, that he sat like a bird on the bough; and sang forth, free and offhand, never knowing the troubles of other men. Not so; with no man it is so. How could a man travel forward from rustic deer-poaching to such tragedy-writing, and not fall in with sorrows on the way? Or, still better, how could a man delineate a Hamlet, a Coriolanus, a Macbeth, so many suffering heroic hearts, if his own heroic heart had never suffered? (p. 92)

In 1844, Matthew Arnold wrote in his sonnet 'Shakespeare': 'Others abide our question. Thou art free. / We stand and ask – Thou smilest and art still, / Out-topping knowledge.' As the Victorian period continued, there were different attempts to escape Arnold's sense of the ultimate unknowability of Shakespeare, and instead to explicate aspects of his writing. Many of these were influenced by the new quasi-scientific methods of bibliographic scholarship expounded by the New Shakspere Society, founded in 1874. The Society's aims were set out by its director, F. J. Furnivall, in the Prospectus:

> To do honour to Shakspere [Footnote: This spelling of our great Poet's name is taken from the only unquestionably genuine signatures of his that we possess [...] Though it has hitherto been too much to ask people to suppose that Shakspere knew how to spell his own name, I hope the demand may not prove too great for the imagination of the Members of the new Society], to mark out the succession of his plays, and thereby the growth of his mind and art; to promote the intelligent study of him, and to print Texts illustrating his works and his times, this *New Shakspere Society* is founded.

Furnivall made explicit the connections between this new branch of literary criticism and the scientific temper of the age:

> Dramatic poet though Shakspere is, bound to lose himself in his wondrous and manifold creations; taciturn 'as the secrets of Nature' though he be; yet in this Victorian time, when our geniuses of Science are so wresting her secrets from Nature as to make our days memorable for ever, the faithful student of Shakspere need not fear that he will be unable to pierce through the crowds of forms that exhibit Shakspere's mind, to the mind itself, the man himself, and see him as he was. (Furnivall, 1874, n.p.)

One attempt to classify and develop Shakespearean study can be seen in a new edition of the plays, introduced by Furnivall: *The Leopold Shakspere. The Poet's Works in Chronological Order. From the Text of Professor Delius* (1879). This edition divided the plays into four chronological groups, with the tragedies largely placed in the third period (1601–8). Furnivall's introduction stressed the scientific investigation of Shakespeare's development and the importance of studying his whole oeuvre 'as parts of a whole, and in relation to the other parts, as well as singly' (p. cxvii). Of the tragic period, Furnivall wrote 'The fierce and stern decree of that Period seems to me to be, "there shall be vengeance, death, for misjudgement, failure in duty, self-indulgence, sin," and the innocent who belong to the guilty shall suffer with them: Portia, Ophelia, Desdemona, Cordelia, lie beside Brutus, Hamlet, Othello, Lear' (p. lxvii). Furnivall found Brutus noble, and took a dim view of Hamlet: 'the hesitating, philosophising, duty-shirking, excuse-seeking Hamlet he has given us [is] a type of the weakness of every one amongst us' (p. lxx); and of Othello: 'Behind the nobleness of his nature were yet the jealousy, the suspicion, the mean cunning of the savage' (p. lxxvii); like Othello, Macbeth shows us how 'man remains the same, mean, tempted, falling, sinning, murdering, with the vengeance of death falling on him and the wife who here has shared his crimes' (p. lxxvii). In *Antony and Cleopatra*

> Shakspere has poured out the glory of his genius in profusion, and makes us stand by, saddened and distresst, as the noble Antony sinks to his ruin, under the gorgeous colouring of the Eastern sky, the vicious splendour of the Egyptian queen; makes us look with admiring hate on the wonderful picture he has drawn, certainly the most wonderful study of woman he has left us. (p. lxxxii)

Furnivall also wrote an introduction to an influential account translated from the German of G. G. Gervinus: *Shakespeare Commentaries* (1877). Gervinus' commentaries covered all the plays. On *Romeo and Juliet* he argued for a moralistic reading:

> excess in any enjoyment, however pure in itself, transforms its sweet into bitterness; that devotion to any single feeling, however noble, bespeaks its ascendancy; that this ascendancy moves the man and woman out of their natural spheres; that love can only be an accompaniment to life, and that it cannot fill out the life and business of the man especially. (Gervinus, 1877, p. 211)

In *Othello* we see a crime 'committed by a man who united the two natures, calmness and ardour, rashness and circumspection – the traits which make the murder possible, and those which allow us to admire and to pity the murderer' (p. 510). Gervinus stops short of blaming Desdemona for the tragedy:

> The same nature and qualities were at work in her when she gave the fatal blow to the life of her father as when she gave occasion for the suspicion of her husband [...] she falls sacrifice to her own nature, and not to the law of any arbitrary and unjust moral statute; to a nature which, in the strength of that simplicity and originality which excites our interest, oversteps the limitations of social custom, unites guilt and innocence in strange combination, draws death as a punishment upon itself, and endures death like a triumph – a nature which divides our feelings between admiration and pity. It seems as if perfect satisfaction was here afforded to all the demands of tragedy. (p. 546)

Like Hazlitt and Coleridge before him, Gervinus stresses the importance of characterization and again, like the Romantics, he identifies Hamlet as a contemporary:

> In Hamlet a social character of modern times is, as it were, depicted, one which is inclined to abandon the heroic customs of the age in which fate has placed

him, of an age in which everything hinges on physical power and the desire for action, which nature has denied to *him*. All the bloody unnatural events which we see before us – adultery, poisoning, and revenge for bloodshed, and the warlike deeds on which we cast a glance, the combat between the old Hamlet and Norway, when 'he smote the sledded Polack on the ice' – all this transports us to a rude and wild period, from which Hamlet's whole nature recoils, and to which he falls a sacrifice, because, by habit, character, and education he is alienated from it, and like the boundary-stone of a changing civilisation he touches a world of finer feeling. [. . .] Our modern sensibility is anticipated, as it were, by two centuries in Hamlet. (pp. 573–4)

The end of the play is designed as a punishment for Hamlet's inaction: 'this bloody conclusion is not the consequence of an aesthetic fault on the part of the poet, but of a moral fault on that of his Hamlet, a consequence which the sense of the whole play and the design of this character aim at from the first' (p. 582). Gervinus argues that the witches are not external tempters or dark agents, but that they represent Macbeth's own inner ambition:

the poet has endowed these creatures with the power to tempt and delude men, to tangle them with oracles of double meaning, with delusion and deception, and even to try them, as Satan in the book of Job, with sorrow and trouble, with storms and sickness; but they have no authority with fatalistic power to do violence to the human will. Their promises and their prophecies leave ample scope for freedom of action; [. . .] they are weird sisters only in the sense that men carry their own fates within their own bosoms. Macbeth, in meeting them, has to struggle against no external power, but only with his own nature; they bring to light the evil side of his character, which was not to be read in his face; he does not stumble on the plans of his royal ambition, because the allurement approaches him from without; but this temptation is sensibly wakened in him, because those plans have long been slumbering in his soul. (p. 592)

He sees *King Lear* as a play without Christian comfort:

Special weight is laid upon the fact that it is a heathenish time; nature is the goddess of Lear as well as of Edmund; chance reigns above, power and force below. The best of this race know of no inner strength, of no noble will, of no calmness and self-command, and of no moral principle, whereby the power of the blood can be broken, the impulse of passion controlled, and immoderate desires bridled. All, and especially the best, with fatalistic feeling attribute the acts of men to the influence of nature and the stars [. . .] There is no other tragedy in which almost all the main acting characters are, as in this, equally the prey of violent mental emotions, vehement feelings, or insurmountable desires. (pp. 619–21)

As the Victorian period advanced, such commentaries on Shakespeare multiplied, and the task of accounting for and explicating not just individual plays but their progress and place in the author's career became more pressing. Following Gervinus' commentaries, a number of booklength studies of Shakespeare's work appeared, of which Edward Dowden's influential *Shakspere: A Critical Study of his Mind and Art* (1875) was pre-eminent. Eschewing the scientific methodologies advocated by Furnivall and later by Moulton, Dowden states his intention: 'To approach Shakspere on the human side is the object of this book' (Dowden, 1875, p. vi): the human side is of Shakespeare himself, as the study is concerned 'to connect the study of Shakspere's works with an inquiry after the personality of the writer, and to observe, as far as is possible, in its several stages the growth of his intellect and character from youth to full maturity' (p. v), and also of his characters. Dowden's study stressed a Shakespeare who prompts questions rather than providing easy or comfortable answers. He cannot be co-opted to orthodox beliefs, because of the time in which he wrote:

> Poetry in this Elizabethan period is put upon a purely human basis. No Fate broods over the actions of men and the history of families; the only fatality is the fatality of character. Luck, an outstanding element, helping to determine the lives of mortals, and not reducible to known law, luck good and bad Shakspere readily admits; but luck is strictly a thing in the course of nature. The divinity which shapes our ends works efficiently, but secretly. [. . .] If we recognise in the moral order of the world a divine presence, then the divine presence is never absent from the Shaksperian world. (p. 24)

Rather than providing a moral framework, Shakespeare stimulates our moral sense:

> Thus Shakspere, like nature and like the vision of human life itself, if he does not furnish us with a doctrine, has the power to free, arouse, dilate. Again and again, we fall back into our little creed or our little theory. Shakspere delivers us; under his influence we come anew into the presence of stupendous mysteries, and, instead of our little piece of comfort, and support, and contentment, we receive the gift of solemn awe, and bow the head in reverential silence. (pp. 34–5)

The tragedies deal with questions beyond comprehension:

> Tragedy as conceived by Shakspere is concerned with the ruin or the restoration of the soul, and of the life of men. In other words its subject is the struggle of good and evil in the world. Thus strikes down upon the roots of things. The comedies of Shakspere had, in comparison, played upon the surface of life [. . .] Now, in the tragedies, Shakspere has flung himself abroad upon the dim sea

which moans around our little solid sphere or the known [. . .] Here, upon the earth, evil *is* – such was Shakspere's declaration in the most emphatic accent. Iago actually exists. There is also in the earth a sacred passion of deliverance, a pure redeeming ardour. Cordelia exists. This Shakspere can tell for certain. But how Iago can be, and why Cordelia lies strangled across the breast of Lear – are these questions which you go on to ask? [. . .] Shakspere prefers to let you remain in the solemn presence of a mystery. He does not invite you into his little church or his little library brilliantly illuminated by philosophical or theological rush-lights. You remain in the darkness. But you remain in the vital air. And the great night is overhead. (pp. 224–6)

This is not, however, to say that they are devoid of comfort: 'his faith in good-ness had never been so strong and sure. [. . .] Now, with every fresh discovery of crime Shakspere made discovery of virtue which cannot suffer defeat' (p. 229).

Dowden views *Hamlet* as inexplicable, and argues, against the positivism of the New Shakspere approach, that this unknowability is intrinsic to the work:

When Shakspere completed Hamlet, he must have trusted himself and trusted his audience; he trusts himself to enter into relation with his subject, highly complex as that subject was, in a pure, emotional manner. Hamlet might so easily have been manufactured into an enigma, or a puzzle; and then the puzzle, if sufficient pains were bestowed, could be completely taken to pieces and explained. But Shakspere created it a mystery, and therefore it is for ever suggestive; for ever suggestive and never wholly explicable [. . .] The obscurity itself is a vital part of the work of art which deals not with a problem but a life. (pp. 126–7)

Dowden's account of tragedy sees its deaths not as failures or occasions for regret, but as larger-than-life triumphs: 'the theme of tragedy, as conceived by the poet, is not material prosperity or failure; it is spiritual; fulfilment or failure of a destiny higher than that which is related to the art of getting on in life. To die under certain conditions may be a higher rapture than to live' (pp. 123–4). Something of the popularity of Dowden's account can be traced in its frequent reissuing, going through a dozen editions by the end of the nineteenth century.

Dowden's rival for this market was the poet A. C. Swinburne, whose *A Study of Shakespeare* was first published in 1880. Swinburne had his own division of Shakespeare's writing, into a first period, 'lyric and fantastic', a second period, 'comic and historic', and a third, 'tragic and romantic'. Swinburne elaborates that 'it is not, so to speak, the literal but the spiritual order which I have studied to observe and to indicate: the periods which I seek to define belong not to chronology but to art' (Swinburne, 1880, p. 16). He argued against the New Shakspere Society's preferred scientific metrical analysis as the approach of the 'horny eye and the callous finger of a pedant' (p. 7). Swinburne's criticism was concerned with the change of Shakespeare's language, the growth and development of his verse and tone, but these were modulations that 'can only be traced by ear and not by finger' (p. 16). He identifies *Hamlet* as 'the bridge between the middle and the final period of Shakespeare' (p. 160), with the first quarto text of 1600 (Q1) as part of the middle period, citing as evidence the difference 'between the straightforward agents of their own destiny whom we meet in the first *Hamlet* and the obliquely moving patients who veer sideways to their doom in the second' (p. 162). He argues, however, for the particular stageworthy qualities of the earlier text: 'Every change in the text of *Hamlet* has impaired its fitness for the stage and increased its value for the closet in exact and perfect proportion' (p. 164).

Summarizing the great tragedies, Swinburne wrote that 'if *Othello* be the most pathetic, *King Lear* the most terrible, *Hamlet* the subtlest and deepest works of Shakespeare, the highest in abrupt and steep simplicity is *Macbeth*' (p. 182). However, he placed *King Lear* at the pinnacle of Shakespeare's achievement:

> Of all Shakespeare's plays, *King Lear* is unquestionably that in which he has come nearest to the height, and to the likeness of the one tragic poet on any side greater than himself whom the world in all its ages has ever seen born of time. It is by far the most Æschylean of his works; the most elemental and primæval, the most oceanic and Titanic in conception. [. . .] But in one main point it differs radically from the work and spirit of Æschylus. Its fatalism is of a darker and harder nature [. . .] Requital, redemption, amends, equity, explanation, pity and mercy, are words without a meaning here. (pp. 170–2)

Swinburne's comments on *Coriolanus* are trenchant: it is

> rather a private and domestic than a public or historical tragedy [. . .] the final impression is not that of a conflict between patrician and plebeian, but solely that of a match of passions played out for life and death between a mother and a son. [. . .] The subject of the whole play is not the exile's revolt, the rebel's repentance, or the traitor's reward, but above all it is the son's tragedy. (pp. 187–8)

Elsewhere he finds flashes of tragedy, arguing that *Measure for Measure* 'is in its very inmost essence a tragedy' (p. 203), and that 'In *Troilus and Cressida* we found too much that Swift might have written when half inspired by the genius of Shakespeare; in the great and terrible fourth act of *Timon* we find such tragedy as Juvenal might have written when half deified by the spirit of Æschylus' (214).

1904: A. C. Bradley

Swinburne's summoning of the ultimate Greek tragedian is elaborated in one of the most significant and influential works of criticism on Shakespeare's tragedies, A. C. Bradley's *Shakespearean Tragedy*, deriving from lectures delivered to university audiences in Liverpool, Glasgow and as Professor of Poetry at Oxford. This study was first published in 1904, and never out of print for the rest of the century. Bradley's work can be seen in the context of the nineteenth century's interest in characterization, but it has cast its shadow over twentieth-century approaches to the genre. Bradley's introduction stresses his interest in 'our understanding and enjoyment of these works as dramas', arguing that the 'right way' to read Shakespeare is as if an actor studying the parts (Bradley, 1904, p. xxv), coupled with a 'process of comparison and analysis' (p. xxvi). For his purposes he identifies 'Shakespearean tragedy' as represented by *Hamlet*, *Othello*, *King Lear* and *Macbeth*.

Bradley argues that 'the tragic story [is] concerned primarily with one person'; it is 'a tale of suffering and calamity conducting to death'; such suffering is exceptional in that it befalls 'a conspicuous person' and in that it is itself 'unexpected and contrasted with previous happiness or glory'. The fate of the tragic individual has broader implications, affecting 'the welfare of the whole nation or empire' (p. 5). His account of the agency of tragedy is clear: 'the calamities of tragedy do not simply happen, nor are they sent; they proceed mainly from actions, and those the actions of men . . . the hero [. . .] always contributes in some measure to the disaster in which he perishes' (p. 6). He argues that Shakespeare's main interest 'may be said with equal truth to lie in action issuing from character, or in character issuing in action' (p. 7). Together with this stress on character, however, is an acknowledgement of other tragic agents. 'Fate' in Shakespeare's tragedies is to Bradley 'a mythological expression for the whole system or order, of which the individual characters form an inconsiderable and feeble part; which seems to determine, far more than they, their native dispositions and their circumstances, and, through these, their action' (p. 21). It is a mistake, Bradley argues, to discuss tragedy in terms of justice or moral deserts: 'when we are immersed in a tragedy, we feel towards dispositions, actions, and persons such emotions as attraction and repulsion, pity, wonder, fear, horror, perhaps hatred; but we do not *judge*' (p. 24). Rather, Shakespeare's tragedies are concerned with good and evil, not with justice and merit. Ultimately, 'tragedy would not be tragedy if it were not a painful mystery' (p. 28).

Crucial to Bradley's theory is the concept of conflict derived from Hegel (see pp. 27–8), the conflict between and within characters: 'as a rule, the hero, though he pursues his fated way is, at least at some point in the action and sometimes at many, torn by an inward struggle' (p. 12). Bradley argues that Shakespearean tragic characters

> are made of the stuff we find within ourselves [. . .] but, by an intensification of the life which they share with others, they are raised above them [. . .]. In almost all we observe a marked one-sidedness, a predisposition in some particular direction; a total incapacity, in certain circumstances, of resisting the force which draws in this direction; a fatal tendency to identify the whole being with one interest, object, passion, or habit of mind. This, it would seem, is, for Shakespeare, the fundamental tragic trait. (p. 13)

Bradley's book contains two chapters on each of the four tragedies *Othello*, *King Lear*, *Macbeth* and, first, *Hamlet*, where he argues briskly against the view taken by Dowden and others of the intrinsic mystery of Hamlet:

> The mysteriousness of life is one thing, the psychological unintelligibility of a dramatic character is quite another; and the second does not show the first, it shows only the incapacity or folly of the dramatist. [. . .] Of course *Hamlet* appeals powerfully to our sense of the mystery of life, but so does *every* good tragedy; and it does so not because the hero is an enigma to us, but because, having a fair understanding of him, we feel how strange it is that strength and weakness should be so mingled in one soul, and that this soul should be doomed to such misery and apparent failure. (p. 73)

The cause of Hamlet's irresolution is not 'an habitual excess of reflectiveness' but rather 'a state of profound melancholy' (p. 86) which can be diagnosed according to Elizabethan ideas of the disease. This condition is prompted or exacerbated by

> the moral shock of the sudden ghastly disclosure of his mother's true nature [. . .] not only an astounding shallowness of feeling but an eruption of coarse sensuality [. . .] It brings bewildered horror, then loathing, then despair of human nature. His whole mind is poisoned. He can never see Ophelia in the same light again: she is a woman, and his mother is a woman. (pp. 94–5)

However, Bradley argues that 'no reasonable doubt can, I think, be felt [that] Hamlet was at some time sincerely and ardently in love with Ophelia' (p. 123), and, with equal certainty: '[Gertrude] was not a bad-hearted woman, not at all the woman to think little of murder. But she had a soft animal nature, and was very dull and very shallow. She loved to be happy, like a sheep in the sun' (pp. 134–5). Ultimately, Bradley identifies 'the feeling of a supreme power of destiny' (p. 140) at work.

Othello Bradley terms 'the most painfully exciting and the most terrible' of Shakespeare's tragedies (p. 143). He concedes, however, that it is not rated as highly as the other tragedies he discusses, given its 'comparative confinement of the imaginative atmosphere. *Othello* has not equally with the other three the power of dilating the imagination by vague suggestions of huge universal powers working in the world of individual fate and passion. It is, in a sense, less "symbolic"' (p. 150). However, its emotional pull is strong. 'The suffering of Desdemona' is 'the most nearly intolerable thing that Shakespeare offers us ... We are never wholly uninfluenced by the feeling that Othello is a man contending with another man; but Desdemona's suffering is like that of the most loving of dumb creatures tortured without cause by the being he adores' (p. 145). Bradley identifies Iago as 'supreme among Shakespeare's evil characters because the greatest intensity and subtlety of imagination have gone into his making' (p. 190) – in terms of his psychological complexity, Bradley suggests he is equalled only by Hamlet – but goes on to argue that 'the tragedy of *Othello* is in a sense his tragedy too. It shows us not a violent man, like Richard [III], who spends his life in murder, but a thoroughly bad, *cold* man, who is at last tempted to let loose the forces within him, and is at once destroyed' (pp. 177–8).

Turning to *King Lear*, Bradley echoes Lamb: the play 'as a whole is imperfectly dramatic, and there is something in its very essence which is at war with the senses, and demands a purely imaginative realisation' (p. 202). The blinding of Gloucester provokes in a theatre audience

> a sensation so violent as to overpower the purely tragic emotions, and therefore the spectacle would seem revolting or shocking. But it is otherwise in reading. For mere imagination, the physical horror, though not lost, is so far deadened that it can do its duty as a stimulus to pity, and to that appalled essence of the tragedy to excite. (p. 205)

The play is structured by its double plot, which gives the sense that 'we [are] witnessing something universal, – a conflict not so much of particular persons as of the powers of good and evil in the world', represented by groups of selfish and selfless characters in conflict, 'almost as if Shakespeare, like Empedocles, were regarding Love and Hate as the two ultimate forces of the universe' (p. 215). Lear owes his new awareness of humanity and love

> to those sufferings which made us doubt whether life were not simply evil, and men like the flies which wanton boys torture for their sport. Should we not be at least as near the truth if we called this poem *The Redemption of King Lear*, and declared that the business of 'the gods' with him was neither to torment him, nor to teach him a 'noble anger', but to lead him to attain through apparently hopeless failure the very end and aim of life? (p. 235)

Bradley argues that Lear's final words over the body of Cordelia represent an agony 'not of pain but of ecstasy', and 'unbearable *joy*' (p. 241) of belief that she is still alive. This is one of the reasons the play is not ultimately pessimistic.

In *Macbeth*, Bradley writes, Shakespeare 'no longer restricts the action to purely human agencies': 'The reader who looks unwillingly at Iago gazes at Lady Macbeth in awe, because though she is dreadful she is also sublime. The whole tragedy is sublime' (p. 277). The tone of the play is particularly marked: 'Darkness, we may say even blackness, broods over this tragedy. It is remarkable that almost all the scenes which at once recur to memory take place either at night or in some dark spot' (p. 279). Flashes of colour punctuate this blackness, however, and

> above all, that colour is the colour of blood. It cannot be an accident that the image of blood is forced upon us continually, not merely by the events themselves, but by full descriptions, and even by reiteration of the word in unlikely parts of the dialogue [. . .] It is as if the poet saw the whole story through an ensanguined mist, and as if it stained the very blackness of the night. (pp. 280–1)

These qualities are developed in the play's use of 'irony on the part of the author himself [. . .] especially the "Sophoclean irony" by which a speaker is made to use words bearing to the audience, in addition to his own meaning, a further and ominous sense, hidden from himself, and, usually, from the other persons on the stage' (p. 283). Of Macbeth and Lady Macbeth, Bradley writes that 'theirs is an *egoïsme à deux*. They have no separate ambitions [. . .] they remain to the end tragic, even grand' (p. 293). In the short Notes which he appends to *Shakespearean Tragedy*, Bradley addresses a number of specific questions and answers them with close reference to the texts. His Notes on *Macbeth* are indicative: 'Did Lady Macbeth Really Faint?' ('Is it not likely [. . .] that the expression on the faces of the lords would force her to realise, what before the murder she had refused to consider, the horror and the suspicion it must excite?' (p. 418); 'Duration of the Action in *Macbeth*. Macbeth's age. "He has no Children."' ('There is no unmistakable indication of the ages of the two principal characters; but the question, though of no great importance, has an interest. I believe most readers imagine Macbeth as a man between forty and fifty, and his wife as younger but not young' (p. 420)); 'The Ghost of Banquo' ('I think that Shakespeare (1) meant the judicious to take the Ghost for an hallucination, but (2) knew that the bulk of the audience would take it for a reality' (p. 426)).

Terence Hawkes has described Bradley's *Shakespearean Tragedy* as 'one of the most influential texts of our century: one which by now ranks as almost synonymous with the study of "English" and which, despite earnest efforts to unseat it, remains a key and vastly formative work' (Hawkes, 1996, p. 30). Gary Taylor observes that 'in Bradley's hands, Shakespearian criticism became a philosophical novel' (Taylor, 1991, p. 230). Katherine Cooke (1972) discusses Bradley's extensive influence on twentieth-century criticism, and, while his focus on character has been challenged, what Jonathan Dollimore terms his 'metaphysic of tragedy' (Dollimore, 1984, p. 53) has remained dominant. Almost all of the works discussed in Part II of this Guide are influenced by Bradley's critical achievement, which sits, Janus-faced, looking back over Victorian and Romantic criticism, and forward, into the increased institutionalization of Shakespeare studies in the twentieth century.

Further Reading

Bate, Jonathan. *Shakespearean Constitutions: Politics, Theatre, Criticism 1730–1830*. Oxford: Clarendon Press, 1989.
—— *The Romantics on Shakespeare*. London: Penguin, 1992.
Bell, John. *Bell's Edition of Shakespeare's Plays, 1774*. London: Cornmarket Press, 1969.
Bradley, A. C. *Shakespearean Tragedy: Lectures on Hamlet, Othello, King Lear, Macbeth*. London: Macmillan, 1904.
Carlyle, Thomas. *On Heroes, Hero-worship, & the Heroic in History*. Berkeley; Oxford: University of California Press, 1993.
Clark, Sandra. *Shakespeare Made Fit: Restoration Adaptations of Shakespeare*. Everyman's Library. London: Dent, 1997.
Coleridge, Samuel Taylor. *Lectures 1808–1819: On Literature*. Bollingen series; 75th edn., 2 vols, R. A. Foakes (ed.), London; Princeton: Routledge & Kegan Paul; Princeton University Press, 1987.
——, and Foakes, R. A. *Coleridge's Criticism of Shakespeare: A Selection*. London: Athlone Press, 1989.
Cooke, Katharine. *A. C. Bradley and His Influence in Twentieth-century Shakespeare Criticism*. Oxford: Clarendon Press, 1972.
De Quincey, Thomas, et al. *The Works of Thomas De Quincey*. London: Pickering & Chatto, 2000.
Delius, Nikolaus, and Furnivall, Frederick James. *The Leopold Shakspere: The Poet's Works, in Chronological Order, from the Text of Professor Delius, with 'The Two Noble Kinsmen' and 'Edward III'*. London: Cassell Petter & Galpin, 1877.
Dennis, John. *An Essay on the Genius and Writings of Shakespear, with some Letters of Criticism to the Spectator*. London, 1712.
Dobson, Michael. *The Making of the National Poet: Shakespeare, Adaptation and Authorship, 1660–1769*. Oxford: Clarendon Press, 1992.
Dollimore, Jonathan. *Radical Tragedy: Religion, Ideology and Power in the Drama of Shakespeare and his Contemporaries*. London: Harvester Wheatsheaf, 1984.
Donaldson, Ian. *Ben Jonson*. Oxford: Oxford University Press, 1985.

Dowden, Edward. *Shakspere: A Critical Study of his Mind and Art.* London: Henry S. King, 1875.

Dryden, John. *Of Dramatick Poesie, an Essay.* Menston: Scolar Press, 1969.

Fuller, Thomas. *The History of the Worthies of England.* London, 1662.

Furnivall, F. J. 'New Shakspere Society Prospectus.' *Transactions of the New Shakspere Society* 1 (1874).

Gervinus, Georg Gottfried, and Bunnett, Fanny Elizabeth. *Shakespeare Commentaries; tr. by F.E. Bunnètt.* London, 1877.

Gildon, Charles. *The Complete Art of Poetry.* London, 1718.

Griffith, Elizabeth. *The Morality of Shakespeare's Drama Illustrated.* London: Frank Cass, 1971.

Hawkes, Terence. *Alternative Shakespeares,* vol. 2. London: Routledge, 1996.

Hazlitt, William, and Wu, Duncan. *The Selected Writings of William Hazlitt.* London: Pickering & Chatto, 1998.

Hogan, Charles Beecher. *Shakespeare in the Theatre, 1701–1800.* Oxford: Clarendon Press, 1952.

Jameson, Anna Brownell. *Characteristics of Women, Moral, Poetical and Historical,* 2 vols. London, 1832.

Johnson, Samuel. *The Plays of William Shakespeare in Eight Volumes: with the corrections and illustrations of various commentators; to which are added notes by Sam Johnson.* London: Printed for J. and R. Tonson, 1765.

Lamb, Charles, Lamb, Mary, and Lucas, E. V. *The Works of Charles and Mary Lamb.* London: Methuen, 1903.

LeWinter, Oswald. *Shakespeare in Europe.* Harmondsworth: Penguin, 1970.

Marsden, Jean I. *The Appropriation of Shakespeare: Post-Renaissance Reconstructions of the Works and the Myth.* New York; London: Harvester Wheatsheaf, 1991.

Meres, Francis. *Palladis tamia. Wits treasury, the second part of Wits commonwealth.* London: 1598.

Montagu, Elizabeth Robinson. *An Essay on the Writings and Genius of Shakespear, compared with the Greek and French Dramatic Poets: With some Remarks upon the Misrepresentations of Mons. de Voltaire.* London: Cass, 1970.

Pope, Alexander, and Rowe, Nicholas. *The Works of Shakespear: In Six Volumes.* London: Printed for Jacob Tonson in the Strand, 1725.

Rowe, Nicholas. *The works of mr. William Shakespear; revis'd and corrected, with an account of the life and writings of the author, by N. Rowe.* London, 1709.

——*The works of mr. William Shakespear; revis'd and corrected, with an account of the life and writings of the author, by N. Rowe. Vol. 7 [containing the poems] to which is prefix'd an essay on the art, rise and progress of the stage in Greece, Rome and England.* London, 1710.

Rymer, Thomas. *A Short View of Tragedy, 1693.* Menston: Scolar Press, 1970.

Schlegel, August Wilhelm von, Black, John, and Morrison, Alexander James William. *A Course of Lectures on Dramatic Art and Literature.* London: H. G. Bohn, 1846.

Scolokar, Anthony. *Diaphantus.* London. 1604.

Shakespeare, William, Hinman, Charlton, and Hooker, Richard. *The First Folio of Shakespeare.* London: Hamlyn, 1968.

Swinburne, Algernon Charles. *A Study of Shakespeare*, 2nd. edn. London: Chatto & Windus, 1880.

Taylor, Gary. *Reinventing Shakespeare: A Cultural History, from the Restoration to the Present.* London: Viking, 1991.

Taylor, Michael. *Shakespeare Criticism in the Twentieth Century.* Oxford: Oxford University Press, 2001.

Theobald, Lewis. *The Works of Shakespeare: In Seven Volumes. Collated with the Oldest Copies, and Corrected; With notes, Explanatory and Critical*, 1733.

——*Shakespeare Restored, or a Specimen of the many errors as well Committed as Unamended.* London: Cass, 1971.

Thompson, Ann, and Roberts, Sasha. *Women Reading Shakespeare, 1660–1900: An Anthology of Criticism.* Manchester: Manchester University Press, 1997.

Vickers, Brian. *Shakespeare: The Critical Heritage.* London: Routledge & Kegan Paul, 1974.

Whiter, Walter. *A Specimen of a Commentary on Shakespeare, 1794.* Menston: Scolar Press, 1972.

Part II

Twentieth-century Criticism

2

Genre: An Overview

Accounts of the genre of tragedy able to incorporate all eleven plays listed as 'tragedies' in the First Folio catalogue (see p. 6) have been thin on the ground. Following Bradley's stress on *Macbeth*, *Hamlet*, *King Lear* and *Othello*, many critics have debated whether tragedy is usefully considered in the singular – *Shakespearean Tragedy*, as both Bradley and a collection of recent criticism edited by John Drakakis (1992), would have it – or in the plural, as Zimmerman's alternative collection *Shakespeare's Tragedies* (1998) proposes.

One approach to genre has been historical. Lily Campbell, in *Shakespeare's Tragic Heroes: Slaves of Passion* (1930) argues that 'the problem of tragedy has always been the problem of evil in the world' (Campbell, 1930, p. 3). She contextualizes Shakespeare's tragedies in their historical period, drawing on material from anatomy, humoral physiology, philosophy and humanism to interpret the plays. In 1947, Campbell published an article on 'Bradley Revisited: Forty Years After' in which she discusses the logical failings of Bradley's argument: 'he by definition makes a tragic hero set the tragic circle in motion while he is morally responsible and then proves that he must have been morally responsible when he set the forces of destruction at work or else he could not have been a tragic hero' (Campbell, 1947, p. 178). E. M. W. Tillyard's *The Elizabethan World Picture* (1943) briefly discusses the tragedies as part of his thesis about the 'chain of being' which positioned humanity between beasts and angels: 'the conflicts of mature Shakespearean tragedy are those between the passions and reason' (Tillyard, 1943, p. 76). More recently, T. McAlindon's *Shakespeare's Tragic Cosmos* (1991) stresses the importance of the 'violent conflict and confusion of opposites' in the tragedies (McAlindon, 1991, p. 6). He describes a divergent cosmological tradition which could equally account for a view of the universe as hierarchically ordered and stable, or as a system of interdependent and dynamic opposites, and traces these different inheritances across the plays. Other historicized accounts, which consider Shakespeare's plays alongside those of other contemporary playwrights, include Dollimore (1984, see pp. 60–73), Neill (1997) and Watson (1994).

Irving Ribner's 1960 volume, *Patterns in Shakespearian Tragedy*, discusses the development of Shakespeare's tragedies throughout his career. Ribner argues for Shakespeare's development as 'a growth in moral vision' (Ribner, 1960, p. 7), and tragedy as a form akin to religion in seeking 'affirmation of order' (p. 9). Identifying *Titus Andronicus*, *Romeo and Juliet* and *Richard III* as tragedies still formed by their debt to Senecan models, it is with *Hamlet* and, ultimately, *Othello* – 'the prototype of tragedy in Christian Europe, that of Adam in the garden of Eden' (p. 115) – that Shakespearean tragedy reaches its truest maturity. Susan Snyder also draws on chronology for her discussion of *The Comic Matrix of Shakespeare's Tragedies* (1979), arguing for the inter-penetration of comedy in Shakespearean tragedy:

> Shakespeare [. . .] had thoroughly explored and mastered the comic form while he was still finding his way in tragedy. Add to that the taste for mixing comic with serious that was part of his theatrical heritage, and it seems probable that he would use the dramatic convention in which he was most at home, the world of romantic comedy, as a point of reference and departure in developing tragic forms. (Snyder, 1979, p. 4)

Written out of the conventions of Italianate love-comedy on the stage in the 1580s and early 1590s *Romeo and Juliet* is a play which 'becomes, rather than is, tragic' (p. 57); and *Othello*, in which a complete comic forepart is condensed into the first act, is followed by a tragic dénouement: 'Othello's disintegration of self is the dark side of comedy's rejection of singleness, its insistence on completing oneself with another' (pp. 82–3). Snyder goes on to discuss the intrusions of absurdity in *Hamlet* and *King Lear*'s relation to its tragicomic source in *King Leir* and its tragicomic successor in Tate's popular revision (see p. 14). Also on the chronology of Shakespeare's tragedy is Nicholas Brooke's *Shakespeare's Early Tragedies* (1968), which challenges the idea that the tragedies before *Hamlet* are merely 'exercises prior to the great achievement that was to follow' (Brooke, 1968, p. 1). Brooke argues that 'we need to free [the early tragedies] from the monolithic idea of Tragedy and regard them simply on their own account' (p. 5), and his study emphasizes connections and differences between the plays he analyses. Kristin Smidt's *Unconformities in Shakespeare's Tragedies* (1989) argues for the early plays as experiments dating from a period 'before Shakespeare fully realised the potentials of the inner conflict and developed a sufficiently mature artistry to portray individuals with a semblance of completeness' (Smidt, 1989, p. 17). Her focus is on problems, inconsistencies and lapses and what they can tell us about the plays and their production.

Dieter Mehl's approach in his *Shakespeare's Tragedies: An Introduction* (1986) begins with an overview of tragedy as a genre, arguing that 'the spectator is not put at his ease by a comforting distribution of reward and punishment; he is confronted, without homiletic soft-soaping, with the reality of wickedness and its power to corrupt the good, to make the world poorer and more hopeless' (Mehl, 1986, p. 7). No single theory is otherwise advanced, as Mehl goes on to discuss the early plays, the 'great tragedies' and the Roman plays. Also arguing that tragedies do not apportion punishment fairly is White's *Innocent Victims: Poetic Injustice in Shakespearean Tragedy* (1986). By contrast, Ruth Nevo's *Tragic Form in Shakespeare* (1972) argues that 'the structure of a Shakespearean tragedy is to be apprehended as an unfolding five-phase sequence, continuous, accumulative, and consummatory, rather than as a simple up-down movement, or even a more complex thesis-antithesis-synthesis' (Nevo, 1972, p. 17). The 'axis of development' throughout this structure is 'the tragic hero', whose journey ends in 'final passion and death, in which he in some way discovers, identifies, bears witness to or affirms the authenticity of the human value his experience in the play has realized' (pp. 21–2). In *Shakespeare and Tragedy* (1981) John Bayley also argues for the centrality of death in tragedy as something which paradoxically confirms rather than extinguishes the existence of its characters, and for the common tragic incompatibility of protagonist and situation. Also focusing on death as constitutive of tragedy are chapters on *Macbeth* and *Hamlet* in Robert Watson's *The Rest is Silence* (1994), and Michael Neill's *Issues of Death* (1997) which discusses *Hamlet*, *Othello* and *Antony and Cleopatra* as part of its thesis that 'tragedy [. . .] was one of the principal instruments by which the culture of early modern England reinvented death' (Neill, 1997, p. 3). The sense of identity as a key theme in tragedy and the dominance of the model of the tragic hero can be seen in Ure's *Shakespeare and the Inward Self of the Tragic Hero* (1961) and in Sanders' and Jacobson's *Shakespeare's Magnanimity: Four Tragic Heroes, their Friends and Families* (1978): see also chapter 4 on 'Character'.

In 1948, H. B. Charlton's view of *Shakespearian Tragedy* was that of a self-confessed 'devout Bradleyite' (Charlton, 1948 p. 4). Charlton argued that 'there emerges through the grief a growing sense of the immeasurable spiritual potentiality within man [. . .] the nobility of man triumphs over tragedy through tragedy [. . .] Shakespearian tragedy is the apotheosis of the spirit of man' (p. 13). A more explicit form of spirituality is identified by G. Wilson Knight, who suggests that 'each of Shakespeare's tragic heroes is a miniature Christ' and that the 'unique act of the Christ sacrifice' is central to Shakespearean tragedy (Knight, 1936, pp. 232–4). Roland Mushat Frye's *Shakespeare and Christian Doctrine* (1963) demonstrates Shakespeare's 'easy and intimate familiarity with Christian theology' (Frye, 1963, p. 13), but that the deployment of this knowledge is always for dramatic, rather than theological or doctrinaire, purposes. Ivor Morris's *Shakespeare's God: the role of religion in the tragedies* (1972) tends towards a Christian interpretation. Northrop Frye's *Fools of Time: Studies in Shakespearean Tragedy* (1967) reads Shakespeare as an exemplar of mythic, cross-cultural, ahistorical narratives:

> tragedy revolves around the primary contract of man and nature, the contract fulfilled by man's death, death being, as we say, the debt he owes to nature. What makes tragedy tragic, and not simply ironic, is the presence in it of a counter-movement of what we call the heroic, a capacity for action or passion, for doing or suffering, which is above ordinary human experience. (Frye, 1967, pp. 4–5)

His study emphasizes the ritual aspects of scapegoating, of rebellion, of the killing of the 'order-figure': a suggestion taken up in Maynard Mack's study *Killing the King* (1973).

Stanley Cavell, in his *Disowning Knowledge* (1987), argues that 'Shakespeare's plays interpret and reinterpret the skeptical problematic – the question whether I know with certainty of the existence of the external world and myself and others in it', and that therefore they 'find no stable solution to skepticism, in particular no rest in what we know of God' (Cavell, 1987, p. 3). Cavell's essay on *King Lear* sees this scepticism in its 'extreme precipitousness [. . .], the velocity of the banishments and of the consequences of the banishments' (p. 5), whereas in *Othello* it is jealousy which figures as the structure and allegory of scepticism. Cavell's essay on *Coriolanus* is reprinted in chapter 3 (p. 73). Timothy Reiss's *Tragedy and Truth* (1980) argues that 'tragedy can be read as a discourse of knowledge and truth' (Reiss, 1980, p. 17). His chapter on *Hamlet* argues that the opening scene of the play establishes its central themes:

> the opposition of speech and silence, or the encounter of speech with mis-understanding (wilful or accidental), constitutes at one level the entire action of the tragedy – at least until the final scene. The space of speech is one of disorder, confusion, and distraction. To it will be opposed a sphere of action, a place of order and firmness, of reason – and unjust tyranny. (p. 163)

The play traces the passing of one discursive order – Hamlet's – into another: Fortinbras's. Reiss' analysis of *King Lear* also reads a dramatization of a clash of values: 'of different classes of discourse, of different ways of acting and thinking, or different conceptions of power, of the place of the self and the role of the other' (p. 183). The gap between these binaries is 'the tragic space' (p. 202): what the discourse of tragedy performs is 'the production of a solution to such incomprehension from within its own elaboration' (p. 203).

Foakes, in his *Hamlet versus Lear: Cultural Politics and Shakespeare's Art* (1993) observes that around 1960, *King Lear* began to supplant *Hamlet* as Shakespeare's greatest play and that, simultaneously, 'the main tradition of criticism up to the 1950s had interpreted [*King Lear*] as Lear's pilgrimage to redemption, as he finds himself and is "saved" at the end, but in the 1960s the play became Shakespeare's bleakest and most despairing vision of suffering' (Foakes, 1993, pp. 3–4). Foakes' exploration of the reasons for this double shift historicizes reactions to tragedy and discusses the cultural reasons for their variable popularity. In his introduction to the New Casebook on the play, Kiernan Ryan (1993) offers an interesting account of the shift in perceptions of *King Lear*, and reprints some crucial stages in the movement from 'overtly or implicitly Christian accounts' (Ryan, 1993, p. 1) shattered by Everett's sceptical article in the journal *Critical Quarterly* (1960) and Elton's *King Lear and the Gods* (1966), which saw the last act destroying 'the foundations of faith itself' (Elton, 1966, p. 337). The critical differences between Kermode's selection for the Casebook series (1992) and Ryan's for the New Casebook only a year later are revealing. John Drakakis' collection *Shakespearean Tragedy* (1992) includes a thorough introduction on the tragic theories of Nietzsche, Hegel, Freud and Derrida. Hawkes (1986) contextualizes a number of critics on tragedy as a way of historicizing their contribution (see chapter 10: History and Politics). Performance histories (see pp. 330–2) have also explored the interplay between topical specificity and universality in the reinterpretation of the tragedies.

In his *Tragedy: Shakespeare and the Greek Example*, Adrian Poole also stresses the importance of diversity within tragedy, offering a reading of Greek tragedy through and in distinction to Shakespearean. 'Greek and Shakespearean tragedy [. . .] affirms with savage jubilation that man's state is diverse, fluid, and unfounded' (Poole, 1987, p. 2). Poole offers readings of *Lear* alongside *Oedipus at Colonus* and *Bacchae*, *Hamlet* alongside *Oedipus Tyrannus*, *Macbeth* alongside the *Oresteia*. Robert S. Miola takes a different antecedent in his *Shakespeare and Classical Tragedy: The Influence of Seneca* (1992), but rather than confining this to an apprentice period at the beginning of Shakespeare's career, Miola traces the influence of Senecan models of tyrannical rule, of revenge tragedy and of rage or *furor* in plays including *Othello*, *Macbeth* and *King Lear*.

Further Reading

Bayley, John. *Shakespeare and Tragedy*. London: Routledge & Kegan Paul, 1981.
Bradbrook. M. C. *Themes and Conventions of Elizabethan Tragedy*, 2nd edn. Cambridge: Cambridge University Press, 1980.

Bradley, A. C. *Shakespearean Tragedy: Lectures on Hamlet, Othello, King Lear, Macbeth.* London: Macmillan, 1904.

Brooke, Nicholas. *Shakespeare's Early Tragedies.* London: Methuen, 1968.

Campbell, Lily Bess. *Shakespeare's Tragic Heroes: Slaves of Passion.* Cambridge: The University Press, 1930.

——'Bradley Revisited: Forty Years After.' *Studies in Philology* 44 (1947): 174–94.

Cavell, Stanley. *Disowning Knowledge: In Six Plays of Shakespeare.* Cambridge: Cambridge University Press, 1987.

Charlton. H. B., and Trinity College (University of Cambridge). *Shakespearian Tragedy.* Cambridge: The University Press, 1948.

Dollimore, Jonathan. *Radical Tragedy: Religion, Ideology and Power in the Drama of Shakespeare and his Contemporaries.* London: Harvester Wheatsheaf, 1984.

Drakakis, John. *Shakespearean Tragedy.* London: Longman, 1992.

Elton, William R. *King Lear and the Gods.* San Marino, Calif: Huntington Library, 1966.

Everett, Barbara. 'The New *King Lear*.' *Critical Quarterly* 2 (1960): 325–39.

Foakes, R. A. *Hamlet versus Lear: Cultural Politics and Shakespeare's Art.* Cambridge: Cambridge University Press, 1993.

Frye, Northrop. *Fools of Time: Studies in Shakespearean Tragedy.* The Alexander lectures, 1966–7. Toronto: University of Toronto Press, 1967.

Frye, Roland Mushat. *Shakespeare and Christian Doctrine.* Princeton: Princeton University Press, 1963.

Hawkes, Terence. *That Shakspeherian Rag: Essays on a Critical Process.* London: Methuen, 1986.

Kermode, Frank. *Shakespeare: King Lear: A Casebook.* Casebook series, revsd edn. Basingstoke: Macmillan, 1992.

Knight, George Wilson. *Principles of Shakespearian Production: with especial reference to the tragedies.* London: Faber and Faber, 1936.

McAlindon, T. *Shakespeare's Tragic Cosmos.* Cambridge: Cambridge University Press, 1991.

Mack, Maynard. *Killing the King: Three Studies in Shakespeare's Tragic Structure.* New Haven: Yale University Press, 1973.

Mehl, Dieter. *Shakespeare's Tragedies: An Introduction.* Cambridge: Cambridge University Press, 1986.

Miola, Robert S. *Shakespeare and Classical Tragedy: The Influence of Seneca.* Oxford: Clarendon Press, 1992.

Morris, Ivor. *Shakespeare's God: the role of religion in the tragedies.* London: Allen and Unwin, 1972.

Neill. Michael. *Issues of Death: Mortality and Identity in English Renaissance Tragedy.* Oxford: Clarendon Press, 1997.

Nevo, Ruth. *Tragic Form in Shakespeare.* Princeton: Princeton University Press, 1972.

Poole, Adrian. *Tragedy: Shakespeare and the Greek Example.* Oxford: Basil Blackwell, 1987.

Reiss, Timothy J. *Tragedy and Truth: Studies in the Development of a Renaissance and Neoclassical Discourse.* New Haven: Yale University Press, 1980.

Ribner, Irving. *Patterns in Shakespearian Tragedy*. London: Methuen, 1960.

Ryan, Kiernan. *King Lear, William Shakespeare*. New Casebook series. Basingstoke: Macmillan, 1993.

Sanders, Wilbur, and Jacobson, Howard. *Shakespeare's Magnanimity: Four Tragic Heroes, their Friends and Families*. London: Chatto and Windus, 1978.

Smidt, Kristian. *Unconformities in Shakespeare's Tragedies*. Basingstoke: Macmillan, 1989.

Snyder, Susan. *The Comic Matrix of Shakespeare's Tragedies: Romeo and Juliet, Hamlet, Othello, and King Lear*. Princeton: Princeton University Press, 1979.

Tillyard, E. M. W. *The Elizabethan World Picture*. London: Chatto & Windus, 1943.

Ure, Peter. *Shakespeare and the Inward Self of the Tragic Hero*. Durham: University of Durham, 1961.

Watson, Robert N. *The Rest is Silence: Death as Annihilation in the English Renaissance*. Berkeley; London: University of California Press, 1994.

White, R. S. *Innocent Victims: Poetic Injustice in Shakespearean Tragedy*, 2nd edn. London: Athlone Press, 1986.

Zimmerman, Susan. *Shakespeare's Tragedies*. Basingstoke: Macmillan, 1998.

3

Genre: Critical Extracts

King Lear (c.1605–6) and Essentialist Humanism

Jonathan Dollimore

This chapter is taken from Dollimore's 1984 book, Radical Tragedy: Religion, Ideology and Power in the Drama of Shakespeare and his Contemporaries. *Here, he argues against the view of* Lear *as a story of Christian redemption, and against revisionist humanist claims that it dramatizes self-redemption through knowledge. Rather, he shows that the play insists on social hierarchies and that it displaces the tragic subject in favour of a more widely politicized account of position and consciousness.*

Jonathan Dollimore, '*King Lear* (c.1605–6) and Essentialist Humanism', in *Radical Tragedy: Religion, Ideology and Power in the Drama of Shakespeare and his Contemporaries*. London: Harvester Wheatsheaf, 1984.

When he is on the heath King Lear is moved to pity. As unaccommodated man he feels what wretches feel. For the humanist the tragic paradox arises here: debasement gives rise to dignity and at the moment when Lear might be expected to be most brutalised he becomes most human. Through kindness and shared vulnerability human kind redeems itself in a universe where the gods are at best callously just, at worst sadistically vindictive.

In recent years the humanist view of Jacobean tragedies like *Lear* has been dominant, having more or less displaced the explicitly Christian alternative. Perhaps the most important distinction between the two is this: the Christian view locates man centrally in a providential universe;[1] the humanist view likewise centralises man but now he is in a condition of tragic dislocation: instead of integrating (ultimately) with a teleological design created and sustained by God, man grows to consciousness in a universe which thwarts his deepest needs. If he is to be redeemed at all he must redeem himself. The humanist also contests the Christian claim that the suffering of Lear and Cordelia is part of a providential and redemptive design. If that suffering is to be justified at all it is because of what it reveals about man's intrinsic nature – his courage and integrity. By heroically enduring a fate he is powerless to alter, by insisting, moreover, upon *knowing* it, man grows in stature even as he is being destroyed. Thus Clifford Leech, an opponent of the Christian view, tells us that tragic protagonists 'have a quality of mind that somehow atones for the nature of the world in which they and we live. They have, in a greater or lesser degree, the power to endure and the power to apprehend' (*Shakespeare's Tragedies*, p. 15). Wilbur Sanders in an influential study argues for an ultimately optimistic Shakespeare who had no truck with Christian doctrine or conventional Christian conceptions of the absolute but nevertheless affirmed that 'the principle of health – grace – is not in heaven, but in nature, and especially in human nature, and it cannot finally be rooted out'. Ultimately this faith in nature and human nature involves and entails 'a faith in a universal moral order which cannot finally be defeated' (*The Dramatist and the Received Idea*, pp. 336–7).

Here as so often with the humanist view there is a strong residue of the more explicit Christian metaphysic and language which it seeks to eschew; comparable with Sanders' use of 'grace' is Leech's use of 'atone'. Moreover both indicate the humanist preoccupation with the universal counterpart of essentialist subjectivity – either ultimately affirmed (Sanders) or recognised as an ultimate tragic absence (Leech).[2] The humanist reading of *Lear* has been authoritatively summarised by G. K. Hunter (he calls it the 'modern' view of the play):

[it] is seen as the greatest of tragedies because it not only strips and reduces and assaults human dignity, but because it also shows with the greatest force and detail the process of restoration by which humanity can recover from degradation . . . [Lear's] retreat into the isolated darkness of his own mind is also a descent into the seed-bed of a new life; *for the individual mind is seen here as the place from which a man's most important qualities and relationships draw the whole of their potential'* (*Dramatic Identities and Cultural Tradition*, pp. 251–2, my italics).

What follows is an exploration of the political dimension of *Lear*. It argues that the humanist view of that play is as inappropriate as the Christian alternative which it has generally displaced – inappropriate not least because it shares the essentialism of the latter. I do not mean to argue again the case against the Christian view since, even though it is still sometimes advanced, it has been effectively discredited by writers as diverse as Barbara Everett, William R. Elton and Cedric Watts.[3] The principal reason why the humanist view seems equally misguided, and not dissimilar, is this: it mystifies suffering and invests man with a quasi-transcendent identity whereas the play does neither of these things. In fact, the play repudiates the essentialism which the humanist reading of it presupposes. However, I do not intend to replace the humanist reading with one which rehearses yet again all the critical clichés about the nihilistic and chaotic 'vision' of Jacobean tragedy. In *Lear*, as in *Troilus*, man is decentred not through misanthropy but in order to make visible social process and its forms of ideological misrecognition.

Redemption and Endurance: Two Sides of Essentialist Humanism

'Pity' is a recurring word in *Lear*. Philip Brockbank, in a recent and sensitive humanist reading of the play, says: 'Lear dies "with pity" (IV. vii. 53) and that access of pity, which in the play attends the dissolution of the senses and of the self, is a condition for the renewal of human life' ('Upon Such Sacrifices', p. 133). Lear, at least when he is on the heath, is indeed moved to pity, but what does it mean to say that such pity is 'a condition for the renewal of human life?' Exactly whose life is renewed? In this connection there is one remake of Lear's which begs our attention; it is made when he first witnesses 'You houseless poverty' (III. iv. 26): 'Oh, I have ta'en / Too little care of this!'. Too little: Lear bitterly reproaches himself because hitherto he has been aware of yet ignored the suffering of his deprived subjects. (The distracted use of the abstract – 'You houseless poverty' – subtly suggests that Lear's disregard has been of a general rather than a local poverty). He has ignored it not through callous indifference but simply *because he has not experienced it*.

King Lear suggests here a simple yet profound truth. Far from endorsing the idea that man can redeem himself in and through an access of pity, we might be moved to recognise that, on the contrary, in a world where pity is the prerequisite for compassionate action, where a king has to share the suffering of his subjects in order to 'care', the majority will remain poor, naked and wretched. The point of course is that princes only see the hovels of wretches during progresses (walkabouts?), in flight or in fairy tale. Even in fiction the wheel of fortune rarely brings them that low. Here, as so often in Jacobean drama, the fictiveness of the genre or scene intrudes; by acknowledging its status as fiction it abdicates the authority of idealist mimesis and indicates the better the reality it signifies; resembling in this Brecht's alienation effect, it stresses artifice not in the service of formalism but of realism. So, far from transcending in the name of an essential humanity the gulf which separates the privileged from the deprived, the play insists on it. And what clinches this is the exchange between Poor Tom (Edgar) and Gloucester. The latter has just arrived at the hovel; given the circumstances, his concern over the company kept by the king is faintly ludicrous but very telling: 'What, hath your Grace no better company?' (III. iv. 138; cf. Cordelia at IV. vii. 38–9). Tom tells Gloucester that he is cold. Gloucester, *uncomprehending rather than callous*, tells him he will keep warm if he goes back into the hovel (true of course, relatively speaking). That this comes from one of the 'kindest' people in the play prevents us from dismissing the remark as individual unkindness: judging is less important than seeing how unkindness is built into social consciousness. That Gloucester is unknowingly talking to his son in this exchange simply underscores the arbitrariness, the woeful inadequacy of what passes for kindness; it is, relatively, a very precious thing but as a basis for human kind's self-redemption it is a non-starter. Insofar as Lear identifies with suffering it is at the point when he is powerless to do anything about it. This is not accidental: the society of *Lear* is structured in such a way that to wait for shared experience to generate justice is to leave it too late. Justice, we might say, is too important to be trusted to empathy.

Like Lear, Gloucester has to undergo intense suffering before he can identify with the deprived. When he does so he expresses more than compassion. He perceives, crucially, the limitation of a society that depends on empathy alone for its justice. Thus he equates his earlier self with the 'lust-dieted man . . . *that will not see / Because he does not feel*' (IV. i. 69–71, my italics). Moreover he is led to a conception of social justice (albeit dubiously administered by the 'Heavens', l. 68) whereby 'distribution should undo excess, / And each man have enough' (IV. i. 72–3).

By contrast, Lear experiences pity mainly as an inseparable aspect of his own grief: 'I am mightily abus'd. I should e'en die with pity / To see another thus' (IV. vii. 53–4). His compassion emerges from grief only to be obliterated by grief. He is angered, horrified, confused and, above all dislocated. Understandably then he does not empathise with Tom so much as assimilate him to his own derangement. Indeed, Lear hardly communicates with anyone, especially on the heath; most of his utterances are demented mumbling interspersed with brief insight. Moreover, his preoccupation with vengeance ultimately displaces his transitory pity; reverting from the charitable reconciliation of V. iii to vengeance once again, we see him, minutes before his death, boasting of having killed the 'slave' that was hanging Cordelia.

But what of Cordelia herself? She more than anyone else has been seen to embody and symbolise pity. But is it a pity which significantly alters anything? To see her death as *intrinsically* redemptive is simply to mystify both her and death.[4] Pity, like kindness, seems in *Lear* to be precious yet ineffectual. Far from being redemptive it is the authentic but residual expression of a scheme of values all but obliterated by a catastrophic upheaval in the power structure of this society. Moreover the failure of those values is in part due to the fact that they are (or were) an ideological ratification of the very power structure which eventually destroys them.

In *Lear*, as we shall see in the next section, there is a repudiation of stoicism similar to that found in Marston's *Antonio's Revenge*. Yet repeatedly the sceptical treatment, sometimes the outright rejection, of stoicism in these plays is overlooked; often in fact it is used to validate another kind of humanism. For convenience I call the kind outlined so far ethical humanism and this other one existential humanism. The two involve different emphases rather than different ideologies. That of the latter is on essential heroism and existential integrity, that of the former on essential humanity, the universal human condition. Thus, according to Barbara Everett (in another explicitly anti-Christian analysis):

> In the storm scene Lear is at his most powerful and, despite moral considerations, at his noblest; the image of man hopelessly confronting a hostile universe and withstanding it only by his inherent powers of rage, endurance and perpetual questioning, is perhaps the most purely 'tragic' in Shakespeare. ('The New King Lear', p. 333)

Significantly, existential humanism forms the basis even of J. W. Lever's *The Tragedy of State*, one of the most astute studies of Jacobean tragedy to date. On the one hand Lever is surely right in insisting that these plays 'are not primarily treatments of characters with a so-called "fatal flaw", whose downfall is brought about by the decree of just if inscrutable powers . . . the fundamental flaw is not in them but in the world they inhabit: in the political state, the social order it upholds, and likewise, by projection, in the cosmic state of shifting arbitrary phenomena called "Fortune"' (p. 10). By the same criteria it is surely wrong to assert (on the same page) that: 'What really matters is the quality of [the heroes'] response to intolerable situations. This is a drama of adversity and stance . . . The rational man who remains master of himself is by the same token the ultimate master of his fate'. In Lever's analysis Seneca is the ultimate influence on a drama (including *King Lear*) which celebrate man's capacity inwardly to transcend oppression (p. 9).

If the Christian mystifies suffering by presenting it as intrinsic to God's redemptive and providential design for man, the humanist does likewise by representing suffering as the mysterious ground for man's *self*-redemption; both in effect mystify suffering by having as their common focus an essentialist conception of what it is to be human: in virtue of his spiritual essence (Christian), essential humanity (ethical humanist), or essential self (existential humanist), man is seen to achieve a paradoxical transcendence: in individual extinction is his apotheosis. Alternatively we might say that in a mystifying closure of the historical real the categories of idealist culture are recuperated.

This suggests why both ethical and existential humanism are in fact quasi-religious: both reject the providential and 'dogmatic' elements of Christianity while retaining its fundamental relation between suffering, affirmation and regeneration. Moreover they, like Christianity, tend to fatalise social dislocation; its causes are displaced from the realm of the human; questions about them are raised but only rhetorically, thus confirming man's impotence to alleviate the human condition. This clears the stage for what really matters: man's responsive suffering and what it reveals in the process about his essential nature. Recognisable here is the fate of existentialism when merged with literary criticism as a surrogate or displaced theology; when, specifically, it was co-opted to the task most symptomatic of that displacement, namely the obsession with defining tragedy. It will be recalled that for the existentialist existence precedes essence, or so said Sartre, who later tried to develop this philosophy in the context of Marxism. In literary criticism the social implications of existentialism, such as they were, were easily ignored, the emphasis being instead on a modernist angst and man's thwarted spiritual potential. This is another sense in which existential humanism is merely a mutation of Christianity and not at all a radical alternative; although it might reluctantly have to acknowledge that neither Absolute nor Essence exist, it still relates man to them on a principle of Augustinian privation: man understands his world only through the grid of their absence.

King Lear: A Materialist Reading

More important than Lear's pity is his 'madness' – less divine furor than a process of collapse which reminds us just how precarious is the psychological equilibrium which we call sanity, and just how dependent upon an identity which is social rather than essential. What makes Lear the person he is – or rather was – is not kingly essence (divine right), but, among other things, his authority and his family. On the heath he represents the process whereby man has been stripped of his stoic and (Christian) humanist conceptions of self. Consider what Seneca has to say of affliction and philosophy:

> Whether we are caught in the grasp of an inexorable law of fate, whether it is God who as lord of the universe has ordered all things, or whether the affairs of mankind are tossed and buffeted haphazardly by chance, it is philosophy that has the duty of protecting us. (*Letters*, p. 64)

Lear, in his affliction, attempts to philosophise with Tom whom he is convinced is a 'Noble philosopher', a 'good Athenian' (II. iv. 168 and 176). It adds up to nothing more than the incoherent ramblings of one half-crazed by just that suffering which philosophy, according to the stoic, guards against. It is an ironic subversion of neo-stoic essentialism, one which recalls Bacon's essay 'Of Adversity,' where he quotes Seneca: '*It is true greatness to have in one the frailty of a man, and the security of a god*' only to add, dryly: 'This would have done better in poesy, where transcendences are more allowed' (*Essays*, p. 15). As I have already shown (chapter 4) Bacon believed that poesy implies idealist mimesis – that is, an illusionist evasion of those historical and empirical realities which, says Bacon, 'buckle and bow the mind unto the nature of things' (*Advancement*, p. 83). He seems to have remained unaware that Jacobean drama was just as subversive of poesy (in this sense) as he was, not only with regard to providentialism but now its corollary, essentialism. Plays like *Lear* precisely disallow 'transcendences': in this at least they confirm Edmund's contention that 'men / Are as the time is' (V. iii. 31–2). Montaigne made a similar point with admirable terseness: 'I am no philosopher: Evils oppresse me according as they waigh' (*Essays*, III. 189). The Fool tells Lear that he is 'an O without a figure' (I. iv. 192); both here and seconds later he anticipates his master's eventual radical decentredness, the consequence of having separated 'The name, and all th' addition' of a king from his real 'power' (I. i. 129, 135): 'Who is it that can tell me who I am?' cries Lear; 'Lear's shadow' replies the Fool.

After he has seen Lear go mad, Gloucester offers this inversion of stoicism:

> Better I were distract
> So should my thoughts be sever'd from my griefs,
> And woes by wrong imagination lose
> The knowledge of themselves.
>
> (IV. vi. 281–4)

For Lear dispossession and displacement entail not redemptive suffering but a kind of suffering recognition – implicated perhaps with confession, depending on how culpable we take this king to have been with regard to 'the great *image* of authority' which he now briefly demystifies: 'a dog's obey'd in office' (IV. vi. 157, my italics). Lear does acknowledge blame, though deludedly believing the power which made him blameworthy is still his: 'Take that of me, my friend, who have the power / To seal th' accuser's lips' (IV. vi. 169–70). His admission that authority is a function of 'office' and 'power', not intrinsic worth, has its corollary: power itself is in control of 'justice' (l. 166) rather than vice versa:

> The usurer hangs the cozener.
> Through tatter'd clothes small vices do appear;

Robes and furr'd gowns hide all. Plate sin with gold
And the strong lance of justice hurtless breaks;
Arm it in rags, a pigmy's straw doth pierce it.

(IV. vi. 163–7)

Scenes like this one remind us that *King Lear* is, above all, a play about power, property and inheritance. Referring to Goneril, the distraught Lear cries: 'Ingratitude thou marble-hearted fiend, / More hideous when thou show'st thee in a child / Than the sea-monster' (I. iv. 259–61). Here, as throughout the play, we see the cherished norms of human kindness shown to have no 'natural' sanction at all. A catastrophic redistribution of power and property – and, eventually, a civil war – disclose the awful truth that these two things are somehow prior to the laws of human kindness rather than vice-versa (likewise, as we have just seen, with power in relation to justice). Human values are not antecedent to these material realities but are, on the contrary, in-formed by them.[5]

Even allowing for his conservative tendency to perceive all change as a change for the worse, Gloucester's account of widespread social discord must surely be taken as at least based on fact: 'These late eclipses in the sun and moon portend no good to us . . . Love cools, friendship falls off, brothers divide, in cities, mutinies; in countries, discord; in palaces, treason . . . there's son against father; the King falls from bias of nature: there's father against child' (I. ii. 100–11). ''Tis strange', concludes the troubled Gloucester and exits, leaving Edmund to make things somewhat less so. Significantly, Edmund does not deny the extent of the discord, only Gloucester's mystified sense of its cause. In an earlier soliloquy Edmund has already repudiated 'the plague of custom . . . The curiosity of nations' which label him bastard (I. ii. 3–4). Like Montaigne he insists that universal law is merely municipal law. Here he goes further, repudiating the ideological process whereby the latter is misrecognised as the former; he rejects, that is, a way of thinking which represents the con-tingent as the necessary and thereby further represents human identity and the social order as metaphysically determined (and therefore unalterable): 'When we are sick in fortune, often the surfeits of our own behaviour, we make guilty of our disasters the sun, the moon, and stars; as if we were villains on neces-sity, fools by heavenly compulsion . . . by a divine thrusting on' (I. ii. 122–31). Closely related to this refusal of the classical ideological effect is the way Edmund also denaturalises the theatrical effect: 'Pat! He comes like the catas-trophe of the old comedy. My cue is villainous melancholy' (I. ii. 128). Yet this revolutionary scepticism is discredited by the purpose to which it is put. How are we to take this? Are we to assume that Edmund is simply evil and therefore so is his philosophy? I want to argue that we need not. To begin with we have to bear in mind a crucial fact: Edmund's scepticism is made to serve an *existing* system of values; although he falls prey to, he does not introduce his society to its obsession with power, property and inheritance; it is already the material and ideological basis of that society. As such it in-forms the consciousness of Lear and Gloucester as much as Cornwall and Regan; consider Lear first, then Gloucester.

Lear's behaviour in the opening scene presupposes first, his absolute power, second, the knowledge that his being king constitutes that power, third, his refusal to tolerate what he perceives as a contradiction of that power. Therefore what Lear demands of Cordelia – authentic familial kindness – is precluded by the very terms of the demand; that is, by the extent to which the occasion as well as his relationship to her is saturated with the ideological imperatives of power. For her part Cordelia's real transgression is not unkindness as such, but speaking in a way which threatens to show too clearly how the laws of human kindness operate in the service of property, contractual, and power relations:

> I love your Majesty
> According to my bond . . .
>
> I
> Return those duties back as are right fit . . .
> Why have my sisters husbands, if they say
> They love you [i.e. Lear] all?
> (I. i. 91–2; 95–6; 98–9)

Presumably Cordelia does not intend it to be so, but this is the patriarchal order in danger of being shorn of its ideological legitimation – here, specifically, a legitimation taking ceremonial form. (Ironically yet predictable, the 'untender' (1. 105) dimension of that order is displaced on to Cordelia). Likewise with the whole issue of dowries. Prior to Lear's disowning of Cordelia, the realities of property marriage are more or less transmuted by the language of love and generosity, the ceremony of good government. But in the act of renouncing her, Lear brutally foregrounds the imperatives of power and property relations: 'Here I disclaim all my paternal care, / Propinquity and property of blood' (I. i. 112–13; cf. ll. 196–7). Kenneth Muir glosses 'property' as 'closest blood relation' (ed. *King Lear*, p. 11). Given the context of this scene it must also mean 'ownership' – father owning daughter – with brutal connotations of the master / slave relationship as in the following passage from *King John*: 'I am too high-born to be *propertied* / To be a . . . serving man' (V. ii. 79–81). Even kinship then – indeed *especially* kinship – is in-formed by the ideology of property relations, the contentious issue of primogeniture being, in this play, only its most obvious manifestation. Later we witness Lear's correlation between the quantity of retainers Goneril will allow him and the quality of her love: Regan offers twenty-five retainers, upon which Lear tells Goneril: 'I'll go with thee. / Thy fifty yet doth double five-and twenty, / And thou art twice her love' (II. iv. 257–9).

Gloucester's unconscious acceptance of this underlying ideology is conveyed at several points but nowhere more effectively than in Act II scene i; even as he is coming to terms with Edgar's supposed treachery he is installing Edmund in his place, offering in *exchange* for Edmund's 'natural' behaviour – property:

> of my land
> Loyal and natural boy, I'll work the means
> To make thee capable.
>
> (II. i. 83–5)

Thus the one thing which the kind Gloucester and the vicious Cornwall have in common is that each offers to reward Edmund's 'loyalty' in exactly the same way (cf. III. v. 16–18). All this would be ludicrous if it were not so painful: as their world disintegrates Lear and Gloucester cling even more tenaciously to the only values they know, which are precisely the values which precipitated the disintegration. Hence even as society is being torn apart by conflict, the ideological structure which has generated that conflict is being reinforced by it.

When Edmund in the forged letter represents Edgar complaining of 'the oppression of aged tyranny' which commands 'not as it hath power, but as it is suffered' (I. ii. 47–8), he exploits the same personal anxiety in Gloucester which Cordelia unintentionally triggers in Lear. Both fathers represent a challenge to their patriarchal authority by offspring as unnatural behaviour, an abdication of familial duty. The trouble is they do this in a society where 'nature' as ideological concept is fast losing its power to police disruptive elements – for example: 'That nature which contemns its origin / Cannot be border'd certain in itself' (IV. ii. 32–3). No longer are origin, identity and action a 'natural' ideological unity, and the disintegration of that unity reveals something of fundamental importance: when, as here (also, e.g. at I. ii. 1–22) nature is represented as socially disruptive, yet elsewhere as the source of social stability (e.g. at II. iv. 176–80), we see an ideological construct beginning to incorporate and thereby render visible the very conflicts and contradictions in the social order which it hitherto effaced. In this respect the play activates a contradiction intrinsic to any 'naturalised' version of the Christian metaphysic; to abandon or blur the distinction between matter and spirit while retaining the basic premises of that metaphysic is to eventually construe evil as at once utterly alien to the human condition (unnatural) yet disturbingly and myste-riously inherent within it (natural) and to be purged accordingly. If deep per-sonal anxiety is thus symptomatic of more general social dislocation it is also what guarantees the general reaction formation to that dislocation: those in power react to crisis by entrenching themselves the deeper within the ideol-ogy and social organisation responsible for it.

At strategic points in the play we see how the minor characters have also internalised the dominant ideology. Two instances must suffice. The first occurs in Act II scene ii where Kent insults Oswald. He does so almost entirely in terms of the latter's lack of material wealth, his mean estate and consequent dependence upon service. Oswald is, says Kent, a 'beggarly, three-suited, hundred-pound, filthy, worsted-stocking . . . superserviceable . . . one-trunk-inheriting slave' (II. ii. 15 ff; as Muir points out, servants were apparently given three suits a year, while gentlemen wore silk as opposed to worsted stockings). The second example involves the way that for the Gentleman attending Cordelia even pity (or more accurately 'Sorrow') is conceived as a kind of passive female commodity (IV. iii. 16–23).[6]

We can now see the significance of Edmund's scepticism and its eventual relationship to this dominant ideology of property and power. Edmund's scep-tical independence is itself constituted by a contradiction: his illegitimate exclusion from society gives him an insight into the ideological basis of that society even as it renders him vulnerable to and dependent upon it. In this respect Edmund resembles the malcontents already encountered in previous chapters: exclusion from society gives rise both to the malcontent's sense of its worthlessness and his awareness that identity itself is dependent upon it. Similarly, Edmund, in liberating himself from the myth of innate inferiority, does not thereby liberate himself from his society's obsession with power, property and inheritance; if anything that obsession becomes the more urgent: 'Legitimate Edgar, I *must* have your land' (I. ii. 16, my italics). He sees through one level of ideological legitimation only to remain the more thoroughly enmeshed with it at a deeper level.

Edmund embodies the process whereby, because of the contradictory conditions of its inception, a revolutionary (emergent) insight is folded back into a dominant ideology. Witnessing his fate we are reminded of how, his-torically, the misuse of revolutionary insight has tended to be in proportion to its truthfulness, and of how, as this very fact is obscured, the insight becomes entirely identified with (or as) its misappropriation. Machiavellianism, Gramsci has reminded us, is just one case in point (*Selections from Prison Notebooks*, p. 136).

The Refusal of Closure

Lionel Trilling has remarked that 'the captains and kings and lovers and clowns of Shakespeare are alive and complete before they die' (*The Opposing Self*, p. 38). Few remarks could be less true of *King Lear*. The notion of man as tragic victim somehow alive and complete in death is precisely the kind of essentialist mystification which the play refuses. It offers instead a decentring of the tragic subject which in turn becomes the focus of a more general exploration of human consciousness in relation to social being – one which discloses human values to be not antecedent to, but rather in-formed by, material conditions. *Lear* actually refuses then that autonomy of value which humanist critics so often insist that it ultimately affirms. Nicholas Brooke, for example, in one of the best close analyses of the play that we have, concludes by declaring: 'all moral structures, whether of natural order or Christian redemption, are invalidated by the naked fact of experience', yet manages in the concluding sentence of the study to resurrect from this unaccommodated 'naked experience' a redemptive autonomy of value, one almost mystically inviolable: 'Large orders collapse; but values remain, and are independent of them' (*Shakespeare: King Lear*, pp. 59–60). But surely in *Lear*, as in most of human history, 'values' are shown to be terrifyingly dependent upon whatever 'large orders' actually exist; in civil war especially – which after all is what *Lear* is about – the two collapse together.

In the closing moments of *Lear* those who have survived the catastrophe actually attempt to recuperate their society in just those terms which the play has subjected to sceptical interrogation. There is invoked, first, a concept of innate nobility in contradistinction to innate evil and, second, its corollary: a metaphysically ordained justice. Thus Edgar's defeat of Edmund is interpreted as a defeat of an evil nature by a noble one. Also nobility is seen to be like truth – it will out: 'Methought thy very gait did prophesy / A royal nobleness' (V. iii. 175–6). Goneril is 'reduced' to her treachery ('read thine own evil', l. 156), while Edmund not only acknowledges defeat but also repents, submitting to Edgar's nobility (ll. 165–6) and acknowledging his own contrary nature (ll. 242–3). Next, Edgar invokes a notion of divine justice which holds out the possibility of rendering their world intelligible once more; speaking to Edmund of Gloucester, he says:

> The gods are just, and of our pleasant vices
> Make instruments to plague us:
> The dark and vicious place where thee he got
> Cost him his eyes.
>
> (V. iii. 170–3)

Thus is responsibility displaced; but perhaps Edgar is meant to wince as he says it since the problem of course is that he is making his society supernaturally intelligible at the cost of rendering the concept of divine justice so punitive and 'poetic' as to be, humanly speaking, almost unintelligible. Nevertheless Albany persists with the same process of recuperation by glossing thus the deaths of Goneril and Regan: 'This judgement of the heavens, that makes us tremble, / Touches us not with pity' (V. iii. 230–1). But when he cries 'The Gods defend her!' – i.e. Cordelia – instead of the process being finally consolidated we witness, even before he has finished speaking, Lear re-entering with Cordelia dead in his arms. Albany has one last desperate bid for recuperation, still within the old punitive / poetic terms:

> All friends shall taste
> The wages of their virtue, and all foes
> The cup of their deservings.
> (V. iii. 302–4)

Seconds later Lear dies. The timing of these two deaths must surely be seen as cruelly, precisely, subversive: instead of complying with the demands of formal closure – the convention which would confirm the attempt at recuperation – the play concludes with two events which sabotage the prospect of both closure and recuperation.

Notes

1   Thus Irving Ribner (for example) argues that the play 'affirms justice in the world, which it sees as a harmonious system ruled by a benevolent God' (*Patterns in Shakespearean Tragedy*, p. 117).

2   Other critics who embrace, invoke or imply the categories of essentialist humanism include the following: A. C. Bradley, *Shakespearean Tragedy*, lectures 7 and 8; Israel Knox, *The Aesthetic Theories of Kant, Hegel and Schopenhauer*, p. 117; Robert Ornstein, *The Moral Vision of Jacobean Tragedy*, p. 264; Kenneth Muir, ed. *King Lear*, especially p. lv; Grigori Kozintsev, *King Lear: The Space of Tragedy*, pp. 250–1. For the essentialist view with a pseudo-Nietzschean twist, see Michael Long, *The Unnatural Scene*, pp. 191–3.

Jan Kott suggests the way that the absurdist view exists in the shadow of a failed Christianity and a failed humanism – a sense of paralysis in the face of that failure (*Shakespeare Our Contemporary*, pp. 104, 108, 116–17).

3   Barbara Everett, 'The New King Lear'; William R. Elton, *King Lear and the Gods*; Cedric Watts, 'Shakespearean Themes: The Dying God and the Universal Wolf'.

4   For John Danby, Cordelia is redemption incarnate; but can she really be seen as 'allegorically the root of individual and social sanity; tropologically Charity "that

suffereth long and is kind"; analogically the redemptive principle itself'? (*Shakespeare's Doctrine of Nature*, p. 125; cf. p. 133).

5   In-form rather than determine: in this play material factors do not determine values in a crude sense; rather, the latter are shown to be dependent upon the former in a way which radically disqualifies the idealist contention that the reverse is true, namely, that these values not only survive the 'evil' but do so in a way which indicates their ultimate independence of it.

6   By contrast compare Derek Traversi who finds in the imagery of this passage a 'sense of value, of richness and fertility . . . an indication of redemption . . . the poetical transformation of natural emotion into its spiritual distillation' (*An Approach to Shakespeare*, II. 164).

Coriolanus and Interpretations of Politics ('Who does the wolf love?')

Stanley Cavell

Cavell's essay, from his 1987 collection Disowning Knowledge: In Six Plays of Shakespeare, *begins with the suggestion that the mystery of* Coriolanus *is its closeness, rather than its actual fit, with notions of tragedy. Drawing on philosophical ideas about scepticism, on psychoanalytical ideas, and on political notions of the hierarchical Roman society, Cavell discovers a religious ritual significance which unites the play's disparate strands, as well as stressing its surprisingly comic elements.*

Stanley Cavell, 'Coriolanus and Interpretations of Politics', in *Disowning Knowledge: In Six Plays of Shakespeare*. Cambridge: Cambridge University Press, 1987.

Something that draws me to *Coriolanus* is its apparent disdain of questions I have previously asked of Shakespearean tragedy, taking tragedy as an epistemological problem, a refusal to know or to be known, an avoidance of acknowledgment, an expression (or imitation) of skepticism. Coriolanus's refusal to acknowledge his participation in finite human existence may seem so obviously the fact of the matter of his play that to note it seems merely to describe the play, not at all to interpret it. It may be, however, that this lack of theoretical grip itself proposes a moral, or offers a conclusion, namely that *Coriolanus* is not exactly to be understood as a tragedy, that its mystery – supposing one agrees to something like a mystery in its events – will be located only in locating its lack or missing of tragedy, hence its closeness to tragedy.

But systematically to pursue this possibility would require – from me – following out a sense that this play presents a particular interpretation of the problem of skepticism as such (skepticism directed toward our knowledge of the existence of others), in particular an interpretation that takes skepticism as a form of narcissism. This interpretation does not in itself come to me as a complete surprise since a book I published a few years ago – *The Claim of Reason* – begins with an interpretation of Wittgenstein's *Philosophical Investigations* that takes his move against the idea of a private language (an idea that arises in his struggle against skepticism) as a move against a kind of narcissism, a kind of denial of an existence shared with others; and my book ends with a reading of *Othello* as a depiction of the murderous lengths to which narcissism must go in order to maintain its picture of itself as skepticism, in order to maintain its stand of ignorance, its fear or avoidance of knowing, under the color of a claim to certainty.[1] What surprised me more in *Coriolanus* was its understanding of narcissism as another face of incestuousness, and of this condition as one in which language breaks down under one's sense of becoming incomprehensible, of the sense of oneself as having lost the power of expression, what I call in *The Claim of Reason* the terror of inexpressiveness; together with the thoroughness with which Narcissus's fate is mirrored in the figure of Coriolanus, a figure whose every act is, by that act, done to him so perfectly that the distinction between action and passion seems to lose its sense, a condition in which human existence becomes precarious, if perhaps transcendable. I mention these connections with the philosophical issue of skepticism not because I pursue them further in the essay to follow but only to attest my conviction that a work such as a play of Shakespeare's cannot contribute the help I want from it for the philosophical issues I mention unless the play is granted the autonomy it is in one's power to grant, which means, seen in its own terms. What does this mean? What is a play of Shakespeare's? I shall try to say something about these questions.

Something else also draws me. The way I have been understanding the conflicts the play engenders keeps sending me back over paths of thought that I believe many critics have found to be depleted of interest, or conviction; three paths, or branches of paths, in particular: (1) those that look in a Shakespearean play for something like an idea of theater, as it were for the play's concept of itself; (2) those that sense Christian stirrings and murmurings under the surface of the words; and (3) even those paths of thought that anticipate something you might call the origins of tragedy in religious ritual. I am, I suppose, as drawn to critical paths that others find empty as some poets are to words that others find flat. But to say fully why one is drawn to a work, and its work of interpretation, can only be the goal of an interpretation; and the motive of an interpretation, like what one might call the intention of the work it seeks, exists fully only in its satisfaction.

I expect, initially, general agreement on two facts about *Coriolanus*. First, compared with other Shakespearean tragedies this one lacks what A. C.

Bradley called "atmosphere" (in his British Academy lecture on the play, the decade after his *Shakespearean Tragedy*). Its language, like its hero, keeps aloof from our attention, as withdrawn, austere, as its rage and its contempt permit. Second, the play is about the organization of the body politic and about how that body is fed, that is, sustained. I expect, further, that readers from opposed camps should be willing to see that the play lends itself equally, or anyway naturally, to psychological and to political readings: Both perspectives are, for example, interested in who produces food and in how food is distributed and paid for. From a psychological perspective (in practice this has in recent years been psychoanalytic) the play directs us to an interest in the development of Coriolanus's character. From a political perspective the play directs us to an interest in whether the patricians or the plebeians are right in their conflict and in whether, granted that Coriolanus is unsuited for political leadership, it is his childishness or his very nobility that unsuits him.

In the critical discussions I have read so far, the psychoanalytic perspective has produced more interesting readings than the political. A political reading is apt to become fairly predictable once you know whose side the reader is taking, that of the patricians or that of the plebeians; and whose side the reader takes may come down to how he or she sees Menenius's fable of the organic state, the parable of the belly, and upon whom we can place the blame for Coriolanus's banishment. If few will consider it realistic to suppose that Coriolanus would have made a good political leader, fewer will deny that in losing him the city has lost its greatest hero and that this loss is the expression of a time of crisis in the state. It is a time of famine in which the call for revolt is made moot by the threat and the fact of war and invasion, followed by a time in which victory in the war, and bitterness over its conduct, creates the call for counterrevolt by the state's defender and preserver. In such a period of crisis everyone and no one has good arguments, everyone and no one has right on their side. In Aufidius's great description of Coriolanus at the end of Act IV he summarizes as follows:

> So our virtues
> Lie in th' interpretation of the time; . . .
> One fire drives out one fire; one nail, one nail;
> Rights by rights founder, strengths by strengths do fail.

One might say that just this division of fire and right is the tragedy, but would that description account for the particular turns of just these events, as distinct from the losses and ironies in any revolutionary situation? Even the most compelling political interpretation – in my experience this is given in Bertolt Brecht's discussion with members of his theater company of the opening scene of the play [2] – seems to have little further to add, in the way of interpretation, once it makes clear that choosing the side of the plebeians is dramatically and textually viable. This is no small matter. It shows that Shakespeare's text – or what we think of as Shakespeare's humanity – leaves ample room for distinctions among the "clusters" of citizens, and it shows the weight of their common position in opposition to that of the patricians. And I take this in turn to show that the politics of the play is essentially the politics of a given production, so that we should not expect its political issues to be settled by an interpretation of what you might call "the text itself."

Exactly the power of Brecht's discussion can be said to be its success in getting us *not* to interpret, not, above all, to interpret food, but to stay with the opening fact of the play, the fact that the citizens of Rome are in revolt because there is a famine (and because of their interpretation of the famine). They and their families are starving and they believe (correctly, for all we know) that the patricians are hoarding grain. Not to interpret this means, in practical or theatrical terms, that we come to see that this cluster is of human beings, individual human beings, who work at particular trades and who live in particular places where specific people await news of the outcome of their dangerous course in taking up arms. This fact of their ordinary humanity is the most impressive fact that can be set against the patricians' scorn of them – a fact that ought not to be visible solely to a Marxist, a fact that shows up the language of the leaders as mysterious and evasive, as subject to what one may think of as the politics of interpretation.

Yet we also feel that the pervasive images of food and hunger, of cannibalism and of disgust, do mean something, that they call upon us for some lines of interpretation, and that the value of attending to this particular play is a function of the value to individual human beings of tracing these lines.

Psychoanalysts naturally have focused on the images of food and feeding that link Coriolanus and his mother. In a recent essay, "'Anger's My Meat': Feeding, Dependency, and Aggression in *Coriolanus*,"[3] Professor Janet Adelman has given so clear and fair an account of some two decades of psychoanalytic interpretations of food and feeding in the play, in the course of working out her further contributions, that I feel free to pick and choose the lines and moments bearing on this aspect of things that serve my somewhat different emphases.

Twice Volumnia invokes nursing. Early she says to Virgilia, rebuking her for worrying about her husband:

> The breasts of Hecuba
> When she did suckle Hector, look'd not lovelier
> Than Hector's forehead when it spit forth blood
> At Grecian sword, contemning.
>
> (I, iii, 43–6)

And in her first intercession with her son:

> Do as thou list.
> Thy valiantness was mine, thou suck'st it from me,
> But owe thy pride thyself.
>
> (III, ii, 127–9)

Both invocations lead one to think what it is this son learned at his mother's breast, what it is he was fed with, particularly as we come to realize that both mother and son declare themselves to be starving. It is after Coriolanus's departure upon being banished, when Menenius asks Volumnia if she'll sup with him, that she comes out with

> Anger's my meat; I sup upon myself
> And so shall starve with feeding.
>
> (IV, ii, 50–1)

As Coriolanus mocks and resists the ritual of asking for the people's voices, his being keeps revolting, one time as follows:

> Better it is to die, better to starve,
> Than crave the hire which first we do deserve.
>
> (II, iii, 118–19)

I say that mother and son, both of them, *are* starving, and I mean throughout, always, not just when they have occasion to say so. I take Volumnia's vision of supping upon herself not to be a picture simply of her local anger but of self-consuming anger as the presiding passion of her life – the primary thing, accordingly, she would have to teach her son, the thing he sucked from her, of course under the name of valiantness. If so, then if Volumnia and hence Coriolanus are taken to exemplify a Roman identification of virtue as valor, they should further be taken as identifying valor with an access to one's anger. It's "in anger, Juno-like," godlike, that Volumnia laments (IV, ii, 52–3); and it is this anger that the tribune Sicinius is remarking as, in trying to avoid being confronted by her, he says, "They say she's mad" (IV, ii, 9). Along these lines, I emphasize Coriolanus's statement about deserving rather than craving not as

> Better it is to *die*, better to *starve*,
> Than crave . . .

as if he is asserting the rightness of a particular choice for the future; but as

> *Better* it is to die, *better* to starve,
> Than crave . . .

as if he is reaffirming or confessing his settled form of (inner) life. I expect that the former is the more usual way of emphasis, but I find it prejudicial.

Coriolanus and Volumnia are – I am taking it – starvers, hungerers. They manifest this condition as a name or a definition of the human, like being mortal. And they manifest this as a condition of insatiability (starving by feeding, feeding as deprivation). It is a condition sometimes described as the infiniteness of desire, imposing upon the finiteness of the body. But starving for Volumnia and her son suggests that this infiniteness is not the cause of human insatiability but is rather its effect. It is the effect not of an endless quantity, as though the self had, or is, endless reserves of desire; but of an endless structure, as though desire has a structure of endlessness. One picture of this structure is given by Narcissus for whom what is longed for is someone longing, who figures beauty as longing. Starving by feeding presents itself to Coriolanus as being consumed by hunger, and his words for hungering are desiring and craving. And what he incessantly hungers for is . . . not to hunger, not to desire, that is, not to be mortal. Take the scene of interview by the people:

Coriolanus.	You know the cause, sir, of my standing here.
Third Citizen.	We do, sir; tell us what hath brought you to't.
Coriolanus.	Mine own desert.
Second Citizen.	Your own desert?
Coriolanus.	Ay, not mine own desire.
Third Citizen.	How not your own desire?

(II, iii, 66–72)

If you desire to be desireless, is there something you desire? If so, how would you express it; that is, tell it; that is, ask for it? Coriolanus's answer to this paradox is to become perfectly deserving. Since to hunger is to want, to lack something, he hungers to lack nothing, to be complete, like a sword. My speculations here are an effort to do justice to one's sense of Coriolanus as responding not primarily to his situation with the plebeians, as if trapped by an uncontrollable disdain; but as responding primarily to his situation with himself, as befits a Narcissus; trapped first by an uncontrollable logic. Although I shall come to agree with Plutarch's early observation or diagnosis in his *Life of Caius Martius Coriolanus* that Coriolanus is "altogether unfit for any man's conversation," I am in effect taking this to mean not that he speaks in anger and contempt (anger and contempt are not unjustifiable) but that whereas under certain circumstances he can express satisfaction, he cannot express desire and to this extent cannot speak at all: The case is not that he will not ask for what he wants but rather that he can want nothing that he asks. His solution amounts, as both patricians and plebeians more or less note, to becoming a god. What god? We have to get to this.

Let us for the moment continue developing the paradox of hungering. To be consumed by hunger, to feed upon oneself, must present itself equally as being fed upon, being eaten up. (To feed means both to give and to take nourishment, as to suckle means both to give and to take the breast.) So the other fact of Coriolanus's and Volumnia's way of starving, of their hunger, is their sense of being cannibalized.[4]

The idea of cannibalization runs throughout the play. It is epitomized in the title question I have given to these remarks: "Who does the wolf love?" Menenius asks this of the tribunes of the people at the opening of Act II. One of them answers, with undeniable truth: "The lamb." And Menenius, ever the interpretive fabulist, answers: "Ay, to devour him, as the hungry plebeians would the noble Marcius." The other tribune's answer – "He's a lamb, indeed, that baas like a bear" – does not unambiguously deny Menenius's interpretation. The shock of the interpretation is of course that it is from the beginning the people, not the patricians, and least of all Coriolanus, who are presented as lambs, anyway as food for patrician wolves. In Menenius's opening effort to talk the people out of revolt he declares that "The helms o' the state . . . care for you like fathers," to which the First Citizen replies, "Care for us! . . . If the wars eat us not up, they will; and there is all the love they bear us." This fantasy is borne out when the general Cominius speaks of Coriolanus's coming to battle as to a feast (I, ix, 10). And the idea of the warrior Coriolanus feeding on a weaker species may be raised again in the battle at Corioli in his threat to any soldier who holds back, "I'll take him for a Volsce / And he shall feel mine edge," allowing the suggestion of his sword as a piece of cutlery. The idea of an ungovernable voraciousness is furthered by Volumnia's association of her son with his son's tearing apart a butterfly with his teeth. On the other hand, when Coriolanus offers himself to Aufidius at Antium he expresses his sense of having been devoured, with only the name Caius Marcius Coriolanus remaining, devoured by "the cruelty and envy of the people" (IV, v, 77–8). And Menenius, whose sense of justice is constricted, among other things by his fear of civil disorder, is accurate in his fears, in the consequences they prophesy for Rome, and he will repeat his vision of civil cannibalism:

> Now the good gods forbid
> That our renowned Rome, whose gratitude
> Towards her deserved children is enrolled
> In Jove's own book, like an unnatural dam
> Should now eat up her own.
>
> (III, i, 288–92)

All readers of this aspect of the play will recognize in this description of Rome as potentially a cannibalistic mother an allusion to Volumnia; and the identification of Volumnia and Rome is enforced in other ways, not least by Volumnia herself when in the second and final intercession scene she says to her son:

> . . . thou shalt no sooner
> March to assault thy country than to tread
> (Trust to't, thou shalt not) on thy mother's womb
> That brought thee to this world.
> (V, iii, 121–4)

It is very much to the point to notice that in Menenius's vision of Rome as an "unnatural dam" an identity is proposed between a mother eating her child and a mother eating herself: If Rome eats up all Romans there is no more Rome, for as one of the tribunes asks, "What is the city but the people?" (III, i, 198).

The paradox and reciprocity of hungering may be found registered in the question "Who does the wolf love?" If the question is asking for the object of the wolf's affection, the more nearly correct grammar would seem to be "Whom does the wolf love?"[5] But this correctness (call it a patrician correctness, a refinement in which the plebeians apparently do not see the good) would rule out taking the question also in its opposite direction, grammatically strict as it stands, namely as asking whose object of affection the wolf is. (Who does love the wolf?) The answer given directly, "The lamb," does not rule out either direction, but as the ensuing discussion demonstrates, the direction will be a function of what or whom you take the lamb to be, hence what the wolf. Both directions, the active and the passive constructions of the play's focal verbs, are operative throughout the action. I have mentioned this explicitly in the cases of feeding and suckling. But it is, I find, true less conspicuously, but pertinently, in such an odd moment as this:

> CORIOLANUS.   Let them hang.
> VOLUMNIA.   Ay, and burn too.
> (III, ii, 23-4)

One of the functions in providing Volumnia with this amplification here strikes me as suggesting her sense of the inevitable reflexiveness of action in their Rome: Are hanging and burning actions done to someone, or something "they" are, or will be, doing?

The circle of cannibalism, of the eater eaten by what he or she eats, keeps being sketched out, from the first to the last. You might call this the identification of narcissism as cannibalism. From the first: At the end of Coriolanus's first long speech he says to the citizens:

> You cry against the noble Senate, who
> (Under the gods) keep you in awe, which else
> Would feed on one another.
>
> (I, i, 187–9)

And at the last: Rome devouring itself is the idea covered in the obsessive images of Coriolanus burning Rome. It was A. C. Bradley again who at the end of his British Academy lecture pointed up the sudden and relentless harping, principally after the banishment, on the image of fire, of Rome burning. Bradley makes nothing further of the point, but it is worth noting, in view of the theme of starving and cannibalism, that fire in this play is imagined under the description of it as *consuming* what it burns.

You may say that burning as a form of revenge is Coriolanus's projection onto Rome of what he felt Rome was doing to him. This cannot be wrong, but it so far pictures Coriolanus, in his revenge, to be essentially a man like Aufidius, merely getting even; the picture requires refining. Suppose that, as I believe, in Coriolanus's famous sentence of farewell, "I banish you!" (III, iii, 123), he has already begun a process of consuming Rome, incorporating it, becoming it. Then when the general Cominius tried in vain to plead with him to save Rome, and found him to be "sitting in gold, his eye / Red as 'twould burn Rome" (V, i, 63–4), he somewhat misunderstood what he saw. He took Coriolanus to be contemplating something in the future whereas Coriolanus's eye was red with the present flames of self-consuming. Consuming the literal Rome with literal fire would accordingly only have been an expression of that self-consuming. Thus would the city understand what it had done to itself. He will give it – horribly – what it deserves. Thus is the play of revenge further interpreted.

These various understandings of cannibalism all illustrate the ancient sentiment that man is wolf to man. (The Roman Plautus, to whom Shakespeare is famously indebted, is credited with being the earliest namable framer of the sentiment. A pertinent modern instance occurs in Brecht's *Threepenny Opera*.) But the question "Who does the wolf love?" has two further reaches which we must eventually consider. First, there is the repetition of the idea that devouring can be an expression of love. Second, if, as I think, there is reason here to take the image of the wolf as the figure of the mythical animal identified with Rome, the one who suckled the founders of Rome (Volumnia is the reason), there is reason to take the lamb it is said to love (or that love it) as the mythical animal identified with Christ.

Before this, I should make explicit a certain way in which the account of Coriolanus's motivation I have been driving at is somewhat at odds with the direction of psychoanalytic interpretation summarized and extended by Janet Adelman.[6] She understands Coriolanus's attempt to make himself inhumanly independent as a defense against his horror of dependence, and his rage as converting his wish to be dependent against those who render him so. A characteristic turn of her argument consists of a reading of some lines I have already had occasion to quote:

> The breasts of Hecuba
> When she did suckle Hector, look'd not lovelier
> Than Hector's forehead when it spit forth blood
> At Grecian sword, contemning.

Adelman reads as follows:

> Blood is more beautiful than milk, the wound than the breast, warfare than peaceful feeding. . . . Hector is transformed immediately from infantile feeding mouth to bleeding wound. For the unspoken mediator between breast and wound is the infant's mouth: in this imagistic transformation, to feed is to be wounded; the mouth becomes the wound, the breast the sword. . . . But at the same time as Volumnia's image suggests the vulnerability inherent in feeding, it also suggests a way to fend off that vulnerability. In her image, feeding, incorporating, is transformed into spitting out, an aggressive expelling; the wound once again becomes the mouth that spits. . . . The wound spitting blood thus becomes not a sign of vulnerability but an instrument of attack. (p. 131)

This is very fine and it must not be denied. But the transformation of Hector's mouth into a wound must not in turn deny two further features of these difficult lines. First, when Hector contemns Grecian swords, he is also to be thought of as fighting, as wielding a sword, so the mouth is transformed into, or seen as, a cutting weapon: The sucking mother is presented as being slashed by the son-hero, eaten by the one she feeds. Suffering such a fantasy would constitute some of Volumnia's more normal moments. Second, the lines set up an equation between a mother's milk and a man's blood, suggesting that we must understand the man's spitting blood in battle not simply as attacking but equally, somehow, as providing food, in a male fashion. But how? Remember that Coriolanus's way to avoid asking for something, that is, to avoid expressing desire, is by what he calls deserving the thing. His proof of desert is his valiantness, so his spitting blood in battle is his way of deserving being fed, that is to say, being devoured, being loved unconditionally. (War and feeding have consistently been joined in the words of this play. A plebeian says: "If the wars eat us not up they will" [I, i, 85–6]. And Cominius: Coriolanus "cam'st to . . . this feast having fully dined before" [I, ix, 10–11]; but again Cominius does not get the connection complete.) To be fed by Volumnia is to be fed *to* her. But since the right, or effective, bleeding depends (according to the equation of blood and milk) upon its being a form of feeding, of giving food, providing blood identifies him with his mother. His mother's fantasy here suggests that the appropriate reciprocation for having nourished her son is for him to become her, as if to remove the arbitrariness in her having been born a woman; and since it is a way of putting her into the world it is a way of giving birth to her. Her son's companion fantasy of reciprocation would be to return Rome's gift, to nurse Rome with the valiantness he sucked from it.

This fantasy produces contradictions that are a match for the fury of contradictions one feels in Coriolanus's position (for example, between the wishes for dependence and for independence). For he can only return his nourishment if Rome – taken as the people – deserves it. Hence the people's lack of desert entails his lack of desert, entails that he cannot do the thing that acquires love; he is logically debarred form reciprocating. The fact that he both has absolute contempt for the people and yet has an absolute need for them is part of what maddens him. (This implies again that I cannot understand Coriolanus's emotions toward the people as directed simply to, say, their cowardice, their being poor fighters. I am taking it that he needs their desert for, so to speak, private reasons as much as public.) The other part of what maddens him is that neither the people nor his mother – neither of the things that mean Rome – will understand his position. Neither understands that his understanding of his valiantness, his virtue, his worth, his deservingness, is of himself as a provider, and that this is the condition of his receiving his own sustenance. (This assumes that he shares his mother's fantasy of the equation of milk and blood – as if there is nothing in her he has not taken in.) The people, precisely on the contrary, maddeningly accuse him of *withholding* food; and his mother precisely regards his heroism purely as toughness, devoid of tenderness; or pure fatherhood devoid of motherhood; and as deserving something more than acknowledging what he provides, more than the delicate balance of his self-account, as if being made consul were indeed something more. ("Know, good mother, / I had rather be their servant in my way / Than sway with them in theirs" [II, i, 107–9.]) In these misunderstandings they have both already abandoned him, weaned him, before the ritual of being made consul comes to grief and he is formally banished. This prior rejection, not just once but always, inherently, would allow the understanding of his anger as his mother interprets anger, that is, as lamentation ("Anger's my meat . . . lament as I do, / In anger, Juno-like"). We may not contradict her interpretation, though we may interpret it further. We might go on to interpret it as depression.

I might characterize my intention in spelling out what I call these fantasies as an attempt to get at the origin of words, not the origin of their meaning exactly but of their production, of the value they have when and as they occur. I have characterized something like this ambition of criticism variously over the years, and related it to what I understand as the characteristic procedure of ordinary language philosophy. And do my spellings-out help? Do they, for example, help comprehend Coriolanus's subsequent course – how he justifies his plan to burn Rome and how he is talked out of his plan by his mother? It is not hard to encourage oneself in the impression that one understands these things. To me they seem mysteries. I shall sketch the answers I have to these questions and then conclude by indicating how these answers serve to interpret our relation to this play, which means to me, to understand what a Shakespearean play is (as revealed in this instance).

I pause, in turning to these questions, to make explicit an issue that at any time may nag our consciousness of the play. The mother relation is so overwhelmingly present in this play that we may not avoid wondering, at least wondering whether we are to wonder, what happened to the father. The play seems to me to raise this question in three ways, which I list in decreasing order of obviousness. First, Menenius is given a certain kind of fatherly role, or a role as a certain kind of father, but the very difficulty of conceiving of him as Coriolanus's real father, which is to say, as Volumnia's husband and lover, keeps alive our imagination of what such a figure might look like. Second, Coriolanus's erotic attachment to battle and to men who battle suggests a search for the father as much as an escape from the mother. This would afford an explanation for an otherwise, to me, insufficiently explained use in the play of the incident from Plutarch's life in which Coriolanus asks, exhausted from victorious battle, that a man in the conquered city of Corioli be spared slavery on the ground that Coriolanus had "sometime lay at the poor man's house," a man whose name Coriolanus discovers he has forgotten. The vagueness of the man's identity and Coriolanus's expression of confusion in the Shakespeare – distinct differences from the occurrence of the incidents in Plutarch – suggest to my mind that the unnamed figure to whom Coriolanus wishes to provide reparation is, vaguely, transiently, an image of his father.[7]

Third, and so little obvious as to be attributable to my powers of hallucination, Coriolanus's effort at mythological identification as he sits enthroned and entranced before Rome is an effort – if one accepts one stratum of description I shall presently give of him – to come unto the Father. (I shall not go into the possibilities here, or fantasies, that a patrician matron is simultaneously father-mother, or that, in replacing his father, he becomes his own father.)

I was about to ask how we are to grasp Coriolanus's return and his change of heart. My answer depends on plotting a relation between him and the other sacrificial lamb I have mentioned, the lamb of God, Christ. I say plotting a relation between the figures, not at all wishing to identify them. I see Coriolanus not so much as imitating Christ as competing with him. These are necessarily shadowy matters and although everything depends on accuracy in defining this relation all I can do here is note some elements that will have to figure in the plotting.

Earlier I spoke of Coriolanus's solution to the paradox of hungering not to hunger, of wanting not to want, of asking not to ask, as one of becoming a god. Now we may see that Christ is the right god because of the way he understands his mission as providing nonliteral food, for the spirit, for immortality; and because it is in him that blood must be understood as food. If one is drawn to this as a possibility, one may find surprising confirmation for it in certain of Coriolanus's actions and in certain descriptions of his actions. (I am not interested in claiming that Coriolanus is *in some sense* a scapegoat, the way perhaps any tragic hero is; but in claiming that he is a specific inflection of *this* scapegoat.)

First his actions, two especially. First is his pivotal refusal to show his wounds. I associate this generally with the issue of Christ's showing his wounds to his disciples, in order to show them the Lord – that is, to prove the Resurrection – and specifically with his saying to Thomas, who was not present at the first showing and who made seeing the wounds a condition of believing, that is, of declaring his faith, "Thomas, because thou hast seen me, thou believest: blessed are they that have not seen, and have believed" (John 20:29). (Thomas would not believe until he could, as he puts it and as Jesus will invite him to, "put mine hand into his side"; Aufidius declares the wish to "wash my fierce hand in's heart" (I, x, 27). I make no further claims on the basis of this conjunction; I can see that some good readers may feel that it is accidental. I do claim that good reading may be guided, or inspired, by the overexcitement such conjunctions can cause.) The second action is the second intercession, in which Volumnia, holding her son's son by the hand, together with Virgilia and Valeria appears to Coriolanus before Rome. I take this to invoke the appearance, while Christ is on the cross, of three women whose names begin with the same letter of the alphabet (I mean begin with M's, not with V's), accompanied by a male he loves, whom he views as his mother's son (John 19:25–7). (Giving his mother a son presages a mystic marriage.)

I do not suppose that one will be convinced by these relations unless one has antecedently felt some quality of – what shall I say? – the mythic in these moments. This is something I meant in calling these relations "shadowy matters": I meant this not negatively but positively. It is a way to understand Volumnia's advice to Coriolanus that when he makes his appeal to the people he act out the meaning of his presence:

> . . . for in such business
> Action is eloquence, and the eyes of th'ignorant
> More learned than the ears.

> (III, ii, 75–7)

I accept this as advice Shakespeare is giving to his own audience, a certain hint about why the words of this particular play may strike one as uncharacteristically ineloquent.

The second source of confirmation for Coriolanus's connection with the figure of Christ lies, I said, in certain descriptions of his actions. I specify now only some parallels that come out of Revelation. In that book the central figure is a lamb (and there is also a dragon), and a figure who sits on a special horse and on a golden throne, whose name is known only to himself, whose "eyes were as a flame of fire," and who burns a city that is identified as a woman; it is, in particular, the city (Babylon) which in Christian tradition is identified with Rome. And I associate the opening of Coriolanus's opening diatribe against the citizens, in which he rebukes their wish for "good words" from him – glad tidings – accusing them of liking "neither peace nor war," with the message Christ dictates to the writer of Revelation: "I know thy works, that thou art neither cold nor hot; . . . Therefore, because thou art luke warm, and neither cold nor hot, it will come to pass that I shall spew thee out of my mouth" (Revelation 3:15–16). (An associated text from Plutarch would be: "So Martius, being a stowte man of nature, that never yelded in any respect, as one thincking that to overcome allwayes, and to have the upper hande in all matters, was a Token of magnanimities, and of no base and fainte corage, which spitteth out anger from the most weake and passioned parte of the harte, much like the matter of an impostume: went home." Whatever the ambiguities in these words, the general idea remains, indelibly, of Coriolanus's speech, when angry, as being the spitting forth of the matter of an abscess.[8] This play about food is about revoltedness and disgust. *Coriolanus* and Revelation are about figures who are bitter, disgusted by those whom they have done good, whose lives they have sustained.)

Conviction, or lack of it, in these relations is something one has naturally to assess for oneself. Granted that they are somehow at work, they work to make comprehensible what Coriolanus's identification with the god is (they are identified as banished providers of spiritual food) and what his justification for destruction is (the people lack faith and are to suffer judgment) and why he changes his mind about the destruction. It is, I think, generally felt that his mother prevails with him by producing human, family feeling in him, in effect showing him that he is not inhuman. This again cannot be wrong, but first of all he has his access of family feeling the moment he sees the four figures approaching (a feeling that does not serve to carry the day), and second, his feeling, so conceived, does not seem to me to account for Coriolanus's words of agony to his mother as he relents and "Holds her by the hand, silent."

> O mother, mother!
> What have you done? Behold, the heavens do ope,

The gods look down, and this unnatural scene
They laugh at. O my mother, mother! O!
You have won a happy victory to Rome;
But, for your son – believe it, O, believe it! –
Most dangerously you have with him prevailed,
If not most mortal to him. But let it come.

(V, iii, 182–9)

(I say these are words of agony, but so far as I recall, no critic who cites them seems to find them so. I feel here especially at a disadvantage in never having been at a performance of *Coriolanus*. But I find on reading this passage, or rather in imagining it said [sometimes as by specific actors; Olivier, of course, among them, and the young Brando], that it takes a long time to get through. Partly that has to do with the fact of repetition of words in the passage; partly with the specific words that are repeated, "O," "mother," and "believe it." It has further to do, I feel sure, with my uncertainty about how long the silences before and within this speech are to be held – a speech that may be understood as expressing the silence with which this son holds, and then relinquishes, his mother's hand. Suppose we try imagining that he does not relinquish her hand until just before the last sentence, "But let it come" – as if what is to come is exactly expressive of their separating, or, say, that of Rome from Rome. Then how far do we imagine that he goes through the imagining of what is to come, and how long would the imagining take, before he takes upon himself the words that invite its coming?) What it means that she may be "most mortal" to him cannot be that he may be killed – the mere fact of death is hardly what concerns this man. He must mean somehow that she has brought it about that he will have the wrong death, the wrong mortality, a fruitless death. Has she done this by showing him that he has feelings? But Christ, even by those who believe that he is the Lord, is generally held to have feelings. Coriolanus's speech expresses his agonized sense that his mother does not know who he is, together with an agonized plea for her belief. She has deprived him of heaven, of, in his fantasy, sitting beside his father, and deprived him by withholding her faith in him, for if she does not believe that he is a god then probably he is not a god, and certainly nothing like the Christian scenario can be fulfilled, in which a mother's belief is essential. If it were his father who sacrificed him for the city of man then he could be a god. But if it is his mother who sacrifices him he is not a god. The logic of his situation, as well as the psychology, is that he cannot sacrifice himself. He can provide spiritual food but he cannot make himself into food, he cannot say, for example, that his body is bread. His sacrifice will not be redemptive; hence one may say his tragedy is that he cannot achieve tragedy. He dies in a place irrelevant to his sacrifice, carved by many swords, by hands that can derive no special nourishment from him. It is too soon in the history of the Roman world for the sacrifice to which he aspires and from which he recoils.

And perhaps it is too late, as if the play is between worlds. I know I have been struck by an apparent incorporation in *Coriolanus* of elements from Euripides' *Bacchae*, without knowing how or whether a historical connection is thinkable. Particularly, it seems to me, I have been influenced in my descriptions by feeling under Coriolanus's final plea to his mother the plea of Pentheus to his mother, outside the city, to see that he is her son and not to tear him to pieces. The *Bacchae* is about admitting the new god to the city, present in one who is returning to his native city, a god who in company with Demeter's grain brings nourishment to mankind, one who demands recognition in order to vindicate at once his mother's honor and his being fathered by Zeus; the first in the city to acknowledge his divine descent are two old men. My idea is that Coriolanus incorporates both raging, implacable Dionysus and raging, inconstant Pentheus and that Volumnia partakes both of the chaste yet god-seduced Semele and of the mad and murderous Agave. Volumnia's identifying of herself with Juno (specifically, with Juno's anger) may thus suggest her sensing herself as the cause of her curse. It is not essential to my thought here that Shakespeare knew (of) Euripides' play. It is enough to consider that he know Ovid's account of Pentheus's story and to suppose that he took the story as Euripides had, as about the kind of son (one unable to express desire) to whom the failure of his mother's recognition presents itself as a sense of being torn to pieces.

What is the good of such a tragedy of failed tragedy? Which is to ask: What is this play to us? How is it to do its work? This is the question I have been driving at and now that it is before us I can only state flatly, without much detail, my provisional conclusions on the topic.

They can by now be derived from certain considerations about Menenius's telling of the parable of the belly in the opening scene of the play. Every reader or participant has to make something of this extended, most prominently placed event. Until recent times most critics have assumed that Menenius is voicing a commonplace assumption of the times in which Shakespeare wrote and one that represents Shakespeare's view of the state – the state as a hierarchical organism, understandable on analogy with the healthy, functioning body. It is my impression that recent critics have tended not to dwell on the fable, as though the conservative way is the only way to take it and as though that vision is no longer acceptable, or presentable. But this seems to me to ignore what I take to be the three principal facts about Menenius's telling of the tale, the facts, one may say, of the drama in the telling. (1) The tale has competing interpretations. What the first citizen calls its "application" is a *question*. He and Menenius joke about whether the people or the patricians are better represented by the belly. (2) The tale is about food, about its distribution and circulation. (3) The tale is told (by a patrician) to citizens who are in the act of rising in revolt against a government they say is deliberately starving them; hence the patrician can be said to be giving them words *instead* of food. The first mystery of the play is that this seems to work, that the words stop the citizens, that they stop to listen, as though these citizens are themselves willing, under certain circumstances, to take words for food, to equate them.

Coriolanus's entrance at the end of the argument over the application of the fable confirms this equation of words and food: He has from the early lines of the play been identified as the people's chief enemy, here in particular as chief of those who withhold food; and his opening main speech to them, after expressing his disgust by them, is to affirm that he does withhold and will go on withholding "good words" from them. Accordingly every word he speaks will mean the withholding of good words. He will, as it were, have a sword in his mouth. There are other suggestions of the equation of words and food in the play (for example, the enlivening of the familiar idea that understanding is a matter of digesting) but this is enough for me, in view of my previous suggestions, to take the equation as part of the invocation of the major figure of our civilization for whom words are food. The word made flesh is to be eaten, since this is the living bread. Moreover, the parables of Jesus are characteristically about food, and are always meant as food. The words / food equation suggests that we should look again at Volumnia's intercession speeches, less for their content than for the plain fact of their drama, that they are much the longest speeches Coriolanus listens to, that they cause his mother to show him her undivided attention and him to give her his silence; he is as if filled up by her words. It pleases me further to remember that Revelation also contains a vision of words that are eaten: There is a book the writer swallows that tastes as sweet as honey in the mouth but bitter in the belly (10:10), as if beauty were the beginning of terror, as in, for example, a play of Shakespeare's.

My conclusion about the working of the play, about what kind of play it is, adds up then as follows. I take the telling of the parable of the belly as a sort of play-within-the-play, a demonstration of what Shakespeare takes his play – named for Coriolanus – to be, for *Coriolanus* too is a tale about food, with competing interpretations requiring application, told by one man to a cluster, call this an audience, causing them to halt momentarily, to turn aside from their more practical or pressing concerns in order to listen. Here is the relevance I see in the fact that the play is written in a time of corn shortages and insurrections. The fact participates not just in the imagery of the play's setting, but in the question of the authority and the virtue of portraying such a time, at such a time, for one's fellow citizens; a question of the authority and the virtue in being a writer. I see in Shakespeare's portrayal of the parable of the belly a competition (in idea, perhaps in fact) with Sir Philip Sidney's familiar citing of the tale in his *Defence of Poetry*, or a rebuke of it.[9] Sidney records Menenius's application of the tale as having "wrought such effect in the people, as I never read that only words brought forth but then, so sudden and so good an alteration; for upon reasonable conditions a perfect reconcilement ensued." But in casting his partisan, limited Menenius as the teller of the tale, and placing its telling at the opening of the play, where we have minimal information or experience for judging its events, Shakespeare puts into question both the nature of the "alteration" and the "perfection" of the reconciliation. Since these are the two chief elements of Sidney's defense of poetry, this defense is as such put into question; but hence, since Shakespeare is nevertheless giving his own version of the telling of the fable, making his own story about the circulation of food, he can be understood as presenting in this play his own defense of poetry (more particularly, of plays, which Sidney particularly attacks). It is in this light noteworthy that Sidney finds "Heroical" poetry to be most "[daunting to] all back-biters," who would "speak evil" of writing that presents "champions . . . who doth not only teach and move to a truth, but teacheth and moveth to the most high and excellent truth." But since "the image of such worthies" as presented in such works "most inflameth the mind with desire to be worthy," and since *Coriolanus* is a play that studies the evil in such an inflammation, Shakespeare's play precisely questions the ground of Sidney's claim that "the Heroical . . . is not only a kind, but the best and most accomplished kind of Poetry."

What would this play's defense of poetry be; I mean how does it direct us consider the question? Its incorporation of the parable of the belly I understand to identify us, the audience, as starvers, and to identify the words of the play as food, for our incorporation. Then we have to ask of ourselves, as we have to ask of the citizens: Why have we stopped to listen? That is, what does it mean to be a member of this audience? Do we feel that these words have the power of redemption for us?

They are part of an enactment of a play of sacrifice; as it happens, of a failed sacrifice. And a feast-sacrifice, whether in Christian, pre-Christian, Nietzschean, or Freudian terms, is a matter of the founding and the preserving of a community. A community is thus identified as those who partake of the same body, of a common victim. This strikes Coriolanus as our being caught in a circle of mutual partaking, incorporating one another. And this is symbolized, or instanced, by speaking the same language. A pervasive reason Coriolanus spits out words is exactly that they *are* words, that they exist only in a language, and that a language is metaphysically something shared, so that speaking is taking and giving in your mouth the very matter others are giving and taking in theirs.

It is maddeningly irrelevant to Coriolanus which party the belly represents. What matters to him is that, whoever rules, all are members, that all participate in the same circulation, the same system of exchange, call it Rome; that to provide civil nourishment you must allow yourself to be partaken of. This is not a play about politics, if this means about political authority or conflict, say about questions of legitimate succession or divided loyalties. It is about the formation of the political, the founding of the city, about what it is that makes a rational animal fit for conversation, for civility. This play seems to think of this creation of the political, call it the public, as the overcoming of narcissism, incestuousness, and cannibalism; as if it perceives an identity among these relations.

In constructing and contesting with a hero for whom the circulation of language is an expression of cannibalism, *Coriolanus* take cannibalism as symbolic of the most human of activities, the most distinctive, or distinguished, of human activities. (Sidney cites the familiar conjunction: "Oratio, next to Ratio, . . . [is] the greatest gift bestowed upon mortality.") Coriolanus wishes to speak, to use words, to communicate, without exchanging words; without, let us say, reasoning (with others); to speak without conversing, without partaking in conversation. Here is the conversation for which he is unfit; call it civil speech. Hence I conceive *Coriolanus* to be incorporating Montaigne's interpretation of literal cannibalism as more civilized than our more sophisticated – above all, more pervasive – manners of psychological torture, our consuming others alive.[10] Montaigne's "On Cannibals" is more specifically pertinent to this play: its story of a cannibal prisoner of a cannibal society valorously taunting his captors by reminding them that in previous battles, when he had been victorious over them, he had captured and eaten their ancestors, so that in eating him they will be consuming their own flesh – this is virtually the mode in which Coriolanus addresses himself to the Volscians in putting himself at their mercy. And more variously pertinent: The essay interprets cannibalism as revenge; and it claims (in one of those moods of measured hilarity) that when three men from a cannibal society visited Rouen and were asked what they found most amazing about the ways of Montaigne's countrymen, one of their responses was as follows (I shall not comment on it but quote in Frame's translation):

> Second (they have a way in their language of speaking of men as halves of one another), they had noticed that there were among us men full and gorged with all sorts of good things, and that their other halves were beggars at their doors, emaciated with hunger and poverty; and they thought it strange that these needy halves could endure such an injustice, and did not take the other by the throat, or set fire to their houses.

Within the experience of such a vision of the circulation of language a question, not readily formulatable, may press for expression: To what extent can Coriolanus (and the play that creates him and contests with him) be understood as seeing his salvation in silence? The theme of silence haunts the play. For example, one of Coriolanus's perfectly cursed tasks is to ask for "voices" (votes) that he exactly wishes not to hear. Again, the words "silent" and "silence" are beautifully and mysteriously associated, once each, with the women in his life: with his wife ("My gracious silence, hail!"); and with his mother ("He holds her by the hand, silent"). Toward both, the word of silence is the expression of intimacy and identification; but in his wife's case it means acknowledgment, freedom from words, but in a life beyond the social, while in his mother's case it means avoidance, denial, death, that there is no life beyond the social. The ambiguities here are drilled through the action of the play by the repeated calls "Peace, peace" – hysterical, ineffective shouts of this particular word for silence. The play literalizes this conventional call for silence by implying that speech is war, as if this is the reason that both words and war can serve as food. But the man for war cannot find peace in peace – not merely because he, personally, cannot keep a civil tongue in his head, but because a tongue is inherently uncivil (if not, one hopes, inveterately so). Silence is not the absence of language; there is no such absence for human beings; in this respect, there is no world elsewhere.

Coriolanus cannot imagine, or cannot accept, that there is a way to partake of one another, incorporate one another, that is necessary to the formation rather that to the extinction of a community. (As he cannot imagine being fed without being deserving. This is his precise reversal of Christ's vision, that we cannot in ourselves deserve sustenance, and that it is for that reason, and in that spirit, that we have to ask for it. Thus is misanthropy, like philanthropy, a certain parody of Christianity.) The play *Coriolanus* asks us to try to imagine it, imagine a beneficial, mutual consumption, arguing in effect that this is what the formation of an audience is. (As if *vorare* were next to *orare*).

It seems to me that what I have been saying demonstrates, no doubt somewhat comically, the hypothesis of the origin of tragedy in religious ritual – somewhat comically, because I must seem rather to have deflated the problem, implying that whether the hypothesis is true depends on what is meant by "tragedy," what by "origin," and which ritual is in mind.[11] I have, in effect, argued that if you accept the words as food, and you accept the central figure as invoking the central figure of the Eucharist, then you may accept a formulation to the effect (not that the play is the ritual of the Eucharist, but to the effect) that the play celebrates, or aspires to, the same fact as the ritual does, say the condition of community. Eucharist means gratitude, precisely what Coriolanus feels the people withhold from him. This is another way to see why I am not satisfied to say that Coriolanus is enraged first of all by the people's cowardice. Perhaps one may say that to Coriolanus their cowardice means ingratitude. As for the idea of origin, we need only appeal to Descartes's idea that the origin of a thing is the same thing that preserves it. What preserves a tragedy, what creates the effect of a certain kind of drama, is the appropriation by an audience of this effect, our mutual incorporation of its words. When the sharing of a sacrifice is held on religious ground, the ritual itself assures its effectiveness. When it is shifted to aesthetic ground, in a theater, there is no such preexisting assurance; the work of art has to handle everything itself. You might think of this as the rebirth of religion from the spirit of tragedy. A performance is nothing without our participation in an audience; and this participation is up to each of us.

To enforce the necessity of this decision to participate (a decision which of course has its analogue for the individual reader with the script in his or her hands) is the way I understand the starkness of the words of this play, their relative ineloquence, their lack of apparent resonance. The play presents us with our need for one another's words by presenting withholding words, words that do not meet us halfway. It presents us with a famine of words. This way of seeing it takes it to fulfill a prophecy from the Book of Amos (8:12): "Behold, the days come, saith the Lord God, that I will send a famine in the land, not a famine of bread, nor a thirst for water; but of hearing the words of the Lord."

Notes

1   The *Othello* pages appear in this book as chapter 3.
2   See Bertolt Brecht, *Collected Plays*, vol. 9, ed. Ralph Manheim and John Willett (New York, 1973), pp. 378–94.
3   In *Representing Shakespeare*, ed. Murray Schwartz and Coppelia Kahn (Baltimore, 1980).
4   "There seems to be some question whether one's knowing oneself is something active, something one does . . . or rather something one suffers, something that happens to one" (*The Claim of Reason*, p. 352).
5   A point emphasized by the chairman of the *Coriolanus* panel at the Stanford meetings, Professor Harry Berger, in his remarks introducing my paper.
6   In the essay cited in note 3.
7   This is not meant as an alternative to but as an extension of the fine perception in the last note to Act I, scene ix, by the editor of the Arden edition (Philip Brockbank) that "One name is found in the scene and another is lost." My thought is that both are names held by Caius Martius Coriolanus. I suppose I am influenced in this thought by a further change Shakespeare makes in Plutarch's characterization of the man. In Plutarch Coriolanus speaks of the man as "an old friend and host of mine"; it is at the analogous moment in Shakespeare that Coriolanus speaks of the man as one at whose house he lay. The opening words of Plutarch's Life are "The house of the Martians," where "house" of course means "family," a phrase and passage employed by Shakespeare at the end of Act II where the tri-

bunes invoke Coriolanus's biological descent as if to their sufficient credit for having considered it but to Coriolanus's insufficient credit for election to consul.

8   I quote from North's translation of Plutarch's biography of Coriolanus, which is given in an appendix to the Arden edition of *Coriolanus* (London, 1976). The "impostume" passage occurs on p. 133.

Coriolanus's sense of disgust with the people is more explicitly conveyed by Shakespeare through the sense of their foul smell than of their foul taste. Shakespeare does use the idea of spitting twice: once, as cited, to describe Hector's forehead bleeding in battle, and the second time in Coriolanus's only scene of soliloquy, disguised before Aufidius's house: "Then know me not. / Lest that thy wives with spits and boys with stones / In puny battle slay me" – so that both times spitting is linked with battle and with food. As I have implied, I understand Coriolanus's vision of his death in Antium at the hands of wives and boys as a prophecy of the death he actually undergoes there, spitted by the swords of strange boys.

9   The following remarks on Sidney's tract were reintroduced, expanded from an earlier set on the subject that I had dropped from the paper, as a result of an exchange with Stephen Greenblatt during the discussion period following my presentation at Stanford.

10   Finding the words / food representation so compelling, I am ignoring here the path along which the circulation of words also registers the circulation of money (as in "So shall my lungs / Coin words" (III, i, 77–8); and in "The price is, to ask it kindly" (II, iii, 77). The sense of consuming as expending would relate to Coriolanus's frantic efforts to deny that his actions can be recompensed ("better to starve than crave the hire" – for example, of receiving voices *in return*). Money depends upon the equating of values; Coriolanus, on their lack of equation, on measurelessness, pricelessness.

11   In the discussion period at Stanford, Paul Alpers noted that I seemed to find something like a comic perspective of the play to be more extensive than just here where I am making it explicit, and he asked how far I wished to go in seeking this perspective. I find this a true response to my reading, but it goes beyond anything I can explore now. I mentioned then what I take to be a starting point to such an exploration, Coriolanus's sense that as he and his mother stand silent together "The Gods look down, and this unnatural scene / They laugh at." Does he feel the gods laugh because mother and son are too close or too distant with one another? At least the scene is unnatural because it is social, and because the social is the scene of mazes of meaning as dense as poetry, in which its poor, prosaic, half-human creatures are isolated. The comedic perspective I seek presents itself to me as a totalization, or a kind of transcendentalizing, of dramatic irony – where the omen or allusion is not of some specific, future event, but of the totality of the present, of events as they are, without our being able to specify in advance what individuates or what relates these events.

4

Character: An Overview

In Shakespearean English, 'character' meant graphical mark or representation: it related to writing rather than to persons, and it is not until the mid-seventeenth century that the dominant meaning of 'personality', or 'dramatic personage', appears. Much character study has been about the relationship between the words of the plays – *characters* – and ideas of personality and performance: *characters*. Bradley's stress on character was a clear legacy of the fiction and Shakespearean criticism of the nineteenth century. In 1935, E. E. Stoll could begin an essay on Hamlet by announcing: 'In this essay I turn from Hamlet as part of the play to consider him as a person' (Stoll, 1935, p. 1) – and as a person who must be liked by the audience: 'to render that tragic catastrophe its full effect the reader must be willing to yield to the hero, as ordinary, unlettered audience have for three centuries done, and as the presentation of his character warrants, their admiration and sympathy almost without misgiving or reserve' (p. 29). J. I. M. Stewart's *Character and Motive in Shakespeare: Some Recent Appraisals Examined* (1949) recognized that character study was in a troubled state because of the habit of novel-reading: 'characters in [*Anna Karenina* and *Madame Bovary*] are interpreted for a mode of consciousness and in terms of assumptions and categories which are familiar to us' (Stewart, 1949, p. 3), unlike Shakespearean drama. Dramatic characters 'have often the superior reality of individuals exposing the deepest springs of their action. But this superior reality is manifested through the medium of situations which are sometimes essentially symbolical' (pp. 9–10). Rather than being always individual and coherent psychological portraits, characters are together, according to Stewart, 'composed into a whole [. . .] which is in the total impression an image of life' (p. 110). Peter Ure's 1960 lecture *Shakespeare and the Inward Self of the Tragic Hero* takes up the metaphor of playing a part and the interplay between inner and outer selves. Ure sees *Othello* as 'the tragedy of a man who dedicates himself absolutely to his part' (Ure, 1961, p. 13) and discusses the annulment of 'Richard II's inner self' (p. 21), the transformation of Lear's and the stripping bare of Coriolanus's.

William Kerrigan, in *Hamlet's Perfection* (1994), gives a (partial) account of post-Bradley conceptions of Hamlet's character, arguing that 'to give up the primacy of character in Shakespeare studies [. . .] seems tantamount to giving up individualism' (Kerrigan, 1994, p. 31), and goes on to elaborate a characterological reading of the play as its protagonist. In her *Reading Shakespeare's Characters* (1992), Christy Desmet uses early modern rhetorical texts as well as theories of language and the self from Aristotle to de Man. Her accounts of *King Lear*, *Hamlet* and *Othello* stress characters' rhetorical agency and the ethics of audience identification. In his *Hamlet and the Concept of Character* (1992), Bert States proposes that 'character [is] a way of behaving rather than as a "depth" of motive or a complexity of traits. Thus read, character takes us to the human base of drama on which all of its subtleties of motive and morals are built' (States, 1992, p. 19).

Derek Cohen's *Shakespearean Motives* (1988) declares its dominant interest in characterization. The chapter on *Othello* discusses the 'two Othellos who dominate his world – the historic other self and the present evident self' (Cohen, 1988, p. 94); on *King Lear* Cohen discusses 'some twenty-four allusions and direct references to the characters' physical existence before the events of the play' which serve to 'anchor them in a real, if almost imperceptible personal and political history' (p. 119). In his *The Passions of Shakespeare's Tragic Heroes* (1990), Arthur Kirsch uses Renaissance and more recent concepts of character to 'renew an appreciation of the timelessness of Shakespeare's genius in dramatizing human actions and feelings' (Kirsch, 1990, p. ix). Kirsch focuses on *Hamlet*, *Lear*, *Othello* and *Macbeth* to argue that the main feature of these tragedies is the inner drama of the suffering protagonist. In *Young Hamlet: Essays on Shakespeare's Tragedies* (1989), Barbara Everett takes as her subject the four major tragedies and 'their truth to ordinary human experience' (Everett, 1989, p. 1). She discusses *Hamlet* as the story of 'a son who must – as the young always must – by living accept an inheritance largely unwanted from the generation of the fathers' (p. 8); in *Othello* Shakespeare makes 'the social susceptible of profundities of experience' (p. 51). A. D. Nuttall's philosophically informed *A New Mimesis: Shakespeare and the Representation of Reality* (1983) discusses Shakespearean verisimilitude with reference to criticism he dubs 'Opaque', characterized by a constant formal awareness of the artifice of the work, and 'Transparent', which explains 'fictitious behaviour by analogy with real-life equivalents' (Nuttall, 1983, p. 81). Nuttall favours the 'Transparent': Coriolanus, Brutus, Antony are products of an 'intuitive psychology' (p. 120). Othello 'was perplexed in the extreme before Iago went to work on him. Marriage itself disoriented him' (p. 139).

Psychoanalysis has given character-study a new vocabulary and new areas of interest. Freud's own comments on *Hamlet* in *The Interpretation of Dreams* (1900) discussed the play's exhibition of Oedipal neurosis. Freud argues that, far from being unable to act in a general sense as the Romantics saw him, Hamlet is inhibited from fulfilling the particular demand of the ghost because Claudius 'shows him the repressed wishes of his own childhood realized. Thus the loathing which should drive him on to revenge is replaced in him by self-reproaches, by scruples of conscience, which remind him that he himself is literally no better than the sinner whom he is to punish' (Freud, 1976, p. 367). These ideas were developed in *Hamlet and Oedipus* by Ernest Jones, published in book form in 1949 as an enlarged version of essays published in 1910 and 1923. Jones proposed that 'no dramatic criticism of the personae in a play is possible except under the pretence that they are living people, and surely one is well aware of this pretence', and goes on to argue that 'in so far and in the same sense as a character in a play is taken as being a living person, to that extent must he have had a life before the action in the play began, since no-one starts life as an adult' (Jones, 1949, pp. 18–19). He discusses aspects and possible explanations of the perennial question of Hamlet's delay, concluding, with Freud, that the repressed urge to kill his father is crucial for Hamlet, as in 'the real Hamlets who are investigated psychologically' (p. 70). In the work of Jacques Lacan, in his 'Desire and the Interpretation of Desire in *Hamlet*', the tragedy is one of desire. Ophelia, whose role is changed subtly from the source material, 'becomes one of the innermost elements in Hamlet's drama, the drama of Hamlet as the man who has lost the way of his desire' (Felman, 1982, p. 12). Lacan argues that 'Hamlet just doesn't know what he wants', and that this figures the unknowability of the object of desire. He notes also that 'all anyone talks about is mourning' (p. 39), and that rites of burial and mourning are all truncated in the play, revisiting and developing Freudian paradigms.

In his *The Tragic Effect: the Oedipus Complex in Tragedy* (1979), André Green takes up psychoanalytic ideas about the spectator and the gaze, about family romance and about language and representation, arguing that 'the family, then, is the tragic space *par excellence*' (Green, 1979, p. 7). Much of Green's book is most directly concerned with Greek tragedy, but his chapter on *Othello* establishes its 'context of alienation' (p. 91) in a discussion of Freudian ideas of jealousy, narcissism, desire and foreclosed homosexuality: 'Othello is a brother of Oedipus and Orestes' whose oedipal relationship to his own father is transferred to Brabantio. Lupton and Reinhard's *After Oedipus: Shakespeare in Psychoanalysis* (1993) is informed by Lacanian psychoanalytical theories of the subject. The study discusses Hamlet, melancholia and mourning, Freud's interpretation of *Hamlet* and the Oedipus complex, the Freudian contexts of Olivier's 1948 film of the play as opposed to the Lacanian dynamic of Zeffirelli's (1990), attitudes to the feminine in *King Lear* and the relationship between psychoanalysis and Shakespeare. Janet Adelman's essay ' "This Is and Is Not Cressid": The Characterization of Cressida' also uses psychoanalytic theory to discuss the ways in which 'Cressida's inconstancy is accompanied by a radical inconsistency of characterization' (Adelman, 1985, p. 120). Adelman argues that her soliloquy in 2.5 'establishes in us a keen sense both of Cressida's inwardness and of our own privileged position as the recipient of her revelations' (p. 122). Like Cordelia, Cressida is, however, split, as Troilus' remark used as Adelman's title enacts: fractured in order to preserve the fantasy of chastity needed by the male characters for their own creation of self: 'Cressida as a whole character must be sacrificed' (p. 140). There is an extensive bibliography of psychoanalytic writings on Shakespeare from 1964 to 1978 compiled by David Willbern (1980).

In the collection of essays edited by Norman Holland, Sidney Homan and Bernard J. Paris as *Shakespeare's Personality* (1989), the argument is that 'the psychoanalyst studies an individual in the Renaissance as psychoanalysis defines the individual, not as the Renaissance defines it' (Holland, 1989, p. 5). By contrast, J. Leeds Barroll's *Artificial Persons: the Formation of Character in the Tragedies of Shakespeare* (1974) argues for a more historicized sense of psychology in an 'attempt to recover some notion of the psychological organizations conceivably familiar to Shakespeare and his contemporaries' (Barroll, 1974, p. 251). Barroll warns that 'even if *Hamlet* does strike us as "Freudian," Shakespeare nevertheless had not read Freud; and while Shakespeare may have observed traits that modern psychology generally accepts as extant in human nature, the structure of ideas by which he sought to account for such phenomena would have been quite importantly different' (p. 21). Peter Murray's *Shakespeare's Imagined Persons* (1996) suggests that the plays invite audiences to register their characters as imagined persons, drawing on early modern psychology to support the thesis. His chapter on *Hamlet* argues that the prince 'has the divided and only partially self-aware and self-controlling subjectivity that in Shakespeare's time was said to characterize human beings' (Murray, 1996, p. 57).

Other challenges to Bradley's brand of character analysis have been numerous. Levin Schücking's *Character Problems in Shakespeare's Plays* (1922; 1959) discusses characterization through soliloquy, through plot and through other characters. Schücking uses the example of Lady Macbeth's swooning in 2.3 to argue that the dramatic medium must be recalled: super-subtle psychological explanation was not the province of the Renaissance theatre. L. C. Knights' famous retort to what he saw as Bradley's excessive focus on 'character' was published as 'How Many Children Had Lady Macbeth?' in 1933, reprinted in his *Explorations* (1946). Knights advocates the understanding of the plays as poetic wholes, and warns against 'mistaking the *dramatis personae* for real persons' (Knights, 1946, p. 29). Wilson Knight's stress on symbolist-poetic structure of the plays led him to propose that 'it is dangerous to abstract the personal history from his environment as a basis for interpretation' (Knight, 1930, p. 141). Caroline Spurgeon's analysis of Shakespeare's language (*Shakespeare's Imagery and What it Tells Us* (1935), see p. 142) stressed patterns of imagery over the idiolect of characterization. Muriel Bradbrook's *Themes and Conventions of Elizabethan Tragedy* (1934) stressed the specific concepts of characterization current in the theatre of Shakespeare and his contemporaries: 'the superhuman nature of heroes, the definition of character by decorum, and the theory of Humours' (Bradbrook, 1980, p. 54) as an antidote to the application of modern ideas of personality.

More recently, Alan Sinfield's *Faultlines* (1992) argues that 'the character of Macbeth, then, is not a mysterious natural essence. Rather he is situated at the intersection of discourses and historical forces that are competing, we might say, to fill up his subjectivity' (Sinfield, 1992, p. 63). Sinfield redefines the concept of character as 'continuous consciousness', and suggests that readers' experience of 'unified psychological density can only be a chimera' (p. 65), willed over the actual inscription of 'radically insecure subjectivity, one swaying between divergent possible selves and vulnerable to manipulation' (p. 64). In his *The Tremulous Private Body: Essays on Subjection* (1984), Francis Barker argues that

> interiority remains, in *Hamlet*, gestural [. . .] at the centre of Hamlet, in the interior of his mystery, there is, in short, nothing. The promised essence remains beyond the scope of the text's signification: or rather, signals the limit of the signification of the world by marking out the site of an absence it cannot fill. It gestures towards a place for subjectivity, but both are anachronistic and belong to a historical order whose outline has so far only been sketched out. (Barker, 1984, pp. 32–3)

The play promises an essential subjectivity, but in its failure to produce it 'the text scandalously reveals the emptiness at the heart of that bourgeois trope' (p. 34). Barker suggests that generations of criticism on *Hamlet* have been trying, blindly, to fill this void. Catherine Belsey's *The Subject of Tragedy* (1985) concurs: 'Hamlet is precisely not a unified subject' (Belsey, 1985, p. 42). In her study *Notorious Identity: Materializing the Subject in Shakespeare* (1993), Linda Charnes discusses Richard III, Antony and Cleopatra, and Troilus and Cressida as already-notorious and commodified 'brand names' before Shakespeare took them over. The characters respond to these earlier textual versions of themselves as an investigation of the relationship between identity and subjectivity. Maus' *Inwardness and Theater* (1995) attempts to recover a 'history of the subject' (Maus, 1995, p. 3) after post-structuralist and materialist assaults by Sinfield, Barker and Dollimore by studying historical analogues for Hamlet's 'that within which passes show'. Lisa Jardine's study of Desdemona in her *Reading Shakespeare Historically* (1996) also draws on historical material, including court records, on early modern defamation cases.

Character-study, however, seems still much in evidence. Much of it has emerged as part of performance criticism, particularly in commentaries by actors (see pp. 330–1). Accounts of particular characters include Porter's study *Shakespeare's Mercutio* (1988) which investigates Mercutio's textual origins, the significance of his name and gives a detailed account of his role in the play and its afterlife. James P. Driscoll considers *Identity in Shakespearean Drama* (1983) with reference to Jung's theory of archetypes and symbols. He discusses characters' real, social, conscious and ideal identities, and the Jungian distinction between *persona* – the performed and projected identity which varies according to the social situation; *anima* – that which lies within; and *shadow* – the repressed negative aspects of the real identity activated by characters such as Iago and Edmund. There are a number of studies of character-types, such as Eldred Jones' *Othello's Countrymen* (1965) and Jack d'Amico's *The Moor in English Renaissance Drama* (1991), and Bernard Spivack's *Shakespeare and the Allegory of Evil* (1958), which traces Iago's predecessors in the Vice characters of medieval drama. A particular interest in female characters is the subject of Heilbrun (1990), Dusinberre (1975), French (1981) and Callaghan (1989), and these are discussed in more detail in chapter 8: Gender and Sexuality. G. M. Pinciss' book *Literary Creations: Conventional Characters in the Drama of Shakespeare and his Contemporaries* (1988) stresses stock figures rather than individuated stage personalities, including the ideal courtier, the savage man, the overreacher, the Machiavel, the tool-villain whose crimes are in the service of another and the married woman. Robert Weimann's essay 'Society and the Individual in Shakespeare's Conception of Character' (1981) develops an account of interplay between social context and the individual.

Despite extensive challenges, character criticism recognizable to the first Romantic progenitors is also still present. Harold Bloom's *Shakespeare: The Invention of the Human* (1998) argues that 'Shakespeare will go on explaining us, in part because he invented us' (Bloom, 1998, p. xviii): 'Shakespeare, by inventing what has become the most accepted mode for representing character and personality in language, thereby invented the human as we know it.' Bloom identifies Shakespeare as 'the original psychologist' (p. 714): his most comprehensive male characters are Hamlet and Falstaff; Cleopatra dominates the women. Bloom's study concludes:

> Whether we are male or female, old or young, Falstaff and Hamlet speak most urgently for us and to us. Hamlet can be transcendent or ironic; in either mode his inventiveness is absolute. Falstaff, at his funniest or at his most reflective, retains a vitalism that renders him alive beyond belief. When we are wholly

human, and know ourselves, we become most like either Hamlet or Falstaff.
(p. 745)

And in a book of essays entitled *Shakespeare and the Twentieth Century* Edward
Pechter ends his contribution 'Why should we call her whore? Bianca in
Othello' by arguing for renewed engagement with the 'characters from inside':
'This is Bradley-talk. Whatever was misdirected in Bradley, treating characters as isolated monads abstracted from the action, an intense affective engagement underwrote his criticism and the traditions culminating in his work. In
this sense, my modest proposal for the critical new world order at the end of
the millennium is: *back to the nineteenth century*' (Pechter, 1998, p. 372).

Further Reading

Adelman, Janet. '"This Is and Is Not Cressid": The Characterization of Cressida'. *The
    (M)other tongue: Essays in Feminist Psychoanalytic Interpretation*. Eds Shirley Nelson
    Garner, Claire Kahane and Madelon Sprengnether. Ithaca; London: Cornell
    University Press, 1985. 119–141.
Barker, Francis. *The Tremulous Private Body: Essays on Subjection*. London: Methuen,
    1984.
Barroll, J. Leeds. *Artificial Persons: The Formation of Character in the Tragedies of
    Shakespeare*. Columbia: University of South Carolina Press, 1974.
Belsey, Catherine. *The Subject of Tragedy: Identity and Difference in Renaissance Drama*.
    London: Methuen, 1985.
Bloom, Harold. *Shakespeare: The Invention of the Human*. New York: Riverhead Books,
    1998.
Bradbrook, M. C. *Themes and Conventions of Elizabethan Tragedy*, 2nd edn Cambridge:
    Cambridge University Press, 1980.
Callaghan, Dympna. *Woman and Gender in Renaissance Tragedy: A Study of Othello,
    King Lear, the Duchess of Malfi and the White Devil*. Hemel Hempstead: Harvester
    Wheatsheaf, 1989.
Charnes, Linda. *Notorious Identity: Materializing the Subject in Shakespeare*. Cambridge,
    Mass; London: Harvard University Press, 1993.
Cohen, Derek. *Shakespearean Motives. Contemporary Interpretations of Shakespeare*.
    Basingstoke: Macmillan, 1988.
D'Amico, Jack F. *The Moor in English Renaissance Drama*. Tampa Gainesville, FL:
    University Presses of Florida, 1991.
Desmet, Christy. *Reading Shakespeare's Characters: Rhetoric, Ethics, and Identity*.
    Massachusetts studies in early modern culture. Amherst: University of Massachu-
    setts Press, 1992.
Driscoll, James P. *Identity in Shakespearean Drama*. Lewisburg: Associated University
    Presses, 1983.
Dusinberre, Juliet. *Shakespeare and the Nature of Women*. London: Macmillan, 1975.

Everett, Barbara. *Young Hamlet: Essays on Shakespeare's Tragedies*. Oxford: Clarendon Press, 1989.

Felman, Shoshana. *Literature and Psychoanalysis: The Question of Reading: otherwise*. Baltimore: Johns Hopkins University Press, 1982.

French, Marilyn. *Shakespeare's Division of Experience*. New York: Summit Books, 1981.

Freud, Sigmund, and Strachey, James. *The Interpretation of Dreams*. Pelican Freud Library, vol. 4. Harmondsworth: Penguin Books, 1976.

Green, André. *The Tragic Effect: The Oedipus Complex in Tragedy*. Cambridge: Cambridge University Press, 1979.

Heilbrun, Carolyn G. *Hamlet's Mother and Other Women*. Gender and Culture. New York: Columbia University Press, 1990.

Holland, Norman N., Homan, Sidney, and Paris, Bernard J. *Shakespeare's Personality*. Berkeley: University of California Press, 1989.

Jardine, Lisa. *Reading Shakespeare Historically*. London: Routledge, 1996.

Jones, Eldred Durosimi, and Fourah Bay College. *Othello's Countrymen: The African in English Renaissance Drama*. London: Oxford University Press, 1965.

Jones, Ernest. *Hamlet and Oedipus*. London: Gollancz, 1949.

Kerrigan, William. *Hamlet's Perfection*. Baltimore; London: Johns Hopkins University Press, 1994.

Kirsch, Arthur. *The Passions of Shakespeare's Tragic Heroes*. Charlottesville; London: University Press of Virginia, 1990.

Knight, George Wilson. *The Wheel of Fire; Essays in Interpretation of Shakespeare's Sombre Tragedies*. London: Oxford University Press, 1930.

Knights, L. C. *Explorations: Essays in Criticism, Mainly on the Literature of the Seventeenth Century*. London: Chatto & Windus, 1946.

Lupton, Julia Reinhard, and Reinhard, Kenneth. *After Oedipus: Shakespeare in Psychoanalysis*. Ithaca; London: Cornell University Press, 1993.

Maus, Katharine Eisaman. *Inwardness and Theater in the English Renaissance*. Chicago; London: University of Chicago Press, 1995.

Murray, Peter B. *Shakespeare's Imagined Persons: The Psychology of Role-playing and Acting*. Lanham; Basingstoke: Barnes & Noble; Macmillan, 1996.

Nuttall, A. D. *A New Mimesis: Shakespeare and the Representation of Reality*. London: Methuen, 1983.

Pechter, Edward. 'Why should we call her whore? Bianca in *Othello*'. *Shakespeare in the Twentieth Century*. Eds Jonathan Bate and Jill Levenson, 1998. 364–77.

Pinciss, G. M. *Literary Creations: Conventional Characters in the Drama of Shakespeare and his Contemporaries*. Woodbridge: D. S. Brewer, 1988.

Porter, Joseph Ashby. *Shakespeare's Mercutio: His History and Drama*. Chapel Hill; London: University of North Carolina Press, 1988.

Schücking, Levin Ludwig. *Character Problems in Shakespeare's Plays: A Guide to the Better Understanding of the Dramatist*. Gloucester: Peter Smith, 1959.

Sinfield, Alan. *Faultlines: Cultural Materialism and the Politics of Dissident Reading*. Oxford: Clarendon Press, 1992.

Spivack, Bernard. *Shakespeare and the Allegory of Evil: The History of a Metaphor in Relation to his Major Villains*. New York: Columbia University Press, 1958.

Spurgeon, C. F. E. *Shakespeare's Imagery: And What it Tells Us*. Cambridge: University Press, 1935.

States, Bert O. *Hamlet and the Concept of Character*. Baltimore; London: Johns Hopkins University Press, 1992.

Stewart, J. I. M. *Character and Motive in Shakespeare: Some Recent Appraisals Examined*. London: Longmans Green, 1949.

Stoll, Elmer Edgar. *Hamlet the Man*. Oxford: Oxford University Press, 1935.

Ure, Peter. *Shakespeare and the Inward Self of the Tragic Hero*. Durham: University of Durham, 1961.

Weimann, Robert. 'Society and the Individual in Shakespeare's Conception of Character'. *Shakespeare Survey* 34 (1981): 23–31.

Willbern, David. 'A Bibliography of Psychoanalytic and Psychological Writings on Shakespeare: 1964–78'. *Representing Shakespeare: New Psychoanalytic Essays*. Eds Murray M. Schwartz and Coppélia Kahn, 1980. 264–88.

5

Character: Critical Extracts

The Resources of Characterization in *Othello*

Peter Holland

Like Goldman, Holland has a particular interest in Shakespeare in performance: his other writings include theatre review articles in the journal Shakespeare Survey *volumes 44–9, and* English Shakespeares: Shakespeare on the English Stage in the 1990s *(1997). Here, Holland is concerned to review the shortcomings of the methodology of character-study, and to combine historicism – his analysis of quarto / Folio variants, for example – with a consciousness of the play's ongoing theatrical life. Ultimately his account of characterization would seem to endorse some kind of 'method' acting in which the hidden 'history' of each minor character could be unfolded, but there are other different and stimulating suggestions about the question of types versus individuals and of naturalistic staging versus presentation, which might interestingly be applied to other plays.*

Peter Holland, 'The Resources of Characterization in *Othello*', in *Shakespeare Survey: An Annual Survey of Shakespeare Studies and Production* 41. Cambridge; New York: Cambridge University Press, 1982.

At the beginning of the last act of Ben Jonson's *The Alchemist*, Lovewit, returning to his house from the country now that the plague has abated, is met by a crowd of his neighbours. The neighbours are eager to tell him all about the peculiar events that have gone on in the house during his absence. As with great excitement and more than a little credulity – as one might expect in the play that finds credulousness to be a universal feature of the city – the six neighbours trip over each other breathlessly with yet more fragments of gossip and corroborating detail, their comments grow together until they become a chorus of Londoners:

> [LOVEWIT] Has there beene such resort, say you?   NEI. 1 Daily, sir.
> NEI. 2 And nightly, too.   NEI. 3 I, some as braue as lords.
> NEI. 4 Ladies, and gentlewomen.   NEI. 5 Citizens wiues.
> NEI. 1 And knights. NEI. 6 In coches.   NEI. 2 Yes, & oyster-women.

Nei. 1 Beside other gallants.   Nei. 3 Sailors wiues.   Nei. 4 *Tabacco*-men.
Nei. 4 Another *Pimlico*.[1]

The anonymous group of undifferentiated and undifferentiable voices can only vaguely be defined, even corporately, as a group. They are plainly of a lower social class than Lovewit himself; they keep addressing him as 'sir'. One of them, Neighbour 3, is a tradesman, 'a smith, and't please your worship' (line 43). But they are hardly individualized; their characters are dissolved into their choric function, a credulous chorus and they can claim no greater identity than that.

All that is, except one, Neighbour 6. As Lovewit questions them about the whereabouts of Jeremy the butler, Neighbour 6 chips in with his gory fears: 'Pray god, he be not made away!' (line 31). Like many of us, Neighbour 6 is only too ready to contemplate the most macabre possibility. But he has a reason for his fear: 'About / Some three weeks since, I head a dolefull cry' (lines 33–4). Lovewit questions him about it: 'Didst thou heare / A cry, saist thou?' 'Yes, sir, like unto a man / That had been strangled an houre, and could not speake' (lines 35–7). It is a deliciously comic moment. But I have suppressed, momentarily, the line that marks Neighbour 6 out, that changes his status so completely: 'About / Some three weeks since, I heard a dolefull cry, / As I sate up, amending my wives stockings' (lines 32–4). With entirely characteristic Jonsonian brilliance, that single line transforms Neighbour 6. Suddenly and with no preparation, the character loses the anonymity of the crowd and has a history, a personality, a differentiated self-hood. Out of the single line we can start to sketch him: poor, with a domineering wife who gets him to do the tasks that are rightly or conventionally hers, he sits up till 2 a.m. (the time Neighbour 2 says he heard the cry) working at his domestic chores and in the quiet of the middle of the night his mind begins to run riot and his thoughts become bloodthirsty. Any bit-part actor, any hireling in the King's Men who was given Neighbour 6, would surely recognize straight away that he had been given something very different from his fellows.

I am inordinately fond of Neighbour 6, but the way he appears out from the crowd defines the change in the nature of characterization conse-quent on the beginnings here of an increased definition, a visibility of individuality. As that particular individuality flourishes for a moment here, so that separateness from the crowd is particular, individual, different. Neighbour 6 is both a part of the group and a unique member of it, perhaps significantly the only member to proclaim in his language his uniqueness. It is not, crucially for my argument, that Neighbour 6 is a character and the other neighbours are not – that would be an unhelpful distinction since it would necessitate remarkably factitious lines of demarcation between certain modes of speaking role, allowed the status of characters, and others who sink back into a mass of something else, unlabelled and unimportant. Instead, the gap that his one defining line opens out is sufficient to change the type of character he is, change the actor's and the audience's response to him, and ought to change in consequence the critical tools appropriate to our description and analysis of him.

As I have read more widely in the critical tradition of the analysis of Shakespearian characterization, I have become more and more troubled by the inability of the methods used, and of the presuppositions implicit in the writing, to cope with the problem posed by Jonson's Neighbour 6, let alone the far more complex and sophisticated problems that seem to me to be posed in Shakespeare himself. In so many senses there is little difference between the critical language tried out falteringly in the eighteenth century and typified for us by, say, Maurice Morgann's *Essay on the Dramatic Character of Sir John Falstaff* (London, 1777) and such recent analyses as those collected in *Shakespeare Survey 34* (1981), devoted to papers from the International Shakespeare Conference on 'Characterization in Shakespeare', or the essays on Shakespeare's styles collected in honour of Kenneth Muir.[2] The critical language has of course become immeasurably subtler and many of the recent essays display a sensitivity and perceptiveness that I unashamedly envy. Yet I hope my arrogance will be excused if I rather glibly declare that while the terms have changed the scope of the analysis has not. Too much has been left out.

I can best arrange my anxieties under six heads:

(i)   There seem to be too few characters in the traditional model. It is obvious that Hamlet deserves far far more attention than Second Gentleman and the dominance of the major roles in the creation of the performance is entirely right and proper. But the methods appropriate to the analysis of the major rarely fit the minor, and the extrapolated synoptic generalizations about Shakespeare inadequately express or consider the range of roles performed. We are left with an apparent ability to analyse most of the lines spoken, but unable to analyse most of the characters in any one play, assuming somehow that the few characters we can analyse will adequately represent the others.

(ii)   These has been little concern to identify the way in which distinctive qualities in characterization emerge at different stages in Shakespeare's career, that his view, in effect, is not static but changing. There have been, under this heading as under the first, isolated exceptions: Anne Barton's fine essay on 'Language and Speaker in Shakespeare's Last Plays' develops, with satisfying results, the perception that 'for whatever reason, Shakespeare at the end of his writing life chose to subordinate character to action in ways that seem to give Aristotle's conviction of the necessary primacy of μνθος a new twist'.[3] But it is nonetheless true that far too little attention has been paid to this chronological change.

(iii)   The relationship of actor to character is seen within a static perspective governed critically early and late by what actors might see as a ravening Stanislavskian maw. Broadly naturalist, heavily psychologized, and occasionally but all too rarely social (in for example the work of Robert Weimann[4]), the method of characterization is recuperated within developing senses of the actor's self. It is assumed that there is a wholeness of interpenetration of actor and role, consequentially powerfully engaged as a model of performance with an assumed emotional reaction on the part of the actor – and hence of the audience in relation to that actor. Even when actors attempt to describe their mode of working, there is usually an unquestioned psychologism, a particular relation to the actor's own psyche very near the surface, throughout the tradition of British and American Shakespeare performance.

Michael Pennington, for instance, describing his preparatory work on Hamlet, generalizes that 'the player is working in a specially subjective way, and the production is likely to be reflecting his own basic personality. It would be surprising to find him reaching very far from his theatrical self'.[5] Though I would want to quiz quite closely the implications of the word 'theatrical' here, Pennington is still describing a mode of interconnection of actor and character that, for all its possible appropriateness to Hamlet, will not work for many characters outside an obvious few. Must an actor approach, say, Claudius 'in a specially subjective way'? Indeed it could be argued that Hamlet *necessitates* and Claudius *denies* that premise of actor subjectivity. Stanislavskian dictates, such as finding the good in the bad, the bad in the good, are a subjectivized normalization of characterization, accommodating character within limited socio-psychological ranges of behaviour. They still provide the basis for most actors' work in classic drama.

(iv)   The relationship of character to audience is trapped within a similarly unitary vision. At times, indeed, it has seemed that the consideration of the audience at all has been completely absent, that character study is still based on an assumption that the theatrical must be suppressed in favour of the fictional, and that Shakespeare only wrote plays through the misfortune of having been born too early to have written novels. The novelistic stress on character is still dominantly visible in a recent work as intelligent and influential as John Bayley's *Shakespeare and Tragedy* (London, 1981).

The study of the relationship of character to audience will have complex parameters depending on such factors as the position of actor on stage, with its own specific consequences in, for example, the degree of directness of audience address. Yet this relationship is rarely considered critically. The relationship of audience to particular actors or roles, the role of clown for example, is similarly potent and largely uncharted. Again there are exceptions: Weimann's work on locus / platea distinctions in the tradition of popular theatre has enormous and as yet largely unrealized consequences for the study of dramatic character.[6] Other work has meant that we can now accept that Hamlet establishes a peculiarly close and direct rapport with the audience from his very first lines, and we can see that as manifesting an attitude towards the action, a commentary status which deserves enquiry. But it is not related to other parallel modes of communication with the audience so that its specific resources can be checked and corroborated. It seems to me, for instance, that in this case the closeness of comparability with the interaction of clown and audience is highly significant and will allow the ways in which we are starting to observe the place of comic method in the development of Hamlet's character to emerge with a wholly different bias.

(v)   In the analysis of character we have not yet built on the highly stimulating work done in the last few years on Shakespeare's methods and art of construction. We could by now have developed the implications of such comments as Anne Barton's, which I quoted on the relation of character to action, to pin-point a remarkable variety of modes of relationship between character and narrative – a relationship in which we could afford to borrow with due circumspection from the development of narrative theory over the past twenty years. Actantial analysis, which can trace as one of its antecedents Vladimir Propp's work on Russian folk-tale (subsequently reformulated by A.-J. Greimas),[7] can also see a root in Etienne Souriau's book *Les Deux Cents Milles Situations Dramatiques* (Paris, 1950). But the analysis of dramatic situation has not profited from formalist actantial analysis. I am not proposing for a moment that we should develop diagrammatic formulations of Shakespearian narrative that identify which character is the villain, donor, helper, dispatcher, hero, and false hero of Greimas's model, or the lion, sun, earth, Mars, scale, and moon of Souriau's, but rather that a flexible perception of the balance between character and action will allow the actantial forces to be observed surfacing at particular moments with significant results.

I am suggesting specifically the use of pre-structuralist and indeed structuralist work of actantial analysis rather than any post-structuralist and deconstructionist modes. It is repeatedly significant to me that the attempts to dissolve subjectivity, as a concept in the analysis of character in narrative fiction in so much recent analysis, have been oddly unhelpful for the analysis of character in drama. It always seems to me consequent on the physical presence of the body, the body of the actor, that the separation of subject from corporeality is impossible in dramatic analysis. Those odd, by which I mean occasional as well as eccentric, recent attempts to dissolve the concept of the subject in the analysis of dramatic character have always been heavily tinged with the experience of reading rather than the theatre. The coherence of character is marked by the integrity and coherence of the unity of the physical existence of the actor, whether that actor plays one or fifteen roles in a particular play. The relation of that coherence to extra-dramatic principles of the coherence of the subject in the social construction of normality in behavioural individuality is consistently subordinated to the face of the unitary presence foregrounded in the actor.

(vi) While some of the very best work on Shakespearian characterization recently has focused on relationships between language and character, even a work as provocative and subtle as Giorgio Melchiori's piece on 'The Rhetoric of Character Construction: *Othello*'[8] treats the creation of dramatic idiolects out of specific rhetorical tropes as if the relationship of a character to its language were undeviatingly single. Obviously this can overlap with my last point. But it does come as a refreshing comment to read Nicholas Brooke's remark on the First Murderer's lines in Macbeth: 'The west yet glimmers with some streaks of day. / Now spurs the lated traveller apace / To gain the timely inn' (3.3.5–7) – that these lines 'belong absolutely to the play and are absolutely alien to the speaker'.[9] The discrepancy, repeated and significantly so amongst minor characters, is also part of the dissociation of line from character that we can find surfacing in the traditional core group of characters usually analysed.

My six points are of course neither exhaustive nor discrete. They interact with each other in various configurations time and again. Similarly their interaction is not of a fixed mode but instead varies between different characters in the same play, consistently within individual roles and, with potent effects, inconsistently, within a scene, a speech, or a line, across the expanse of a play. But the drift of my critique should by now be clear. We have not yet begun to take on the true extent of the infinite variety of Shakespearian characterization. We have not yet charted the parameters of that problem in a manner that convinces me that we can represent its breadth of vision and its potential. Until we have the bases for such analysis comprehensively and systematically available, we are producing character analysis that is limiting and constrictive rather than enlarging and inclusive.

Obviously it will not be possible here to suggest fully what that set of axes might be like or even to chart some of the parameters for any of the axes. My generalizations here suggest investigations well beyond the scope of a single article; all I shall do is sketch some of the possibilities in relation to the resources of characterization in a single play, *Othello*. With a proper openness of response to the wider problem of character we should however be able to see, for instance, how the relation of character to function operates and learn for our critical practice the sort of lesson that actors often understand better than critics.

At its most reduced, character is a mute piece of set-dressing, filling the stage with people and using those people to define status and circumstance. Kings are accompanied by attendant lords, few of whom are given anything to say but whose presence is part of the definition of the court surrounding the king. Most actors begin their careers as this sort of human wallpaper. There was a tendency in the productions of Shakespeare which Stanislavsky staged for the Moscow Art Theatre with Vladimir Nemirovich-Danchenko, to build on the work of the Meiningen company until every member of a large and largely silent crowd had an individual identity and history. That was an act of humane generosity as well as theatrical theory, but it strikes me as essentially opposed to Elizabethan practice. Yet the precise definition of these groups of anonymous characters is something over which Shakespeare appears to have been concerned, and even in the variants between the quarto text of 1622 and Folio text of 1623 for *Othello* there seem to be suggestions of significant change.

The precise source of these q and f variants is obviously unclear. Not until there is substantial change in the words spoken by a character could I feel confident about the possibility of ascribing the variants to Shakespeare. But my checking of q / f variants in a number of other plays has shown that the sort of variants in the identification of a character (in speech-prefixes and stage-directions) that I shall be describing for *Othello* is surprisingly uncommon. Since we cannot deny their authorial status and since, as I shall be suggesting, some of these variants are potentially significant I am prepared to claim that they are at least as likely to be authorial as to reflect non-authorial playhouse influence. Their most likely source seems to me to have been the fruitful interaction between playwright and company in the process of rehearsal and repertory performance.

It does for instance make a difference whether in Act 1 Scene 2 Brabanzio and Roderigo, arriving to find Othello, are accompanied by 'others with lights and weapons' as in q or with 'Officers, and Torches' as in f. In q they arrive with those members of Brabanzio's household woken by Iago in the first scene, with 'all my kindred' that Brabanzio wants raised (1.1.169) and those he has found at 'every house . . . / I may command at most' (1.1.182–3). It makes the effect of their arrival in 1.3 into a street brawl with rival groups of attendants trying to take Othello off to prison or to prevent the kidnap. In f, Brabanzio has had time to collect officers on the way, 'some speciall Officers of night' (1.1.184; 'night' derives from q; f has 'might'). This makes the threat of prison much more official and contrasts his officers with those who arrived with Cassio as messengers from the Duke, two forms of social authority, the Duke and the law, set against each other and anticipating the double demands on state business made in the next scene.

There are similar distinctions to be made according to whether Othello enters to stop the night riot in Cyprus accompanied by Gentlemen as in Q or attendants as in F. The Gentlemen might well include some of those who wait with Montano for news of incoming ships in 2.1 – at least those who are not actually rioting; the 'attendants' suggest a different group entirely. It may indicate a difference in social status and social relationship that is very much a part of the play's inquiry. The more precisely we are aware of social status, as G. K. Hunter has reminded us,[10] the more such moments are illuminated. It may have mattered far more, originally, than it does to us, whether the messages that reach the Senate in 1.3 are carried by a sailor and a messenger or by two messengers, whether the line 'A messenger from the galleys' is spoken by the sailor himself (as in Q) or by one of the Duke's officers (as in F), or whether the news of Iago's ship's arrival in 2.1 is brought by a messenger or another of the gentlemen who accompany Montano in this scene. In each and every case there are small, but nonetheless noticeable, consequences dependent on which character it is, what social group he belongs to, and what his relationship is to the other characters around him on stage in the scene. This too must be a part of character analysis.

We can sense this kind of change more strongly in the difference between Othello's proclamation, which constitutes the single-speech scene 2.2, being spoken by a Herald (F) or read by a Gentleman (Q). This first is an official statement spoken by an officer of Othell's quasi-court; it requires automatically and unalterably a strong, direct, and impersonal delivery, the Herald as mouthpiece through which Othello's pleasure is made known. The Quarto version with a Gentleman reading it could be the same. The Herald could be a Gentleman, I suppose, or the Gentleman speech-prefix may indicate that Q's proclaimer belongs to a different social group. But it could also be played by the Gentleman as a commentary on it, someone reading the proclamation to himself as well as to the audience, with perhaps the last line, 'Heaven bless the isle of Cyprus and our noble general, Othello', separated from the official language into a genuine benediction or even an ironic one. Either way there are possibilities in Q's version that are not available in F's.

Much more significant is the change between Q and F in the use of the First Senator in the Senate scene. F gives him eight more lines, enabling him to offer carefully considered reasons for his belief that the Turkish fleet is heading towards Cyprus rather than Rhodes (1.3.25–31), allowing him to cut across the messenger's speech to show that the true information matches his perception of Turkish strategy ('Ay, so I thought'), and making him question the messenger to elicit further information ('How many, as you guess?', 1.3.37). It means that by the time Brabanzio and Othello arrive at the Senate, the First Senator has spoken considerably more than the Duke, spoken wisely and accurately and seemed to participate in the operation of the Venetian state with great dignity and assuredness. It is this dignified and responsible figure who is plainly marked throughout the rest of the scene as being on Othello's side from his first greeting, 'Here comes Brabanzio and the valiant Moor' (1.3.47), to his specific invitation, not the Duke's, for Othello to defend himself against these charges:

> But Othello, speak,
> Did you by indirect and forcèd courses
> Subdue and poison this young maid's affections,
> Or came it by request and such fair question
> As soul to soul affordeth?
>
> (1.3.110–14)

Even Othello's willingness to leave immediately on the state's business is differently managed. Q's dialogue runs:

Du.   . . . you must hence to night,
DESD.   To night my Lord?
Du.   This night.
OTH.   With all my heart.
                                                   (1.3.277–8)

F's allows the First Senator yet another intervention and deletes Desdemona's line:

SEN.   You must away to night.
OTHE.   With all my heart.

This actually removes the instruction from the Duke to the Senator and makes Othello's immediate agreement directed towards his friend and supporter in the Senate, the man who will later advise him 'Adieu, brave Moor. Use Desdemona well' (1.3.291). I do not believe that any actor would be terribly thrilled by the prospect of playing First Senator in either text but the increased status and significance of the role in F mean that there are substantial consequential changes in the relationship between Othello and Venetian authority as exemplified in the Senate. The changes, to my mind unequivocally deliberate and consistent, alter subtly how Othello is treated, where authority is vested, how the state operates, and whether it can cope with the problems posed by the stranger, the alien Othello.

Character here is functional, outward-looking. The significance of the First Senator is not essentially in what his role reveals about himself, nor even what sort of people are senators in Venice. Instead the actor's task, in playing First Senator, is to use him unselfishly – almost selflessly – as a mediation between Ducal Senate and Othello, to make him indicate those facets of the state and its General that he alone can mediate. This absence of intrinsic significance, an actantial purpose without self-hood, is the principal denominator of the majority of characters in the play.

None of these roles is really very significant. They all belong to the broad group of anonymous actors whose presence we hardly even deign to notice. But they belong in the same group from which come those moments of shattering import in other plays, when minor characters determine to take part in the action or when those previously mute speak. There is nothing of this in *Othello*, but only from the perspective of such work here can we see what happens when the human wallpaper demands the right to take part in the play's centre. This technique, the sudden transition of actor from one type of role, one type of character, to another is present from Aeschylus onwards. On two familiar occasions in the *Oresteia*, for instance, Aeschylus plays on the novelty of the availability of a third actor, the innovation of Sophocles that the older dramatist learnt from. When Agamemnon and Clytemnestra, in the first play of the trilogy, leave the stage along the sea-red, blood-red carpet, the audience must have assumed that what would follow would be a choric ode. Nothing in their experience could have prepared them for the cry that bursts from an actor, the actor playing Cassandra, mute till now and assumed to be mute throughout, but suddenly and transformingly changed from mute to actor, screaming from the pain of her vision of what Apollo has done to her: 'otototoi popoi da / Apollo Apollo'.[11] In the second play of the trilogy something remarkably similar occurs as Orestes, wrestling with the crisis of whether to kill Clytemnestra or not, turns to his friend Pylades and asks 'Pylades! What shall I do?' The audience does not expect him to receive an answer, but the previously mute actor speaks 'Remember Apollo and all that you swore' (p. 79). Not only does the mute speak but the mute speaks for the god, acting oracularly as Apollo's mouth-piece, reminding Orestes that his duty to Apollo is greater than his bond to his mother. Pylades does not speak again.

This virtuosity, moments of enormous theatrical power created by the use of a new device – having three actors available – is not possible in Shakespeare. But there is an obvious moment in *King Lear* which builds on a remarkably similar transition of character from one state to another, when one of the mute servants who have aided and abetted Cornwall in the seizing and blinding of Gloucester is compelled to intervene, unable to remain passive and acquiescent in his master's actions. The first servant changes from being human wallpaper, claims his part in the action, demands that we see that Cornwall's men are not to be identified with Cornwall. As he cuts across his lord's line:

> Hold your hand, my lord.
> I have served you ever since I was a child,
> But better service have I never done you
> Than now to bid you hold;
>
> (Q: 14.70–3; F: 3.7.70–3)

so Regan's furious comment, 'A peasant stand up thus!' (line 78), indicates something of the transition accomplished, the change from mute to speaker, the denial of generalized inhumanity in favour of a real concern. The caring is extended at the end of the scene, in Q at least, by the servants who will 'fetch some flax and whites of eggs / To apply to his bleeding face' (14.104–5). The first servant's intervention has, of course, strong structural parallels, parallels that tie character to actantial function and dramatic situation, with Kent's refusal to acquiesce in Lear's treatment of Cordelia. The first servant's lines that I have quoted fit just as well the situation in which Kent found himself, if without Kent's magnificent anger. Kent's breaking into the ceremonial ritual of Lear's love-test has metamorphosed into the first servant's breaking into the hideous violence of Cornwall. The functional interconnection of the moments (which could be developed) places *its* strain on the creation of character for both Kent and the servant. It is a moment at which the director's responsibility, as much as the actors', is to point up the link, to make the audience observe the situational parallel and the substitution of one attendant's humane concern by another, lesser character's similar refusal to remain silent. There is nothing as shattering or as consoling in the treatment of the minor characters in *Othello*.

The only other minor character in *Othello* on whom I would like to comment poses a very different problem indeed: the Clown. No one has much good to say about Othello's Clown: critics usually ignore him completely, productions usually cut him. He is eminently forgettable even though he has two scenes (3.1.3–29 and 3.4.1–22) late enough in the play and extensive enough to warrant some thought. We can see, of course, that there are extremely complex and resonant implications in the Clown's discussion of music and sex. The weight given to Iago's lines on Othello and Desdemona 'O, you are well tuned now, / But I'll set down the pegs that make this music, / As honest as I am' (2.1.200–2) carries heavily on into the dialogue on syphilis, tails, wind-music, and silent music that the Clown provides in 3.1.[12] There is incidentally yet another Q and F variant here in which the Clown's wit is directed either at the First Musician or at a Boy (F and Q respectively). He also ends his first scene mocking the affectation of Cassio's language: 'If she will stir hither, I shall seem to notify unto her' (lines 27–8). The Clown's quibbles in his second scene, with their punning on lying, have a similar resonance when Othello will soon fall into his epileptic fit, punning on the same word in similar ways, and when a soldier's lines, Iago's rather than Cassio's (though Iago's about Cassio), have already begun to work their evil.

But our evaluation of the function of the scene disguises the status of the Clown who speaks them. Clown is not just another character but a character of a very different type. He may be Othello's servant but he is also the Clown of the company and identified as such by the speech-prefixes. He has then a clear social role within the play's fiction and an even stronger theatrical role through the play's relation to the theatre company. Though he probably did not thank Shakespeare for the part, it was presumably designed for Armin. No one else would have been able to take roles called Clown at that time. Like Feste he jests with the ladies, enjoys quibbles and catechisms and music. The part has, in other words, many of the characteristics that we have learnt to associate with the parts Shakespeare wrote for Armin.[13] Clown is then not a signifier of a role in the play, but a role in the King's Men, a role in the theatre company. The scenes have, therefore, an external, theatrical basis that is in a conventionalized tension with their fictional form. They are the routines of the company's Clown, their comedian, claiming his usual place in another play the company is putting on. Armin is, after all, the only member apart from Burbage of whose role in the first performance of *Othello* we can be reasonably sure. There is, then, a certain visibility of the actor here over the character, a connection from type of role to player, that evidently had an immediacy of perceptibility for the original audience that it does not have for us. Its place along the axis of *audience* to character is substantially different from that of every other character in the play: the Clown is the way he is because he *is* Armin, the company's Clown. Othello is the way he is with help from the abilities of Burbage, but without being so indissolubly linked to him. It makes no sense at all to begin looking at the character of the Clown by identifying him as Othello's servant and wondering why on earth Othello employs such a peculiar and unlikely door-keeper. He wanders into the play because Armin is needed – and also, I suspect, because Armin demanded some sort of part however small, possibly even a part he could embroider slightly in performance, even though Armin was never such a dangerous ad-libber as Will Kemp. The mixing of the Clown and tragedy is so unhomogeneous here, unlike, say, the gravediggers in *Hamlet* a few years previously, that the theatrical origins of the scene are all the more glaringly visible, both to us and to its audience. The Clown's function within this, or indeed almost any comparable play, cannot be defined by reference to the traditional individualist parameters of character analysis.

There is one further implication in the Clown that I want to mention. The Clown is the first of the characters I have glanced at in the play to be played by an actor-sharer in the King's Men rather than a hireling. We know little enough about the internal organization of the company, and the massive labours expended recently on trying to puzzle out the ways in which plays were cast have done little more than make us draw back from the worst excesses of earlier critics' work. But it does seem likely to me that the actor-sharers were a recognizably distinct group, automatically claiming the largest roles and probably largely free from the dreary necessities of doubling, vexed issue though that has now become. My point is that the hierarchy of control within the organization of the King's Men has substantial effects on character, not only hierarchically, but also typologically. It is not only that the senior actor-sharers, other than the Clown, take roles that are larger, more dominant, and, in a sense, more noticeable, but also that their roles may be qualitatively different, belonging to different modes of characterization, different qualities of intrinsic significance, different ranges of selfhood and consciousness. A typology of Shakespearian characterization would, I suspect, have to hypothesize a correlation between the sharer / hireling division in the company and differing points along the axes I have been implying.

There will of course also be divisions between boys and adults, between those who play women's parts and those who do not. So far, there has been remarkably little sustained and thoughtful consideration of the effects of boy actresses on the creation of female roles in English Renaissance drama; too little for us to be able to assess yet what effects they may have had on the development and formation of gender roles within the drama or the mode of interaction, and the distinctions in that interaction, between the actor and the character and the audience, the triangle of theatrical relationship. The status of Shakespeare as sharer in the company, bound to them and producing on average two plays a year for them, must have had profound effects on the range of characterization he developed. It is another still undervalued feature of the problem.

It is time now to face up to the single largest problem for the analysis of character in *Othello*: the figure of Iago. It is not after all that there has been any shortage of attempts from many different angles to provide an answer. Indeed the history of Iago criticism has often seemed to me a remarkable example, in another mode, of what Richard Levin in his mocking attack on thematic criticism dubbed the 'my theme can lick your theme' school.[14] Each critic triumphantly brandishes aloft the new key that will unlock all the mysteries once and for all. But the result, self-defeatingly, has usually been to lock the character away into a different cell of the critic's own devising and the effect is as separating and limiting, as opposed as ever to the variety of possibility in the role.

In part, the mechanics of the attempts have tended to be associative. In the title for this article I deliberately used the word 'resources' of characterization rather than 'sources' in order to indicate a *potentiality* in the available materials rather than an identifiable single antecedent or group of antecedents. If we identify the basis of Iago's character as, for instance, the inheritance of the figure of Vice from the tradition of sixteenth-century morality drama, we can find in the model one rich vein of possibility. It will in some senses *account* for the wicked humour in the role, our sense of the trickster, the stage-manager of intrigue, manipulatively pushing the characters around the stage. We can see immediately the analogy with Edmund, in *Lear*, spotting Edgar arriving 'like the catastrophe of the old comedy' (Q: 2.129–30; F: 1.2.131). This energetic humorous attractiveness of Vice will have consequential effects on our perception of the operation of morality in the play. That tendency is so brilliantly explored in a play like *Mankinde*, for there, the immorality of Vice enables it to disguise itself into a supposedly harmless amorality, a joyful cynicism at the expense of those for whom morality is of great significance, and is in turn transformed into the cold harshness of the pain of Mankinde's humiliation. It is a moral and dramatic trajectory that has strong similarities with the audience's dynamic in its response to *Othello*. The Vice figure finds in its dramatic antecedents the very notion of morality as play-genre and socio-religious problematic that is its dramatic field of operations. Vice as *source* suggests a character *resource* of a certain staginess, a conscious theatricality that is then available for the actor to use. It enforces a particular mode of close connection with the audience, a deliberate sharing of the malign joy of the corruption of Othello's joy, a position downstage mediating the action through this shared observation of the trick. It creates a remarkably strong dissociation of character from the mechanics of the social world of the play, replacing it with a sustained pose of authoritative and knowledgeable observation. Vice has overlapping links with the choric presenter, the disengaged watcher.

The terms of this approach have of course been varied. It has been suggested that the rich vein of satanic language in the play, the depiction of Iago as more than Vice and more like Devil, can too see its antecedents dramatically, finding its roots in the devils of the cycle drama.[15] But the creative results of the diabolic analogy or direct satanic representation have often been for critics to push the play into an emblematic struggle of absolute good and absolute evil. This has an immense and rebounding effect on, for instance, the characterization of Desdemona: the more diabolic Iago is, the more 'enskied and sainted' (*Measure*, 1.4.33) Desdemona becomes. She has, then, to be played as similarly abstracted and exemplary, with Othello caught dramatically between his play's versions of the good and evil angels. Stanley Edgar Hyman, in his fascinating study of approaches to Iago,[16] separates these two modes, Vice and Devil, into different chapters, the Vice mode belonging to what he calls 'genre criticism' – Iago as 'stage villain' – and the Devil mode as 'theological criticism' – Iago as 'Satan'. But the two more properly connect at the level of source and resource, in both cases an essentially similar dramatic root rather than a root in contemporary theological debate.

There is a deep incompatibility between such approaches and such equally enticing explanations as, in all their variant forms, the psychologistic readings. These reach, of course, some sort of apotheosis in the full-scale pseudo-psychoanalytic studies, creating the whole history of the character as case-study and discovering in Iago, most notoriously, latent homosexual attachments to Othello, Cassio, and even Roderigo. Yet, while critical antipathy has tended to dub such analyses extraneous and novelistic, they have obviously offered res-onant possibilities for actors throughout this century, and there are traces of a perception of its potential in pre-Freudian performances by Edwin Booth and others. It did not need Freud to teach actors such a method, any more than it needed Stanislavsky. My concern is not qualitative judgement and I firmly believe that there are plenty of indications, even in Elizabethan psychological theory, to enable us to contemplate such an approach as available and com-prehensible in its stopping up of certain channels of emotional desire and its scooping out of new ducts to carry its powerful affects into action. But the effect of such a method on the interaction of audience and character – and hence actor and character – is substantially at variance.

The Vice encourages the audience towards an adoption of his perspective, teaches the audience or persuades them to adopt his point of view as a monoc-ular vision of human behaviour. It is a participatory mode. The psychologistic is distancing in its relationship, prescriptively separate from and observed by the audience, as complete an inclusion of the character into the drama as the other is separate and dissociating. They suggest, for instance, opposing degrees of directness of audience address and contact.

It may well be that the mode of Jacobean performance of such realist roles is more closely analogous to a quasi-Brechtian *presentation* of the character than to a pseudo-Stanislavskian *representation*, but the effect of that is to create a link between actor and audience (rather than between actor and character). Such a model, rather than seeing the identification of actor and character as identifiably whole, marks out the continual separation of the actor from the role to such an extent that the audience is encouraged to share the actor's observation of the character, located now as separably external to the mind that presents it, a separation in effect of character's consciousness from actor's consciousness. This form of sharing connects actor and audience almost at the expense of character. Crucially, by contrast with the Vice mode, the psychol-ogistic mode replaces the character into the play, denying the dissociation of actor from character or from play.

Analogously, though in a delightfully contrary way, Empson's astonishing analysis of the implications of the word 'honest'[17] turns the word into an index of social structure. When the word is seen as being used patronizingly, in a way which 'carried an obscure social insult' (p. 219), then the play's use of the word, which 'amounts to a criticism of the word itself', is both a representation of the difficulty of the association of honesty with double-dealing and, at the same time, an analysis of the social organization that builds so extensively and confidently on the socially superior use of the word without being able to control its soft vulnerability to Iago's actions. The relationship established in the play between honest and Iago is then a means of the character's acting as index of social thought and class insult. Iago as honest soldier, the reliable man who is not officer material in the way that Cassio's gentlemanly manner makes the lieutenancy so naturally his, becomes oddly less intrinsically interesting for Iago himself than for what the character's social position reveals about others and about the society that created him. What such a view of the character necessitates theatrically is a strong creation of the Venetian social system, its closed ranks of aristocratic control, turning Iago, just as much as Othello, into the outsider. The social creation of character creates in its turn an ambivalent engagement and disengagement of character to a play, an indexical functionality explicable in broadly realist terms – associative with play in its own social location, but dissociative in its indexical mode.

Oddly, then, Empson's approach, the richest and most resourceful of all attempts to engage singly and reductively with Iago, has the paradoxical effect of enciphering the character, reducing him to this indexicality, a pointer to something else, where the Vice mode, while similarly placing Iago as pointer also identifies intrinsic and consequential interest and significance in the identity of the pointer itself. Empson's view is passive in its function, the Vice approach equally active.

The variety of the approaches to Iago which I have sketched, the multiple resources which each claims, and the hierarchized dominance which each annexes, have not countenanced the various points on the axes actor–audience, actor–character, and character–audience, to which each belongs. We can of course out of our own critical prejudices align ourselves with each one to a greater or lesser extent. We can see the way each claims single control over individual lines in the play and we can see, as Hyman does with some success, how each climactic moment is an interaction of these oppositional resources, so that, as he suggests, Iago's line 'I am your own forever' is:

> simultaneously a pinnacle of duplicity for the stage villain, Satan's revelation of Othello's eternal damnation, William Shakespeare's oath of fealty to his own imaginative creation, the repressed homosexual's marriage vow, and the Machiavel's veiled boast that he is not servant but master. (p. 139)

But are these contradictory dramatic and theatrical relationships that I perceive as endemic in the contradictory approaches in any sense simultaneously playable and perceptible, or is the modern audience's normal desire for a simplifying model of performance control entirely correct? In many respects, the conditions of Jacobean performance make the contradictions I am exploring here more easily available within a single mode of performance technique than such obviously incompatible psychologized or individualistic models as have tended to accrete around Othello. I cannot see the same lines, the same actions, and the same gestures being potentially indicative of nobility and gullibility in the same performance, but the Iago possibilities can co-exist, if not moment by moment then certainly distributed across the play.

The multiple and opposing ways in which an actor playing Iago is able to play out his, and the character's, relationship to the audience reach their most acute state of tension not in the interactive dialogue with the other characters but in the interactive monologues with the audience. In a recent article Raymond Williams began, with only limited success, the massive task of suggesting how we might systematize the modes of dramatic monologue, creating a typology of dramatic language like the one I have suggested we need for dramatic character.[18] Iago's language partakes of all the types he defines, slipping and sliding between them with a virtuosity unparalleled in the rest of the play, indeed in the rest of Shakespeare. The traditional concept of the sort of relationship between speech and character that soliloquy is supposed to represent, the spoken thoughts of a realized character, the overheard internal speech, simplifies inordinately the dazzling variety of resources of speech Shakespeare give to Iago. It is a rhetoric to whose multiple theatricalities we have been inadequately responsive. Character shifts with the possibilities available in the forms of its speech. The actor must transform himself from, say, anguished internal doubt for 'I do suspect the lusty Moor / Hath leapt into my seat, the thought whereof / Doth, like a poisonous mineral, gnaw my inwards' (2.1.294–6), to perhaps a direct, amused mockery for 'And what's he then that says I play a villain?' (2.3.327) – though the earlier example is, of course, just as open to such a mode as this is. There are very different resources of characterization operative here.

It may seem odd that I have reached the end of an article on *Othello* without any consideration of Othello himself. One comment I will make, however. Emrys Jones has noted how Othello's reality is tightly bound up with performance, that he 'acquires full reality only in the presence of a theatre audience'.[19] Othello exhibits the passion, elemental and powerful, in which the audience takes delight. It is a provocative and, I believe, accurate comment. The assumption has been that the creation of character occurs on stage and is communicated to the audience. Jones makes it an interactive quality, depending not simply on complicity from the audience, but rather on their emotional hunger, their demand for the theatre to satisfy their emotions. The significance of this in placing the onus of the creation of character so firmly with the audience is huge.

When the Duke in *Measure for Measure* tells Angelo 'There is a kind of character in thy life / That to th'observer doth thy history / Fully unfold' (1.1.27–9) he had no idea yet of the extent of the character whose history the play would proceed to unfold to the observers. My interest is in extending this unfolding history to those characters and those forms of characterization whose history has not yet been unfolded. Even Jonson's Neighbour 6 has a history.

Notes

1   Ben Jonson, *The Works*, eds C. H. Herford and P. E. Simpson, 11 vols. (Oxford, 1925–52), vol. 5 (1937), 5.1.1–6.

2   P. Edwards, I.-S. Ewbank and G. K. Hunter, eds, *Shakespeare's Styles* (Cambridge, 1980).

3   In *Shakespeare's Styles*, 131–50, p. 137.

4   Robert Weimann, 'Society and the Individual in Shakespeare's Conception of Character', *Shakespeare Survey 34* (1981), 23–31.

5   'Hamlet', in *Players of Shakespeare*, ed. P. Brockbank (Cambridge, 1985), 115–28, p. 122.

6   R. Weimann, *Shakespeare and the Popular Tradition in the Theatre* (Baltimore, 1978); see, for example, pp. 224–37. See also M. E. Mooney, '"Edgar I nothing am": *Figurenposition* in *King Lear*', *Shakespeare Survey 38* (1985), 153–66.

7   See for example Vladimir Propp, *Morphologie du conte* (Paris, 1965) and A.-J. Greimas, *Sémantique structurale* (Paris, 1966).

8   *Shakespeare Survey 34* (1981), 61–72.

9   *Shakespeare's Styles*, 67–77, p. 69.

10   G. K. Hunter, 'Flatcaps and Bluecoats: Visual Signals on the Elizabethan Stage', *Essays and Studies*, NS 33 (1980), 16–47 (especially pp. 25–37).

11   Aeschylus, *The Oresteia*, translated by Tony Harrison (London, 1981), p. 31.

12   See also L. J. Ross, 'Shakespeare's "Dull Clown" and Symbolic Music', *Shakespeare Quarterly*, 17 (1968), 107–28.

13   On Armin see M. C. Bradbrook, *Shakespeare the Craftsman* (London, 1969), chapter 4; Gareth Lloyd Evans, 'Shakespeare's Fools: the Shadow and the Substance of Drama', in *Shakespearian Comedy*, eds. M. Bradbury and D. Palmer, Stratford-upon-Avon Studies, 14 (London and New York, 1972), pp. 142–59; David Wiles, *Shakespeare's Clown* (Cambridge, 1987), chapter 10.

14   R. Levin, *New Readings vs Old Plays* (Chicago, 1979), p. 28.

15   Leah Scragg, 'Iago – Vice or Devil?', *Shakespeare Survey 21* (1968), 53–65.

16   S . E. Hyman, *Iago: Some Approaches to the Illusion of his Motivation* (New York, 1970).

17   W. Empson, *The Structure of Complex Words* (London and New York, 1951), pp. 218–49.
18   Raymond Williams, *Writing in Society* (London, 1983), pp. 31–64.
19   Emrys Jones, *Scenic Form in Shakespeare* (Oxford, 1971), p. 132.

The Woman in Hamlet: An Interpersonal View (1978)

David Leverenz

Leverenz's article, published in a collection subtitled New Psychoanalytic Essays, *develops some of the approaches outlined above in the work of Freud, Lacan and Lupton. Leverenz discusses the patriarchal world of the Ghost, Polonius, Hamlet and Laertes set against the female imagery in the play, the role of Gertrude, and Ophelia's madness. Male and female elements are seen as figures for the play's dissociation and for its exploration of the idea of the divided self. Leverenz argues that the play's past events affect identity itself: Hamlet finds his identity 'stifled' 'by structures of rule that no longer have legitimacy'. Leverenz has published widely on psychoanalytic approaches to a range of literary texts, and his work is particularly interested in masculinity and the role of the father. Here, his method weaves close textual analysis with psychoanalytic paradigms from a range of authorities to produce a stimulating and readable interpretation of the play.*

David Leverenz, 'The Woman in Hamlet: An Interpersonal View', in *Representing Shakespeare: New Psychoanalytic Essays*, Coppélia Kahn and Murray M. Schwartz (eds). Baltimore; London: Johns Hopkins University Press, 1980.
   (This article first appeared in *Signs: Journal of Women in Culture and Society* 4 (Winter 1978). Copyright © 1978 by The University of Chicago. Reprinted by permission of the University of Chicago Press.)

> John, I guess there are some people around here who think you have some little old lady in you.
>
> John Dean, *Blind Ambition*

"Who's there?" Bernardo's anxious shout, which begins Shakespeare's most problematic play, raises the fundamental question of Hamlet's identity. Various male authority figures advance simple answers. For the Ghost, Hamlet is a dutiful son who should sweep to his father's revenge and forget about his mother. For Claudius, Hamlet is a possible rebel who should be either made tractable or banished and killed. For Polonius, Hamlet is the heir gone mad through frustrated love for Ophelia, whom Polonius has denied him partly for reasons of state. But for Hamlet, the roles of dutiful son, ambitious rebel, or mad, lovesick heir are just that: roles, to be played for others but not felt for himself. The "who" remains unsettled within and without, "the heart of my mystery" (III.ii.351).[1]

The mixed and contradictory expectations of these father figures – the Ghost, Claudius, Polonius – reflect their own divided image of dutiful reason and bestial lust. At times their power seems to be defined by their ability to order women and children around. Hamlet sees Gertrude give way to Claudius, Ophelia give way to Polonius, and himself at last yield to the Ghost. But Hamlet also sees duplicity and falseness in all the fathers, except perhaps his own, and even there his famous delay may well indicate unconscious perception, rather than the unconscious guilt ascribed to him by a strict Freudian interpretation. Hamlet resists his father's commands to obey. Despite his illusory idealization of the senior Hamlet as pure and angelic, he senses the Ghost's complicity in the paternal doublespeak that bends Gertrude and Ophelia, indeed bends feelings and the body itself, to self-falsifying reason and filial loyalty. Hamlet is part hysteric, as Freud said, and part Puritan in his disgust at contamination and his idealization of his absent father. But he is also, as Goethe was the first to say, part woman. And Goethe was wrong, as Freud was wrong, to assume that "woman" means weakness. To equate women with weak and tainted bodies, words, and feelings while men possess noble reason and ambitious purpose is to participate in Denmark's disease that divides mind from body, act from feeling, man from woman.

Hamlet's tragedy is the forced triumph of filial duty over sensitivity to his own heart. To fulfill various fathers' commands, he has to deny his self-awareness, just as Gertrude and Ophelia have done. That denial is equivalent to suicide, as the language of the last act shows. His puritanical cries about whoredom in himself and others, his hysterical outbursts to Ophelia about nunneries and painted women, are the outer shell of a horror at what the nurtured, loving, and well-loved soul has been corrupted to. From a more modern perspective than the play allows, we can sense that the destruction of good mothering is the real issue, at least from Hamlet's point of view.

Freudians, too many of whom have their own paternal answers to "Who's there?", see Hamlet as an unconscious Claudius-Oedipus, or as a man baffled by pre-Oedipal ambivalences about his weak-willed, passionate, fickle mother.[2] While acknowledging Hamlet's parricidal and matricidal impulses, we should see these inchoate feelings as responses, not innate drives. Interpersonal expectations, more than self-contained desires, are what divide Hamlet from himself and conscript him to false social purposes. In this perspective, taken from Harry Stack Sullivan, R. D. Laing, and D. W. Winnicott, Hamlet's supposed delay is a natural reaction to overwhelming interpersonal confusion.[3] His self-preoccupation is paradoxically grounded not so much in himself as in the extraordinary and unremitting array of "mixed signals" that separate role from self, reason from feeling, duty from love.

Hamlet has no way of unambiguously understanding what anyone says to him. The girl who supposedly loves him inexplicably refuses his attentions. His grieving mother suddenly marries. His dead father, suddenly alive, twice tells him to deny his anger at his mother's shocking change of heart. Two of his best friends "make love to this employment" of snooping against him (V.ii.57). Polonius, Claudius, and the Ghost all manifest themselves as loving fathers, yet expect the worst and even spy on their children, either directly or through messengers. Who is this "uncle-father and aunt-mother" (II.ii.366), or this courtier-father? They preach the unity of being true to oneself and others yet are false to everyone; each can "smile, and smile, and be a villain" (I.v.108). Gertrude's inconstancy not only brings on disgust and incestuous feelings, it is also the sign of diseased doubleness in everyone who has accommodated to his or her social role. The usurping Claudius is the symbol of all those "pretenders," who are now trying to bring Hamlet into line. No wonder Hamlet weeps at the sight of a genuine actor – the irony reveals the problem – playing Hecuba's grief. The male expressing a woman's constancy once again mirrors Hamlet's need. And the role, though feigned, at least is openly played. The actor's tears are the play's one unambiguous reflection of the grief Hamlet thought his mother shared with him before the onset of so many multitudinous double-dealings.

The question of whether to kill or not to kill cannot be entertained when one is not even sure of existing with any integrity. Being, not desiring or revenging, is the question. Freudians assume that everyone has strong desires blocked by stronger repressions, but contemporary work with schizophrenics reveals the tragic variety of people whose voices are only amalgams of other people's voices, with caustic self-observation or a still more terrifying vacuum as their incessant inward reality. This is Hamlet to a degree, as it is Ophelia completely. As Laing says of her in *The Divided Self*: "In her madness, there is no one there. She is not a person. There is no integral selfhood expressed through her actions or utterances. Incomprehensible statements are said by nothing. She has already died. There is now only a vacuum where there was once a person."[4] Laing misrepresents her state only because there are many voices in Ophelia's madness speaking through her, all making sense, and none of them her own. She becomes the mirror for a madness-inducing world. Hamlet resists these pressures at the cost of a terrifying isolation. Once he thinks his mother has abandoned him, there is nothing and no one to "mirror" his feelings, as Winnicott puts it.[5] Hamlet is utterly alone, beyond the loving semiunderstanding of reasonable Horatio or obedient Ophelia.

A world of fathers and sons, ambition and lust, considers grief "unmanly," as Claudius preaches (I.ii.94). Hamlet seems to agree, at least to himself, citing his "whorish" doubts as the cause of his inability to take manly filial action. This female imagery, which reflects the play's male-centered world view, represents a covert homosexual fantasy, according to Freudian interpretation.[6] Certainly Hamlet's idealizations of his father and of Horatio's friendship show a hunger for male closeness. Poisoning in the ear may unconsciously evoke anal intercourse. And the climactic swordplay with Laertes does lead to a brotherly understanding. But these instances of covert homosexual desire are responses to a lack. Poisoning in the ear evokes conscious and unconscious perversity to intimate the perversion of communication, especially between men. The woman in Hamlet is the source of his most acute perceptions about the diseased, disordered patriarchal society that tries to "play upon this pipe" of Hamlet's soul (III.ii.336), even as a ghost returning from the dead.

The separation of role from self is clear in the opening scene. Anxiety precipitates a genuine question: "Who's there?" It is answered not with "Francisco," the natural rejoinder, but with "Nay, answer me. Stand and unfold yourself" (I.i.2). Francisco restores public ritual by the prescribed challenge of a guard, not the response of a friend. To private uneasiness he responds with public norms. Bernardo's answer to the command to "unfold yourself" is equally self-avoiding. "Long live the King!" he cries (I.i.3). His identity, in the prescribed convention, is equivalent to respect for the King. Yet the not-so-long-lived King has just died, and the new one, who was to have been Hamlet the younger, has been displaced by the old one's brother. Who *is* the rightful King? Who *is* there? The question returns, under the formulaic phrase that denies any problems of loyalty or succession.

Francisco departs with an odd and disconcerting addition to a conventional farewell: "For this relief much thanks. 'Tis bitter cold, / And I am sick at heart" (I.i.8–9). Tensions between the head and the heart, noble reason and diseased emotion, center the play. Yet this first expression of heartsick feelings has no explanation. The watch has been "quiet" – "Not a mouse stirring," Francisco gratuitously adds (I.i.10). By Act III, Hamlet will be devising a play he calls "The Mousetrap," which would make the new King a mouse and suggest that royal stability is corroded at its base. But for now these jagged interchanges, like the half-lines staggered on the page and the roles confused by the guards, seem simply "out of joint," with no clear perspective on who has been guarding what, why Bernardo seems scared, and why Francisco feels sick at heart. The darker questions recede into the comfortable self-definitions of Horatio and Marcellus, who respond to the next "Who is there?" with "Friends to this ground" (Horatio), "And liegemen to the Dane" (Marcellus, I.i.15). Horatio, whose first word is "friends," is the only one of this group to define himself both within and beyond conventional public deference. As yet we cannot sense the incompatibility between being friends and being liegemen. By Act V the gap is so wide that Horatio declares himself "more an antique Roman than a Dane" (V.ii.330) and tries to drink from the poisoned cup to follow his friend both from and to a poisoned state. All we know now, though, is that more seems afoot than simply the changing of a guard.[7]

Identity, in the first scene, is defined as role, specifically as loyalty among functionaries of a state. But feelings have been partly voiced that are curiously disconnected from roles. There is no coherent voice for more private feelings – in this case, fear; rote is the norm. The polarity between mind and passions reflects larger polarities in the social order, or rather in a society pretending to be ordered along the father's lines. These polarities become more apparent in the contrast between Claudius's opening speech and Hamlet's first soliloquy. Claudius speaks in the language of public command, with phrases tailored and balanced, the royal "we" firmly affixed to his crown. Oxymorons prescribe a unity of opposites, and his balanced phrasing is only twice disrupted with the reality of seized power: "Taken to wife," and "So much for him" (I.ii.14, 25). For Claudius, reason, nature, and submission are joined in a facile unity.

> Fie, 'tis a fault to heaven,
> A fault against the dead, a fault to nature,
> To reason most absurd, whose common theme
> Is death of fathers, and who still hath cried,
> From the first corse till he that died to-day,
> "This must be so."
>
>   (I.ii.101–06)

To personify an abstraction, reason, is characteristic of Claudius' perspective, in which abstract states are more real than persons. Unfortunately, reality intrudes; in the rush of his logic he misrepresents "the first corse," who was obviously Abel, not a father but a brother killed by a brother, as in Claudius's crime. The heart will intrude its guilt, no matter how speech tries to deny fact and feeling. The rhetoric of formal obedience avoids, while suggesting, the simple stark reality of a father's murder, a son's grief, and a murderer's guilt.

Claudius' speech reveals a second assumption already sensed in the personification of reason. When he speaks of "our whole kingdom . . . contracted in one brow of woe" (I.ii.3–4), he presents his kingdom as a single person. He further connects the language of personal love with the language of public war, since making war among states has the same unity of opposites that he wants to prescribe for individuals, even for his wife. Gertrude, whom he defines only in her disjointed roles as "our sometime sister, now our queen," is thus "Th' imperial jointress to this warlike state" (I.ii.8–9). Marriage is simply the prelude to aggression. The only arena for "joining" is the ordering of the state for war, not the expressing of desire in the marriage bed. Polonius continues the inversion of love and war more explicitly in his advice to Ophelia: "Set your entreatments at a higher rate / Than a command to parley" (I.iii.122–23). Laertes also echoes the language of war in speaking of love to her: "Keep you in the rear of your affection, / Out of the shot and danger of desire" (I.iii.34–35). In this collusion of ambitious functionaries, the state is the only real person, whose war with other person-states can be told as love, while human loves and fears can be expressed only as warlike obedience to the purposes of states.[8]

Hamlet's first private discourse opposes, point for point, the dehumanizing unities of the King's public preaching. Where Claudius assumes the oneness of reason and nature in filial subjection, Hamlet piles contrary on rebellious contrary, especially that of mind and body. Indeed, Hamlet's soliloquy is obsessed with language of the body – sullied (or solid) flesh, appetite, feeding, father's dead body, tears, incestuous sheets, "gallèd eyes" (I.ii.155), and finally the heart and tongue: "But break my heart, for I must hold my tongue" (I.ii.159), an intuition that precisely describes his fate. Parts of the body, rank, gross, and unweeded, overwhelm any pretense at understanding.

Elsewhere Hamlet attempts to recast the language of public ritual as personal feeling. When his friends say farewell with the conventional "Our duty to your honor," Hamlet responds with a half-ironic inversion: "Your loves, as mine to you" (I.ii.253–54). Duty and love still have something in common, he hopes. But his language in the first act more broadly participates in the most pervasive assumption of Claudius, that reason is what makes a man. Hamlet is disgusted at the thought of "some complexion . . . breaking down the pales and forts of reason" (I.iv.27–28). Those "pales and forts" echo Claudius' equation between war and love. Here is the inward castle of the mind on which, metaphorically, Bernardo and Francisco stand guard, though against what is still uncertain. "Nobility" connotes the mind's royalty, as befits a prince's role. "Nature," on the other hand, is associated with the rabble, reveling in the bestial dregs of "swinish phrase" and scandal, "some vicious mole of nature in them" (I.iv.19, 24) that cannot help but get out. Just as Claudius falsely conjoins nature and obedience into the smooth illusory primacy of reason, so Hamlet, searching for truth at the other extreme, lumps nature, feeling, beasts, and body together, all as negatives.

Hamlet is "unsocialized," a psychiatrist might say, hearing reports of his hostile puns, asides, and soliloquies. Unfortunately, he is far more socialized than he can perceive. He still takes refuge in the shared assumptions of those around him, who locate the self in the mind's obedience to patriarchal order, the body's obedience to abstractions. Whether speaking as Polonius, who can talk so glibly of "wit" as having "soul" and "limbs" (II.ii.90–91) and swear that

"I hold my duty as I hold my soul" (II.ii.44), or as Rosencrantz, who expounds so eloquently on how the "single and peculiar life" is only part of the "massy wheel" of majesty (III.iii.11–23), or as Laertes, who takes such pains to instruct Ophelia that Hamlet is "circumscribed / Unto the voice and yielding of that body / Whereof he is the head" (I.iii.22–24), this common public voice denies private feeling and private identity, while asserting the false union of all the parts of the social body in subjection to majesty. As Rosencrantz declares (III.iii.12–13), this power is "much more" than "the strength and armor of the mind" itself. Again the warlike image is symptomatic.

The Ghost seems to be the one father who speaks straight, and Hamlet's encounter with him precipitates clarity about what has happened and what he must do. But while confirming Hamlet's perception of external wickedness, the Ghost invalidates Hamlet's feelings. He speaks to the mind's suspicions of Claudius while denying Hamlet's more profound heartsickness over Gertrude. Claudius' villainy is clear and clearly stated. But many other aspects of the Ghost's account are mixed signals denying simple feeling. After hearing of the "sulph'rous and tormenting flames" awaiting his father, Hamlet cries "Alas, poor ghost!" – a Gertrude-like response (I.v.4). "Pity me not," the Ghost rejoins, rejecting the empathy he has just solicited. He wants only "serious hearing" and revenge. Yet the Ghost then gratuitously describes "my prison house" and forces its horrors on Hamlet by suggesting that knowledge of the truth would shatter his son's body. This is already a Laingian "knot,"[9] designed to exaggerate the father's strength and the son's weakness. Feelings are frivolous; manly endurance is true fortitude. As he will do with Gertrude, the Ghost implies that his son is too frail to hear; so is anyone with "ears of flesh and blood" (I.v.22). Don't pity me, runs the message – but boy, what you *would* feel. . . . Yet why is father in Purgatory? Not because of his heroic or virtuous strength but because of "the foul crimes done in my days of nature" (I.v.12). So in these first few lines the father has: (1) told his son not to pity, yet encouraged him to pity, (2) accentuated his son's earthly weakness and his own immortal strength, yet told Hamlet of "foul crimes," and (3) equated pity with frivolity and dutiful hearing with seriousness, while picturing Hamlet's feelings in language that dismembers the body in its exaggerated seriousness.

The mixed signals persist. We never learn what the "foul crimes" consist of, though they are apparently extensive enough to have the Ghost cry out "O, horrible! O, horrible! Most horrible!" at the thought of his "account" for "my imperfections" (I.v.78–80). Yet the major burden of his discourse is to contrast his "dignity" and "virtue" with Claudius' crimes. We have already heard from others, notably Horatio, about King Hamlet's warlike "frown" and armor (I.i.60–62). There is very little in the Ghost's own speech, however, to support a sense of virtuous integrity. His surprisingly weak affirmation of his love's "dignity" states only that "it went hand in hand even with the vow / I made to her in marriage," presumably to remain faithful (I.v.48–50). Even his love can be fully summarized not by feeling but by "vow" or public ritual. And as King, his peacetime behavior seems to have been primarily sleeping on the job. Otherwise he would not have been killed as he was "Sleeping within my orchard, / My custom always of the afternoon" (I.v.59–60). He is also viciously uncharitable to the Queen, while at the same time forbidding his son from having that same feeling.[10] Throughout his speech, the Ghost is preoccupied with the body, and, as with Hamlet, Gertrude is the focus for that concern. Her change from "seeming-virtuous" behavior to "lust" puts the Ghost into a paroxysm of disgust, not so much at the vile seducer as at the woman who could move from "a radiant angel" to a beast who preys "on garbage" (I.v.46, 55–57). The king of "foul crimes" presents himself as an angel now.

Hamlet's idealization of his father and disgust with Claudius reveals, as Freudians have rightly argued, a splitting of the son's ambivalence toward the father. But the various mixed signals in the Ghost's speech show how the father's communication, not the son's intrapsychic repressions, fosters ambivalence. Father is, in fact, more like Claudius than the Ghost can dare admit. They both speak with the arrogant abstractedness of majesty – "So the whole ear of Denmark / Is . . . / Rankly abused" (I.v.36–38) – yet they both show their particular bodies, in word or deed, subverting the false nobility of royal role. And the Ghost is particularly ambivalent about "nature" itself. Though he invokes his own "foul crimes done in my days of nature" (I.v.12), he concludes: "If thou hast nature in thee, bear it not" (I.v.81). From "Pity me not" to "Bear it not," the Ghost's commands falsify both the father's reality and the son's "nature." They exaggerate father's virtues, demean Hamlet's responses, and establish a confusing set of connections between nature, lust, feeling, and Gertrude, all of which must be resolutely disowned to follow the father's directives toward filial revenge, a "natural feeling" unnatural to Hamlet.[11] Even the minor father figures, like old Priam and Yorick, are vivid in their infirm bodies, not in their dignified precepts. Yet precepts are the "me" that Hamlet has to remember.

Through her impossible attempt to obey contradictory voices, Ophelia mirrors in her madness the tensions that Hamlet perceives. As in Laing's *Sanity, Madness, and the Family*, Ophelia's "madness" is a natural response to the unacknowledged interpersonal falsities of the group.[12] Her history is another instance of how someone can be driven mad by having her inner feelings misrepresented, not responded to, or acknowledged only through chastisement and repression. From her entrance on, Ophelia must continually respond to commands that imply distrust even as they compel obedience. "Do you doubt that?" she opens, after Laertes has told her: "Do not sleep, / But let me hear from you" (I.iii.3–4). The body's natural desire to sleep must yield to the role of always-attentive sister. Without responding, perhaps not even hearing her rejoinder to his demand, Laertes immediately tries to plunge her into a more severe doubt of Hamlet's affection, and therefore of her own. It is simply toying with lust, he says, "a fashion and a toy in blood" (I.iii.6). Reflecting the division between mind and body forced on children by fathers themselves divided, Laertes speaks magisterially of how "nature crescent" in Hamlet must be "circumscribed" to the larger "body" of the state "Whereof he is the head" (I.iii.11, 22–24). Hamlet's voice can go "no further / Than the main voice of Denmark goes withal" (I.iii.27–28). A prince can express no feeling except as it furthers his social role; the rest is transient sensuality, "The perfume and suppliance of a minute, / No more." "No more but so?" Ophelia responds, questioning but trusting, and Laertes rejoins ambiguously: "Think it no more" (I.iii.9–10). So the Ghost speaks to Hamlet and of Gertrude, emphasizing their weakness and strength.

Ophelia accepts Laertes's commands as a "lesson" to "keep / As watchman to my heart . . ." (I.iii.45–46). Yet her advice to him shows her awareness of his possible double self, the pastor and the libertine, the very division he used in describing Hamlet. Punning on "recks" and "reckless," she displays an independent wit, much like Hamlet's more constricted opening puns. But her sense of the necessity for a "watchman" over probable evils of the heart is as unquestioned as her acceptance of the military terminology. The fortress of the female heart needs its Barnardos. She *will* doubt her feelings henceforth. When Polonius reinterprets what she calls Hamlet's "tenders / Of his affection to me" (I.iii.99–100) as monetary transactions leading only to her father's exposure as "a fool," Ophelia hesitantly asserts the "honorable fashion" of Hamlet's loving speech to her (I.iii.111). Yet she mutely accepts her father's assumption that to "tender yourself more dearly" is essential to protect father's self-image (I.iii.107). Polonius is deliberately unconcerned with what his daughter feels. His command to refuse Hamlet any "words or talk" flies in the face of everything Ophelia has said (I.iii.134). Yet she has no choice but to say, "I shall obey, my lord" (I.iii.136).

For his part, Polonius is preoccupied only with how he looks. Always the fawning courtier, the man who can say "I hold my duty as I hold my soul" in return for being called "the father of good news" by the new King (II.ii.42–44), his response to Claudius' questions about Ophelia flagrantly reveals his unconcern for anything but his own position. "But how hath she / Received his love?" Claudius inquires. "What do you think of me?" is Polonius' answer; "What might you think?" he anxiously repeats (II.ii.128–29, 139). For Polonius, his daughter is an animal whom he can "loose" (II.ii.162) to catch Hamlet's motive. He cares for Claudius, for his role as "assistant for a state" (II.ii.166), not for his daughter's feelings. The subplot makes clear what the main plot obfuscates: Fathers perceive children as they do their wives and bodies, as beasts to be controlled for the magnification of their self-images, or rather, for the expression of their divided selves, their reason and their lust. These divisions grow from their complicity in playing a leading role in a corrupt state. Polonius, putting the issue squarely, says to Ophelia: "You do not understand yourself so clearly / As it behooves my daughter and your honor" (I.iii.96–97). Ophelia must accept the role of honorable possession and deny her love for Hamlet. This is not a question of repressed sexual desire, though certainly her anxieties, like Hamlet's, have to do with feelings denied. It is a question of what it means to understand oneself when the price is falseness to others.

Hamlet himself fosters Ophelia's crisis, to be sure. He sends her an ambiguous poem that can be read as "Never doubt that I love" or "Never suspect that I love" (II.ii.119). He tells her he loved her; then, "I loved you not" (III.i.119). He seems to confirm Laertes' suspicions by warning her of his lust and ordering her to a nunnery, which of course – another mixed signal – could also be a whorehouse. His crude jokes about "country matters" (III.ii.111) as he lies in her lap, at the play, toy with her role as honorable daughter, confirm his lust, yet contradict the piteous picture he makes of himself in her room, wordless, his clothes in disarray. His oscillating acts of need and aggression are Hamlet's nasty mirroring of what he perceives to be her mixed signals to him: her loving talks, then her inexplicable denial and silence. First he mirrors her silence, then he mirrors the self that Polonius and Laertes have warned her against. More profoundly, her behavior to him – since he has no knowledge of her obedience to Polonius' command – so evokes Gertrude's inconstancy that Hamlet's double messages to Ophelia take on a frenzied condemnation of all women. His soliloquies extend that condemnation to the woman in himself. This Laingian knot of miscommunications compounded, of false selves intensified, leads finally to self-mistrust, even to madness.

Not allowed to love and unable to be false, Ophelia breaks. She goes mad rather than gets mad. Even in her madness she has no voice of her own, only a discord of other voices and expectations, customs gone awry. Most obviously, she does what Hamlet preaches, or at least what he feigns in going mad. Thinking she is not loved by him, she becomes him, or at least what she conceives to be his "noble mind . . . o'erthrown" (III.i.150). Just as his absence in Act IV is reflected in the absence of her reason, so her suicide embodies what Hamlet ponders in his soliloquies. After all, Polonius has instructed her that love denied leads to madness (II.i.110), and Ophelia is forever faithful to her contradictory directives. She herself is a play within a play, or a player trying to respond to several imperious directors at once. Everyone has used her: Polonius, to gain favor; Laertes, to belittle Hamlet; Claudius, to spy on Hamlet; Hamlet, to express rage at Gertrude; and Hamlet again, to express his feigned madness with her as a decoy. She is only valued for the roles that further other people's plots. Treated as a helpless child, she finally becomes one, veiling her perceptions of falsehood and manipulation in her seemingly innocent ballads.

Ophelia's songs give back the contradictory voices lodged within her and expose the contradictions. "Where is the beauteous majesty of Denmark?" she asks of Gertrude as she enters (IV.v.21) – a question Hamlet has often asked of the state, as well as of his mother. She then shifts to her first interchange with Polonius, expressed as his question and her answer:

> How should I your true-love know
> From another one?
> By his cockle hat and staff
> And his sandal shoon.
>
> (IV.v.23–26)

Polonius has told her that men are all alike, and Ophelia replies that Hamlet has the constancy of a pilgrim. The first verse also expresses Hamlet's query to Gertrude about her switch in lovers, while the second says goodbye to all faithful true loves, whether brothers, lovers, or fathers. "He is dead and gone, lady" could refer to Polonius, Prince Hamlet, Laertes, Hamlet the King, or the mythical pilgrim. Her next songs replace this faithful male with lusting lovers who deflower young maids, then depart without fulfilling their vows of marriage. "Young men will do't if they come to't. By Cock, they are to blame" (IV.v.60–61). Most readings take this song for Ophelia's own sensual desires under her dutiful exterior – "For bonny sweet Robin is all my joy" (IV.v.185), where Robin is a colloquial Elizabethan term for penis.[13] But "all" implies it is the only joy allowed her. The speaker is Gertrude's helpless, manipulated lust, veering suddenly to Polonius and Laertes telling her about the dangers of male desire, and back again to Hamlet's sense of loss. The songs mirror every level of the play, even Polonius's "flowery" speech; yet they do not express what Ophelia feels, except as sadness. Laertes is right to say, "Thought and affliction, passion, hell itself, / She turns to favor and to prettiness" (IV.v.186–87). Merging with everyone, she speaks in a collage of voices about present sensuality and absent faithfulness, yet dies, as Gertrude says so empathetically, "incapable of her own distress" (IV.vii.177).

Ophelia's suicide becomes a little microcosm of the male world's banishment of the female, because "woman" represents everything denied by reasonable men. In responding to Ophelia's death, Laertes, patently the norm for filial behavior, is embarrassed by his womanly tears. He forbids himself to cry, "but yet / It is our trick; nature her custom holds, / Let shame say what it will." To be manly is to be ashamed of emotion and nature. Saying farewell to her, he says farewell to that part of himself: "When these [tears] are gone, / The woman will be out" (IV.vii.185–88). His genuine feeling cannot be told except as a wish to get rid of the feeling. Even Hamlet, so much more sensitive than others to "nature" and "heart," equates woman with "frailty" (I.ii.146) or worse. "Whore" is his word for changeable feelings, whether those of Gertrude, of "strumpet" Fortune (II.ii.233), or even of himself. Hamlet echoes his stepfather's association of painted woman and painted word (III.i.51–53) as he rails against himself for not being the dutiful son:

> Why, what an ass am I! This is most brave,
> That I, the son of a dear father murthered,
> Prompted to my revenge by heaven and hell,
> Must like a whore unpack my heart with words
> And fall a-cursing like a very drab,
> A stallion!
>
> (II.ii.568–73)

That women, grief, words, and the heart should be confused with nature, guilt, whoredom, and the body, while filial obedience is equated with noble reason in opposition, is what is rotten in Denmark. Linguistic disorders express social disorders. Ophelia's drowning signifies the necessity of drowning both words and feelings if Hamlet is to act the role prescribed for him, and that is the real tragedy in the play.

Hamlet's focus on ears that are abused stands as a metaphor for the violation of female receptivity. By that token, Hamlet in the end becomes his own violator. Far from being a catharsis or a resolute confrontation, or an integration of the underlying issues, the play's end is a study in frustration and failure.[14] Hamlet retreats to filial duty, allowing the "machine" of his body (II.ii.124) to accomplish the acts required of him. Coming back to a world of fathers and usurpers, where ambition and lust have been defined as the only valid motives, he can speak that language without a qualm. "It is as easy as lying," he has told Rosencrantz and Guildenstern before (III.ii.343). Surrounded by "Examples gross as earth," of sons "with divine ambition puffed," like Fortinbras, who can breezily risk everything "Even for an eggshell" (IV.iv.46, 49, 53), Hamlet at last resolves himself into a Do by obeying the dictates of his father and of "providence," another abstracted father. "I shall win at the odds," he tells Horatio (V.ii.200). It is a world where winning is the only thing; all else is "foolery" for women. "But thou wouldst not think how ill all's here about my heart," he tells uncomprehending Horatio. "But it is no matter. . . . It is but foolery, but it is such a kind of gaingiving as would perhaps trouble a woman" (V.ii.201–05). To Hamlet's four-times-repeated "but," Horatio ignores the "woman," and responds only: "If your mind dislike anything, obey it." Concerns for mind and obedience are part of the male world, to which Hamlet's stifled heart now responds not with whorish "unpacking" but with silence.

Silence is really the theme of the last act, not the almost farcical excess of deeds and rhetoric. The graveyard scene shows the last perversion of reason, as clowns chop logic over the dead. These mini-Claudiuses at least have the merit of not pretending grief, and their wit calls a spade by asserting the absoluteness of law and power, and of class distinctions even in death. Their jokes have to do with the strong and the weak – the gallowsmaker or the gravemaker "builds stronger" (V.i.40, 55) – because their social roles abet the permanence of death. "Has this fellow no feeling of his business, that 'a sings at grave-making?" Hamlet inquires (V.i.62–63). "Custom hath made it in him a property of easiness," Horatio replies. Feeling and custom, as ever opposed but now with greater clarity, cannot be reconciled. Those who are most at home with "wit" are also most at ease with custom, reasoning, and playing their roles. Words come as glibly to them as to Osric, in proportion as feelings are denied.

It is clear to Hamlet now that words are of no use. "Nay, an thou'lt mouth, / I'll rant as well as thou," he throws back at Laertes (V.i.270–71). This is the posturing of animals, nothing more:

> Let Hercules himself do what he may,
> The cat will mew, and dog will have his day.
> (V.i.278–79)

Like Ophelia, Hamlet can mirror how others talk, though with a savage irony that emphasizes the distance between his inward feelings and outward rhetoric. He mocks the foppish Osric, who "did comply, sir, with his dug before 'a sucked it" (V.ii.179). He seems calm, controlled, at arm's length from what he says. Only Gertrude senses the truth:

> This is mere madness;
> And thus a while the fit will work on him.
> Anon, as patient as the female dove
> When that her golden couplets are disclosed,
> His silence will sit drooping.
> (V.i.271–75)

What seems like a manic-depressive "fit" to Gertrude (a better diagnosis than Freud's "hysteria") is actually Hamlet's response to "the fit" of a senseless society. He mouths its language and assumes its stance of male combat, while the "female dove" in him prepares for a final silence. Earlier he had berated himself for his dove-like gentleness: "But I am pigeon-livered and lack gall / To make oppression bitter" (II.ii.562–63). Now, while he puts on the necessary gall, the unspoken woman in him outwardly obeys paternal commands ("my purposes . . . follow the king's pleasure" (V.ii.190–91)), whether of Claudius, the Ghost, or Providence. Inwardly he has already left the world of fathers, roles, and mixed messages to rejoin Ophelia and Gertrude in death's constancy. Not until Gertrude dies does Hamlet, dying, fulfill the Ghost's instructions. To kill Claudius as an afterthought to the Queen's death is his last little "dig" at the "old mole" (I.v.162).

So much for Hamlet's "golden couplets," the fledgling poetry of the self he has tried to "disclose." Ending his drama as he begins it, with a play on words, he expires with "the rest is silence" (V.ii.347). That gnomic phrase could mean that there is no afterlife, despite Hamlet's earlier scruples; that "rest" is equivalent to silence; that my rest is silence; or that the rest of my story is untold. All of these ambiguities are true, or at least more true in their ambiguity than the interpretations that so quickly falsify Hamlet's story. Horatio immediately invalidates the connection between rest and silence by invoking singing angels: "And flights of angels sing thee to thy rest!" The noise of war, the "warlike volley" of drums and guns (V.ii.344), drives out the silence utterly. We are back in the male world of ambitious sons advancing to their fathers' footsteps.

The play ends in a mindless sequence of ritual male duties, roles without meaning. The ambassador informs the court that the King's "commandment is fulfilled / That Rosencrantz and Guildenstern are dead." Staring at the dead bodies of the King, Queen, Hamlet, and Laertes, he can think only of saying, "Where should we have our thanks?" (V.ii.359–61). Horatio responds not with the story of Hamlet's struggle to keep the integrity of his "noble heart" (V.ii.348) but with the narrative of Claudius' villainy, and perhaps of Hamlet's as well:

> So shall you hear
> Of carnal, bloody, and unnatural acts,
> Of accidental judgments, casual slaughters,
> Of deaths put on by cunning and forced cause,
> And, in this upshot, purposes mistook
> Fall'n on th'inventors' heads. All this can I
> Truly deliver.
>
> (V.ii.369–75)

This is the public story of an unnatural world, not the private record of a heart unspoken. It is a tale of deeds, not feelings. Yet it may be the story Hamlet knows will be told. After all, Horatio himself, "As th'art a man" (V.ii.331), is manfully following his duty to Hamlet's command, sacrificing his wish for suicide. A story born of duty must be a man's story.

All the women are dead, and there are not more womanly tears. Young "Strong-in-arm," who inherits an irrevocably corrupted world, is the arrogant, stupid, blundering finale to the theme of filial duty, to which both the Ghost and Claudius had demanded Hamlet's conformity. His tribute to Hamlet is cast in the rhetoric of a military command: "Let four captains / Bear Hamlet like a soldier to the stage" (V.ii.384–85). Here Hamlet is finally "fit" to the alien mold of soldier in the stage world of the "captains." At the play's close, Fortinbras ludicrously undercuts Hamlet's final words.

> For he was likely, had he been put on,
> To have proved most royal; and for his passage
> The soldiers' music and the rites of war
> Speak loudly for him.
>
> (V.ii.386–89)

How right for this man without a touch of the female in him to have such confidence in "the rites of war" as confirmation of Hamlet's identity! We are back in the world of the first act, with a more ironic consciousness of what it means for Fortinbras to say, "had he been put on." A body politic cannot take off its clothes and venture, like Hamlet, "naked" and "alone" (IV.vii.50–51); it can only "put on" more roles. From the first anxious question of the guards to the last pointless order to "Go, bid the soldiers shoot," the military atmosphere pervades the language of the play.

Having learned how cruel one must be to be "kind" (I.ii.65), Hamlet puts on a "most royal" corruptedness (V.ii.387). He acts as the world does, speaks as the world speaks. Yet what a mockery it is, a self-mockery, to say of Fortinbras, "He has my dying voice" (V.ii.345). The illegitimate succession instituted by Claudius concludes with the triumph of the son against whom these fathers were at war. It is final proof of the interchangeability, in language and body, of all those in authority, whether enemy or friend. It is also the concluding irony of Hamlet's struggle for speech. His last soliloquy is a voice dying into accord with the senseless ambition and mindless "honor" of Fortinbras: "O, from this time forth, / My thoughts be bloody, or be nothing worth!" (IV.iv.65–66). But now that the guns "Speak loudly for him" (V.ii.389), Fortinbras pompously distinguishes between carnage in field and in court, as if Hamlet's death in battle would have been eminently acceptable: "Such a sight as this / Becomes the field, but here shows much amiss" (V.ii.390–91). Hamlet is right; Fortinbras does inherit his "dying voice," while the rest *is* silence. Just as the hawkish voices of blood, honor, and ambition inherit the world of the fathers, with its false roles and false proprieties, so Hamlet the dove joins Gertrude and Ophelia as a much-too-ravished bride of quietness.

Hamlet is not so much a full-throated tragedy as an ironic stifling of a hero's identity by structures of rule that no longer have legitimacy. It is the most frustrating of Shakespeare's plays precisely because it is the one most specifically about frustration. Shakespeare uses the opposition between male and female to denote the impossibility of speaking truly in a public role without violating or being violated. Too aware of paternal duplicity, Hamlet remains wordlessly modern in his excess of words, unable to center himself in a society whose "offence is rank" (III.iii.36) in every sense, and where the quest for self-knowledge is womanishly at odds with the manly roles he must put on. Even Ophelia only loved his mind. Hamlet's final assumption of a swordsman's identity is not a healthy solution to Oedipal conflicts but a mute submission to his father's command to "whet thy almost blunted purpose" (III.iv.112). The manly identity is imposed, not grown into. Hamlet delays revenging his father's death because his real struggle is to restore his mother's validation of his feelings, though "whore" is the only word available to him for his heartsick disgust. For Freudians to call Hamlet a mini-Claudius, to accept his male world's perspective of ambition and lust as sufficient motives, is to do what all the fathers want to do: explain Hamlet by their own divided selves. Perhaps even incest fantasies, as Laing tells us, may be defenses against the dread of being alone.[15]

What T. S. Eliot took for *Hamlet*'s failure, Shakespeare took for theme, as I have tried to show.[16] It is a play "dealing with the effects of a mother's guilt upon her son," not as sexuality but as identity itself. Hamlet's self-doubt is joined to Gertrude's insufficiency. Her "negative and insignificant" character "arouses in Hamlet the feeling which she is incapable of representing," Eliot rightly says, while the demand of his father for revenge calls Hamlet to a clear, though false, role.[17] But these are not flaws in the drama. They are flaws in the patriarchal order, which has cracked all the mirrors for self-confirmation. *Hamlet* succeeds so well, and has lasted so long, because it speaks so keenly to the dissociation of sensibility Eliot elsewhere describes.[18] Whether we call it role and self, reason and nature, mind and body, manly and womanly, or the language of power and the language of feeling, we recognize these dichotomies in our world and in ourselves. How poisonous rule o'ercrows every person's spirit (V.ii.342) is indeed the fundamental answer to "Who's there," as Eliot's critique implies. To pursue the question, Hamlet learns much too well, is not only to fail, but to participate in the collusion.

Notes

1   I am using the Pelican edition of *Hamlet*, ed. Willard Farnham (New York: Pelican Books, 1957). The 1605 edition's title is *The Tragicall Historie of Hamlet, Prince of Denmarke*. The epigraph is taken from John Dean, *Blind Ambition: The White House Years* (New York: Simon and Schuster, 1976), p. 47. I thank Domna Stanton, of *Signs: Journal of Women in Culture and Society*, where this essay first appeared

(vol. 4, Winter 1978, pp. 291–308) for her thoughtful and attentive editorial work.

2   See Norman N. Holland, *Psychoanalysis and Shakespeare*, rev. ed. (1964; rpt. New York: Octagon Books, 1976), pp. 163–206, for various parricidal and matricidal interpretations. Erik Erikson discusses Hamlet's identity as delayed adolescent in "Youth: Fidelity and Diversity," *Daedalus*, 91 (1962), 5–27. Neil Friedman and Richard M. Jones develop further psychosocial perspectives, to which my essay is indebted, in "On the Mutuality of the Oedipus Complex: Notes on the Hamlet Case," *American Imago*, 20 (1963), 107–31. More recent psychoanalytic studies include Theodore Lidz, *Hamlet's Enemy: Madness and Myth in "Hamlet"* (New York: Basic Books, 1975), and Norman N. Holland, "*Hamlet* – My Greatest Creation," *Journal of the American Academy of Psychoanalysis*, 3 (1975), 419–27. Avi Erlich's *Hamlet's Absent Father* (Princeton, N.J.: Princeton Univ. Press, 1977) came to my attention after this essay was first drafted. It argues that Hamlet unconsciously fears his mother and needs his father, a conclusion directly opposed to mine. Though Erlich's book has many useful insights, psychoanalytic theory leads him to mistake a wishful male fantasy for interpersonal reality.

3   See Harry Stack Sullivan, *The Interpersonal Theory of Psychiatry* (New York: W. W. Norton, 1953); R. D. Laing, *The Divided Self: An Existential Study in Sanity and Madness* (London: Tavistock Press, 1960); D. W. Winnicott, "Mirror-Role of Mother and Family in Child Development," in *The Predicament of the Family*, ed. P. Lomas (London: Hogarth Press, 1967), pp. 26–33; and D. W. Winnicott, *The Maturational Processes and the Facilitating Environment* (New York: International Univ. Press, 1965). I recognize that the interpersonal approach is in some ways tangential to the major post-Freudian development in psychoanalysis, the British object-relations school. Nevertheless, I believe it is more useful for literary criticism. A quasi-Laingian study of Shakespeare is Terence Eagleton's *Shakespeare and Society: Critical Essays on Shakespearean Drama* (New York: Schocken Books, 1971).

4   Laing, *Divided Self*, p. 95. Laing's dismissal of Ophelia's statements as "incomprehensible" is odd, given his extraordinary sensitivity to the meanings in schizophrenic voices.

5   See Winnicott, "Mirror-Role." pp. 26–33.

6   Ernest Jones, *Hamlet and Oedipus* (London: Victor Gollancz Press, 1949), pp. 86–87, sees "repulsion against woman" as coming from repressed sexual feelings and a "splitting of the mother image"; he connects Hamlet's diatribes against women to unconscious fear of incest wishes. Avi Erlich, in *Hamlet's Absent Father*, explores pre-oedipal dynamics more thoroughly.

7   See Roy Walker, "*Hamlet*: The Opening Scene," in *The Time is Out of Joint* (Folcroft, Pa.: Folcroft Library Editions, 1948), reprinted in *Shakespeare: Modern Essays in Criticism*, ed. Leonard F. Dean (New York: Peter Smith, 1961), pp. 216–21. For broader commentaries on the play's "interrogative mood," see also Maynard Mack, "The World of Hamlet," *The Yale Review*, 41 (1952), 502–23, widely reprinted; Harry Levin, *The Question of Hamlet* (New York: Oxford Univ. Press, 1959); and Bernard McElroy, *Shakespeare's Mature Tragedies* (Princeton, N.J.: Princeton Univ. Press, 1973), pp. 29–88.

8   Laing defines "collusion" as a process by which members of an intimate group, such as the family, conspire knowingly or unknowingly to validate one member's "false self," that self which conforms to other people's expectations. Eagleton's *Shakespeare and Society* analyzes how various false unities in *Hamlet* force the hero's subjectivity into being manipulated as an object.

9   See R. D. Laing, *Knots* (London: Tavistock Press, 1970). This is an extension of Gregory Bateson's "double bind" theory; see G. Bateson et al., "Toward a Theory of Schizophrenia," *Behavioural Science*, 1 (1956), 251–64.

10 Harold C. Goddard, in *The Meaning of Shakespeare* (Chicago: Univ. of Chicago Press, 1951), vol. 1, develops an interpretation along parallel lines, with the Ghost as devil imposing a "divided mind" on Hamlet. Goddard's reading is finally a Christian one, arguing that Art, or the play within the play, could have converted Claudius to repentance if Hamlet's uncontrollable vengefulness had not intervened. Another Christian reader sensitive to the Ghost's duplicity is Eleanor Prosser, in *Hamlet and Revenge* (Stanford, Calif.: Stanford Univ. Press, 1967). Christian readings, like too many Freudian readings, tend to substitute the false answer of duty for the real question of identity.

11 The Ghost has occasioned immense controversy. Of those who see the Ghost as other than benign, see above, and also Richard Flatter, *Hamlet's Father* (New Haven, Conn.: Yale Univ. Press, 1949); G. Wilson Knight, *The Wheel of Fire*, 2nd ed. (London: Methuen, 1965); and J. Dover Wilson, *What Happens in Hamlet* (Cambridge: At the Univ. Press, 1967). Most critics see the Ghost as the good father to whom Hamlet should submit. In *Fools of Time: Studies in Shakespearean Tragedy* (Toronto: Univ. of Toronto Press, 1967), p. 80, Northrop Frye concludes that "God's main interest, in Elizabethan tragedy, is in promoting the revenge, and in making it as bloody as possible." For a Jungian view, which superficially resembles my own in its prescription for men to encounter the woman in themselves, see Alex Aronson, *Psyche and Symbol in Shakespeare* (Bloomington, Ind.: Indiana Univ. Press, 1972). In Aronson's view, the Ghost is Hamlet's dramatized unconsciousness, as Hamlet tries to free himself from "his entanglement with a Hecate-like Magna Mater" (p. 235).

12 R. D. Laing and Aaron Esterson, *Sanity, Madness, and the Family* (London: Tavistock Press, 1964). Esterson expanded one chapter into *The Leaves of Spring: A Study in the Dialectics of Madness* (London: Tavistock Press, 1970).

13 See Harry Morris, "Ophelia's 'Bonny Sweet Robin,'" *PMLA*, 73 (1958), 601–03; also see Carroll Camden, "On Ophelia's Madness," *Shakespeare Quarterly*, 15, (1964), 247–55; and Maurice Charney, *Style in Hamlet* (Princeton N.J.: Princeton Univ. Press, 1969), pp. 107–12.

14 There is near-unanimous critical agreement, except for Goddard, that the last act promotes integration. See Mack, pp. 518–23; McElroy, pp. 85–86; Harold Fisch, *Hamlet and the Word: The Covenant Pattern in Shakespeare* (New York: Ungar, 1971), pp. 85–86; Irving Ribner, *Patterns in Shakespearian Tragedy* (London: Methuen, 1960); Wilson, p. 272; and Michael Goldman, *Shakespeare and the Energies of Drama* (Princeton, N.J.: Princeton Univ. Press, 1972). Goldman goes so far as to say, "The play ends with a final unambiguous discharge of energy,"

and the gunshots prove that "the air has been cleared" (p. 90). Reuben Brower's more sensitive reading, in *Hero and Saint: Shakespeare and the Graeco-Roman Heroic Tradition* (New York: Oxford Univ. Press, 1971), finds the tension between soldier hero and moral hero reduced to soldier in the end. For a stronger dissent from the consensus, see L. C. Knights, *Some Shakespearean Themes and an Approach to "Hamlet"* (Stanford, Calif.: Stanford Univ. Press. 1966), who finds Hamlet engulfed by evil and the cause of further evil. T. McAlindon, in *Shakespeare and Decorum* (New York: Barnes and Noble, 1973), p. 67, notes that Fortinbras is just "a crude strong-arm," and Frye (pp. 29–30) sees Hamlet as selfish to the end. Lidz's *Hamlet's Enemy* (see n. 2 above) reflects the characteristic adaptive bias of lesser Freudians by discussing the play as a ritual reestablishing appropriate social defenses; he sees Fortinbras as a "direct and uncomplicated hero" who "brings hope for the rebirth of the nation" (p. 112).

15 Laing, *Divided Self*, p. 57. Laing's system suffers from its romanticization of "true self" as aloneness rather than the positive interdependence taught by Winnicott. For a psychoanalytic critique of Laing, see David Holbrook, "R. D. Laing and the Death Circuit," *Encounter*, 31 (1968), 35–45. In *Shakespeare and Society*, Eagleton offers a similar critique of Hamlet himself: "Hamlet's insistence on not being a puppet leads, finally, to a delight in resisting any kind of definition; it becomes, in fact, socially irresponsible, a merely negative response" (p. 61). My own sense is that Hamlet looks to women rather than to men for self-definition and that structures of male rule induce his negation.

16 T. S. Eliot, "Hamlet" (1919), reprinted in *Selected Essays*, 3rd ed. (London: Faber and Faber, 1951), pp. 141–46. In *The Tiger's Heart: Eight Essays on Shakespeare* (New York: Oxford Univ. Press, 1970), p. 76, Herbert Howarth finds Eliot mistaken because the play is about "the helplessness of what is gentle before the onrush of what is rank," a nice formulation. Richard A. Lanham's *The Motives of Eloquence: Literary Rhetoric in the Renaissance* (New Haven, Conn.: Yale Univ. Press, 1976), pp. 129–43, concludes that *Hamlet* is two plays with "two kinds of self," revenger and self-conscious actor looking for the "big scene." Charney's *Style in Hamlet* says Hamlet responds to his world with four styles: self-consciously parodic, witty, passionate, and simple. In my interpretation, the clash Lanham sees between the role-playing "rhetoric" self and the "serious" revenger self mirrors Hamlet's role-inducing world, with no mirror for the real self. In some respects Eliot is right to question Gertrude as an "objective correlative"; she is so much more constant in Hamlet's hopes than in her weak, sensual actuality that she raises the question of whether the woman in *Hamlet* is only in Hamlet.

17 Eliot, "Hamlet," p. 146.

18 Eliot, "The Metaphysical Poets" (1921), reprinted in *Selected Essays*, pp. 281–91.

6

Language: An Overview

Shakespeare's plays are, firstly, words on the page. D. H. Lawrence's poem 'When I read Shakespeare' opens: 'When I read Shakespeare I am struck with wonder / that such trivial people should muse and thunder / in such lovely language'. The different approaches to this 'lovely language', through the varied lenses of historical linguistics, studies of imagery and post-structuralism, have produced extremely varied criticism over the last century, and some of the key movements in this critical history are described in this chapter.

There have been many studies of early modern English and Shakespeare's plays. Margreta de Grazia's overview 'Shakespeare and the craft of language' in de Grazia and Wells (2001) provides an introduction to rhetoric, punning and historical linguistics. Hussey (1992), Blake (1983) and Salmon and Burness (1987) all offer more detailed studies or collections of essays on Shakespeare's language. The historical context of Shakespeare's language is discussed by Hope (1999) and Barber (1997), and Cercignani (1981) writes about Elizabethan pronunciation. Wright (1988) and Houston (1988) discuss Shakespeare's metre and syntax. Lanham (1969, 2nd edn 1991) is the standard work on rhetorical terms. Vickers (1968) discusses Shakespeare's prose; Ness (1941) catalogues Shakespeare's use of rhyme. There are interesting approaches to Shakespeare's language from the point of view of actors speaking the verse in Barton (1984) and Berry (1993).

Literary studies of Shakespeare's language have made a major contribution to criticism over the last century. L. C. Knights' argument that 'the only profitable approach to Shakespeare is a consideration of his plays as dramatic poems' (Knights, 1946, p. 6), Wilson Knight's attempt 'to see each play as an expanded metaphor' (Knight, 1930, p. 16), and C. S. Lewis' injunction 'to surrender oneself to the poetry and the situation' (Lewis, 1964, p. 208) are all instances of a critical reaction against the stress on character promoted by Bradley and his Romantic antecedents. Wilson Knight's influential essay 'The

Othello Music' argues that 'in first analysing Othello's poetry, we shall lay the basis for an understanding of the play's symbolism' (Knight, 1930, p. 98). The music is that of 'the extreme, slightly exaggerated beauty of Othello's language' (p. 103). There is, Wilson Knight argues, 'something sentimental in Othello's language, in Othello. Iago is pure cynicism' (p. 117). Wilson Knight sees language contributing to theme and to characterization. In her study *Shakespeare's Imagery and What it Tells us* (1935), however, Caroline Spurgeon is less concerned with individual characters than with the overall linguistic mood of a play. She offers 'suggestions as to the light thrown by the imagery (1) on Shakespeare's personality, temperament and thought, (2) on the themes and characters of the plays' (Spurgeon, 1935, p. ix). The book groups image clusters together by theme and also indentifies dominant strains of imagery in specific plays. A chapter on 'Leading Motives in the Tragedies' elucidates 'the part played by recurrent images in raising, developing, sustaining and repeating emotion' (p. 309), light and dark in *Romeo and Juliet*, 'images of sickness, disease or blemish of the body' (p. 316), in *Hamlet*, 'continuous use made of the simplest, humblest, everyday things, drawn from the daily life in a small house, as a vehicle for sublime poetry' (p. 324) in *Macbeth*, the image in *Othello* 'of animals in action, preying upon one another, mischievous, lascivious, cruel or suffering, and through these, the general sense of pain and unpleasantness is much increased and kept constantly before us' (p. 335). The sharpness of focus in *King Lear* is intensified by the presence of a single dominating image of suffering, 'chiefly by means of the verbs used, but also in metaphor, of a human body in anguished movement, tugged, wrenched, beaten, pierced, stung, scourged, dislocated, flayed, gashed, tortured, and finally broken on the rack' (pp. 338–9). A similar focus on unifying symbolism and imagery is found in Cleanth Brooks' chapter on *Macbeth* in his *The Well Wrought Urn: Studies in the Structure of Poetry* (1949). Brooks argues that 'what is at stake is the relation of Shakespeare's imagery to the total structure of the plays themselves' (Brooks, 1968, p. 24), and discusses the imagery of clothing and of the 'naked babe' as representative of disguised and stripped humanity, used 'to encompass an astonishingly large area of the total situation' (pp. 38–9).

Wolfgang Clemen's *The Development of Shakespeare's Imagery* (1951) developed both the character focus of Wilson Knight and Spurgeon's index of imagery study, arguing that isolated images needed to be seen in their context, that the form of speech in which they occur is important, as is their speaker: 'In [Shakespeare's] hands metaphors grew more and more effective instruments: at first fulfilling only a few simple functions, they later serve several aims at one and the same time and play a decisive part in the characterization of the figures in the play and in expressing the dramatic theme' (Clemen, 1951, p. 5). Clemen argues that in the early plays, such as *Titus Andronicus*, the 'words are not yet necessarily individual to the character by whom they are uttered'

(p. 21), and often they do not serve either characterization or plot. It was in the great tragedies, beginning with *Hamlet*, that Shakespeare's control of language was at its most subtle and impressive: 'In the early plays, it was his aim to make everything as obvious and plain as possible [. . .] in the work of the mature Shakespeare by a more subtle and indirect method. Things are suggested, intimated, hinted at; they are seldom expressly stated (pp. 89–90). In the tragedies, rhetoric which might have seemed bombastic in the earlier plays is shown to be 'borne by great passion and correspond[s] to the depth and immensity of human emotion' (p. 92). [Man] appears in relationship to certain forces determining and guiding his very existence. Be they called fate, doom, time or metaphysical powers, these occult forces have a hand in every tragedy; man appears to be surrounded by them. Their vivid reality often becomes perceptible in the imagery' (p. 97). Clemen proposes that imagery needs to be judged according to 'the degree of harmony existing between the image and the dramatic situation producing it': often the imagery goes virtually unnoticed because it is 'so wholly adapted to the situation and emotion of the speaker' (pp. 102–3). In place of the classical dramatic unities, Shakespeare substitutes a 'unity of atmosphere' created by the imagery 'binding the separate elements of the play together into a real organic structure' (p. 105).

Shakespeare's puns and wordplay have also received attention, notably by William Empson in his 'Honest in Othello' (1951). M. M. Mahood revisits Johnson's repugnance at Shakespeare's 'weakness' for puns (see p. 20) in her essay 'The Fatal Cleopatra', in *Shakespeare's Wordplay* (1957). Puns are also discussed by Michel Grivelet in his essay 'Shakespeare as "Corrupter of Words"' (1963), which argues that puns in tragedies 'place darkness at the heart of bright vision' (Grivelet, 1963, p. 73), whereas in comedies they aid the plot movement towards enlightenment and resolution. Bawdy innuendo can be excavated with reference to Partridge's *Shakespeare's Bawdy*, an essay and an extensive glossary first published in 1947 with revised editions in 1968 and 2001. For Terry Eagleton (1986), however, puns are a challenge to the ostensible ideological values of Shakespeare's drama:

> Even those who know very little about Shakespeare might be vaguely aware that his plays value social order and stability, and that they are written with extraordinary eloquence, one metaphor breeding another in an apparently unstaunchable flow of what modern theorists might call 'textual productivity'. The problem is that these two aspects of Shakespeare are in potential conflict with one another. For a stability of signs – each word securely in its place, each signifier (mark or sound) corresponding to its signified, (or meaning) – is an integral part of any social order: settled meanings, shared definitions and regularities of grammar both reflect, and help to constitute, a well-ordered political state. Yet it is all this which Shakespeare's flamboyant punning, troping and riddling

threaten to put into question. His belief in social stability is jeopardized by the very language in which it is articulated. It would seem, then, that the very act of writing implies for Shakespeare an epistemology (or theory of knowledge) at odds with his political ideology. This is a deeply embarrassing dilemma, and it is not surprising that much of Shakespeare's drama is devoted to figuring out strategies for resolving it. (Eagleton, 1986, p. 1)

Patricia Parker's work in *Shakespeare from the Margins* (1996) and *Literary Fat Ladies* (1987), has been exemplary in its sophisticated discussion of puns and language within a post-structuralist and feminist framework.

Frank Kermode's *Shakespeare's Language* (2000) echoes Clemen in finding a crucial shift in Shakespeare's writing around the time of *Hamlet*. Before this, Kermode argues, Shakespeare's language relies heavily on the rhetorical arts of non-dramatic poetry, preferring literary figures of speech over individual characterization. In *Hamlet*, Kermode praises the limitless variety of the play's register, from blank verse to prose, from friendship to suspicion, from philosophical speculation to bawdy punning. Kermode returns to the importance of one particular rhetorical device:

> [*Hamlet*] is obsessed with doubles of all kinds, and notably by its use of the figure known as hendiadys. This means, literally, one-through-two, and can be illustrated by some common expressions such as 'law and order' or 'house and home' [. . .] My purpose in drawing attention to hendiadys is largely to show that in the rhetoric of *Hamlet* there may be a strain, virtually unnoticed, a kind of compulsion that reflects the great and obvious topics, adultery and incest, deep preoccupations given external representation. These preoccupations seem to be related to a concern with questions of identity, sameness, and the union of separate selves [. . .] as in marriage, and, in a pathologised form, incest. (Kermode, 2000, pp. 100–1)

James Calderwood makes a similar point about *Hamlet's* language and its 'incestuous uses of words: his puns, riddles, equivocations' (Calderwood, 1983, p. 71). On *Macbeth*, Kermode argues that the 'distinctive character of the language [. . .] is largely dictated by its structure. From the first suggestion of a plot on Duncan's life until his murder, the play exists in a world of nightmare doubt and decision: to kill or not to kill' (p. 202). In the repetition of key words, the play enacts its own theme: 'all may be said to equivocate, and on their equivocal variety we impose our limited interpretations' (p. 216). Kermode's chapter on *Antony and Cleopatra* is reprinted in chapter 7. Also concerned with the development of Shakespeare's language over his career is *The Heroic Idiom of Shakespearean Tragedy* (1985), where James Bulman argues that Shakespeare's early plays conceive 'tragic heroism entirely through the conventions of the received heroic idiom', but that 'his greatest achievement was to free tragedy from that servitude and move it towards the dramatisation of the hero's inner life' (Bulman, 1985, p. 213).

R. A. Foakes' 'Suggestions for a New Approach to Shakespeare's Imagery' (1952) tackles a lack of methodological sophistication in the work on Shakespeare's imagery. He argues that there has been little assessment of the difference between 'poetic' and 'dramatic' imagery (Foakes, 1952, pp. 81–2), and that a definition of imagery derived from drama is needed:

> While it is possible for a poem to be a metaphor, to exist only in an image or images, this cannot properly be said of a Shakespearian play. The poetic image in a play is set in a context not of words alone, but of words, dramatic situation, interplay of character, stage-effect, and it is also placed in a time sequence. (pp. 85–6)

Thus, a

> discussion of dramatic imagery then would include reference to the subject-matter and object-matter of poetic imagery, to visual and auditory effects, iterative words, historical and geographical placing, and to both the general and particular uses of these things. Dramatic imagery would be examined primarily in relation to context, to dramatic context, and to the time-sequence of a play; the general or overall patterns of word and image would be examined in relation to other effects as well as for their own value. (p. 90)

Also on methodological questions is Robert Weimann's essay 'Shakespeare and the Study of Metaphor' (1974), which reminds us that 'The essence of metaphor is to connect' (Weimann, 1974, p. 150) and that the study of metaphor cannot therefore be separated from these points of reference. Weimann suggests that the formalist study of Shakespeare's language has 'not considered the theatrical functions of dramatic speech and the way it is correlated to non-verbal means of expression. To read the figures in the carpet is to see them in their two-dimensional extension, not as part of a process in time, and on the stage' (pp. 158–9). He argues for the interrelation of metaphor in 'the total meaning of Shakespeare's poetry in the theater' (p. 167).

Much of the work described so far sees the study of Shakespeare's language in terms of its unifying imagery, or its perceived change through his career. Post-structuralist ideas about the instability of words and their referents, however, influenced a different style of criticism. Terence Hawkes discusses *Shakespeare's Talking Animals* (1973):

> In the course of their exhaustive probing after the nature of human reality, Shakespeare's tragic plays seem to take as their starting-point the notion that man is fundamentally a communicator; that talking and listening make a man

human. In them, the tragedy seems to involve a denial, by villainy or circumstance, of man's communicative functions; a prohibition of the essential 'talking and listening' aspects of his nature. (Hawkes, 1973, p. 105)

Hawkes sees Denmark as 'a world which destroys words, reducing them to a formless "rhapsody" incapable of a truly human function' (p. 111), as the deterioration in language throughout the play brings 'with it a breakdown in exactly those personal relationships which underpin society and make man human' (p. 113). Ultimately, 'release from the tyranny of "words, words, words" remains the reward of the dead Hamlet, for whom the rest is silence', whereas the play *Hamlet*, 'perhaps as the ultimate play on words, continues to try to speak' (p. 126).

A number of contributors to G. Douglas Atkins and David M. Bergeron (eds), *Shakespeare and Deconstruction* (1988), are also concerned with similar issues. Waller explains that deconstructive readings of Shakespeare 'concentrate not on thematization or meanings but on the linguistic *struggle* for meaning: not on what the text can be made to reveal, but the inevitable play of revelation and concealment in language' (Waller, 1988, p. 23), and in his article on *King Lear*, Jonathan Goldberg argues that in Edgar's lines looking over 'Dover Cliff': 'the limits that *Dover* presents in the text are the limits of representation themselves' (Goldberg, 1988, p. 247). Jackson I. Cope's article 'Shakespeare, Derrida, and the End of Language in *Lear*' suggests 'a certain timid rapprochement between the metaphoric language about language of Derrida and the more furious poetry and radical claims against the paradox of language in *Lear*' (Cope, 1988, p. 275). Patricia Parker's essay on *Othello* in the collection *Shakespeare and the Question of Theory* (edited by Patricia Parker and Geoffrey Hartman, 1985) combines theoretical and rhetorical approaches to argue for the significance of the theme of disclosure to the play. Most recently, close studies of Shakespeare's language have tended to be integrated with other approaches: historicism, feminism and performance.

Further Reading

Atkins, G. Douglas, and Bergeron, David M. (eds). *Shakespeare and Deconstruction*. New York: Lang, 1988.

Barber, Charles Laurence. *Early Modern English*. Edinburgh: Edinburgh University Press, 1997.

Barton, John, *Playing Shakespeare*. London: Methuen, 1984.

Berry, Cicely. *The Actor and the Text*, rev. edn. London: Virgin, 1993.

Blake, N. F. *Shakespeare's Language: An Introduction*. London: Macmillan, 1983.

Brooks, Cleanth. *The Well Wrought Urn: Studies in the Structure of Poetry*, rev. edn. London: Dobson, 1968.

Bulman, James C. *The Heroic Idiom of Shakespearean Tragedy.* Newark; London: University of Delaware Press; Associated University Presses, 1985.

Calderwood, James L. *To Be and Not to Be: Negation and Metadrama in Hamlet.* New York: Columbia University Press, 1983.

Cercignani, Fausto. *Shakespeare's Works and Elizabethan Pronunciation.* Oxford; New York: Clarendon Press; Oxford University Press, 1981.

Clemen, Wolfgang. *The Development of Shakespeare's Imagery.* London: Methuen, 1951.

Cope, Jackson I. 'Shakespeare, Derrida, and the End of Language in *Lear'*. *Shakespeare and Deconstruction*, eds G. Douglas Atkins and David M. Bergeron, 1988, pp. 267–83.

de Grazia, Margreta, and Stanley W. Wells. *The Cambridge Companion to Shakespeare.* Cambridge: Cambridge University Press, 2001.

Eagleton, Terry. *William Shakespeare.* Rereading Literature. Oxford: Blackwell, 1986.

Empson, William. *The Structure of Complex Words.* London: Chatto & Windus, 1951.

Foakes, R. A. 'Suggestions for a New Approach to Shakespeare's Imagery'. *Shakespeare Survey* 5 (1952): 81–92.

Goldberg, Jonathan. 'Perspectives: Dover Cliff and the Conditions of Representation'. *Shakespeare and Deconstruction*, eds G. Douglas Atkins and David M. Bergeron, 1988, pp. 245–65.

Grivelet, Michel. 'Shakespeare as "Corrupter of Words"'. *Shakespeare Survey* 16 (1963): 70–6.

Hawkes, Terence. *Shakespeare's Talking Animals: Language and Drama in Society.* London: Edward Arnold, 1973.

Hope, Jonathan. 'Shakespeare's "Natiue English"'. *A Companion to Shakespeare*, ed. David Scott Kastan. Oxford: Blackwell, 1999, pp. 239–55.

Houston, John Porter. *Shakespearean Sentences: A Study in Style and Syntax.* Baton Rouge: Louisiana State University Press, 1988.

Hussey, S. S. *The Literary Language of Shakespeare*, 2nd edn. London: Longman, 1992.

Kermode, Frank. *Shakespeare's Language.* London: Allen Lane, 2000.

Knight, George Wilson. *The Wheel of Fire; Essays in Interpretation of Shakespeare's Sombre Tragedies.* London: Oxford University Press, 1930.

Knights, L. C. *Explorations: Essays in Criticism, mainly on the Literature of the Seventeenth Century.* London: Chatto & Windus, 1946.

Lanham, Richard A. *A Handlist of Rhetorical Terms: A Guide for Students of English Literature.* Berkeley: University of California Press, 1969; 2nd edn 1991.

Lewis, C. S. 'Hamlet: The Prince or the Poem'. *Studies in Shakespeare: British Academy Lectures*, ed. Peter Alexander, 1964, pp. 201–18.

Mahood, M. M. *Shakespeare's Wordplay.* London: Methuen, 1957.

Ness, Frederic W., *The Use of Rhyme in Shakespeare's Plays.* New Haven; London: Yale University Press; Oxford University Press, 1941.

Parker, Patricia. *Literary Fat Ladies: Rhetoric, Gender, Property.* London: Methuen, 1987.

——, *Shakespeare from the Margins: Language, Culture, Context.* Chicago; London: University of Chicago Press, 1996.

——, and Hartman, Geoffrey H. *Shakespeare and the Question of Theory.* London: Methuen, 1985.

Partridge, Eric. *Shakespeare's Bawdy: A Literary & Psychological Essay, and a Comprehensive Glossary*. Revised and enlarged edn. London: Routledge & Kegan Paul, 1968.

Salmon, Vivian, and Burness, Edwina. *A Reader in the Language of Shakespearean Drama: Essays*. Amsterdam: John Benjamins Publishing Company, 1987.

Spurgeon, C. F. E. *Shakespeare's Imagery and What it Tells us*. Cambridge: University Press, 1935.

Vickers, Brian. *The Artistry of Shakespeare's Prose*. London: Methuen, 1968.

Waller, Gary. 'Decentering the Bard: The Dissemination of the Shakespearean Text'. *Shakespeare and Deconstruction*, eds G. Douglas Atkins and David M. Bergeron, 1988, pp. 21–46.

Weimann, Robert. 'Shakespeare and the Study of Metaphor'. *New Literary History* 6 (1974): 149–67.

Wright, George T. *Shakespeare's Metrical Art*. Berkeley: University of California Press, 1988.

7

Language: Critical Extracts

Antony and Cleopatra

Frank Kermode

Kermode's book Shakespeare's Language, *from which this chapter is excerpted, proposes that the life of Shakespeare's play is 'in the linguistic detail', and his detailed analyses are written in response to our wish 'to understand as much of this as we can. We don't just want to hang on to the general sense as if we were watching an opera in Czech' (p. 7). Kermode draws out interesting points from a register of word frequency – the word 'become' and its derivatives, for example, or 'world'. This is not number-crunching but clever and sensitive use of statistics to reveal the skein of connections which give the play its particular character.*

Frank Kermode, '*Antony and Cleopatra*', in *Shakespeare's Language*. London: Penguin Press, 2000.

Perhaps we should not trouble ourselves too much about dates and the exact order of composition of Shakespeare's plays, but it is important that *Antony and Cleopatra*, usually dated towards the end of 1606, is very close in time to *King Lear, Macbeth*, and *Timon of Athens*, with *Coriolanus* soon to follow. The composition of these plays within a span of a couple of years is astonishing, and would be so even if one left *Timon* out of account. And perhaps we should also congratulate the anonymous but marvellous boy who played Lady Macbeth, Cleopatra, and possibly also Volumnia in *Coriolanus*.[1]

In theme, structure, and rhetoric *Antony and Cleopatra* is strikingly different from the others. It is a history play, but its principal source is Plutarch's *Life of Antonius*, treated with the same blend of fidelity and freedom we find in Shakespeare's rehandling of English historians. It treats of Roman history at its turning point, the time between the effective end of the republic and the establishment of empire. Its theme, therefore, is world history, and in its deliberate grandeur and political scope the play keeps us continually aware of the greatness of its subject. When Octavius prophesies that "The time of universal peace is near" (IV.vi.4), he may simply mean that the period during which the Roman world was divided between him and Antony was about to end; but his auditors would recall the familiar idea of the "Augustan peace," the years when providence ensured conditions favourable to the birth of Christ and the foundation of an empire that would ultimately become the Christian empire. Of course Octavius, later Augustus, had to win; otherwise the centre of empire would have been Alexandria, and the style of empire Oriental and pagan. The defeat of Antony and Cleopatra was as necessary as the silencing of the pagan oracles, the replacement of the Roman gods by Christ.

In that sense the victory of Octavius at Actium was held to change the world. The play continually reminds us of the tremendous historical alteration produced by the ending of the war between him and Antony. A. C. Bradley calls the play "the picture of a world catastrophe," and so it is. Friendship between the two leaders would be "a hoop" to hold them "staunch from edge to edge / A' th' world" (II.ii.115–16). Menas repeatedly tells Pompey during the drinking party that by an act of murder, by killing "These three world-sharers" (II.vii.70),[2] he can be "lord of the whole world" (61, 62, 65). Octavia remarks that war between her husband and brother would be "As if the world should cleave" (III.iv.31), and Antony at Actium loses "half the bulk o' th' world" (III.xi.64).

Shakespeare's use of a particular word or set of words to give undercurrents of sense to the dramatic narratives is, of course, a device used in later literature – it is a feature of E. M. Forster's novels and a trick also of Virginia Woolf's. Bernard, the writer in *The Waves*, says he is tired of stories and longs "for some little language such as lovers use, broken words, inarticulate words, like the shuffling of feet upon the pavement." The "little language" may be a muttered undersong to the main tune of the narrative, as it is in *Between the Acts* and sometimes in Shakespeare, or it may blare out like a trumpet entry.

An example of the quieter mode is the use, in *Antony and Cleopatra*, of the word "become" and its derivatives; they occur seventeen times in the play (as against three times in *Lear*, six times in *Macbeth*, four times in *Timon*, nine in *Coriolanus*; "became" is the sole occurrence in *Hamlet*). What is to be made of this? The first occurrence is in the ninth line of the play: "his captain's heart / . . . is become the bellows and the fan / To cool a gipsy's lust" (I.i.6–10). Antony, hearing of his wife's death, reflects that "The present pleasure, / By revolution low'ring, does become / The opposite of itself" (I.ii.124–26). Cleopatra taunts Antony: "Look . . . / How this Herculean Roman does become / The carriage of his chafe" (I.iii.83–84). "Since my becomings kill me when they do not / Eye well to you" (I.iii.96–97). "Good Enobarbus, 'tis a worthy deed, / And shall become you well . . . " (II.ii.1–2). "She makes hungry / Where most she satisfies; for vildest things / Become themselves in her"

(II.ii.236–38). "Near him, thy angel / Becomes a fear . . . " (II.iii.22–23). "Till I shall see you in your soldier's dress, / Which will become you both . . . " (II.iv.4–5). "Enjoy thy plainness, / It nothing ill becomes thee" (II.vi.78–79). "Observe how Antony becomes his flaw" (III.xii.34). "A good rebuke, / Which might have well becom'd the best of men, / To taunt at slackness" (III.vii.25–27). And so on.

Some of these occurrences would normally escape notice; "become" is a useful word not earnestly to be dwelt upon. Yet it has many senses, as the *OED* demonstrates. "What's become of Waring?" "The powers given us by Nature are little more than a power to become." "Nothing in his life / Became him like the leaving of it" (*Macbeth*, I.iv.7–8). "She will become thy bed" (*The Tempest*, III.ii.104). In *Antony and Cleopatra* the word is often used, as it were naturally, in these senses, but occasionally it has enough strain on it to make one pause. For example, Cleopatra's "my becomings kill me when they do not / Eye well to you" is a noun usage noted as "rare" by the *OED*, which cites only Shakespeare's Sonnet 150 ("Whence hast thou this becoming of things ill . . . ") as a second example. The strain on the noun is enhanced by the peculiar use of "Eye" as a verb to mean "appear under scrutiny." This is so out of the way that I think it fails to illustrate the sense it is cited to exemplify in the dictionary (I.5a), which offers nothing else very like it.

The strangeness of Cleopatra's remark arises from its remoteness from the plain sense of the sentiment. She has just explained that the change in their situation has so disconcerted her that she hardly knows what she is saying. The speaker in the sonnet is saying that his friend has the ability to make unworthy things seem pleasant. Cleopatra calls her demeanour in general her "becomings," which, like her speech, are out of order when Antony treats her coldly, as he has just done. But the train of the words is very Shakespearian; one often, in these later plays, has the choice of pondering or passing on. "Vildest things / Become themselves in her" is a little easier, but here "become" means rather more than it usually does in this kind of context: "make themselves becoming" or even "become becoming." There is no special difficulty in Antony's use of the word in I.ii.124, although the sentiment in which it figures is not expressed simply: in the turn of the wheel, pleasure, brought low, finds itself transformed into pain. "Thy angel / Becomes a fear" is very striking; the guardian angel becomes a shapeless, abstract menace, and the verb, with an initial stress, is very conspicuous.

"Becomes / becoming" is, then, identifiable as part of *Antony and Cleopatra*'s "little language," and even its commonplace occurrences reinforce this sense of a semantic subplot. It may nag gently at us, reminding us how much the play is concerned with "becoming": what becomes a Roman, in manners, including the manner of dying; what will become of the world when this contention is over and the entire history of Europe and Roman-Christian empire opens up. There is the question of what kind of behaviour "O'erflows the measure" (I.i.2) (like the Nile) – behaviour such as submission to a "gipsy," and endless Egyptian carousing. To stay within measure is to live as Antony once did, when he bore adversity "with patience more / Than savages could suffer" (I.iv.60–61). It is to conduct oneself with the habitual chilly reserve of Octavius, and that is becoming conduct, since it presages the morality and power of the world to come or, in the now obsolete expression, the becoming world.

The use of the word "world," however, is a different matter. The trumpets sound; attention is continually drawn to it. The same device, using "dog," is something of a failure in *Timon*, but here, with "world," it is a success because of its manifest relevance to the theme and ambitions of the play. It is sounded at once: Antony is "The triple pillar of the world transform'd / Into a strumpet's fool" (I.i.12–13). The antithetical relation between the two significant parts of the world, Rome and Egypt, is also put before us immediately, not only in Antony's negligent treatment of the messenger from Octavius but also in his language: "Let Rome in Tiber melt," he says, "Here is my space" (34–35). He chooses to be where Egypt melts into the fertilising Nile, and the point about the voluptuous flooding of Egypt is made vividly in later passages: "Melt Egypt into Nile! and kindly creatures / Turn all to serpents!" cries Cleopatra in her anger at the news that Antony has married Octavia (II.v.78–79). The Nile has serpents (Antony considers her one of them [I.v.25]), and "kindly creatures" is a contracted idea: creatures, each in its natural kind, should turn into snakes; the other sense of "kind" is also present.[3]

What will decide the fate of the world? The answers are multiple; there is the cowardice of Cleopatra at Actium; the weakness of Antony in fleeing with her; and "the luck of Caesar." The second scene of the play seems lighthearted but is serious in so far as it is about luck, the hope of good fortune. The word "fortune" recurs (14, 26, 33, 45, 63, 74)[4] and is related at once to the "o'erflowing Nile" (49–50). Antony's angel becomes a cloud; he loses to Caesar at cards and cockfighting. Fortune is leading him into "dotage" – a word pronounced in the first line of the play and taken up by Antony himself (117). This is a word now associated mostly with old age, but in Shakespeare it normally (though not in *Lear*) means "infatuation," as often in *A Midsummer Night's Dream*.

These brilliant opening scenes put all the cards on the table: Antony is still capable of a Roman thought: he would not dream of mistreating a messenger bringing unwelcome tidings (later he has one whipped, in Cleopatra's manner); and he is aware of his unbecoming conduct: "O then we bring forth weeds / When our quick winds lie still" (109–10). Here the very energy of the figure is Roman; it refers to labour, the labour of the plough; it is full of force, opposed to the relaxation of Egypt.

So the possession of the world is at risk; the politics of the piece is of universal import. The ribaldry of Enobarbus has to be stilled, and Sextus Pompeius has to be resisted. Octavius and Antony agree; Antony thinks of the fickle populace:

> Our slippery people,
> Whose love is never link'd to the deserver
> Till his deserts are past, begin to throw
> Pompey the Great and all his dignities
> Upon his son . . .
> . . .
> whose quality, going on,
> The sides o' th' world may danger.
> (I.ii.185–92)

One notes the freedom, the unconfined mental force of this, the conversational compression of "whose quality, going on," and the quick figure of a world with two sides – sides not in the competitive sense but in the physical, as when Leontes, in *The Winter's Tale*, says that he is like one who, having drunk, sees a spider in the cup, and "cracks his gorge, his sides, / With violent hefts" (II.i.44–45). And Octavius, also brooding on the news of Pompey's successes, is no less vigorous:

> It hath been taught us from the primal state
> That he which is was wish'd, until he were;
> And the ebb'd man, ne'er lov'd till ne'er worth love,
> Comes dear'd by being lack'd.
> (I.iv.41–44)[5]

The sentiment is the same, the imagery different, and even more energetic, with its mixed figures of tide and price. The marriage of Antony to Octavia is of course a political move. A Machiavellian sense of political reality tempers Antony's licence and is the entirety of Octavius's mentality; a lack of it causes Pompey to reject the advice of Menas to murder the triumvirs, an out-and-out Machiavellian prescription. When Ventidius declines to pursue the defeated Parthians, he tells us something new about the megalomaniac Antony: subordinates must not be threateningly famous. The temperaments, though not the ambitions, of the great men are very different, and Octavius's is the more Roman, but Antony's is Roman, too, with an Egyptian inclination. Hence the force of the comparison between them: a version of Virtue opposed to a version of Pleasure.

But these comparisons are not allowed to be simple. Dryden's version of the story of Antony and Cleopatra is called *All for Love, or The World Well Lost*.

Shakespeare offers Antony his choice, the choice made by his supposed ancestor and patron, Hercules, between Virtue on its hilltop and Pleasure, with hell's
bonfire at the end of the path. It is plain that Antony finally makes the wrong
choice, but it is clearly the business of the play also to complicate the issue by
making pleasure admirable as well as weakeningly seductive and, sometimes,
in the presentation, amusing. The characters of the lovers must be aggrandised.
Antony is "The demi-Atlas of this earth" (I.v.23) – Atlas, whom Hercules
relieved of his burden, the world – and Cleopatra, self-described as "A morsel
for a monarch" (I.v.31),[6] is allowed, in the extraordinary last act, all the poetic
excesses associated with the language of the East, the Asiatic as compared
with the Attic. She is to Octavia as Pleasure is to Virtue; she is Isis and Venus
(as in Enobarbus's famous passage about her barge (II.ii.206ff.), she "makes
hungry / Where most she satisfies" (II.ii.236–37)). Octavia's "beauty, wisdom,
modesty" (240) can offer no real competition; "I' th' East my pleasure lies"
(II.iii.41). Antony is Hercules to Cleopatra's Omphale; she dresses him as a
woman (II.v.22), in Roman eyes a gross effeminacy and so recognised by the
Renaissance poets (Spenser, for example), who signify the loss of manhood,
virtus, in the same way.

In the confrontations of Octavius and Antony the former occupies the
high moral ground. At Pompey's party Caesar doesn't get drunk; "Be a child
o' th' time," says Antony; "Possess it, I'll make answer," replies Octavius
(II.vii.100–1). The division between them soon declares itself. War between
them, with Octavia the ostensible occasion of it, will be "As if the world should
cleave" (III.iv.31); it will be ground between "a pair of chaps" (III.v.13). But
so it must be, and the noble characters grow, in their own ways, nobler.
Octavius becomes shrewder, and gets rid of Lepidus. Cleopatra appears in the
habiliments of Isis; Antony, though more proudly Herculean than ever, has
"given his empire / Up to a whore" (III.vi.66–67) but levied "The kings o' th'
earth for war" (68). There is an epic catalogue, lifted from Plutarch and not
without its irony, of many kings of the earth. Antony is "the Emperor"
(III.vii.20) – a term reserved for him throughout the play until the quiet,
scheming entry of Octavius in the last scene, when he is greeted by the title
only a moment after Cleopatra's ecstatic eulogy of Antony as a lord of
universal bounty, the true emperor.

Antony's defeat in the naval battle is called his "wounded chance" (III.x.35),
but luck comes into the matter only because Octavius has it all; it is against
his luck that Antony, under Cleopatra's influence, made so disastrous a bet. He
has "lost command" (III.xi.24). Now, he says, he must "dodge / And palter in
the shifts of lowness, who / With half the bulk o' th' world play'd as I pleased,
/ Making and marring fortunes" (III.xi.62–65). Yet one notes the *power* of this
complaint, the vigorous self-contempt of "dodge and palter," the compression

of "the shifts of lowness" (the mean tricks forced on those without power), and finally the recollection of the possession of power as a power to *play*, as if at cards. In such games, we have been told, he always lost to Caesar, who has now made his fortune and marred Antony's. Antony is left to defy fortune: "Fortune knows / We scorn her most when most she offers blows" (73–74).

But Octavius is now "Lord of his [Antony's] fortunes" (III.xii.11). In that brief scene of only thirty-six lines, "fortune" or "fortunes" occurs three times. In the next, when Cleopatra is answering Caesar's messenger Thidias, we hear again of "the universal landlord" Caesar's "fortunes," and Thidias offers advice that might have come direct from Machiavelli: "Wisdom and fortune combating together, / If that the former dare but what it can, / No chance may shake it" (III.xiii.79–81). As it happens, Thidias's own luck has run out, and Antony has him whipped; another indication that his "wisdom" has been depleted.

"Authority *melts* from me," he says (90), melting being another recurrent idea in this play – the Nile, and Antony's empire. He turns on Cleopatra, and the verse here is remarkable:

ANT.   Cold-hearted toward me?
CLEO.   Ah, dear, if I be so,
From my cold heart let heaven engender hail,
And poison it in the source, and the first stone
Drop in my neck; as it determines, so
Dissolve my life! The next Caesarion smite,
Till by degrees the memory of my womb,
Together with my brave Egyptians all,
By the discandying of this pelleted storm,
Lie graveless, till the flies and gnats of Nile
Have buried them for prey!
                                    (III.xiii.158–67)

Here she begins by taking up the accusation of a cold heart, imagines it as shedding poisoned hail which melts ("determines," meaning comes to an end, a remote way of saying "melts" or "dissolves," which is reserved for the next line). The destruction then becomes more general; her son – whose mention suggests "womb" and its "memory," preserved in her children – will "discandy"[7] or, once more, dissolve as the hailstones melt; finally the whole pride of Egypt will be consumed, no longer by the hail but by the insects of the Nile. Antony is pacified by this transcendental rant, and swears to be wildly courageous, though understanding that his "hours" are no longer "nice and lucky" (178–79). As for Octavius Caesar, he is "twenty times of better fortune" (IV.ii.3).

In IV.iii, one of those scenes used by Shakespeare that comment on rather than advance the action, like the Parthian scene (III.i), the soldiers on watch hear the ominous music that means Hercules is abandoning Antony. (In Plutarch the god is Bacchus; Shakespeare takes the moment to emphasise Antony's claim to protection from his ancestor god.) In twenty-one lines it does much, giving to the fate of Antony a quasi-mythological grandeur which henceforth infuses much of the verse. Enobarbus deserts: "O, my fortunes have / Corrupted honest men!" (IV.v.16–17). But the tones of imperial grandeur persist. Antony scores an inconclusive victory and greets Cleopatra as if she were more than human, calling her "this great fairy" (IV.viii.12), while she gives him the welcome due to a god:

> Lord of lords!
> O infinite virtue, com'st thou smiling from
> The world's great snare uncaught?
>
> (16–18)

The marvel is that in this play bombast, or what ought to be at best nickel silver, is somehow transmuted into fine gold. Given infinite virtue, unlimited manly power, Antony hardly deserves congratulations on managing, like an animal, to escape the hunter; there is a deliberate glory in the greeting, but it has a faintly ill-omened sound.

Fighting by sea again, with all the omens bad, "Antony / Is valiant, and dejected, and by starts / His fretted fortunes give him hope and fear / Of what he has, and has not" (IV.xii.6–9). This is absolutely typical of the mature Shakespeare, part of the run of his mind; it sounds like *Macbeth*. The point is made by the time we have heard "hope and fear," but Shakespeare ties another knot in the concluding line, as if to make sure the sense cannot be unbound; this trick gives the reader or listener work to do, relating "what he has" to "hope," and "what he has not" to "fear."

The final battle lost ("Fortune and Antony part here" (IV.xii.19)), Antony again turns on Cleopatra. Deserted by so many of his followers, he utters a very remarkable complaint:

> All come to this? The hearts
> That spannell'd[8] me at heels, to whom I gave
> Their wishes, do discandy, melt their sweets
> On blossoming Caesar; and this pine is bark'd,
> That overtopp'd them all.
>
> (20–24)

Here is a strange mixture of metaphors: hearts (of course a synecdoche for "men" or, ironically, "brave men" or "friends") that followed him like dogs now melt themselves, and also melt the sweets he has given them, slavering them over Caesar, represented as a tree in blossom compared with Antony, a taller tree but doomed to die by having had its bark stripped away, with a hint of the usual attention dogs give to trees. There are few passages even in this play that whirl so dizzily from one association to another. Antony heard Cleopatra's "discandying" speech, quoted above, and echoes it in this unrelated passage some time later. Melting is his fate, and it impregnates this complaint.

And so Antony himself melts. The intellectual energy of the verse is now probably more intense than anywhere else in Shakespeare, except possibly in *Coriolanus*, yet it is never completely wild. Antony asks Eros to consider shapes seen in clouds: "That which is now a horse, even with a thought / The rack dislimns, and makes it indistinct / As water is in water" (IV.xiv.9–11). "Rack" is drifting cloud; "dislimns" is an essential, irreplaceably apt new word (later uses are quotations of this one, as the *OED* notes); an artist "limns" and the cloud breaking up does the opposite for the horse. Antony is dislimned like the shapes in the cloud; he "cannot hold this visible shape" (14). He adds another complaint against fortune: he has been cheated at cards by the swindler Cleopatra and the lucky Caesar.

Antony's death calls forth verse of an exalted tone peculiar to this play. "The star is fall'n. / And time is at his period," say the guards (IV.xiv.106–7). Here the note of apocalypse differs from that sounded in *Lear* ("Is this the promis'd end? Or image of that horror?") because it suggests an enormous hyperbole – here the death of one godlike man, "the greatest prince o' th' world" (IV.xv.54), is the death of the entire world.

Octavian, however, remains to rule the world, for he is "the full-fortun'd Caesar" (IV.xv.24). But his luck doesn't quite hold out, for he is thwarted by Cleopatra. She utters her astonishing, almost triumphing lament:

> The crown o' th' earth doth melt. My lord!
> O, wither'd is the garland of the war,
> The soldier's pole is fall'n. Young boys and girls
> Are level now with men; the odds is gone,
> And there is nothing left remarkable
> Beneath the visiting moon.
>
> (IV.xv.63–68)

The grandeur of Antony entitles him to be called the crown of the earth, but again this crown *melts*; he adorned the war like a victor's wreath, but the wreath is withered. "Pole" is of grandly uncertain meaning: the pole star (the guard, over Antony's not quite dead body, says "The star is fall'n" (IV.xiv.106)), possibly the tent pole that upheld the soldier's world. Each of these figures elevates Antony from ordinary humanity: he is a melting crown, a withered garland suggesting a defeated hero; a heavenly guide or a prop. The rest of the passage says that with Antony all distinction of merit or achievement dies; children are equal to grown men, the unevenness that allows a man to be great, to be an emperor, is abolished. And the conclusion drops into an extra-ordinary simplicity ("nothing left remarkable"), qualified only by the strange redundancy of "visiting" – though Cleopatra, resolved on suicide, will also renounce "the fleeting moon" (V.ii.240) as the woman's "planet." What is altogether striking about the speech is that it conveys a kind of keening, quite unlike the formal expressions of mourning and lamentation found in the mouths of women in the earlier history plays; in place of rhetorical pattern one has a diversity of figure, that restless movement of intelligence that char-acterises the later verse of Shakespeare.

There is a contrast with Caesar's expressions of regret that follow shortly. He undercuts Cleopatra's extravagances by saying that the death of Antony should have been more portentous: "The round world / Should have shook lions into civil streets . . . The death of Antony / Is not a single doom, in the name lay / A moi'ty of the world" (V.i.15–19). His Antony was not the whole world, only half of it; his portents signify not universal collapse but a tempo-rary interference with the civic peace of Rome and his own imperial progress. The eulogy is formal, but always attentive to the importance of victorious Caesar: "we could not stall together / In the whole world . . . my mate in empire" (39–43). He breaks off his tribute at the call of business: "Hear me, good friends – / But I will tell you at some meeter season" (48–49). And he plans to lead Cleopatra in his triumph.

She, however, has seen how she must triumph over Caesar: "'Tis paltry to be Caesar; / Not being Fortune, he's but Fortune's knave, / A minister of her will" (V.ii.2–4). She has it in her power to do the deed "Which shackles accidents and bolts up change" (6) – a wonderfully vigorous line, imprisoning chance and forcing change into a cell like a despised convict. To Caesar's messenger she is crafty enough to say she is "his fortune's vassal" (28). Seized by Romans, she tells Dolabella her dream of the Emperor, the universal hero, the god. It has been suggested that the imagery derives from the Book of Revelation and from a mythographer's description of the god Jupiter.[9] This is plausible, and the passage is like the vision of a god or an angel:

> His face was as the heav'ns, and therein stuck
> A sun and moon, which kept their course, and lighted

The little O, th' earth.

. . .

His legs bestrid the ocean, his rear'd arm
Crested the world, his voice was propertied
As all the tuned spheres, and that to friends;
But when he meant to quail and shake the orb,
He was as rattling thunder. For his bounty,
There was no winter in't; an autumn[10] it was
That grew the more by reaping. His delights
Were dolphin-like, they show'd his back above
The element they liv'd in. In his livery
Walk'd crowns and crownets; realms and islands were
As plates dropp'd from his pocket.

(V.ii.79–92)

This colossal figure is credited with power over the world and then over the universe; his very voice expressed the harmony of the spheres, inaccessible to mortal ears. The rapid switch from the seasonal imagery to that of the dolphin leaping out of the sea is again typical of Shakespeare's late style – no laborious working out of the figures, instead a sort of impatience at the unexplored resources of language. Then another move, to kings and princes as servants wearing his livery, and finally a cosmic image of liberality, "realms and islands" carelessly dropped, like coins from his pocket. Cleopatra defends herself against Dolabella's gentle scepticism: this was not a mere dream; it is true that fancy or imagination produces in dreams stranger stuff than nature can contrive, but in this case we are talking about reality, about nature's masterpiece, something real and actual, not the mere shadows produced by dreaming.

With the entry of the new, actual Emperor, she reallocates the title she conferred on Antony: "Sole sir o' th' world," she calls him (120), for all the world is now his (134). The episode of Seleucus and the inventory reminds us that Cleopatra has not lost her cunning. She is trying to trick Caesar into believing that her withholding of much property signifies her intention to live; and he wants her for his triumph. Cleopatra wins this bout. Her last hours have the kind of splendour she attributed to Antony. It is at this point that her women, Charmian and Iras, catch the tone of royal magniloquence: "Finish, good lady, the bright day is done, / And we are for the dark" (193–94). She gets the asps from the Clown and is dressed as a queen, an "eastern star," "A lass unparallel'd" (308, 316); at last she can mock "The luck of Caesar" (286). Evidence of Shakespeare's eye for a wonderful line can be found in Plutarch, where the soldier, seeing Cleopatra dead, asks, "Is that well done, Charmian?" and she answers, "Very well . . . and meet for a Princess descended from the race of so many noble kings." "She said no more, but fell down dead . . ." This becomes:

> It is well done, and fitting for a princess
> Descended of so many royal kings.
> Ah, soldier!   *Charmian dies.*
>   (326–28)

All that was needed was the substitution of the apparently pleonastic "royal" for Plutarch's mere "noble." One needs to add the notion of beautiful excess to Coleridge's famous account of the style of this play, "happy valiancy." *Antony and Cleopatra* takes the world-sharers, exposes them as they are, both ruthless politicians and one a libertine, and with controlled hyperbole elevates them to a status so grand that only an exercise of linguistic genius could prevent their seeming inflated or absurd.

Notes

1   Andrew Gurr states that one boy continued to play women's parts till he was twenty-one, though others switched to male parts much earlier (*The Shakespearean Stage*, p. 95). Muriel Bradbrook is convinced that Cleopatra and Volumnia were played by a man (*Shakespeare: The Poet in his World* (1978), pp. 213–14).

2   Cf. "The senators alone of this great world" (II.vi.9).

3   In II.v.94–95, Cleopatra tells the messenger she would be happier if he were lying, "So half my Egypt were submerg'd and made / A cestern [lake, pond] for scal'd snakes!"

4   It is used forty-four times in the play; no other play has even half as many occurrences.

5   Note also the lines that follow: "This common body / Like to a vagabond flag upon the stream, / goes to and back, lackeying the varying tide, / To rot itself with motion" (44–47). This metaphor was too compactly apt to be forgotten; Antony says of Octavia as they part: "Her tongue will not obey her heart, nor can / Her heart inform her tongue – the swan's down feather, / That stands upon the swell at the full of tide, / And neither way inclines" (III.ii.47–50), the feather remaining constant as the tide changes, unlike the "flag" of Octavius's lines.

6   Later on Antony, in a rage, describes her as "a morsel, cold upon / Dead Caesar's trencher" (III.xiii.116–17), and Enobarbus calls her "his Egyptian dish" (II.vi.126). These words chime with the imagery of Egyptian banqueting and appetite generally. On a favourable view Cleopatra "makes hungry / Where most she satisfies," like an exquisite dinner; on another, she is what is left on the plate when great men have dined.

7   "Discandying" is an eighteenth-century emendation of the Folio's "discandering."
    It admirably joins the sequence "determines," "dissolve," and is soon to be
    significantly echoed in IV.xii.22. A stream could be called "candied" if ice
    formed on the surface, presumably from the use of "candy" to mean a coating of
    sugar.

8   The Folio reads "pannelled," and the eighteenth-century editor Hanmer emended
    this to "spanieled," which suits well with the idea of spaniels fawning and slaver-
    ing (see Caroline Spurgeon, *Shakespeare's Imagery and What It Tells Us* (1935), p.
    195). Moreover, "spanell" was an alternative spelling of "spaniel," and it is normal
    enough for Shakespeare to make a verb of a noun. However, Hilda Hulme argues
    that the word Shakespeare wrote was correctly rendered by F, and that "panel" or
    "pannel" means a prostitute, a sense that survives in some dialects; so the hearts
    follow Antony like whores (*Explorations in Shakespeare's Language*, pp. 102–8).
    This explanation is worth considering, but it forfeits the dog-candy connection,
    and recent editors have not accepted it.

9   The passage from the mythographer Cartari is quoted in *Antony and Cleopatra*,
    ed. John Wilders Arden edition, 1995, p. 281. Revelation 10:1–2: "And I saw
    another mighty angel come down from heaven, clothed with a cloud: and a
    rainbow was upon his head, and his face was as it were the sun and his feet as
    pillars of fire: And he had in his hand a little book, open: and he set his right foot
    upon the sea and his left foot on the earth."

10 F reads "Antony." The eighteenth-century emendation is generally accepted, but
    there are those who defend "Antony" – see Wilders, Arden edition, p. 305. These
    arguments seem forced, and I take "autumn" to be correct. So, in his text, does
    Wilders.

Imperfect Speakers

Malcolm Evans

Evans discusses the different kinds of language in Macbeth *and* Hamlet *as symptomatic of 'the crisis of the sign' and of 'the unified subject'. His chapter, from*
Signifying Nothing: Truth's True Contents in Shakespeare's Text, *exemplifies
linguistic criticism which sees a struggle for meaning as immanent in the very languages of a play, a site of fractured signs rather than of the symbolically unified 'well
wrought urn' of New Criticism. Evans' politically engaged criticism demonstrates
how close linguistic analysis can serve different methodological and ideological
purposes.*

Malcolm Evans, 'Imperfect Speakers', in *Signifying Nothing: Truth's True Contents in
Shakespeare's Text*, 2nd edn. London: Harvester Wheatsheaf, 1989.

Words, words, words! That will be my device as long as I have not been shown
that our languages echo a transcendent reality.

Jutes Laforgue, *Hamlet*

Unless I wish it, not a bird flies in this empire, not a leaf stirs on the trees.

Atahualpa to Pizarro

At the end of his first encounter with the "weyward sisters", Macbeth addresses
them as "imperfect Speakers' (I.iii. 170) and bids them to tell him more. On
the order "Speake, I charge you" (179), they disappear like bubbles into the
earth, leaving Macbeth and Banquo to doubt their own perceptions, and their
language. When Banquo asks if they have "eaten on the insane Root", he also
wonders about the reality of "such things . . . as we doe *speake* about" (185–6).
The tentative moves of Macbeth and Banquo to verbally grasp what has happened are like an old song, a nursery game which recalls the doggerel of the
sisters themselves:

> MACB.   Your Children shall be Kings
> BANQ.   You shall be King
> MACB.   And Thane of Cawdor too: wente it not so?
> BANQ.   To th' selfe-same tune, and words:
> (188–91)

When Rosse, at this point, enters to deliver his report, it is clear that 'imperfect speaking' is not a disorder exclusive to the sisters or to those who have
been in immediate contact with them:

> The King hath happily receiv'd, *Macbeth*,
> The newes of thy successe: and when he reades
> Thy personall Venture in the Rebels fight,
> His Wonders and his Prayses do contend,
> Which should be thine, or his: silenc'd with that,
> In viewing o're the rest o' th' selfe-same day,
> He findes thee in the stout Norweyan Rankes,
> Nothing afeard of what thy selfe didst make
> Strange Images of death, as thick as Tale
> Can post with post, and every one did beare
> Thy prayses in his Kingdomes great defence,
> And powr'd them downe before him.
> (193–204)

The perplexing density of Rosse's report releases imperfections of its own,
while repeating the haste and excitement of the messengers and narratives it

describes, which arrive headlong and inarticulate, "as thick as Tale / Can post on post", leaving Duncan amazed, silent, and finally awash in information. The thickening of Rosse's account is a contagion caught from these other reports or an indication, perhaps, of his own penchant for the "Relation too nice" (IV.iii. 2010) later criticized by Macduff. There is a call here for a performance which incorporates at once a lack and an excess of rhetorical preparation, and the information imparted reproduces this uneasy play of opposites. Verbal and syntactic ambiguities edge the heroic image of Macbeth from the good to the evil cause – "Thy personall venture in the Rebels fight", "He findes thee in the stout Norweyan Rankes". This shifting also applies to Duncan, drawn into the narrative to the extent of occupying its protagonist's position. "When he reades", the King becomes his subject, Macbeth, mirroring in the contention of "Which should be thine, or his" the usurpation that is imminent. The tale thickens further as Macbeth becomes not only protagonist but author, of "Strange Images of death", and reader, in place of the king, of Rosse's narrative about narratives.

Any attempt to relate the content of narratives in the early scenes of *Macbeth* has to negotiate a conflict between two basic linguistic modes which results in a potentially baffling opacity. On the one side is the attempt to construct an unequivocal idiom in which the theory of the divine right of kings and its place in the Great Chain of Being is made one with nature to the extent that the 'unnatural', constitutive operations of language itself are strenuously deleted. On the other there is an inescapable undertow of negation, in which the hurly-burly of language which precedes the construction of these sealed hierarchical categories leaks back to interrupt the 'natural' quality their linguistic mode silently claims for itself. In Rosse's speech the first mode, affirming a positive metaphysical 'order' which can somehow, magically, exist outside language and ideology, appears in the attempt to conjure up a grateful, generous king and his loyal, heroic subject. Its negation is the intractability of language, which intimates a more deeply rooted disorder than the one that has just been quelled, and a potentially unending circulation of subjects through hierarchical positions that only *seem* to be fixed and sovereign – of king and thane, of author, reader and protagonist.

The same 'thickening' of the tale and dispersal of clear ideological categories divides the language of the "bleeding Captaine" at the beginning of the play. The captain's report of the battle opens with a reference to the "choked Art" of spent swimmers who cling together for support and ends with the choking of his own voice and the cacophony of gashes that "cry for helpe" (I.ii. 63). The Arden editor argues that, under these circumstances, some incoherence might be expected (Muir, 1953, p. 8) but the form it takes is no different from that in Rosse's tale. First there is the intention of affirming an ideal of manhood and service validated by reference to natural hierarchies and centred on Banquo and Macbeth, whom the rebels can dismay no more than "Sparrowes, Eagles / Or the Hare the Lyon", (54–5). But the language of the narrative palters "in a double sence" no less than that of the play's central and most conscious "imperfect Speakers", the sisters, incorporating their characteristic blend of confusion and prophecy. The rebels, by the end of the speech, have been compared implicitly with the crucified Christ, and Macbeth and Banquo with his torturers (60–1). In the interim, the narrative production of a "brave *Macbeth* (well hee deserves that Name)" (35) has already been thrown into crisis, if not by a graphic excess in the description of 'legitimate' violence then at least by strategic ambiguities in the test. Seeking the rebel Macdonwald, Macbeth:

> Disdayning Fortune, with his brandisht steele,
> Which smoak'd with bloody execution
> (Like Valours Minion) carv'd out his passage,
> Till hee fac'd the Slave:
> Which nev'r shooke hands, nor bade farewell to him,
> Till he unseam'd him from the Nave to th' Chops,
> And fix'd his Head upon our Battlements.
>
> (36–42)

The clause "Which nev'r shooke hands . . . ", applying equally, and in different senses, to Fortune, Macbeth, or the Slave, disturbs the balance of a complex syntactic structure, which totters to the climactic image of an impaled rebellious head, Macdonwald's but also, proleptically, already that of Macbeth, his own worst enemy.

Such instances of disruption to the harmonious, univocal discourse of Tudor and Stuart absolutism proliferate in the early scenes of *Macbeth*. Rosse's first report to the king anticipates some of the instabilities of his language when he later addresses Macbeth and Banquo. Here another ambiguous 'Macbeth' faces the treacherous thane of Cawdor, a title soon to be his own, confronting him "with selfe-comparisons, / Point against Point, rebellious Arme 'gainst Arme" (I.ii. 80–1). Again too much, and too little, is stated with the result that the image of the defender of right merges into its opposite. Equivocation in these opening scenes is a condition of language, which moves constantly back from the articulated code to an anterior heterogeneity, melting, like the sisters after their encounter with Macbeth and Banquo, "as breath into the Winde" (I.iii. 183). Macbeth's first words in the play, "So foule and faire a day I have not seene" (I.iii. 137), establish his connection with the sisters before they have even met. But the motion of their "faire is foul, and foule is fair" (I.i. 12), which L. C. Knights described as a "metaphysical pitch-and-toss" (1946, p. 18), extends not only to those who become directly implicated in what the language of metaphysics would describe as 'evil'. Even Duncan, the perfect, saintly king of *Macbeth* criticism, unintentionally equivocates himself into complicity with his own downfall, confusion's masterpiece, when he acknowledges to his general, "More is thy due than more than all can pay" (I.iv. 304).

The crisis of the sign and unequivocal discourse in the play is paralleled by that of the unified subject. As Macbeth embarks on the passage from 'Glamis' to 'Cawdor' to 'King', the identity sustained in the hierarchical order is fractured. After the first meeting with the sisters, when the prospect of murder is still only "fantasticall", the thought still "Shakes so my single state of Man / That function is smother'd in surmise: (I.iii. 252–3). By finally daring to do more than "may become a man" (I.vii. 525), he ceases to be a coherent subject, either of Duncan or in the sense of an intact, self-present identity. *Macbeth*, as Catherine Belsey has pointed out, explores the relationship between crisis in the "state", or the social order, and disruption in the "single state" of the subject (1980, pp. 89–90). Once the structures of Duncan's kingdom are wrenched from their place in 'nature', Macbeth himself becomes a plurality, a process rather than a fixity. In the same movement the bonds between the state, the subject and the unequivocal linguistic mode of 'order' and 'nature', always suspended in 'imperfect speaking', are broken. Only the "weyward sisters" who inhabit the heath, outside the closures of the social formation, can properly perform "A deed without a name" (IV.i. 1579). But after Duncan's murder Macduff can speak of a "horror" which "Tongue nor Heart cannot conceive, nor name" (II.iii. 816–17), while Macbeth recognizes that "To know my deed, / 'Twere best not know my selfe" (II.i. 737–8). The semantic volatility of all the earlier narratives, the negative undertow which compromises the ordered, 'natural' discourse of ideology and its unified subjects, finally comes into its own in the "written troubles of the Braine" (V.iii. 2264) that emanate from Lady Macbeth between sleep and waking, madness and reason, and, most crucially, in Macbeth's description of life as "a Tale / Told by an Ideot, full of sound and fury / Signifying nothing" (V.v. 2347–9). The "nothing" signified is not merely an absence but a delirious plenitude of selves and meanings, always prior to, and in excess of, the self-naturalizing signs and subjects of the discourses it calls perpetually to account.

The Macbeths, with the sisters, spill over the limits of 'character' to constitute the text's 'nothing' which, in turn, constantly erodes and undermines the hierarchies of irreducible 'somethings' proposed by metaphysics. To define this space of 'nothing' quite simply as 'evil' is to reprocess the text through a moral discourse it renders problematic. Even in orthodox Christian doctrine, if 'nothing' is identifiable with sin or chaos it is also the ground of all creation,[1] and *Macbeth* also signifies nothing in this paradoxically positive sense. The unequivocal discourse of a metaphysically sanctioned absolutism, even when it succeeds in avoiding self-contradiction and the interpenetration of opposites is 'single' not only in the sense of 'unified' or 'unambiguous' but also in a second sense, exploited here as in other plays, of 'weak' or 'simple-minded'.[2] In the choric scene following the murder of Duncan, Rosse and the Old Man discuss the night which has "trifled former knowings" (II.iv. 928) in terms that permit these "former knowings" to reassert themselves with a vengeance.

The studied theatrical archaism of the scene sets off the credulous rhetoric of Rosse and the geriatric amazement of his interlocutor, who together reconstitute order in a reprise of the bloody Captain's bird and animal lore. The feudal norm is unequivocally reaffirmed in the outrage of Duncan's horses breaking from their stalls and proceeding to "eate each other", a fact the Old Man prefaces with the standard formula for this type of narrative, "'Tis said . . ." (945). The same system of 'natural' correspondences is at work in his image of a falcon, "by a Mowsing Owle hawkt at, and kill'd" (939), but the 'singleness' of this type of language always sits uneasily in the text. It marks the language of Duncan and Banquo when they first arrive at Macbeth's castle, hallowed in their minds by the presence of the birds who make each "Jutty frieze", "buttrice" and "Coigne of Vantage" the place for a "pendant bed, and procreant Cradle, / Where they must breed, and haunt" (I.vi. 439–42). There is clearly a hint here of the 'life-themes' discovered by G. Wilson Knight (1951, p. 125f.), but the situational ironies also tend to strip the rhetoric away from its experiential and 'natural' base, revealing that the birds at least, if not Banquo and Duncan, are a little naive in their literal adherence to the 'Elizabethen World Picture'. There is a similar element of bathos in Macduff's first reaction to the murder of his "pretty chickens, and their Damme" by the "Hell-Kite" Macbeth (IV.iii. 2066–7), particularly in the context of his desertion of his family. After his father's flight, in response to the question "How will you live?", the young Macduff replies "As Birds do, Mother" (IV.ii. 1747–8), an answer in which echoes of the Shakespearean fool mark a limit to the pretensions of one of the text's most insistent images of 'order' – 'Let them eat ideology'.

The choric exchange between Rosse and the Old Man ends, after the play's most sustained burst of 'singleness', with a benediction which is also a curse and which restores to the text its characteristic signification of 'nothing'. As he leaves, the Old Man bids "Gods benyson go with you, and with those / That would make good of bad, and Friends of Foes" (II.iv. 1978–9). His blessing applies equally to those who speak of falcons, owls, eagles and sparrows and to the proponents of "faire is foule, and foule is faire" who bring, from the viewpoint of the bird-watchers, a curse to Scotland. No one makes "good of bad" more forcefully than the Macbeths, who harness the ambiguities of language in the process. Lady Macbeth, for whom the 'single' is the inadequate, courts 'doubleness' in its various senses. In response to Duncan's pedantic greeting to "our honor'd Hostesse", she affirms:

> All our service
> In every point twice done, and then done double,
> Were poore, and single Businesse to contend
> Against those Honors deepe, and broad,
> Wherewith your Majestie loades our house
>   (I.vi. 449–53)

The 'Honors' here connote titles already bestowed on Macbeth, the royal presence which now graces his castle, and the sinister opportunities for further advancement that presence affords. The service done 'double' implies not only the obvious numerical sense but also the involvement of 'strength' and 'duplicity'. Making good out of bad is, at one level, a definition of this type of hypocritical show, in which the sense directed to the naive 'single' hearer is enriched by the speaker's recognition of true intentions. In the case of Macbeth, his "single state" broken open, one utterance may disclose different levels of duplicity and delusion in the process of the same subject. When Duncan's murder is revealed, he announces:

> Had I but dy'd an houre before this chance,
> I had liv'd a blessed time: for from this instant,
> There's nothing serious in Mortalitie:
> All is but Toyes:
>   (II.iii. 852–5)

While the regicide conceals his crime beneath an extravagant show of 'single' piety, unknown to him the Macbeth of "Tomorrow, and tomorrow, and tomorrow" is already, by indirection, speaking an unequivocal truth.

In summary, the density of the narratives that accumulate in the early scenes of *Macbeth* is produced by a conflict between two linguistic modes. The first, which attempts to suppress the constitutive role of language, is the 'single', unequivocal identification of the ideology of divine right with nature. It pertains, in its own terms, to the 'good characters' of the play and the birds. The second, most fully itself in the language of the sisters and the protagonists, is evident elsewhere whenever 'imperfect speaking' cuts into the first mode and restores to it a discordant element of linguistic materiality and heterogeneity. The two modes proceed side by side until the end of the play, never fully resolving themselves into a unity. When Malcolm finally assumes power, the restoration of 'single' discourse is announced in his description of the Macbeths as "this dead Butcher, and his Fiend-like Queene' (V.vii. 2522), the most reductive and parsimonious of all possible definitions, the mark of a speaker whose sole foray into equivocation, in the testing of Macduff in Act 4, Scene 3, lacks altogether the Vice's theatrical panache inherited by his antagonist. In contrast to Macbeth's, his discourse 'knows' and 'sees' very little or, to put it another way, does not know 'nothing'. Malcolm's "single state" is ripe for an encounter with the sisters.[3]

There is an influential strand in *Macbeth* criticism, one particularly suited in the recent past to the practical exegetical requirements of students, which works with the text's unequivocal mode to deliver a clear account of it as a "morality play" (Farnham, 1950, p. 79), a "vision of evil" (Knight, 1949, pl. 40), a "statement of evil" (Knights, 1946, p. 18), or "the story of a noble and valiant man who is brought to his damnation, presented in such a way as to arouse our pity and terror" (Muir, 1953, p. lv). The pandemic 'pitch-and-toss' and 'imperfect speaking' which unseat metaphysics in the play clearly fail to reach out to the critical discourse which can so casually refurbish "morality", "evil" and "damnation". At heart this is still the 'Shakespeare' of the Reverend Sims, embellished with images, themes, characters and a story but directed to the statement of a central, transcendent 'truth' in the text. These secondary narratives, which purport to help the text along in delivering its essential meanings, do so by privileging, at their most fundamental level, its 'single' mode and ignoring, or banishing to the realms of 'evil' or 'exquisite complexity', the 'unnatural' operations of language that divide and 'thicken' narrative in the play itself, which is ultimately no more an affirmation of metaphysical unity and order than a contradictory "Tale / Told by an Ideot, full of sound and fury / Signifying nothing".

Antonin Artaud regarded Shakespeare as the source of 400 years of dramatic "falsehood and illusion", of a "purely descriptive and narrative theatre – storytelling psychology" in which the stage is kept separate from the audience, and administers to its public the dominant cultural and ideological forms (Artaud, 1958, p. 76). This may be true of the 'single' *Macbeth* sustained by much modern criticism and theatrical production but not of the other play which, by fissuring the 'natural' subjects and signs that exist for and in ideology, achieves precisely what Artaud denies a 'Shakespeare' who leaves his audience intact "without setting off one image that will shake the organism to its foundations and leave an ineffaceable scar" (Artaud, 1958, pp. 76–7). But this latter play has much to contend with, quite apart from the critical assumptions that transform ideology into 'human values' and recover from the Shakespearean text, however complex, their suitably harmonious vehicle. A normative criticism will always affirm unity by marginalizing texts, or parts of texts, where 'Shakespeare' is nodding or not speaking perfectly. The Newbolt Report advised teachers to avoid passages which were not "verbally inspired"; for example, "the tediously protracted dialogue" between Malcolm and Macduff in Act 4, Scene 3, of *Macbeth* (Newbolt, p. 314) – a point where the 'singleness' of text and criticism is most at risk. Where pedagogic or discursive exclusion is impossible, another available strategy is the theoretical splits, guaranteed to unseam any commentator from nave to chops. So Kenneth Muir wishes away the contradictory thickening of the bloody Captain's tale by combining naturalism – the wounded man is exhausted and therefore incoherent – with an extreme of conventional formalism in which the character "utters bombastic language, not because he is himself bombastic, but because such language was considered appropriate to epic narration" (Muir, 1953, pp. li, 88). Fair is foul and foul is fair, and in the last instance the text can be recovered from its own imperfect speaking by forms of rewriting and incrustation not dreamed of even in Macherey's philosophy. In nearly all modern editions, Rosse's description of the messages that reach Duncan "as thick as Tale / Can post with post" – words "well within the normal language patterns of this time" (Hulme, 1962, p. 25) – has been excised. Rosse now delivers lines written by Nicholas Rowe in 1709, in which reports "As thick as *hail, / Came* post with post". And what could be more natural?

Wild and Hurling Words

Narratives in *Macbeth* select and organize their detail for specific purposes in the present. The report not only tells or conceals what has taken place, but does so in a way that confirms the relations of a social order into which it is itself inserted as a gift, a form of exchange, or an act of fealty. The narrative constitutes subject positions for a narrator and a receiver, and there are no 'facts', only interpretations conditioned by context. Thus Rosse's report to Duncan of the battle against the rebels and then his account, delivered to Macbeth and Banquo, of the king's reactions to this and other reports are at once confirmations of the proper relations of monarch and loyal subject, and acts of duty or homage. The disruption of a narrative also dislodges the subject-positions it proposes. Through the accounts of Macbeth's victory, Duncan is able in a sense to be present in battle – "In viewing o're the rest o' th' selfe-same day, / He findes thee in the stout Norweyan Rankes" – but their mode of arrival and delivery, both "as thick as Tale", leave him in some consternation. In this confusion Duncan, the only king in Shakespeare apart from the weak Henry VI who sends his forces into battle without being at their head, can only find himself in Macbeth and, in the contention of praise and wonder, experience the uncertainty of "Which should be thine, or his". Duncan, "when he reades", is divided from himself. In another reversal of positions, common in these early scenes, it is really Scotland's, not Norway's, king who finally "craves *composition*" (I.i. 86), an *ordering* and *making whole* that apply equally to the discourse and the subject.

In *Hamlet*, too, narrative is in this sense a form of 'composition' and exchange. Improbably, and in contrast to the story-tellers in Macbeth, one of the most cogent narrators in Shakespeare is Ophelia. The account of Hamlet's assault on her is a rhetorical *tour de force*:

> My Lord, as I was sowing in my Chamber,
> Lord *Hamlet* with his doublet all unbrac'd
> No hat upon his head, his stockings foul'd,
> Ungartred and downe gived to his Anckle,
> Pale as his shirt, his knees knocking each other,
> And with a looke so pitious in purport,
> As if he had been loosed out of hell,
> To speake of horrors: he comes before me.
>
> (II.i. 937–80)

The hearer, Polonius, is arrested by the image of closeted domesticity, the shocking intrusion of disorganized costume, the display of maidenly compassion, and the climactic switch of narrative tense. He is able to muster only open-mouthed, monosyllabic reactions – "Mad for thy Love?" (981), "What said he?" (983) – that propel Ophelia's description of a Hamlet in "the very extasie of Love" (999) forward to its next phase. There is no related dramatic action to verify this narrative, and the answer to Hamlet's question in the nunnery scene, "Are you honest?" (1758)[4] remains something of an enigma throughout the play. But the subject-positions the report creates for speaker and hearer, or its composition of Ophelia and Polonius, are clear. Ophelia registers the reactions of the "greene Girle" (I.iii. 567) Polonius has told her she is during their first exchange in the play, when he advises her "thinke your selfe a Baby" (571) and warns her "You do not understand your selfe so cleerely, / As it behoves my Daughter" (562–3). More firmly placed in the position of 'daughter', Ophelia has now reversed the pattern that holds in the earlier encounter, when all of the passive reaction-shots are hers – "I do not know, my Lord, what I should thinke", "I shall obey my Lord" (I.iii. 570, 602) – but only in the interest of placing Polonius more securely, and unequivocally, in the position of 'father'.

Ophelia's narrative puts back in place the family relations thrown into a mild crisis in Act 1, Scene 3, by the anxieties of Polonius and Laertes about the possibility of her opening her "chast Treasure" to Hamlet's "unmastered importunity" (494–5). An act of obeisance in this context, it is also a gift which Polonius will put to work in the larger network of relations that constitute the state. The image of a Hamlet mad for love will do much to explain the prince's "antic disposition" and to recompose Claudius and Gertrude. It will also confirm the status, and usefulness, of Polonius as Councillor of State, a role he pursues with fastidious and sycophantic single-mindedness. As Hamlet eventually points out to the corpse he drags from behind the arras in Gertrude's chamber, "Thou find'st to be too busie, is some danger" (2415) and as soon as he has received Ophelia's report, Polonius is characteristically busy relaying it to his betters. But what Ophelia accomplishes with consummate skill and economy in twenty-two lines takes her father, with his sententious circumlo-cution, the better part of a scene:

> My Liege, and Madam, to expostulate
> What Majestie should be, what Dutie is,
> Why day is day; night, night; and time time is time,
> Were nothing but to waste Night, Day and Time,
> Therefore, since Brevitie is the Soule of Wit,
> And tediousnesse, the limbes and outward flourishes,
> I will be breefe. Your Noble Sonne is mad:
> Mad call I it; for to define true Madnesse,
> What is't, but to be nothing else but mad.
>
> > (II.ii. 1113–21)

By making so explicit the subject positions and relations that Ophelia incor-porates into the substance of her narrative, Polonius thickens the tale beyond the patience of his hearers. Gertrude immediately cries out "More matter, with less Art" (1123). But this 'art', for Polonius, is what reaffirms his position as councillor, father, bearer of the sententious wisdom of age. Some ninety lines after initiating his report he emphasizes these guarantees of his identity in his prologue to the empirical proof of Hamlet's madness, to be staged for Claudius in the nunnery scene:

> Be you and I behinde an Arras then,
> Marke the encounter: If he love her not,
> And be not from his reason falne thereon;
> Let me be no Assistant for a State,
> And keepe a Farme and Carters.
>
> > (1197–201)

These compositions of the 'truth' behind Hamlet's show of madness trace the network that binds family and state in language, the "instrument of society" which is not so much for the use of its members as the very means by which they are constructed as subjects. This network, and its corruption in Denmark, is made graphically present in the play's most crucial narrative, the Ghost's account of poison poured in through the ear to course through the smooth body of the monarch and his state, leaving it covered with a "vile and loath-some crust" (I.iii. 757). By this act, and doubly in its concealment, "the whole eare of Denmarke" is "rankly abus'd". (723–4). The poisoned ear, as Terence Hawkes has shown, is an image central to a pervasive corruption of the channels of communication in Denmark.[5] Normal patterns of speaking and listening are displaced by Claudius's "most painted words" (II.ii. 1705), by the courtly obfuscations of Polonius and Osric, and by the pattern of strategic concealment, spying and overhearing Polonius calls "the traile of Policie" (II.ii. 1071). In this context, even before the revelations of the Ghost, Hamlet is compelled to suffer in silence – "breake my hearte, for I must hold my tongue" (I.ii. 342). Horatio is distinguished less by what he knows ("There are more things in Heaven and Earth", *etc.*) than by the very fact that Hamlet can talk to him. There is no one else.

The central image of corruption, and the network that radiates from it, make the operations of a self-naturalizing discourse much more obvious in *Hamlet* than in *Macbeth*. The hierarchy of subject positions confirmed by the narratives of Ophelia and Polonius shapes both Claudius's attempt to piece back together an unequivocal order he himself has broken open and Gertrude's desire to reconcile Hamlet to his father's death through the 'single', and ostensibly natural, truth of proverbial wisdom. But again 'single' discourse is compromised by the heterogeneous mode which refuses to delete the constitutive materiality of language, and which unravels all composition. This second mode is in evidence in the 'art' of Polonius's narrative, where the information to which all such messages are directed is blocked by an inept, and insistent, manifesting of the latent structures they keep in place. There is a revealing contradiction even in the cogency of Ophelia's description of a distracted Hamlet. Here, as in her earlier exchange with Laertes, a gap opens between the position of "baby" or "green girl" that her discourse constructs for the speaker and on the other hand, that discourse's inescapable rhetorical finesse.[6] The 'character' is a process in excess of the subject constituted in the family and the larger hierarchical scheme. Even in sanity she is already "Poore *Ophelia* / Divided from her selfe" (2821–2), whose "speech is nothing" (2752) in that it says more than can ever be crammed into the position made available to her by her father, brother and king. But the 'single' mode is least stable, and most open to the deconstructive interventions of Hamlet, in the language of Claudius and Gertrude. When Claudius addresses "our sometimes Sister, now our Queen" (I.ii. 186) and "my Cosin *Hamlet*, and my Sonne" (244), the glib attempt to reconstitute 'order' by glossing over the very differences by which order is constituted becomes easy prey for Hamlet's riddling wordplay about being "too much i' th' Sun" (247), with the king "A little more than kin, and lesse then kinde" (245). Gertrude opens herself to a similar attack when she advises Hamlet not to think about his dead father: "Thou know'st 'tis common, all that lives must dye, / Passing through Nature, to Eternity" (252–3). Hamlet's response, "Madam, it is common" (254), confronts the single with the double, one mode of language with another, the unequivocal statement with its dispersal in a pun.

This ambiguity, and resistance of the 'single', is the keynote of Hamlet's language in a play which contains more quibbles than any of Shakespeare's tragedies (Mahood, 1957, p. 112). After his conversation with the Ghost, the prince begins to reveal what he has heard to his friends but diverts his account into a sequence of enigmas and broken proverbs that Horatio describes as "wild and hurling words" (I.iii. 825). After the assumption of an "antic disposition", Hamlet's language becomes a vortext for all unequivocal discourse and the subject-positions it proposes, drawing them in and throwing them out again in fragments. At the heart of this disintegrative process are the "Unckle Father, and Aunt Mother" (II.ii. 1422–3) to whom he returns time and again. Before departing for England, Hamlet bids Claudius "Farewell deere Mother" and, in response to the baffled reaction, explains: "Father and Mother is man and wife: man & wife in one flesh, and so my mother" (2713–17). In the context of a language already corrupt, Hamlet assumes a negating, complicating function comparable to that of the Fool in other plays, a part described by Feste in *Twelfth Night* as the "corrupter of words" (III.i. 1248). The corrupt language of those in power is at once burlesqued and resisted. Like the 'nothing' of *Macbeth*, Hamlet's 'imperfect speaking' is, as Ophelia points out, "naught" (2014), but its strategic hurly-burly points to the finite, fictive quality of all discursive constructions. Even "the King", as Hamlet points out to Guildenstern, is "a thing . . . Of nothing" (2257–9).

What Laertes says of Ophelia's language in madness, "This nothings more than matter" (2926), is equally true of Hamlet's. The two fundamental linguistic modes, of 'matter' and 'nothing', come into direct open conflict when Claudius initiates what should be a polite, ritual exchange with the question "How fares our Cosin *Hamlet*?" (1948). Hamlet takes "fares" in its unintended sense of 'eats', and his reply leaves Claudius, the commentators, and possibly left the Globe audience dumbfounded with too much and too little meaning: "Excellent Ifaith, of the Camelions dish: I eate the Ayre promise-cramm'd, you cannot feed Capons so" (1949–50). In the best edition of the play to date, Harold Jenkins suggests that there may be an allusion here to Hamlet's unfulfilled hopes for Claudius's support in the succession, with a possible pun on 'Ayre' / 'heir' designed to throw the king off the trail of the true cause of his melancholy. An embedded Elizabethan proverb about love, like the chameleon, being able to feed on air may also bring in Ophelia and her part in Hamlet's feigned madness (Jenkins, 1982, p. 293). The reference to the 'cramming' of the capon could imply that Claudius's polite concern is merely a way of fattening Hamlet up for impending slaughter. But the main impact, as Claudius recognizes, is again that of "wild and hurling words" which, in effect, make up a language different from his own: "I have nothing with this answer *Hamlet*, these words are not mine" (1951–2). Hamlet's reply, "No, nor mine" (1953) is a further refinement and elaboration of the productive "nothing" which is set against the discourse of the king. In one sense it is a confirmation of 'single' language, reproducing the proverb which states that words, once spoken, no longer belong to the speaker (Jenkins, 1982, p. 293). But the words are also not Hamlet's in that this linguistic mode of 'nothing' declines to produce unequivocal meanings for, or from, unified subjects. Because Claudius resists this as not his language, the words also fail to take their subversive toll. In addition to being the adjectival pronoun, "mine" is also the verb 'to undermine',[7] which is the design of Hamlet's 'nothing' on Claudius's ideological closures.

Language in Denmark is like the "vile and loathsome crust" that covers the body of the dead king poisoned through the ear. Hamlet's compounding of corruption, in his role as traditional "corrupter of words", adds to the density of language. Set against the initial corruption, there is a norm of clear speaking, disclosure and reciprocation, of language as an instrument of society in the ideal sense. This is implicit in the order of Old Hamlet. It reappears momentarily in Hamlet's conversations with Horatio, Claudius's private recognition of guilt, and Gertrude's vow of secrecy in the closet scene, where she swears "if words be made of breath, / And breath of life: I have no life to breath / What thou hast said to me" (2573–5).

But the incrustations of language finally overwhelm both "the converse of breath" and any notion of a free subject or a metaphysical certainty it might propose. The voice of metaphysical truth in the play, the Ghost, is itself deeply compromised. The injunction to revenge and its prospect of damnation, coupled with the Protestant view of purgatory as a popish invention, keeps open the possibility that this "Apparition" (I.i. 37) or "Illusion" (127) is a "Goblin damn'd" (I.ii. 624) which, like the sisters in *Macbeth*, tells us truths only to "betray's in deepest consequence" (I.iii. 237).[8] Even if the prince is right in naming the Ghost – "I'le call thee *Hamlet*" (629) – its demands are marked by the dead king's own lack of perception. If its supplementary injunction, "nor let thy Soule contrive / Against thy Mother ought", poses certain difficulties, the stipulation "Taint not thy mind" is, under the circumstances, preposterous (770–1). The fusty Senecan air that clings to this figure is strongest in the closet scene, where the Ghost enters "in his night gowne",[9] appropriately cued in by Hamlet's "A vice of Kings" and "A King of shreds and patches" (2483) to take his place in a disengaging family snapshot. Indeterminacies of language extend from the mortal contortions of the signifier to the transcendental signified from beyond the grave, one whose only ultimate guarantee to the text is to seal it off as the site of an imperfect speaking to which neither Hamlet's language nor any other can offer a solution.

Maimed Rites / Signifying Nothing

In his seminar on *Hamlet*, Jacques Lacan observed that in all instances of death and mourning in the play the appropriate ritual is cut short or omitted (Lacan, 1977b, pp. 40–3). Old Hamlet dies without confession or absolution, Gertrude's mourning is interrupted by her remarriage, Claudius buries Polonius "in hugger mugger" in fear of the suspicions of "the people muddied, / Thicke and unwholesome in their thoughts, and whispers" (2818–19) and the corpse of Ophelia is attended only by the "maimed rites" (1.3408) appropriate to a possible suicide. This breaking of customary forms in *Hamlet* is not, however, exclusive to death and mourning. "Maimed rites" are in evidence everywhere as the correlative of an incrusting and deformation in language, another dimension of what is rotten in the state of Denmark. The curtailment of Gertrude's mourning after a month is also the disruption of her wedding rites, conducted "with Dirge in Marriage" (I.ii. 190), "the Funerall Bakt-meats" coldly furnishing the table of festivity (369). Claudius's attempt to pray is another abortive rite, his thoughts remaining below to free another "rapsidie of words" (2431) into the text's 'nothing'. The play begins with what in the theatre must have seemed for a moment to be an actor's error – a changing of the guard in which Barnardo calls the challenge and Francisco, the sentinel on duty, has to insist "Nay answer *me*" (I.i. 5). It ends with the duel, a noble test of skill with blunted rapiers which, in the event, leaves the stage littered with the bodies of all surviving members of the two main families. At the centre of *Hamlet* is another "maimed rite", the dramatic performance that ends abruptly when "The King rises" (2136).

In the final words of the play, the new social order headed by Fortinbras is announced with the promise of a completed ritual at last, the bearing of Hamlet "like a Soldier to the Stage" accompanied by "the Souldiours Musicke, and the rites of Warre" (3896–900). The 'stage' in question is a platform on the larger stage of the Globe. But the fact that Hamlet, at the end of the play, will be borne not *from* but *to* a stage is itself appropriate. Apart from the arrival of Fortinbras, the other key factor at the end is the survival of Horatio in the role of guardian of the narrative. His task, repeated by Hamlet at the point of death, is to "report me and my causes right / To the unsatisfied" (3823–4) and "in this harsh world" to "draw thy breath in paine. / To tell my Storie" (3834–5). So Fortinbras's final words, which herald the first completed rite in the play, also complete *Hamlet*, in contrast to the 'maimed' play-within-the-play, as a 'rite' of Jacobean society. The rite of *Hamlet* begins just after it ends, with the eventual relaying of Horatio's story to actors – described by Hamlet himself as 'the Abstracts and breefe Chronicles of the time" (II.ii. 1565) – who will tell the prince's story and report his cause right, with all the contradictory 'nothings' that suspend unequivocal narrative, in "The Tragedie of Hamlet, Prince of Denmarke".

Hamlet ends, and begins again, with its tail in its mouth. Narrative time and mimetic action become aspects of a 'single' dramatic discourse, embedded in and mediated by an acknowledgment of the ritual exchange in the theatre and the subject positions it constructs. The meeting of a 'natural', ideologically complicit mode with the material heterogeneity of 'nothing' on the level of language is repeated in a semiotics of dramatic performance. The mimetic content of the 'fable' *is* the forms that mobilize it, *Hamlet* being as much 'about' its own linguistic and theatrical signifiers as anything else. In the text, Saussure's analogy of the signifier and signified as different but indivisible, like the opposite sides of a sheet of paper, is extended into a Möbius strip in which end and beginning, 'inside' and 'outside' are not finally distinguishable.

"Remember thee?" says Hamlet after the account of his father's murder, "I, thou poore Ghost, while memory holds a seate / In this distracted Globe" (I.iii. 780–2). While there is memory in the world, or in the 'globe' of Hamlet's own skull, this narrative will not be forgotten. At the same moment, Richard Burbage scans the "distracted" faces around him in the Globe Theatre and, breaking the illusion only in the 'doubleness' of language and of his own divided presence as actor and protagonist, marks at once a key item in the advance of the narrative of *Hamlet* and the relationship of stage and audience within which it is articulated.

When the players arrive at Elsinore in Act 2, the audience is again reminded of the social transaction involved, and of the building in which its individual members stand or sit. The text's allusion to a 'war of the theatres', and the threat posed to the livelihood of adult actors by the popularity of boys' companies, makes the action of *Hamlet* momentarily contemporary with its performances in the first decade of the seventeenth century. "Do the Boyes carry it away?" asks Hamlet, to which Rosencrantz replies "I that they do, *Hercules* & his load too" (II. ii. 1407–8). The Globe itself, borne by Hercules, survives only because the prosperity of the text, as Rosaline reminds Berowne in *Love's Labour's Lost*, lies in the ear of the hearer. At the end of the play, before Fortinbras's men bear Hamlet "to the Stage", the audience is again in the action. Hamlet's dying words extend once more from those assembled on stage to the whole 'distracted Globe':

> You that looke pale, and tremble at this chance,
> That are but Mutes or audience to this acte:
> Had I but time (as this fell Sergeant Death
> Is strick'd in his Arrest) oh I could tell you.
> But let it be.

> (3818–22)

Horatio resists his suicidal desire to play the "Antike Roman" (3826) with its play on 'antic' – 'antique', 'theatrical', 'burlesque' – only in order to comply with Hamlet's last request, recapitulated in another allusion to the production in progress:

> Give order that these bodies
> High on a stage be placed to the view,
> And let me speake to th' yet unknowing world,
> How these things came about.
>
> (3873–7)

It is by now a commonplace of *Hamlet* criticism that the play is shot through with references, explicit and oblique, to plays and acting. Words like "act", "pro- logue", "theme", "antic", "play", "audience" and "stage" recur in the text in double senses, while "seems" always implies at once deception and display.[10] During 'The murder of Gonzago', the audience watches an audience watching a play, in a characteristic moment of thickening, and disclosure, of the materials and signifiers of drama. By continually accepting its own illusion, and alluding to the contract between stage and audience within which it is put to work, the per- formance becomes a form of true, unconcealed seeming which purges the false. Although this self-reflexive theatrical rite is 'maimed' in the interrupted per- formance of 'The Murder of Gonzago', its completion with the conclusion of *Hamlet* itself, as a rite of Jacobean society, signals again the triumph of an idealized reciprocal exchange between actors and audience in the theatre – the exchange which acts as a foil and a normative frame for the corruption of lan- guage and acting at Elsinore. The illusion *per se* (action, narrative), stripped of these reflexive elements, offers an unresolved confusion, a dark Saturnalia. But into this irredeemably corrupt world of the represented Elsinore comes a stabi- lizing factor – the very conditions of its representation as theatrical illusion (actors, the stage, performance), woven into the 'doubleness' of the play's lan- guage and periodically incorporated in much more explicit ways, through the play within the play, for example, or the references to the Globe itself and the war of theatres. The 'corruption' and 'nothing' that characterize language at Elsinore on the level of plot or the play's represented 'world', carry their own positive value in the larger context of the rite. They constitute a space of excess and, in a double sense, 'play' in the subject and the signifier – a mode of speech and performance which dislodges the unified characters and signs of mimesis and also of the unknowing and undisclosed theatricals that take place in the world outside the theatre. Before the ever-receding horizon of the real, the 'natural' subjects and signs of everyday life as reconstituted in the text of *Hamlet* shimmer like mirages, or like actors on a stage who half pretend to be people whose conversation strays incessantly to the problem of acting.

Macbeth too projects the mediations of 'doubleness' and 'nothing' from language to the theatre. Here again numerous theatrical references emerge on the "bloody Stage" (II.iv. 930) of Scotland in the course of the play,[11] culminating in Macbeth's speech on 'signifying nothing', which moves from an image of the actor who speaks to its final delirium:

> Out, out, breefe Candle,
> Life's but a walking Shadow, a poore Player,
> That struts and frets his houre upon the Stage,
> And then is heard no more. It is a tale
> Told by an Ideot, full of sound and fury
> Signifying nothing.
>
> (V.v. 2344–9)

On the 'single' level of plot and character this may be read as a statement of despair or, giving more credit to the protagonist, a moment of self-awareness when, in the very act of confronting such darkness, "personal life announces its virtue, and superbly *signifies itself*".[12] For those who follow Nietzsche in believing that such basically 'moral' readings dwarf Shakespeare's imaginative concept, this speech becomes a central statement of the meaningless of life, the metaphysical coin's existential obverse, which depicts a Macbeth transported, complete with garbage-can, from the Left Bank to the South Bank.[13] At the limit of such 'single' interpretation, aimed at decoding the 'spirit' of the text and its characters, V. Y. Kantak argues that Macbeth, in this "last moment of deep sentience", reaches for the poor player as "a fitting symbol of what he has become", a fact which "expresses character" in that the image reflects the protagonist's "poetic power" and "radiant self-knowledge" (Kantak, 1963, pp. 51–2).

What this analysis obscures, as it strains to hold on to the category of character, is the 'double' quality of the theatrical signifier itself and the fact that the actor is not just what Macbeth has become but what he has been all along. In this, and other accounts of the speech that are geared to an unproblematic notion of representation, certain key constituents of 'life', transcendentally signified and beyond the play of signs, are recovered from language which, in fact, unravels any such absolute referent of mimesis. Here, as in Jaques's "All the world's a stage" speech in *As You Like It*, a medieval commonplace about the futility of life – the world is *merely* a play, men and women *merely* actors – is transformed by the fact that it is spoken from the stage by an actor. The actor who speaks, or at least the actor he acts – Macbeth dwarfed by the "borrowed Robes" of kingship – *is* the poor player whose mediations block any smooth passage to what is being represented and, like the mad language of the "Ideot", foregrounds the irreducible materials of signification in signifying nothing.

The stage, then, can in no way be simply the means for expressing this commonplace. In this context it negates itself. 'Shadows' cast no light except in a ritual where language is no longer permitted to function 'naturally', where "Faire is foule, and foule is faire" and "nothing is, but what is not" (I.iii. 253). The stage itself, and the actor, enter into the density of 'imperfect speaking', the cauldron in which the syntax of 'nature' is disrupted and reconstituted – "Eye of Newt and Toe of Frogge, / Wooll of Bat, and Tongue of Dogge: / Adder's Forke . . . " (IV.i. 1540–3). As the "single state" of Macbeth is broken, along with the coherence of unequivocal language, so the character itself is placed under erasure. Crossed by the walking shadow of the poor player who struts and frets, it constructs for the audience subject-positions quite unlike those of a purely mimetic drama or a language that affects easy access to its signifieds. The material residue of actors, costumes, movements and characters is thrown into the cauldron of signifiers that will never be fully absorbed in symbolic meanings but remain the ground and negation of all ideological and metaphysical absolutes. It is from within the unperceived closures of the signified – sublime confidence in unshakeable truth – that the voice of kingship and symbolic order finally constricts the limitless transformations of 'nothing' into the "dead Butcher" and the "Fiend-like Queene". The 'character' reaffirmed here is not so much an absolute subjectivity as the literal sense of the term, an *inscription* – the mark of a limited discursive practice. " 'Tis the Eye of Childhood", Lady Macbeth points out, "That feares a painted Devill' (II.ii. 713–14). While embodying this one aspect of the semiotic innocence of childhood, Malcolm's metaphysics of evil, always problematic in a text in which the ravelled sleeve of language is never conclusively knit, displays none of the child's pleasure in nonsense: "Double, double, toyle and trouble; / Fire burne, and Cauldron bubble" (IV.i. 1537–8).

In both *Macbeth* and *Hamlet* naive notions of 'representation' in language and drama, and the given, unified subjects they propose are referred back to the constitutive, and deconstructive, *processes* of the subject and the sign, and the ritual and institutional structures in which these processes are inscribed and take effect. A broad range of Elizabethan sources, from works of literary theory to Puritan attacks on the theatre, allude to the ambiguous operations of 'double' and 'nothing'. Philip Stubbes attacks actors as "doble dealing ambodexters" (Stubbes, 1595, p. 102), pointing to the plurality which, in the theatre, combines with the poetic language described by Puttenham as exceeding "the limits of common utterance" and drawing speech "from plainnesse and simplicitie to a certaine *doublenesse*" (1589, p. 128), to confound the 'single' in all its manifestations. The juxtaposition of unequivocal statement and 'nothing' is also present in Sir Philip Sidney's defence of the poet, who "*nothing* affirms, and therefore never lieth" (Sidney, 1966, p. 52).

Robert Weimann's work suggests that this 'double' linguistic and theatrical quality in Shakespeare's text is related to medieval popular staging, with its mixing of mimesis and ritual and its division of the action between the *locus* of the platform or the stage proper, where dominant ideological forms are held in 'single' language and sustained illusion, and the unlocalized space of the *platea*, where the social production of meaning, obscured in 'innocent' notions of representation, is excavated and displayed through popular forms of burlesque, nonsense, hocus-pocus, and direct contact between actors and audience.[14] In the traditional ritual role of fool as 'corrupter of words", one part of Hamlet is always outside the action, occupying the downstage area which is the equivalent of the *platea* in the Jacobean theatre. From this position the actor / protagonist takes the audience into his confidence and implicitly upstages the work of actors who pretend to be what they seem and whose language strives to keep the 'natural' signs and subjects of ideology in place. In this context the remarks on naturalistic acting, the Fool sticking to the script and the stupidity of the 'groundlings', all made by the *locus* Hamlet, become doubly ironic.[15] As a development of the Vice and the "painted Devill" of the moralities and interludes, Macbeth too is divided between mimetic action and the forms of popular ritual, which are also apparent in his doubling as a carnival king or lord of misrule.[16] When, after the murder of Duncan, he announces that "from this instant, / There's nothing serious in Mortalitie: / All is but Toyes", the triple signification, of 'good subject', hypocrite, and the genuinely despairing Macbeth who will eventually emerge in the *locus*, is set off by a fourth – the reveller who conducts the rites of 'nothing' from the *platea*. If the *locus* contains an action which is no more than a "statement of evil", or something of that order, the *platea* affirms the 'doubleness' of an orgiastic interregnum, which incorporates language, and the theatre itself, as the place where anything can happen. Attached to this is the utopianism of carnival,[17] where nothing is serious while, at the same time, the 'nothing' which banishes hierarchical constraints is pursued in all earnest. The king who presides is characterized by the traditional iconography of festivity – intoxication, an emblematic lechery (IV.iii. 1881) and an appetite which will not be satisfied until he has "supt full" with horrors (V.v. 2334).

"The purpose of Playing", says Hamlet, "is to hold as 'twer the Mirror up to Nature" (1868–70), an act which, once spoken of within the illusion, implies much more than a realistic representation. The critical discourse that cannot go beyond mimesis and its 'natural', intact subjects and signs will inevitably find its own assumptions reflected, and fail to theorize or even describe the text's deconstructive mode without finally pulling it back towards unity and metaphysics. It will also take this reflection to be the play itself in its totality rather than only one of its dimensions. The text, in contrast, manifests the presence of the mirror – surface, frame and illusion of depth – as many reflections as there are spectators, and, in the subject that composes itself for each in the specular image, an uneasy coalescence which is both a momentary reduction of a much more various process and something always other than itself.[18]

So *Hamlet*, like *Macbeth*, addresses the *processes* by which the subjects and signs taken as read by a drama (and criticism) of plot, theme and character are constructed. The post-structuralist and materialist methods that recover these textual operations do so in ways that accentuate the status of all reading as an intervention and a production rather than a simple decoding. After the academic maunderings of 'Is it really a tragedy?' and 'What is the central theme?' criticism, the promise of current literary theory is a transformed, contemporary Shakespeare. But the perspectives it opens up also have a historical specificity – confirmed by Foucault's work on the late sixteenth- and early seventeenth-century crisis in concepts of representation, the work of Weimann and, more recently, Hattaway (1982) on the popular theatre, and Jonathan Dollimore's account of a discontinuity and "irresolution" in English Renaissance drama – a manifestation of conflict between "residual, dominant and emergent conceptions of the real" which is accompanied by an interrogation of mimesis and by what Dollimore calls a "decentring of man".[19]

Any attempt to recover a 'transparent' representation from Shakespeare now has to contend not only with contemporary theory but with this growing body of historical study. So when A. D. Nuttall, for example, defends his programme for *A New Mimesis* (1983) by reference to Shakespeare's dramaturgy, he is able to sustain an argument only by disregarding the ways in which post-structuralism can remain responsive to historical considerations and by ignoring the work of Weimann and others on the popular dramatic tradition, crucial for any serious contemporary study of the plays of this period. Nuttall's doctrinaire attack on contemporary theory creates a straw opponent, the "radical formalist" or mechanically "opaque" critic, who serves as a convenient pretext for trotting out some of the central tenets of the 'great tradition' of English criticism. These are enshrined in the person of Nuttall's "transparent" critic who remains flexible, alive, open to the experiential domain of "people and things", and who is able to engage in a fruitful dialogue with the literary work (1983, pp. 77, 94, 125, 192). Nuttall's own text, secure in its grasp of which cultural practices are 'natural' and which 'artificial',[20] produces a version of Shakespeare in which an unmediated 'self' and 'experience' are shored up against the interventions of discourse and ideology or the fracturing of the unified subject and sign. Unlike the "opaque" adversary, a "transparent" reader runs no risk of imposing his or her theoretical or discursive frameworks on the plays because the text refuses to submit passively to analysis and, for those open to prompting, Shakespeare himself, like the Holy Spirit, "is for ever popping up at one's elbow with suggestions and insights" – insights which, astonishingly, happen to coincide with Nuttall's understanding of modern anthropology, cultural history, psychoanalysis and existential philosophy (pp. 101, 118, 143, 164).

The new mimesis is itself no more than a transparent representation of the old. The unified subject (Shakespeare) addresses an ideal reader ('one') about things out there in the world, and its essential or existential truths. The codes, discourses and ideologies that determine this exchange are presented as secondary – as a supplement that falls away to reveal a transcendental *represented* or *signified* which is underwritten by the irreducible categories of the 'self' and its 'experience'. Where the text puts such certainties in doubt, Nuttall recuperates it as offering special instances of *mimesis*. So the impassioned cry of Troilus confronted with evidence of betrayal, "this is, and is not, Cressid" (*Troilus and Cressida*, 3143)[21] approaches the edge of mimesis only to reassert representation's centrality. Here Shakespeare according to Nuttall, "*knows*, experientially, the possible failure of experiential knowing, and that is what he teaches us, his audience" (p. 77). But if this possible failure can be known experientially, it is no failure but a triumph of experiential knowledge, in which the positive and negative both turn out to have been playing for the same side. 'Experience', Nuttall's mantra, is the true touchstone because he experiences it as such, and nothing in modern psychoanalysis or the theory of ideology will convince him otherwise.[22] But his choice of these particular lines to make his point is a revealing one, as an extended reading of the sequence in question would suggest that Troilus is much more of a proto-Lacanian or -Derridean than a friend of empiricism, the subject and unmediated experience. Everything hinges on whether this is *really* Cressida who bestows her favours on Diomedes – which, at the level of mimesis or the play's *locus*, action, it clearly is. But the truths that follow from this truth remove the metaphysical ground from under it, denying it the right to be purely rational, identical with itself, or part of a stable order of significant differences in language:

> If there be rule in unitie it selfe,
> This is not she: O madnesse of discourse!
> The cause sets up, withe, and against the selfe
> By foule authority: where reason can revolt
> Without perdition, and losse assume all reason,
> Without revolt. This is, and is not *Cressid*:
> Within my soule, there doth conduce a fight
> Of this strange nature, that a thing inseparate,
> Divides more wider than the skie and earth:
> And yet the spacious bredth of this division,
> Admits no Orifex for a point as subtle,
> As Ariachnes broken woofe to enter.
>
> (3138–49)

The dividing of the subject, the questioning of identity and significant difference, the undoing of unities and the association of these processes with an abortive construction of sexuality and gender (the 'orifex' and subtle 'point') open up areas that are not accessible to Nuttall's foreclosed discourse, constituting as they do the site of a textual heterogeneity beyond the subject and the mimetic sign. This particular speech could be as seminal to a post-structuralist Shakespeare criticism as Ulysses's disquisition on 'degree' was to the conservative Shakespeare of the 'Elizabethan world picture'. Troilus on the divided subject and sign also indicates the site from which the self-naturalizing hierarchies of the 'degree' speech can be seen as precisely that – ideology, discourse, closure rather than 'insight' or 'how Shakespeare saw the world'. On stage the intricacies of this position are themselves domesticated in an empirical truth. There is a sense in which "this is, and is not, Cressid" is no momentary loss of experiential bearings but a recovery from the trance of mimesis in a simple statement of fact about acting. This should be the case not only for Jacobean audiences familiar with plays that called for a 'double' vision, incorporating a response to the action *and* a continuing recognition of theatricality, but also for those later theatre-goers who, under the influence of Brecht or Artaud, are unable to wholly forget themselves and their part in a specific social transaction by submitting to the discreet charm of the bourgeois realism many critics and consumers would like Shakespeare's work to be. But historically the plays were more than the "storytelling psychology" Artaud found in the Shakespeare of his day. And the interruptions to what Nuttall calls "the natural *coitus* of reader and work" (p. 83), the mimetic fantasy, come not only from the probings of "mechanical" theorists but from the textual process that can be described, in the terms of Troilus's speech, as making "nature" seem "strange".

Notes

1 For the Renaissance theory that the poet, like God, creates *ex nihilo, see* Puttenham, 1589, p. 1. Cf. *A Midsummer Night's Dream*, V. 1804–9.

2 *Romeo and Juliet*, 1169; *2 Henry IV*, I.ii. 444.

3 Roman Polanski's film version of *Macbeth* (Caliban Productions) ends with a meeting between Donalbain and the Witches. "Ambiguity, whereby evil and good become inextricable, runs through this play in which the hero is at once a 'dead butcher' and the most continually sympathetic character, while Macduff can on the other hand believe Malcolm capable of whoremongering and avarice, and can yet think these not unfit characteristics for Scotland's future hero-king. Confusion reigns and 'nothing is but what is not'" (Somerset, 1975, p. 62). On the contradiction between the traditional Vice's homiletic function and his role as provoker of "Dionysian laughter", *see* Spivack, 1958, pp. 113, 121, 128; Somerset,

pp. 62–9; Weimann, 1978, pp. 151–60. Weimann emphasizes the plebian associations of the Vice and his language, his direct contact with the audience, his status, even in defeat, as "a powerful symbol of negation and unending rebellion" and his role as "an independent instigator of actions and reactions" free, to some extent, of the *locus*'s "balanced contest of allegorical figures".

4   The Folio text of *Hamlet* has no act or scene divisions after Act 2, Scene 2.

5   Hawkes, 1973, pp. 115–16.

6   CF. I.iii. 508–14.

7   CF. "ranke Corruption mining all within" (2531).

8   On the questionable status of the Ghost, *see*: Wilson, 1951, pp. 52–86; Prosser, 1971, pp. 118f.

9   First Quarto stage direction. For the point that follows, *see* Lacan, 1977b, pp. 44–5.

10   Mahood, 1957, p. 43. *See also* Forker, 1963, pp. 215–30.

11   *See* Rosenberg, 1978, pp. 95–7; Van Laan, 1978, p. 190; Wilson, 1978, pp. 107–14; Kantak, 1963, pp. 42–56.

12   Lascelles Abercrombie, *cit*. Wells, 1973, p. 193.

13   *See* Breuer, 1976, pp. 256–71.

14   *See* Weimann, 1978, pp. 73–84.

15   *See* lines 1849–93.

16   Holloway, 1961, p. 73. Cf. note 3 above on the Vice.

17   On the links between carnival and utopia, *see* Bakhtin, 1968, pp. 8f.; and on popular utopianism and topsy-turvydom generally, Weimann, pp. 20–4.

18   Cf. Lacan, 1977a, pp. 1–7, 164–5, 299.

19   Dollimore, 1984, pp. 82, 135f., *passim*.

20   Nuttall, 1983, pp. 83, 97, 169.

21   In Folio 1 there are no act and scene divisions for *Troilus and Cressida* after Act 1, Scene 1.

22   Cf. Belsey, 1980, pp. 11–14, 45–6.

8

Gender and Sexuality: An Overview

In her groundbreaking study, *Shakespeare and the Nature of Women* (1975), Juliet Dusinberre proposes that 'the drama from 1590 to 1625 is feminist in sympathy' (Dusinberre, 1975, p. 5). Chapters on the significance of boy-players, on chastity and virtue and on female authority develop the thesis that the stage reflected changing attitudes to women in contemporary society, and that 'Shakespeare's feminism consists of more than a handful of high-born emancipated heroines: it lies rather in his scepticism about the nature of women' (p. 305): '[Shakespeare] did not divide human nature into the masculine and the feminine, but observed in the individual woman or man an infinite variety of union between opposing impulses. To talk about Shakespeare's women is to talk about his men, because he refused to separate their worlds physically, intellectually, or spiritually' (p. 308).

Having established the specificity of her subject, Dusinberre seems here to conclude by erasing it. But this was only the beginning of a burgeoning critical field. Philip Kolin takes *Shakespeare and the Nature of Women* as the starting point for his bibliography *Shakespeare and Feminist Criticism* (1991), and countless critics cite it in approbation or disagreement. Looking back over the two decades of revisionist literary scholarship since the first edition of her study, Dusinberre cites the book's place in a wider feminist politics, a 'battle about ownership' (Dusinberre, 1996, p. xii), connecting the debate about Shakespeare with modern gendered struggles for a critical and social position from which to speak. She admits that 'if I were rewriting the book I would have to address the theoretical problems surrounding the relation of history to the play as fiction' (p. xxi), that 'I wouldn't now use the language of authorial intention' (p. xxii), and that the need to discuss the plays in performance is now firmly established. This list of additional factors and changing methodologies, as well as Dusinberre's double focus on the historical context of Shakespeare's plays and current feminist debates, makes her review of the state of recent feminist scholarship on Shakespeare a good place to introduce the lively and wide-ranging field of gender criticism.

Following Dusinberre, Marilyn French's *Shakespeare's Division of Experience* (1981) proposed that the 'gender principle' was of fundamental importance to Shakespeare's drama, arguing for a movement from 'profound suspicion of "feminine"' qualities in his early work towards some 'fear' of the 'masculine principle' and an idealization of the feminine (French, 1981, p. 17). French describes the tragedies as 'in a masculine mode' (p. 201). *Othello*, for example, is discussed as a 'profound examination of male modes of thought at behavior, especially with regard to women and "feminine" qualities' (p. 219). In her *Comic Women, Tragic Men: A Study of Gender and Genre in Shakespeare* (1982), Linda Bamber makes it clear that her approach 'locates the feminism in the critic – not in the author or even the work', although her argument proceeds by contrasting an apparently 'feminist' Shakespeare in the comedies with the 'nightmare female figures . . . charged with sexual antagonism' in the tragedies (Bamber, 1982, p. 2). Chapters on *Antony and Cleopatra*, *Hamlet*, *Macbeth* and *Coriolanus* discuss the role of women and the feminine: 'the feminine is the foremost representative in Shakespeare of the challenge by the Other of the Self' (p. 107).

Philippa Berry's *Shakespeare's Feminine Endings: Disfiguring Death in the Tragedies* (1999) also argues that tragedy unsettles its heroes' masculinity:

> By redefining dying as a state that is open rather than closed, these tragedies both problematize and amplify orthodox religious knowledge of and around death, disrupting the orderliness of such established significations in a complex layering of figurative detail that is often emblematically embodied, near the end of the play, by a dead or dying woman. (Berry, 1999, p. 5)

This sophisticated 'tropical interrelationship of woman and death' (p. 9) is discussed in relation to *Romeo and Juliet*, *Macbeth*, *King Lear* and *Othello*. Coppélia Kahn's *Roman Shakespeare: Warriors, Wounds and Women* (1997) appears in the same series, 'Feminist Readings of Shakespeare'. Kahn's gendering of Roman *virtus* and her delineation of the feminized *polis* is developed through readings of *Titus Andronicus*, *Julius Caesar*, *Coriolanus* and, in a postscript, *Cymbeline*.

The most significant form for the development of gender criticism has been the collection of essays rather than the monograph. Lenz, Greene and Neely's *The Woman's Part: Feminist Criticism of Shakespeare* (1980) is an early attempt 'to liberate Shakespeare's women from the stereotypes to which they have too often been confined; [to] examine women's relations to each other; [to] analyze the nature and effects of patriarchal structures; and [to] explore the influence of genre on the portrayal of women' (Lenz, 1980, p. 4). Chapters on the tragedies include Rebecca Smith's account of Gertrude's speeches presenting 'a compliant, loving, unimaginative woman whose only concern is pleasing others' (p. 207), rather than the lusty, treacherous figure generated by Hamlet and often endorsed in performance. Writing on *Othello*, Carol Thomas Neely discusses the play as 'cankered comedy' (p. 234) in which divisions between men and women are reified rather than bridged. Richard Levin's is a dissonant voice against these approaches: his 'Feminist Thematics and Shakespearean Tragedy' (1988) reviews some of this criticism unsympathetically. For Levin, feminist criticism is inevitably 'thematic', concerned with what the plays are *about* – 'the role of gender in the individual and society'– rather than what they *are*: 'dramatizations of actions' (Levin, 1988, p. 126). Levin criticizes books and articles by Kahn (1981), Erickson (1985) and others as selective in their reading of Shakespeare, as reductive in their attitudes to the tragic heroes, who 'emerge as a very sorry lot indeed' (p. 131), and as misguided in their insistence on 'a universal definition of [. . .] gender' (p. 136).

Valerie Wayne's collection *The Matter of Difference: Materialist Feminist Criticism of Shakespeare* (1991) includes articles on the tragedies by Ann Thompson on *King Lear*, Marion Wynne-Davies on *Titus Andronicus* and Wayne on *Othello*. Sara Eaton's article 'Defacing the Feminine in Renaissance Tragedy' (pp. 181–198) discusses the depiction of female sexuality in a range of Jacobean plays and their critics. Other important collections of essays concerned with gender and genre include *Shakespearean Tragedy and Gender* (edited by Shirley Nelson Garner and Madelon Sprengnether, 1996). Here contributors 'demonstrate how significantly gender figures in the construction and devolution of tragic subjectivity and action. For Shakespeare [. . .] *gender* and *genre* (both derived from the Latin *genus*) are as interinvolved in the interpretation of tragedy as they are in their linguistic origins' (Garner, 1996, p. 12). Phyllis Rackin discusses 'History into Tragedy: the case of *Richard III*' (pp. 31–53) via the supposedly effeminating effects of tragic drama on its spectators and the move of the drama towards a tragic form which authorized masculine dominance by centring on a male protagonist. Among the other contributors, Sara Eaton considers the character of Lavinia, and both Lena Cowen Orlin and Mary Beth Rose discuss Shakespeare's women in the light of contemporary conduct literature.

In her introduction to *A Feminist Companion to Shakespeare* (2000), Dympna Callaghan categorizes the contributors to the volume as 'part of an ever-growing body of scholarship that has set out to discover what the world, and in this instance, quite specifically what a hugely influential body of canonical literature, might look like from the perspective of women, from the margins of hitherto patriarchal knowledge' (Callaghan, 2000, pp. xiii–xiv). Essays in the collection include Laurie Maguire on feminist editing of Shakespeare, Katherine Romack on the Shakespeare criticism of Margaret Cavendish,

Susan Zimmerman on 'Duncan's corpse' and Denise Albanese on racial casting in *Othello*, although there is a preponderance of discussion of the comedies. Dympna Callaghan, Lorraine Helms and Jyotsna Singh's *The Weyward Sisters: Shakespeare and Feminist Politics* (1994) asserts collaborative scholarship as a political act, and discusses feminist historiography, the ideology of romantic love in *Romeo and Juliet* and the gendering of performance spaces. Helms ends the volume with a manifesto for a version of *Macbeth* performed at the instigation of the witches, and in which they form the central dramatic attraction. At the head of the collection of essays *Shakespeare and Sexuality* (2001), edited by Catherine Alexander and Stanley Wells, is a review essay by Ann Thompson ('Shakespeare and Sexuality', pp. 1–13). Thompson identifies four key concerns of scholarship in the area of sexuality: 'feminism'; 'men in feminism and gay studies'; 'the boy actor and performance studies'; and 'language'. She offers brief commentary on these areas and makes useful suggestions for further reading. Elsewhere in the volume Lloyd Davis dicusses 'Death and desire in *Romeo and Juliet*' (pp. 35–51), and Michael Hattaway reads *Othello* as part of his 'Male sexuality and misogyny' (pp. 92–115). Kate Chedgzoy's collection of important essays representing a range of approaches to *Shakespeare, Feminism and Gender* (2001) also offers a review of the field in its introduction. The methodological range of gender criticism is showcased in diverse contributions from Ania Loomba on 'The colour of patriarchy: critical difference, cultural difference and Renaissance drama', Steven Mullaney's historicized account 'Mourning and misogyny: *Hamlet* and the final progress of Elizabeth I', and Lizbeth Goodman's essay on feminist performance, 'Women's Alternative Shakespeares and Women's Alternatives to Shakespeare in Contemporary British Theatre'.

The collection *Shakespeare and Gender: A History*, edited by Deborah Barker and Ivo Kamps (1995), offers a range of feminist scholarship framed by an introduction which emphasizes the move towards history and away from essentializing notions of gender. These include articles by Jacqueline Rose on *Hamlet*, Carol Thomas Neely on *Othello* and a reflection by Lisa Jardine on twenty years of feminist scholarship. This historicist approach to gender criticism is an important strand. Jardine's aim in her *Still Harping on Daughters: Women and Drama in the Age of Shakespeare* (2nd edn, 1989) is to suggest 'possibilities for reading the relationship between real social conditions, and literary representation' (Jardine, 1989, p. 7), and she brings extensive historical material to bear on her readings of the plays. Writing in 1987, however, Lynda Boose defended more psychoanalytical approaches in gender criticism against this historicist orthodoxy, arguing that new historicism tended to marginalize issues of gender, and that the stress on male actors often seemed to imply that 'there are no more women in Shakespeare's plays' (Boose, 1987, p. 730). Dympna Callaghan's *Shakespeare without Women: Representing Gender and Race on the Renaissance Stage* (1999) discusses the implications for mimetic representation of the simultaneous absence of women and Africans from the early modern theatre. The idea of impersonation, both gendered and racial, emerges as a crucial example of theatrical representation's paradoxical dependence 'on the absence of the thing it represents' (Callaghan, 1999, p. 9). Depictions of women and of Moors on the stage are no less 'real' than they might have been were they performed by women or black actors; they are 'profoundly cultural and complex rather than biological and essential' (p. 14). *Othello* serves as the paradigmatic instance of race / gender representation in the chapter '"Othello was a white man"'.

Gender criticism has also focused on masculinity. Stephen Orgel's *Impersonations: The Performance of Gender in Shakespeare's England* (1996) discusses the connections between boy-players, cross-dressing within plays, effeminacy and the fragility of gendered identity in the early modern period. Coppélia Kahn's *Man's Estate: Masculine Identity in Shakespeare* (1981) argues that Shakespeare's 'male characters are engaged in a continuous struggle, first to form a masculine identity, then to be secure and productive in it' (Kahn, 1981, p. 1). Janet Adelman's subject in *Suffocating Mothers: Fantasies of Maternal Origin in Shakespeare's Plays, 'Hamlet' to 'The Tempest'* (1992) is related in its stress on perilous masculinity in relation to the maternal presence. Peter Erickson's account of *Patriarchal Structures in Shakespeare's Drama* (1985) is less concerned with individual masculine identity, and instead engages with the social structure – sometimes benevolent, sometimes tyrannical – of patriarchal power in the plays. His chapter on the tragedies stresses male bonding, particularly in the relationship between Hamlet and Horatio as a refuge for the paralysed and paralyzing relationship between Hamlet and his father. Erickson's interpretation of *Othello* sees an elision between state and domestic patriarchy, *Macbeth*'s conclusion valorizes an entirely masculine social order, and in *King Lear* 'the comfort of male bonding' (Erickson, 1985, p. 104) is stressed after Lear has provoked his relationships with his daughters into misogynistic crisis. In his *Shakespeare and Masculinity* (2000), Bruce R. Smith derives from feminist criticism an understanding of gender as historical and social construction, and applies this to concepts of masculinity. Robin Headlam Wells' *Shakespeare on Masculinity* (2000) discusses Shakespeare's plays as responses to and interventions in contemporary debates about militant Protestant heroic masculinity. He argues that, through his career, Shakespeare develops a more sceptical relation to this version of masculinity, and studies Prospero as the ultimate embodiment of this shift. On issues of sexuality, most often discussed in relation to the comedies, see Kate Chedgzoy's *Shakespeare's Queer Children* (1995), Bruce Smith, *Homosexual Desire in Shakespeare's England* (1991) and Jonathan Goldberg's *Sodometries* and *Queering the Renaissance* (1992; 1994).

Further Reading

Adelman, Janet. *Suffocating Mothers: Fantasies of Maternal Origin in Shakespeare's Plays, 'Hamlet' to 'The Tempest'*. New York; London: Routledge, 1992.

Alexander, Catherine M. S., and Wells, Stanley W. *Shakespeare and Sexuality*. Cambridge: Cambridge University Press, 2001.

Bamber, Linda. *Comic Women, Tragic Men: A Study of Gender and Genre in Shakespeare*. Stanford, Calif: Stanford University Press, 1982.

Barker, Deborah, and Kamps, Ivo. *Shakespeare and Gender: A History*. London: Verso, 1995.

Berry, Philippa. *Shakespeare's Feminine Endings: Disfiguring Death in the Tragedies*. London: Routledge, 1999.

Boose, Lynda. 'The Family in Shakespeare Studies; or – Studies in the Family of Shakespeareans; or – The Politics of Politics.' *Renaissance Quarterly* 40 (1987): 707–42.

Callaghan, Dympna. *Shakespeare without Women: Representing Gender and Race on the Renaissance Stage*. London: Routledge, 1999.

——*A Feminist Companion to Shakespeare*. Oxford: Blackwell, 2000.

——, Helms, Lorraine Rae, and Singh, Jyotsna. *The Weyward Sisters: Shakespeare and Feminist Politics*. Oxford: Blackwell, 1994.

Chedgzoy, Kate. *Shakespeare's Queer Children: Sexual Politics and Contemporary Culture*. Manchester: Manchester University Press, 1995.

——*Shakespeare, Feminism and Gender*. Basingstoke: Palgrave, 2001.

Dusinberre, Juliet. *Shakespeare and the Nature of Women*. London: Macmillan, 1975 (2nd edn, 1996).

Erickson, Peter. *Patriarchal Structures in Shakespeare's Drama*. Berkeley: University of California Press, 1985.

French, Marilyn. *Shakespeare's Division of Experience*. New York: Summit Books, 1981.

Garner, Shirley Nelson, and Sprengnether, Madelon. *Shakespearean Tragedy and Gender*. Bloomington: Indiana University Press, 1996.

Goldberg, Jonathan. *Sodometries: Renaissance Texts, Modern Sexualities*. Stanford, Calif: Stanford University Press, 1992.

——*Queering the Renaissance*. Durham, NC; London: Duke University Press, 1994.

Jardine, Lisa. *Still Harping on Daughters: Women and Drama in the Age of Shakespeare*. Brighton: Harvester, 1989.

Kahn, Coppélia. *Man's Estate: Masculine Identity in Shakespeare*. Berkeley: University of California Press, 1981.

——*Roman Shakespeare: Warriors, Wounds and Women*. Feminist Readings of Shakespeare. London: Routledge, 1997.

Kolin, Philip C. *Shakespeare and Feminist Criticism: An Annotated Bibliography and Commentary*. New York; London: Garland, 1991.

Lenz, Carolyn Ruth Swift, Neely, Carol Thomas, and Greene, Gayle. *The Woman's Part: Feminist Criticism of Shakespeare*. Urbana: London: University of Illinois Press, 1980.

Levin, Richard. 'Feminist Thematics and Shakespearean Tragedy'. *PMLA* 103 (1988): 125–38.

Newman, Karen. *Fashioning Femininity and English Renaissance Drama*. Women in culture and society. Chicago; London: University of Chicago Press, 1991.

Orgel, Stephen. *Impersonations: The Performance of Gender in Shakespeare's England*. Cambridge: Cambridge University Press, 1996.

Smith, Bruce R. *Homosexual Desire in Shakespeare's England: A Cultural Poetics*. Chicago: London: University of Chicago Press, 1991.

—— *Shakespeare and Masculinity*. Oxford: Oxford University Press, 2000.

Wayne, Valerie. *The Matter of Difference: Materialist Feminist Criticism of Shakespeare*. New York; London: Harvester Wheatsheaf, 1991.

Wells, Robin Headlam. *Shakespeare on Masculinity*. Cambridge: Cambridge University Press, 2000.

9

Gender and Sexuality: Critical Extracts

The Daughter's Seduction in *Titus Andronicus,* or, Writing is the Best Revenge

Coppélia Kahn

Kahn's Roman Shakespeare: Warriors, Wounds and Women, *from which this essay is taken, was the first sustained feminist reading of the Roman plays. Here she analyses the politics of sexuality in* Titus Andronicus, *particularly in the relationship between Titus and Lavinia and in the familial and political signification attached to Lavinia's chastity and violation. Close reading of the feminized metaphors of enclosure and rupture, of treasure, the family tomb and the pit demonstrates how tragic subjectivity is achieved through female suffering, and Kahn discusses the prominent role of tragic classical precedents in the story.*

Coppélia Kahn, 'The Daughter's Seduction in *Titus Andronicus,* or, Writing is the Best Revenge', in *Roman Shakespeare: Warriors, Wounds and Women.* London: Routledge, 1997.

> The female must never control
> reproduction for herself . . .
> She must also never see, and
> certainly never speak about what
> she learns from her position.
> (Joplin 1990: 21)

Shakespeare was about thirty in 1594 when *Titus Andronicus* was published, but this sensational revenge tragedy is marked by the brashness and bravura of a younger poet, showing off both his knowledge of classical authors and his mastery of a crowd-pleasing popular genre. Weaving an Ovidian tale into a Senecan revenge tragedy, seeding allusions to the *Aeneid* in nearly every scene, Shakespeare revels in the *imitatio* that structured the transmission of Latin literature to the Elizabethan elite and those aspiring to join it.

Leonard Barkan notes "the competitive mode" in which Shakespeare appropriates Ovid:

> What is horrible in Ovid's Tereus story Shakespeare makes twice as horrible in *Titus Andronicus*. Not one rapist but two, not one murdered child but five, not one or two mutilated organs but six, not a one-course meal but a two. (1986: 244)

Furthermore, as T. J. B. Spencer remarked of Shakespeare's appropriation of Roman history in *Titus*,

> It is not so much that any particular set of political institutions is assumed in *Titus*, but rather that it includes *all* the political institutions that Rome ever had. The author seems anxious, not to get it all right, but to get it all in. (Spencer 1957: 32)

Yet this most self-consciously textual of all Shakespearean plays doesn't appropriate, imitate, allude to, and parody a host of classical authors merely to elicit plaudits for its author's learning and virtuosity.[1]

Even while he travesties Romanness, Shakespeare generates his main action from versions of Roman *pietas* and *virtus* – making this play a serious critique of Roman ideology, institutions, and mores. In the hero's character, G. K. Hunter notes, Shakespeare draws on the standard motifs of austere republican virtue that typify Rome's "great ethical heroes, Scipio, Regulus, Brutus" as chronicled by Livy, while placing him in an ambience of imperial decadence like that portrayed by Tacitus, Suetonius, and Herodian (1984: 182, 187). Republican virtue, though, perpetrates as much (if not more) horror than imperial decadence. The play insists on an antithesis between civilized Rome and the barbaric Goths only to break it down: the real enemy lies within.

Moreover, it can be argued, it isn't only Rome as Elizabethan culture knew it that the play attacks, but also the humanistic appropriation of Rome's textual legacy from grammar school through university in Shakespeare's England. As one critic notes,

> Rome is a tradition in which [the characters] have been schooled through school books: the works of Horace, Virgil, Ovid, and Seneca . . . Roman education, which seems to stand for Roman tradition in general, has been twisted to become the teacher and rationalizer of heinous deeds. (West 1982: 65)

In the late empire ambience of this play, even non-Romans can recognize a verse from Horace – but they don't understand what it means. And not only Titus writes copiously, but also Aaron the Moor (sometimes carving his messages on corpses); even Lavinia, though she lacks hands, scratches letters in the earth. In one of the play's eeriest moments, when the revenger-hero is finally empowered by learning the identity of his enemies, the revelation is accomplished through the material presence of a text, significantly a school-boy's copy of Ovid's *Metamorphoses*.

This sophisticated awareness of the politics of textuality is interwoven with the play's central concern: the politics of sexuality. And in the schematically patriarchal world of *Titus*, sexuality is a family matter that only the father can deal with.[2] Of the several crimes against Titus, it is the rape and mutilation of his daughter Lavinia that establishes him in the central position of revenger. He proves his title of *paterfamilias*, one might say, with a vengeance – not only on those who violated and injured her so brutally but on the girl herself, when he murders her. *Titus* configures the father's investment in the daughter, relent-lessly carrying out that "symbolics of blood" according to which, Lynda Boose argues, "A daughter's virginity is perceived to 'belong to' the blood of – and therefore to – the father".[3] Yet Shakespeare makes the hauntingly mute, hideously disfigured Lavinia much more than a patriarchal icon of the dutiful daughter. Deprived of speech and the usual means of writing, Lavinia herself becomes a signifier; as such, Douglas Green asserts, she is "polysemic and dis-ruptive . . . beyond complete containment by the patriarchal assumptions of Shakespeare's time – and in some ways our own" (1989: 325). As Lavinia's male kin struggle to understand her grotesque body language, the cultural logic of the Roman father–daughter complex works itself out in a compelling series of scenes (2.4–4.1). They come to a climax in Lavinia's revelation of her rape and identification of the rapists – whereupon she disappears for four scenes (4.2, 3, 4; 5.1), to return not only mute but veiled, assisting in the revenge that now belongs to her father. Titus's subjectivity as a tragic hero is generated from his daughter's pain inscribed as his own.[4] Moving from sorrow to anger, finding his tortuous way to "revenge's cave," Titus carries out the father's role accord-ing to the "exchange model" of father–daughter sacrifice that Boose delineates: he sacrifices his daughter "to the perceived demands of the patriarchy and thus affirms his membership in it" (1989: 40).

The Father's Treasure

Titus Andronicus opens in high Roman fashion by staging two public cere-monies, an election and a funeral. "With drums and trumpets," Titus is declared the new emperor of Rome. He makes his first entrance, though, not as successful *candidatus* but as grieving father, at the head of a funeral proces-sion. Having lost twenty-one of his twenty-five sons in battle, he brings the last two of the slain home for burial in the monument of the Andronici. His surname "Pius" recalls the epithet that characterizes the first Roman hero,

Aeneas, and his sons total in number half those of Priam, in whose defense Aeneas fought.[5] Clearly he embodies paternal authority and the historical tradition of *pietas* that supports it, as well as the gendered ideals of character typical of early republican *virtus*: "severity, self-conscious masculinity, stoical self-denial" (Hunter 1984: 4). Finally, to complete this composite of typical Roman traits and values, he is a victorious general, returning from a ten-year campaign against the Goths with captives in tow.

As he prepares to sacrifice *ad manes fratrum* – to the spirits of his dead sons – the oldest son of his prisoner Tamora, Queen of the Goths, she pleads with him to spare the boy. She appeals to his love as a father, and to "the mercy of the gods," but Titus is adamant: the honor of the Andronici demands this tribute, which he has exacted five times before.[6] The victim is taken off, his limbs to be "lopp'd." Ironically alluding to Titus's surname, Tamora brands his action "cruel irreligious piety" (1.1.133). A few moments later, Titus's inflexible adherence to primogeniture in backing the elder of two brothers to take his place as emperor leads him, in a sudden eruption of fury, to kill his own son. The two filicides are paralleled: both sons are sacrificed in the name of the fathers, according to a piety that seems not only cruel and irreligious but also a perversion of *virtus*.

Titus's sacrifice of Tamora's son trips off the revenge mechanism that drives the play toward its savage denouement. The *quid pro quo* that Tamora extracts for her murdered son isn't the murder of Titus's son, though she does abet Aaron in murdering two of them, nor even that of a daughter, but rather a daughter's rape and mutilation. Lavinia then becomes the focus of action in the middle part of the play and the most shocking and memorable of its many images of bodily violation. In thus placing dramatic emphasis on her injuries, rather than on the murder of her brothers, Shakespeare calls attention to the role of women in Rome's sexual politics – a role that, overshadowed by the strident patriarchal motif of the opening scene, is nonetheless central. For Titus, Lavinia's worth resides in her exchange value as a virgin daughter. In a larger sense, she is symbolically important to Roman patriarchy: as an emblem of what Joplin calls "sacralized chastity," she is "the sign of her father's or husband's political power" – the power of male kin to control women's sexual desire and reproductive power (Joplin 1990: 53). Both her exchange value and her symbolic value are nullified several times over by what is done to her at Tamora's behest. Not only is she violated by the queen's two sons: her tongue is cut out and her hands are cut off. Thus Tamora gets back at Titus through his daughter by mocking and despoiling his investment in her.

According to Lévi-Strauss, the structure of the patriarchal family derives from the interlocking operation of two cultural imperatives: the incest taboo and exogamy.[7] Forbidden to marry within the family, its sons and daughters must be married out. The sons, however, remain identified with the paternal family, carrying on its name into posterity and inheriting the father's prerogatives, while the daughters pass from their paternal households to those of their husbands, to mediate the continuation of another patriarchal lineage. The only members of the family whose destiny is to leave it, they are thus made liminal, and turned into creatures of passage. Moreover, they are distinguished from sons in another important way. As Boose points out, appropriating Lacan's family script,

> [The mother] is the necessary mediator between [father and son], the empty vessel through whom, in psychoanalytic terms, the father's phallus and sign of the father's authority is passed to the son . . . The son receives the externally evident sign of the father and becomes synonymous with him at birth. By parallel, what the daughter receives from the mother is not the sign *of* maternity but the hidden receptacle *for* it, the so-called empty space . . . a signal passed on to her not *from* the mother but from the phallus that is the sign of the father. (Boose 1989: 21)

The virgin daughter's womb is the hidden, prized treasure of her father, to be guarded, given or exchanged as he determines. What Page DuBois calls "thesaurization," the representation of the female body in Greek culture as vase, oven, and temple – enclosures "for keeping safe, for entreasuring" – is further elaborated in the woman's role in Greco-Roman culture generally: "women preserve and maintain the goods brought to them by the men of their households . . . the wife as treasure ensures the prosperity and endurance of the house" (1988: 97, 103). The Roman worship of Vesta, virgin goddess of the hearth, places thesaurization at the center of the state religion, inscribing both the centrality and the hiddenness of women and their sexualized bodies.[8] The image of the chaste woman as impermeable container was also highly visible in the Renaissance through the legend of Tuccia, first recounted by St Augustine in *The City of God*. This vestal virgin proved her chastity by carrying water from the Tiber in a sieve, a "miraculous inversion of the vessel's ordinary function [that] replicates the prodigy of virginity itself" (Warner 1985: 242). Tuccia reappears notably in the *Trionfi*, Petrarch's sequence of allegorical poems, heading a host of virtues represented by female figures. For Shakespeare's England, she was familiar in portraits of Elizabeth, several times portrayed as Tuccia with a sieve in her hand.

In *Titus*, the problematics of liminality and thesaurization are dramatized in Lavinia's troubled passage from father to husband to violators and back to father. Conspicuous as the only daughter among twenty-five sons, she enters the play after her father completes the solemn sacrificial ritual of burial by placing the last of his slain sons in the family tomb. Greeting her father by repeating his words of farewell to her brothers, offering "tributary tears" for them, and kneeling at his feet, she asks for the blessing of his "victorious hand" (1.1.162–6). Despite these indications of her complete subjection as a model patriarchal daughter, Titus seems curiously negligent in supervising her betrothal – the crucial transmission of his treasure to another male guardian. When Bassianus suddenly declares that Lavinia is his, Titus exclaims, "Lavinia is surpris'd" (288); in the context, surprise seems a delicate euphemism for what is later called "this rape" (409). But it also marks one of the many oddly comic moments in this play, for it is he, not his daughter, who is surprised that she has evidently been party to a previous betrothal.[9] Further, in offering to make Lavinia his empress, Saturninus tells Titus he will "advance / Thy name and honorable family" (242–3) – as though paying him back for supporting his bid for emperor over that of his younger brother. Titus responds to this proposal by offering his sword, chariot, and prisoners – rather than Lavinia herself – as "tribute that I owe" (255) to his prospective son-in-law. Lavinia's betrothal thus takes its place in a sequence of exchanges between her father and the newly elevated emperor that stress Titus's reverence for tradition and authority and his eagerness to garner imperial favor, while effacing or even exploiting her.

Titus's delinquency as a father derives from his over-zealous (and in the killing of his son Mutius, self-contradictory) commitment to those forms of *pietas* specifically involving men: dedicating all his many sons to the service of the state, insisting on the strict observance of blood sacrifice to their spirits despite a mother's plea for mercy, opting for primogeniture without considering a rival claim, and defending imperial power even to the point of slaying his own son. When his brother Marcus asks Titus, "How comes it that the subtle Queen of Goths / Is of sudden thus advanc'd in Rome?" (397–8), the obvious answer is that it happened because Titus failed to oversee properly both the transmission of political power and the exchange of a daughter. The sequence of events in the first scene that connects the election of the emperor with the betrothal and "rape" of Lavinia, and with the double wedding of the emperor and his brother-rival, demonstrates the tight-woven interrelation of the two kinds of passage. Similarly, in the *Aeneid*, the hero's betrothal to Lavinia represents both a vital political alliance between the Trojans and the stable native kingdom of Latium and the acquisition of the female reproductive power that is crucial to the continuity of the state they seek to found. Similarly also, the Virgilian Lavinia's passage from her father to her husband is troubled by a rival suitor (Turnus), and like Lavinia's marriage in *Titus*, gives rise to carnage and civil war (Miola 1983: 55, 45).

The father's exaggerated investment in the patriarchal order is commandingly represented onstage by the tomb of the Andronici, five hundred years old and "sumptuously re-edified" by Titus (1.1.356). It is the site of two separate funerals in the play's first scene, each of them interrupted and troubled: the first by Tamora's pleas that Alarbus be spared, the second by Titus's refusal to bury with his brothers the son whom he has just killed, on the grounds that "Here none but soldiers and Rome's servitors / Repose in fame; none basely slain in brawls" (357–8). The tomb thus represents not simply the continuity of the family so much as the subordination of the family to the military needs of the state – the original and hallowed medium of *virtus*.

The terms of the hero's apostrophe to the tomb, however, also suggest its feminine counterpart:

> O sacred receptacle of my joys,
> Sweet cell of virtue and nobility,
> How many sons of mine hast thou in store,
> That thou wilt never render to me more!
>
> (1.1.95–8)

Like the daughter's virginal womb, it is a receptacle, an enclosed cell, that stores up the joy and sweetness of successive generations, specifically through commemorating for posterity the fame gained by male ancestors through death in battle. The daughter's womb is intended to produce sons for the state; the father's tomb keeps them "in store," to generate ideological as distinct from biological *virtus*.

When Aaron incites Chiron and Demetrius to rape Lavinia in the forest, his language evokes the thesaurization that the rape is intended to undo:

> There speak, and strike, brave boys, and take your turns;
> There serve your lust, shadowed from heaven's eye,
> And revel in Lavinia's treasury.
>
> (1.1.629–31)

Demetrius perpetuates the image when he jeers at Lavinia as "corn" to be harvested; Chiron refers to her "nice-preserved" honesty: and Tamora calls her "the honey we desire" (2.2.123, 135, 131). Lavinia is both the container they would break open and the valued nourishment it stores. Lavinia, totally subjected to this construction of herself, supplies a precipitating cause for the rape when she taunts Tamora for her "goodly gift in horning" (2.2.67), by which Lavinia implies her own unspotted chastity. This slur functions somewhat like Collatine's boast of Lucrece's chastity in *Lucrece*, in that it implicitly sets up a competition centering on a man's possession of his wife's body. Here, however, it is the women who compete. Preening herself as properly "contained" by her husband, Lavinia scorns Tamora's freedom from sexual constraint, thus giving Demetrius a pretext for defending his mother's honor by violating Lavinia's:

> This minion stood upon her chastity,
> Upon her nuptial now, her loyalty . . .
> And shall she carry this unto her grave?
> (2.2.124–5, 127)

The brothers' plan to drag Bassianus "to some secret hole / And make his dead trunk pillow to our lust" travesties the marital chastity of which Lavinia boasts (2.2.129–30) by fusing the scene of marital consummation with the scene of rape, making it obscene. The travesty is furthered when the Andronicus brothers, having fallen into the same pit, remark on the "precious ring" that Lavinia's dead husband wears on his "bloody finger," likening it to "a taper in some monument" (2.2.226–8). This image alludes, again obscenely, to Bassianus's sexual guardianship of his wife, brutally mocked by both his murder and her rape (compare the similar implications of "Nerissa's ring" in *The Merchant of Venice* (Kahn 1985). It also connects and contrasts Lavinia's "treasury," her precious but violated womb, with the monument of the Andronici that Titus obsequiously honored as the "sweet cell" of sons who died for Rome. He venerated one pious place while neglecting another, which will prove to be his undoing as well as his daughter's.

Lavinia's "treasury" and the monument of the Andronici also stand in close, overdetermined relationship to another site already mentioned: the "abhorred pit" that is the scene of the murders, rape, and mutilations committed by Chiron and Demetrius.[10] This pit is first rhetorically conjured into existence by Tamora, who locates it in "A barren detested vale" where "nothing breeds," then associates it with "A thousand fiends, a thousand hissing snakes, / Ten thousand swelling toads, as many urchins" (2.3.93–101). The unwitting Lavinia then connects this locale of nightmarish fecundity to the scene of her own rape when, using the euphemistic language that befits her chastity, she pleads with Tamora,

> 'Tis present death I beg; and one thing more
> That womanhood denies my tongue to tell.
> O, keep me from their worse than killing lust,
> And tumble me into some loathsome pit,
> Where never man's eye may behold my body . . .
> (22.173–7)

When Titus's sons further elaborate the pit as an image of female genitalia, their metaphors evoke virginity and defloration:

> What subtle hole is this,
> Whose mouth is covered with rude-growing briers,
> Upon whose leaves are drops of new-shed blood
> As fresh as morning dew distilled on flowers?
>
> (2.2.198–201)

Though Lavinia is a "a new-married lady" (2.1.15) when she is raped, Tamora uses the term "deflower" (2.2.191) to describe what is done to her, thus representing her as virginal daughter rather than chaste wife, even before her husband is murdered and she returns to her father in the daughter's position (2.2.191). The spoliation of her virginal fertility by rape contrasts with Tamora's wanton fecundity; already the mother of two grown sons, she soon will bear a bastard child by a Moor. To sum up the relationship between chaste daughter and whorish mother implied by the burgeoning metaphoricity of the pit: the virginal daughter's fertility is cut off at a womb-like place that associates rape and murder with the maternal. The father's treasure is stolen and destroyed by the mother.

As several critics have demonstrated, the imagery of the pit proliferates meaning in a way that suggests what I would call the *ur*-meaning of that imagery: maternal fecundity that, eluding patriarchal control, becomes excessive, destructive, and malignant, breeding further evils. The extremely fecund mother of the twenty-six Andronici – never mentioned in the play, and conspicuously absent from the funeral rites of the first scene – has been excised from Rome, displaced onto Tamora, the Gothic outsider, and demonized with a ferocious linguistic and theatrical inventiveness. When Titus offends Tamora's maternity by sacrificing her son and facilitates her incorporation into Rome by mishandling his political and filial responsibilities, she becomes the breeding-ground of outrages, as much a spur to others' wickedness as a source of it herself. Aaron sets on her sons as a way of obscurely realizing his own ambitions to "mount her pitch"; those sons kill, rape, and mutilate to satisfy their mutual rivalry, and assist her in revenge. One crime spawns another, and the ultimate source of all is the offended, alienated mother.[11]

In the composite Romanness of the first scene, maternal presence is entirely excluded, but alienated and given compelling voice in Tamora, while the father's power is foregrounded as rashly, cruelly, and hubristically dominant. As Marion Wynne-Davies notes, however, "The womb is not only the centre of female sexuality, but the repository of familial descent . . . Control of the womb was paramount to determining a direct patrilineal descent" (1991: 136). Under proper patriarchal control, the womb is subordinated to the tomb, to the patriarchal family as configured by the Roman state, its military aims, and the dictates of *virtus*. Eluding that control, the maternal womb burgeons aggressively, pollutes patrilineal descent, and destroys civil order, whereas the daughter's womb, first virginal and then violated, serves as the focal point whereby the father defends patriarchy against the mother's attack and ultimately regains control. *Titus* positions its hero between a rampaging mother and a dutiful daughter.

The play's first scene locates the initiating mechanism of the revenge play not in an injury done to the hero through his kin as in *The Spanish Tragedy* or *Hamlet*, but in the hero's injury to a mother.[12] Once Alarbus's limbs are lopped, Tamora becomes Titus's enemy, and once she conspires against his children – notably, his daughter – he becomes the offended party, the injured father, the avenging hero. The play can be seen as the story of Titus's transformation from Roman hero to revenge hero, which he accomplishes by hacking and hewing his way through the tangled matrix of outrages and injuries that Tamora spawns.

Titus thus bears a strong resemblance to Shakespeare's Richard III who, as Janet Adelman argues, imagines and enacts his masculinity as a response to his mother's depriving, malignant womb, where love "forswore" him. Deformed and unloved, he seeks compensation in the crown. Fantasizing the obstacles to it as "a thorny wood," a suffocating matrix that replicates the hostile womb, he determines to "hew [his] way out with a bloody axe" (*3 Henry VI*, 3.2.153–81). Richard's character localizes what Adelman calls "a whole range of anxieties about masculinity and female power . . . diffused over the whole surface of the text" (1992: 3). Similarly, in Titus's tragic plight Shakespeare tries to focus the anxieties that are diffused (to say the least) in the crimes Tamora sponsors and in the over-elaborated pit metaphorically equated with vagina ("secret hole"), "swallowing womb," tomb ("this deep pit, poor Bassianus' grave"), mouth and hell itself ("this fell devouring receptacle, / As hateful as Cocytus' misty mouth") (2.3.129, 192–240).

As Douglas Green remarks, "It is largely on and through the female characters that Titus is constructed and his tragedy inscribed" (1989: 319). By pitting Gothic mother against Roman daughter, the angry, aggressive maternal womb against the subjected, violated daughterly womb, Shakespeare configures Titus's passage from *pietas* to revenge.

The Handmaiden

In conformity with the usual decorum, the rape of Lavinia is not enacted onstage. She is taken off by her assailants in one scene (2.2) and returns in the next according to the following stage direction: "*Enter the empress' sons, with Lavinia, her hands cut off, and her tongue cut out, and ravish'd*" (2.3.S.D.). Ravishment leaves no outward mark, no visible sign save those contrived by convention: dishevelled dress, unbound hair.[13] From this point on, Lavinia's rape is signified to us as audience or readers by her mutilations, but her male kin take those signs for the thing itself. Until she writes "Stuprum" in the dust, they remain transfixed by her external wounds and ignorant of the internal one, which has the greater symbolic significance. The mutilations are an afterthought, a corollary to the main crime, presumably necessitated by the brothers' desire to conceal the crime and avoid punishment (also, perhaps, marked by Shakespeare's desire to emulate Ovid and Seneca). While the rape was planned and discussed extensively (1.1.599ff., 2.2.122–86), the mutilations come as a surprise to us. Yet it is the mutilations that distract Lavinia's uncle, father, brother, and nephew and keep them from realizing that she has been raped as well.

Or rather, the text voices and then suppresses that realization. When Marcus first encounters his niece he describes the sight she presents in an often-quoted passage that imitates a typically Ovidian mingling of the erotic with the grotesque:

> Speak, gentle niece, what stern ungentle hands
> Hath lopp'd and hew'd and made thy body bare
> Of her two branches, those sweet ornaments,
> Whose circling shadows kings have sought to sleep in,
> And might not gain so great a happiness
> As half thy love? Why dost not speak to me?
> Alas, a crimson river of warm blood,
> Like to a bubbling fountain stirr'd with wind,
> Doth rise and fall between thy rosed lips,
> Coming and going with thy honey breath.
> But, sure, some Tereus hath deflower'd thee,
> And lest thou should'st detect him, cut thy tongue.
>
> (2.3.16–27)

Marcus easily and immediately connects Lavinia's bleeding mouth with Philomel's, the visible wound with the hidden fact of rape.[14] A few lines later, he elaborates the connection by noting that while Philomel only lost her tongue, "A craftier Tereus" has cut off Lavinia's "pretty fingers" to keep her from telling of her rape in needlework (38–43). Just after he mentions Tereus, Marcus says his niece turns away her face "for shame," as if "blushing to be encountered" (2.3.28–32) – her blush implicitly confirming his suspicions. But these moments of truth vanish, to be followed by three successive scenes in which Marcus seems to be just as much in the dark as his male kinsfolk. As Lyn Higgins and Brenda Silver point out, in many representations of rape in western literature, "Rape exists as an absence or gap that is both product and source of textual anxiety, contradiction and censorship . . . [a] constantly deferred origin of both plot and social relations" (Higgins and Silver, 1991: 3). In this play, like Chiron and Demetrius the text flaunts the rape, then conceals it; points it out, then censors it. Here as in other of Shakespeare's Roman works, a wound works like a fetish as a site of undecideability about inscriptions and relations of gender.

Higgins and Silver also comment that "Who gets to tell the story and whose story counts as 'truth' determine the definition of what rape is" (1991: 1). The "absence or gap" that Marcus's amnesia creates is filled by a sequence of scenes in which he and other men try to interpret Lavinia, mistaking her meanings and appropriating her signs for their own. Because we know her hidden truth, however, these scenes ironically serve to dramatize and thematize the erasure of the feminine in patriarchy; to destabilize the language in which women are customarily figured as objects of exchange or vessels for reproduction; and to bring obliquely to light – for us – what has been censored.

In this part of the play, the polluted Lavinia, neither maid nor wife nor simply widow, passes from a state of liminality and passivity to an active role as communicator of her own meaning. When Marcus first glimpses her, she is evidently fleeing from him so that her injuries are hidden. He asks her, "Where is your husband?" (2.3.12), a normal response to the sight of a married woman wandering alone in the woods. Then he pours out the Petrarchan travesty quoted above that moves back and forth between hands and tongue, tongue and hands to blazon her ruination as both marriageable daughter and chaste wife. The shocking disparity between Marcus's rhetoric (he calls Lavinia's arms "circling shadows kings have sought to sleep in," 2.3.19) and the maimed body to which it pertains makes it clear that the Lavinia who existed before the rape as an object of desire and exchange was a construction of the language wielded by the men who exchanged and desired her. Marcus's recourse to that language when it can no longer function both highlights it and the places for women that it normally creates, and indicates that Lavinia can no longer occupy those linguistic or social sites.[15]

Throughout the next two scenes (3.1 and 3.2), Titus tries both to assimilate Lavinia into the losses he is already suffering (his two sons, framed as the murderers of Bassianus, are executed after Aaron tricks him into cutting off his hand to free them) and to project his own meanings onto her gestures. Even before he loses his hand, he takes her amputations as an emblem of Rome's ingratitude towards him, its chief warrior:

> Speak, Lavinia, what accursed hand
> Hath made thee handless in thy father's sight? . . .
> Give me a sword, I'll chop off my hands too;
> For they have fought for Rome, and all in vain . . .

> 'Tis well, Lavinia, that thou hast no hand,
> For hands to do Rome service is but vain.
>
> (3.1.67–8, 73–4, 80–1)

He places her at the top of his hierarchy of woes – two sons killed, one son banished, his brother weeping for him – as "dear Lavinia, dearer than my soul" (103). But as the scene progresses, his attempts and those of his kin to interpret her wounds and her gestures invariably point back from her to the men in her family:

> TITUS.　　Look, Marcus! ah, son Lucius, look on her!
> 　　　　　When I did name her brothers, then fresh tears
> 　　　　　Stood on her cheeks, as doth the honey-dew
> 　　　　　Upon a gath'red lily almost withered.
> MARCUS.　Perchance she weeps because they kill'd her husband;
> 　　　　　Perchance because she knows them innocent.
> 　　　　　　　　　　　　　　　　　　　(3.1.111–16)
> LUCIUS.　Sweet father, cease your tears; for at your grief
> 　　　　　See how my wretched sister sobs and weeps
> 　　　　　　　　　　　　　　　　　　　(3.1.137–8)

Titus's suffering centers in himself, standing "as one upon a rock / Environ'd with a wilderness of sea" (94–5), while he interprets his daughter's anguish as reflexive and empathetic, responding to others. He claims, "I understand her signs" (144), but as he reads them, those signs have nothing to do with her, and in the rhetoric of his grief he eclipses both her and his other kin. He is no longer a rock surrounded by sea but the sea itself and the earth as well:

> I am the sea. Hark how her sighs doth blow;
> She is the weeping welkin, I the earth;
> Then must my sea be moved with her sighs;
> Then must my earth with her continual tears
> Become a deluge, overflow'd and drown'd . . .
>
> (3.1.226–30)

Lavinia does respond to her father's pain, to some extent bearing out his projections: she kneels with him (210). But his every reference to her wounds and her gestures is nonetheless both ambiguous and ironic, because the wounds are both metaphor and metonymy for the hidden, adjacent wound of rape, of which, in his egocentric grief, he remains ignorant. Furthermore, as responsive to Titus as Lavinia is, all her gestures may be construed as in some way self-referential, too. When she seeks to kneel with her father, for instance, her reasons for prayer can't be the same as his. She wears her rue with a difference.

When Titus finally turns from tears to mad laughter, and assembles his remaining family into a circle to swear revenge (267–88), it would seem that her part in this ritual signifies her return to the role of patriarchal daughter. "Bear thou my hand, sweet wench, between thy teeth," he commands, making her the handmaid of his revenge, a metaphor gruesomely literalized both here and later (5.1) when with her stumps she holds a basin to catch the blood while he slits the throats of her attackers.[16] But there are other ways to read this image, as Mary Loughlin Fawcett suggests. The substitution of father's hand for daughter's tongue can indicate the patriarchal origin and status of language, for example; or as parody of the marriage ceremony in which the father gives away his daughter's hand, it can hint at the incestuous return of the daughter to the father (Fawcett 1983: 261–2). Meanings such as these call attention to the social and linguistic structures that make daughters into handmaidens.

When Lavinia sits down at the banquet table in the next scene (3.2), the emphasis shifts from the hero's grief to the problematics of Lavinia as signifier. Though Titus still professes, "I can interpret all her martyr'd signs" (36), it is more obvious than ever that he can't. Since neither he nor his daughter can eat normally, the scene offers further opportunities for wordplay about hands, and gestures complementing it. Marcus rebukes his brother for suggesting, in a grotesque conceit, that she in effect commit suicide: "Fie, brother, fie! Teach her not thus to lay / Such violent hands upon her tender life." Reasonably enough, since she has indeed lost all manual dexterity, Titus replies, "What violent hands can she lay on her life?" (3.2.21–2, 25). Lavinia renders even commonplace metaphors dysfunctional. Furthermore, in the context of Titus's earlier reference to his hands that "fought for Rome and all in vain" (3.1.74), it is evident that the meaning of hands is gender-specific. Even when she still had her hands, Lavinia's use of them was limited to lute-playing and sewing "tedious samplers," the ornaments of her chastity; she had no access to agency.

After continuing, somewhat tediously, to "handle . . . the theme . . . of hands" (3.2.29), Titus now volunteers more modestly to "learn" what Lavinia means:

> Thou shalt not sigh, nor hold thy stumps to heaven,
> Nor wink, nor nod, nor kneel, nor make a sign,
> But I of these will wrest an alphabet . . .
>
> (3.2.42–4)

This list, which isn't comprehensive, indicates the scope of gestures available to the actor playing Lavinia, and the opportunity for possibly disruptive or subversive meanings in her "alphabet."[17] It is not simply through gestures, though, that she finally manages to identify her rapists. The scene closes as father, daughter, and nephew go off to read together – a touching family group – seemingly just for distraction from their overbearing griefs (3.2.82–6). This moment heralds the play's most interesting critique of the linguistic bases of patriarchy.

The next scene opens with a burst of activity emanating from a transformed Lavinia. No longer weeping or kneeling, she chases her nephew around the stage as though possessed by "some fit or frenzy" until she gets hold – in a fashion – of the book she seeks, Ovid's *Metamorphoses*, turns to the tale of Philomel, and finally gets her message across. No longer misled by her visible wounds, Titus now sees the hidden truth through the medium of a text: "And rape, I fear, was root of thy annoy" (4.1.49).

Previously, Lavinia unwittingly disrupted language by conveying meanings she didn't intend, and couldn't tell the story she wanted to tell. Now she tells it, but in the revealingly mediated form of a citation from one of the master texts of Latin culture. Thus she figures the cultural double bind of women, who must either speak in the language of the fathers or improvise some other means of communication in its interstices. When Chiron and Demetrius turned her loose in the woods after raping and maiming her, they jeered:

> So, now go tell, and if thy tongue can speak,
> Who 'twas that cut thy tongue and ravish'd thee.
> Write down thy mind, bewray thy meaning so
> And if thy stumps will let thee, play the scribe.
> See how with signs and tokens she can scrowl.
>
> (2.4.1–5)

The last word "scrowl" is a variant spelling of "scrawl," defined in the *OED* as "to spread the limbs abroad in a sprawling manner." The physical activity of writing that normally passes unremarked becomes in Lavinia's case grotesquely indecorous. To a modern reader it may also suggest other forms of signification such as "scrawl" and "scroll," referring to writing and written text (the *QED* offers no examples contemporary with the play), and "scowl," a facial expression as non-verbal signifier. Lavinia eventually does manage to "scrowl" the Latin word for rape, and the names of the rapists, in the earth; by following her uncle's example, she holds a staff between her teeth and guides it with her stumps. After the prolonged irony of the preceding textual aporia, during which Marcus's initial recognition of rape was effaced, this moment comes as Lavinia's peculiar, hard-won triumph. But it is also true that, as Fawcett argues, "When she takes her uncle's staff into her mouth, she uses the language of the fathers, the cultural dominators" (1983: 269), for she writes in Latin. What

Shakespeare gives with one hand, one might say, he takes away with the other.[18]

Though the story of Philomel supplies the most fully elaborated paradigm of Lavinia's role in the revenge scenario, it is but one in a sequence of classical references in this scene – a sequence that as a whole suggests the complexity of women's relations to texuality in patriarchal culture. More specifically, it reveals Shakespeare's effacement of female agency in his selective retention and deletion of elements in the stories of women.[19] The sequence begins when Marcus, urging his nephew not to be frightened by the aunt who is furiously pursuing him, compares her to Cornelia, mother of the Gracchi, who read to her sons. Just as Cornelia prepared them for their political roles, he implies, so has Lavinia, by reading poetry and Cicero's *De Oratore* to the boy, performed the office of a mother by mediating literacy to the next generation of males (without seizing its power for herself). The boy then compares his aunt to a strikingly different kind of mother, "Hecuba of Troy" who, he has read, "Ran mad for sorrow" (4.1.20–1).[20]

Hecuba's sorrow, interestingly, motivates only the first part of the story Ovid tells in the *Metamorphoses*. After the defeat of Troy, when her only surviving daughter Polyxena is sacrificed to appease Achilles' shade, Hecuba beats her breast and grieves both for her daughter and her lost dignity as queen. But when she discovers that Polydorus, the last of her sons, has been treacherously murdered by Polymestor, to whom he was given to be kept safe from the war, she sets out to avenge him and herself. Ovid stresses the empowerment anger gives her: "In that rage / She towered, a queen again, whose whole employment / Spelled out the images of fitting vengeance" (*Met.* 13.545–7).[21] That vengeance is no less terrible than the one exacted by Titus. Hecuba lures Polymestor to an audience and with the aid of the other captured women, grabs him. Then she not only digs out his eyes from their sockets but keeps on, "In manic fury, with bloody fingers, scooping / The hollows where the eyes had been" (*Met.* 13.563–4). In suppressing the second part of Hecuba's story in the Boy's reference to Lavinia as Hecuba, Shakespeare excises a female agency that takes violent retribution against patriarchy, and retains as the woman's part the ineffectual empathetic sorrow – witness as opposed to agency – that Titus and the others ascribe to Lavinia.

The Philomel story offers a more complex array of parallels and differences. In both the Ovidian tale and the Shakespeare play, "the exchange of women articulates the culture's boundaries" and the woman's sexualized body serves as "the ground of the culture's system of differences" (Joplin 1984: 37, 38). Ovid's tale (*Met.*, 6. 419–672) begins with a father giving his daughter in marriage. Because Tereus, king of Thrace, came to his aid when Athens was threatened with invasion, Pandion gives him his daughter Procne. (Similarly, as noted above, Titus furthers Lavinia's betrothal within a sequence of exchanges

between men.) In making this alliance, Pandion unwisely breaches the bound-
ary between civilized Athens and wild Thrace. Similarly, in taking Tamora,
the licentious and barbarous Goth, as wife, Saturninus opens Rome's gates to
its cultural other, while his brother's marriage to Lavinia, the epitome of chaste
Roman womanhood, marks the difference between Roman and barbarian. But
that difference, already destabilized by the blurring of distinctions between
rape and marriage in the passage of Lavinia from one brother to the other, is
violently confounded when she is raped by two Gothic brothers. In Ovid's
story, Tereus takes two daughters from the same man: he marries Procne, but
he then rapes her sister Philomel, becoming the husband of two women and
changing sisters to rivals (*Met.*, 6.536–9). Thus both the tale and the play point
to exogamy as a perilous marker of cultural difference, and generate their plots
from the disruption of the lawful exchange of women in marriage by the
violent seizure of women in rape.

   The tale and the play diverge importantly, however, in scripting women's
responses to rape. Lavinia, complicit with her patriarchal role as daughter and
wife, helped precipitate rape by boasting of her chastity, and loses her tongue
simultaneously with her chastity. As I have just argued, the text registers
anxiety about rape, rather than protest, by muting not only Lavinia but also
Marcus, whose recognition of her rape as a version of Philomel's is dramatized, then effaced. Philomel, in contrast, speaks out against Tereus, boldly
indicting him and threatening to reveal the rape:

> O wicked deed! O cruel monster,
> Barbarian, savage! . . .
> Now that I have no shame, I will proclaim it.
> Given the chance, I will go where people are,
> Tell everybody; if you shut me here,
> I will move the very woods and rocks to pity.
> The air of Heaven will hear, and any god,
> If there is any god in heaven, will hear me.
> (*Met.* 6.532–3, 545–50)

Moved equally by fear and anger, Tereus cuts off her tongue and hides her in
the forest.

   From this point, Ovid stresses the bonds among women by means of which
a terrible revenge against Tereus is enacted (Joplin 1990). A silenced Philomel
makes the traditionally feminine art of the loom a medium of communication
with her sister. She weaves her story into a tapestry and gives it to an old
woman, who brings it to Procne. Taking advantage of a women's rite, a festival of Bacchus attended by "all the Thracian mothers," dressed in vines and
deerskin Procne joins the raging worshippers and finds her sister, hidden in

the forest. Reunited with Philomel, she immediately begins to plot vengeance, telling her, "This is no time . . . / For tears, but for the sword, for something stronger / Than sword" (*Met.*, 6.613–15) – namely, murdering her son and serving him to his unwitting father as a ritual meal. Procne hesitates only when her son embraces her; at that moment, she explicitly weighs his claim on her, and her husband's, against her ties to her sister: "Since he calls me mother, / Why does she not say Sister? Whose wife are you, / Daughter of Pandion?" She concludes, "But devotion to him [Tereus] is a worse crime," and together the sisters swiftly take their bloody retribution on the rapist – appropriately through his son, his stake in the continuity of patriarchal power (*Met.*, 6.634–8).

In contrast, Lavinia depends not on the feminine art of textiles, but, as I have argued, on the texts authored by men that authorize patriarchal culture. Shakespeare marks the moment in which dramatic focus shifts from Lavinia's communication of rape to Titus' enactment of revenge by making Titus, the avenging father, address the father of the gods in Latin: "*Magni dominator poli, / Tam lentus audis scelera? Tam lentus vides?* (4.1.81–2) (Ruler of the great heavens, art thou so slow to hear and to see crimes?)[22] Titus is the offended party, and it will be Titus who initiates, supervises, and carries out revenge. Construing the injury done to Lavinia as an injury to himself, as he prepares to slaughter Chiron and Demetrius he tells them, "For worse than Philomel you used my daughter, / And worse than Progne I will be revenged" (5.2.194–5).

Wherever the story of Philomel is evoked in Shakespeare, the story of Lucrece is also brought in.[23] Celebrated on adjacent days in Ovid's *Fasti*, the two stories are parallel and complementary in their portrayals of rape and women enacting retribution. While Philomel and Procne act against the rapist only, in killing herself Lucrece also motivates her kinsmen to take retribution. Trying to learn who raped his daughter, Titus turns from Ovid's myth to Livy's history:

> Give signs, sweet girl, for here are not but friends,
> What Roman lord it was durst do the deed:
> Or slunk not Saturnine, as Tarquin erst,
> That left the camp to sin in Lucrece' bed?
>
> (4.1.61–4)

By citing the rape of Lucrece, Titus raises the possibility that Lavinia, like Lucrece, might represent herself, articulate the meaning of sexual violation, and lay the foundation for the revenge that follows. Summoning her husband, her father, and her other male kin, Livy's Lucrece reveals the crime and its perpetrator. She also affirms that "It is my bodye onely that is violated, my minde God knoweth is guiltles," but stresses what it means for the honor of her father and her husband rather than to herself. Most importantly, she declares that, despite her innocence, she nonetheless intends to commit suicide, and links this act to the action she expects them to take, saying:

> I praye you consider with you selves, what punishmente is due for the male-factour. As for my part, though I cleare my selfe of the offence, my body shall feele the punishment: for no unchast or ill women, shall hereafter impute no dishonest act to Lucrece. (Painter's *Pallace*, quoted in Prince 1961: 194–5)

This double move constitutes an exceptionally lucid representation of the role of sacralized chastity, incorporate in the female body, in Roman patriarchy. Lucrece takes it upon herself to maintain the ideological purity of chastity for future generations, by making her suicide a symbolic purification of the pollution of her chastity wrought by the rape.[24] Furthermore, by drawing a parallel between "what is due the malefactour" and "my parte," when she turns the knife against herself she makes it imperative for the men to turn it against the tyrant. Thus she establishes a narrative linkage between rape, revenge, and revolution that, as Stephanie Jed (1989) has argued, reaches back to Thucydides and Aristotle, and forward to Machiavelli and Salutati – and to Shakespeare.

This promise of empowerment for Lavinia, however circumscribed by patriarchal ideology, is not borne out. In the stage action so suggestive of woman's relation to patriarchal language and power, Lavinia follows her uncle's guidance, takes a staff in her mouth, and scratches in the earth the names of the crime and the criminals. Then, instead of inciting her kinsmen to revenge, she becomes part of the ritual her uncle leads, a ritual modeled on the oath-taking in Livy's narrative. Marcus commands:

> My lord, kneel down with me; Lavinia, kneel;
> And kneel, sweet boy, the Roman Hector's hope;
> And swear with me, as with the woeful fere
> And father of that chaste dishonoured dame,
> Lord Junius Brutus sware for Lucrece' rape,
> That we will prosecute by good advice
> Mortal revenge upon these traitorous Goths,
> And see their blood, or die with this reproach.
> (4.1.87–94)

Once Lavinia makes the rape known, the task of avenging it passes into male hands. For her, it remains only to assist her father in killing the rapists, and according to the last of the many textural precedents and parallels cited, not to kill herself but to be killed by her father. If, in Joplin's interpretation, the chaste woman is the sign of her father's or husband's power, when that woman is raped, such power is mocked, challenged, diminished (1984: 33–4). Through revenge, it can be restored.

The Revenger

Curiously, however, once Titus finally has his mandate for revenge, he doesn't seize it. Not he but his brother Marcus leads the Andronici in swearing revenge, and in the next three scenes, Titus repeatedly seeks recourse to actions that, though symbolically potent, don't effect revenge. He sends to the rapist a bundle of weapons wrapped in a scroll on which a famous verse from Horace is written (4.2); together with the weapons, it constitutes an ironic comment on their guilt, but its meaning eludes them. Next he organizes a group of Romans to shoot arrows addressed to various gods toward the court, an elaborate dramatic conceit signifying – again, through a well-known Latin tag – that he can find no justice here on earth (*"Terras Astraea reliquit"* (Ovid, *Met.*, 150), 4.3.4). Finally, he sends Saturninus an oration wrapped around a knife. All these gestures combine texts with weapons to signify ambivalently that while words can work like weapons, they aren't weapons, and weapons, in this case, work like words, signifying but not committing aggression.

This recoil from revenge could be explained generically, for Titus now finds himself in the same position as the revenge tragedy heroes Hieronimo or Hamlet: he knows the identity of his enemies, and they are the ones in power. In acting against them he would commit treason and risk his won destruction. Furthermore, revenge heroes are inherently decent men reluctant to act outside the law. This kind of impasse necessitates the delay standard to the revenge play, delay that creates an ethical and dramatic tension released in the final outburst of bloody retaliations. Titus's reluctance to act, however, is based on more than revenge convention; it fits into the pattern informing the whole play that positions him between the daughter and the mother. Empowered by his daughter's words, Titus must now face Tamora, the evil mother – and here he pauses:

> But if you hunt these bear-whelps, then beware:
> The dam will wake, and if she wind ye once
> She's with the lion deeply still in league,
> And lulls him whilst she playeth on her back,
> And when he sleeps will she do what she list.
>
> (4.1.96–100)

Tamora (and unknown to Titus, her paramour Aaron) have made Rome "a wilderness of tigers." This feral mother, Titus argues, fiercely guards her bearish sons, "lulls" the emperor her husband while she cuckolds him, and can have her way against any who challenge her. Though Marcus thinks his brother won't act because he is "yet so just that he will not revenge" (4.1.128), it is specifically Tamora from whom Titus recoils.

At this point, the half-mad Titus fantasizes making the most futile of textual gestures: writing a version of the Sibyl's prophecies (persumably indicting Tamora), to be blown away "like leaves before the wind" (4.1.102–6). This impotence is contrasted to the Boy's boast: "if I were a man / Their mother's bedchamber should not be safe" (4.1.107–8). He would revenge rape by rape, and, his uncle assures him, "thy father hath full oft / For his ungrateful country done the like" (4.1.110–11). In other words, rape is manly, Roman, and in warfare, surely, a component of *virtus*. This fleeting fantasy of raping a mother as revenge hardly models the action that an upright Roman like Titus would pursue. But it recalls the sexually overdetermined image of the pit as vagina, womb, tomb, and hell, an image that represented a complex of male anxieties primarily surrounding the maternal feminine, unleashed when Tamora became Titus's enemy. It is those fears that Titus must confront in avenging his daughter's rape.

Tamora, absent from the stage since the scene in which the pit figured, the scene of the rape, returns as an offstage presence in the next scene. A trumpet flourish announces that she has given birth to a child, and the Nurse brings the baby onstage. The scene then centers on whether this black baby shall live or die. Tamora and her sons want to do away with it, because the child's skin color proves her mother's adultery; as the Nurse says, the baby is "Our empress' shame, and stately Rome's disgrace" (4.2.60), while Aaron proudly claims it as his own. In ideological terms, what is at stake is the preservation of sacralized chastity in Rome, either through deception by means of infanticide, or through the revelation of Tamora's breach of chastity and the restoration of the real thing. Constant reference to the baby's blackness and many physical threats to its life ("I'll broach the tadpole on my rapier's point," says Demetrius, 4.2.87), make it very much a creature of the flesh and emphasize its fleshly connection to Tamora. Her labor pains are mentioned (4.2.46–7), and Aaron rebukes Chiron and Demetrius by saying,

> He is your brother, lords, sensibly fed
> Of that self blood that first gave life to you;
> And from that womb where you imprisoned were
> He is enfranchised and come to light . . .
> (4.2.124–7)

With every reference to Tamora's maternity, we are also reminded of her lasciviousness. She flaunts sacralized chastity and also the Roman ethnic purity it protects, her bastard child being by blood half-Goth, half-Moor. This nameless infant embodies the anxieties about the unconstrained maternal womb represented by the pit in act two – anxieties that Titus must confront and recontain.

While his last remaining son, Lucius, the representative of unblemished *virtus*, leads an army of Goths against Rome to rid it of the demonized mother, Tamora plans to set father against son by persuading Titus to make his son relent. In the play's cleverest scene, she finds him in contemplative retreat in his study, "ruminat[ing] plots of dire revenge" (5.2.6); that is, he is writing. "What I mean to do / See here in bloody lines I have set down," he says, "And what is written shall be executed" (5.2.13–15). But, he adds sardonically, he lacks "a hand to give it action" (5.2.18). Tamora has disguised herself as Revenge, and her two sons as Rape and Murder; because Titus is mad, she thinks, he won't recognize them. Serving as a sort of anti-muse, she tells him she is "sent from th'infernal kingdom / To ease the gnawing vulture of thy mind" (5.2.30–1) by working vengeance on his enemies. In this scene, as Willbern suggests, Tamora's self-association with hell is more than conventional, given the imagery of the pit that connects hell not only with female sexuality (a connection ubiquitous in the Shakespearean canon as well) but more specifically, as I have argued, with the malign fecundity of the maternal womb. Ascending, perhaps, from the trapdoor that localizes hell on stage, she "stands within the symbol of her dreadful power" and accosts the reclusive Titus (Willbern 1978: 177–8). She would entice him "down" – into the damnable evil of revenge – by offering to put into action for him the plots he has put into writing. Titus first resists her, claiming that he's not mad and that he recognizes her, joking with bitter irony, "Is not thy coming for my other hand?" (5.2.27).

Finally, pretending to be taken in by her transparent ruse, he descends, and meets her on her own ground, materially and morally: he is now ready to act, to perform by his own agency, not hers, the plot that he (with the aid of Ovid and Seneca) has written. In terms of the play's gender politics, he confronts the mother and repossesses the initiative that she had illicitly seized; he reestablishes patriarchal control over a matrix made evil when he lost control. The banquet that she suggests to him as her device he appropriates for his own purposes as a Thyestean banquet of her own flesh, a supremely fitting revenge. She attacked his progeny by supervising the murder of his sons and, more cruelly, the rape of his daughter; she raided his treasury and mocked the sign of his power, his chaste daughter. Now he insults her womb (the word also means stomach), the site of her power, by making her "swallow her own increase" (5.2.191).

Of equal ideological significance in the gender politics of *Titus*, though, is the action that precedes the eating of the forbidden food – the murder of

Lavinia. Here we confront the last of the several textual precedents by which Lavinia is represented. She has been compared to Cornelia, Hecuba, Philomel, and Lucrece; in her final moments she is a Verginia, not mother, sister, or wife but definitively daughter, at last restored to Titus, though only by the knife. In Livy, the long and complex story that reaches its climax with the murder of Verginia is explicitly paralleled with that of Lucrece. Like the Tarquins, the decemvirs (a council of ten that seizes more power than it was originally granted, and, backed by force, refuses to surrender its office) are tyrants; as in the Lucrece narrative, their abuse of political power is figured in a sexual act, the culminating insult to the Roman social order.

The decemvir Appius Claudius conceives a passion for Verginia, daughter of the upright soldier Lucius Verginius; she is already betrothed to Icilius. Through a legal maneuver Appius seeks to claim her as his slave and subject her to his lust. In resisting him, the father and the intended husband function as a pair, occupying complementary positions as Verginia's present and future guardians. Verginia is helpless and unable to speak for herself; her father is away at the front, and in the buildup to confrontation between him and Appius, "the maiden's safety turn[s] on her protector's being at hand in time" (III.xvi.6). So Icilius steps in to act as her protector, articulating precisely his and her father's interest in her chastity:

> This maiden I am going to wed, and I intend that my bride shall be chaste . . .
> If Verginius yields to this man's claim, he will have to seek a husband for her.
> (III.xlv.6–7, 11)

When her father arrives, he makes a public appeal that contrasts the father's legitimate control over his daughter's body in marital exchange to the rape of daughters and wives in war:

> He then began to go about and canvass people . . . saying that he stood daily in
> the battle-line in defence of their children and their wives . . . to what end, if
> despite the safety of the City those outrages which were dreaded as the worst
> that could follow a city's capture must be suffered by their children? (III.xlvii.2)

Just as importantly, Verginius parallels the male role as warrior-protector of Rome with that of *paterfamilias*. The internal order of the city and its safety from external threat both depend, he argues, on the father's guardianship of the daughter.

The crowd to which Verginius appeals is cowed by the decemvir's authority, and Appius prepares to seize Verginia. To prevent him, the father stabs his daughter to the heart, saying "'Tis you, Appius, and your life I devote to destruction with this blood!" (III.xlviii.5). Only then does popular resistance begin to take hold, and Appius retreats; in the end, the decemvirs are forced to abdicate. Even more explicitly than in the story of Lucrece, patriarchal control over female sexuality is linked to the order and safety of the state. In both stories, the body of the slain woman, exhibited to the people, incites them to rise against tyrants.

In *Titus*, a political over-plot – the assault on Rome to unseat Saturninus, led by Titus's son Lucius – is paralleled and interwoven with the revenge plot against Tamora that Titus carries out. Titus doesn't seize political initiative as Verginius does; that falls to his son. But both stories represent filicide as an act that is both personal and political, an act based on a recognition of the social and ideological centrality of the father's control over the virgin daughter. Verginius kills his daughter so as to prevent the loss of her chastity, and makes her blood the sign and ground of resistance – his and that of the people – against the decemvir. When Titus kills Lavinia, he stresses his sorrow (in line with the play's earlier emphasis) and links it with her shame (5.3.45–6), as though only personal feelings matter. But in citing Livy's story as "A reason mighty, strong, and effectual; / A pattern, president, and lively warrant" for the murder (5.3.42–3), Titus supplies a historical context in which chastity has a fully developed political significance.

In her last brief appearance on stage, Lavinia is veiled, so that Tamora and Saturninus won't recognize her and guess what Titus is up to. This veil can also be read to indicate her liminal status as neither maid nor wife, polluted by the stain of rape. When Titus kills her – as Verginius did, "with his own right hand" – he purges her of that pollution, as Lucrece purged herself of her "forced stain" (*Lucrece*, 1700–50), and restores her to the right hand of paternal blessing.[25] What Joplin says of Lucretia's death by her own hand in Livy is equally true of Lavinia's death by her father's hand:

> Lucretia, raped and alive, would be a sign of contradiction that cynical and less virtuous women might interpret to their own ends. Lucretia, raped and dead by her own hand, neatly circumscribes and seals off the potential pollution of her sexual violation. (1990: 63)

Now Lucius can restore her to the Andronici, giving orders that "My father and Lavinia shall forthwith / Be closed in our household's monument," while Tamora, "that ravenous tiger," that murderous mother, be left unburied, prey for beasts and birds (5.3.191–200).

Notes

1   A number of critics have identified classical sources and analogues in *Titus* and interpreted their function in the play. Law (1943) added the *Aeneid* and Plutarch's

"Life of Scipio" to Kittredge's list of sources (Seneca's *Thyestes* and *Troades*, Ovid's tale of Philomel in the *Metamorphoses*, Plutarch's "Life of Coriolanus," and the story of Verginius and Verginia in Livy). Mowat (1981) suggests that the "larger shaping myth [in addition to that of Philomel] is actually . . . Hecuba's revenge, into which the Philomel myth and others are embedded" (59). See also G. K. Hunter (1984) for an important contribution to theories of source material and their meaning, and West (1982) for an interpretation of Latin texts in the play's action, both noted below. James Galderwood (1971) discovers in the transformation of Rome from civilization to barbarism an overarching allegory of Shakespeare's sense of his own descent from the purity of his literary models to "theatrical sensationalism" (41). Richard T. Brucher (1979) argues that by surpassing the violence in his classical sources, Shakespeare "push[es] the audience into an unfamiliar realm of experience where conventionally serious responses are disallowed" (87). Mary Loughlin Fawcett (1983) uses *Titus* "as a primary text to evolve a theoretical account of the relationship between the body, signs, speech, and writing," and comments interestingly on its use of Latin (263–3).

2   Miola, astutely noting Shakespeare's many appropriations of the *Aeneid* and the *Metamorphoses*, reads *Titus* as dramatizing the decline of Roman values from their original *pietas*, and stresses "the importance of familial unity" to those values (1983: 59, 66–7 *et passim*). He does not criticize, as I do, the patriarchal terms of that unity.

3   See Boose (1989) (to which I am much indebted in this chapter) for a cogent analysis of the daughter's position in the patriarchal family, in structural and historical terms.

4   Green's insightful essay, originally prepared for a seminar at the Shakespeare Association of America in 1986, first spurred me to think about Lavinia's role in the construction of her father as hero. Here I have tried to extend Green's argument that "[Lavinia's] mutilated body articulates Titus's own suffering and victimization" (1989: 322).

5   Tracing Virgilian parallels, Jonathan Bate points out that "as in the *Aeneid*, the main threat to [Titus] is an exotic woman from a rival empire," and that "Virgil's Lavinia, the mother of early Rome, becomes the mutilated daughter of late Rome" (1995: 18). In a richly detailed and suggestive intertextual reading, Heather James interprets the entire play in terms of "a discourse of cultural disintegration" in which "Shakespeare first invokes the *Aeneid* as the epic of empire-building, order, and *pietas*, and then allows Ovid's *Metamorphoses* to invade, interpreting the fundamental impulses of Vergil's poem as chaotic, even apocalyptic" (1991: 123).

6   This and all further quotations from *Titus Andronicus* are taken from the Arden Shakespeare, third series, edited by Jonathan Bate (London and New York: Routledge, 1995).

7   Lévi-Strauss's theory of kinship, exchange and culture has been appropriated, revised, and criticized by feminists. For an influential critique of it, see Rubin (1975); also see Greene and Kahn (1985).

8   Lynda Boose's discussion of the daughter's meaning in *Beowulf* suggests the dimensions of thesaurization in *Titus*: "As the means of production for all the

bonds within either her father's or the enemy's group, the daughter is every tribe's central treasure . . . As potentially multiple mediator of bonds inside, outside, or between oppositions, she defines the poem's emblematic nexus of conflicting desires" (29). See also the essays by Traub (1992) and Ziegler (1990).

9 What might seem merely clumsiness in dramatizing the conflict over Lavinia in the play's first scene can be interpreted, in several ways, as implying a comment on the patriarchal exchange of women. David Willbern states that Lavinia's first "rape . . . suggests the unconscious equation of marriage and rape, sexuality and violence, which permeates the play" (1978: 163). On a theoretical level, Patricia Klindienst Joplin's claim that rape, as a failed exchange, is homologous with marriage, can be applied to the rape / marriage of Lavinia. In rape, the woman is taken, not given, but she signifies the same thing: "In truth, they are one: prohibition (sacralized chastity) and transgression (rape by the sacred) are two sides of one coin . . . [in that the] object of desire the female body represents is supreme authority" (1990: 59). Similarly, John Winkler interprets the episodes of sexual violence in Longus's story of Daphnis and Chloe as revealing "the inherent violence of the cultural system . . . in the integration of males and females into the competitive and hostile economy of Greek culture" (1991: 17, 21).

10 In Peter Brook's acclaimed 1955 production of the play (in which Lawrence Olivier played Titus), the set was dominated by large pillars; when moved aside, they revealed an inner recess that first served as the tomb of the Andronici, then as the pit, and finally, as Titus's study or "Revenge's cave" – thus linking the three sites.

11 David Willbern's fascinating psychoanalytic interpretation places the pit, representing the mother's body, at the symbolic core of the play. He views rape and revenge as interlocking parts of a basically oedipal fantasy of attack on and defense of the mother's body: "revenge is both a substitute for sex and a defense against it." In social terms, a maternal Rome (represented by Lavinia) is raped by the Goths, and must be defended by revenge against them. He equates Tamora with a different aspect of the maternal – "the dreaded devouring mother" (1978: 166). In this view, Lavinia and Tamora are in a sense interchangeable representations of the maternal, reflecting the desire and dread of the oedipal subject. In mine, as alienated mother and violated daughter, they enact opposing feminine positions in the patriarchal family. Albert Tricomi notes that Tamora's description of the pit (2.2.94–104) links it to the underworld, as would the use of a trapdoor, "not only a symbol of the demonic power but a theatrical embodiment of it," in the staging of 2.2 (1974: 18).

12 The Longleat manuscript, which may be dated as early as 1595 or later than the Folio of 1633, emphasizes Tamora's importance and, as Alan Dessen points out, portrays her rejected plea as a key moment in the play (1989: 6). Strikingly, in its drawing of Tamora kneeling with her sons before a standing Titus, she is as tall as he is. Transcripts of her plea for Alarbus and Aaron's boastful list of his many crimes are linked by lines from Titus's speech justifying the sacrifice, implying that his action provokes the network of vengeance that Aaron plots. Jonathan Bate comments that the drawing "demonstrates how a contemporary of Shakespeare's

visualized the play," and further interprets Peacham's scene as "an emblematic reading of the whole play" representing Titus and Tamora as opposites, their gestures "the central gestures of the play: authoritative command against supplication on knees" (1995: 41–2).

13   For a different view of Lavinia's mutilation, see Leonard Tennenhouse (1986b: 107–8), who regards it as Shakespeare's "highly self-conscious revision of his classical materials," intended to displace rape so as to make Lavinia's body a symbol of the state.

14   Gail Kern Paster remarks on the "conventional metonymic replacement of mouth for vagina" in this speech, in which "the blood flowing from Lavinia's mutilated mouth stands for the vaginal wound that cannot be staged or represented . . . the sign of an immutable condition – the condition of womanhood . . . ultimately inseparable from the more conventional meaning of vaginal blood as a sign of male mastery over the body of woman, or (as here) of male sexual violence" (1993: 98–9).

15   This speech, to be sure, possesses other dimensions as well. In Deborah Warner's landmark 1987 production, Donald Sumpter as Marcus delivered it uncut and produced the effect described by Stanley Wells: "it became a deeply moving attempt to master the facts, and thus to overcome the emotional shock, of a previously unimagined horror . . . an articulation, necessarily extended in expression, of a sequence of thoughts and emotions that might have taken no more than a second or two to flash through the character's mind, like a bad dream" (Wells quoted in Bate 1995: 62). Jonathan Bate remarks that "a lyrical speech is needed because it is only when an appropriately inappropriate language has been found that the sheer force of contrast between its beauty and Lavinia's degradation begins to express what she has undergone and lost" (1995: 63).

16   Heather James credits me with spotting this visual joke, in a paper I gave in 1988 (1991: 133, 140); Jonathan Bate also remarks on it (1995: 11–12) in passing, without noting how it subsumes Lavinia's injury in her father's, and subordinates her to his heroic mission.

17   Alan Dessen (1989) surveys the range of modes in which the role of Lavinia has been performed and staged. In Peter Brook's 1955 production, crimson ribbons streamed from Lavinia's mouth and arms to signify mutilation, while in Trevor Nunn's (1972), Lavinia was "a pitiable, hunched grotesque crawling out of the darkness like a wounded animal." In her 1985 BBC production, Jane Howell's Lavinia displayed "verisimilar stumps and bloody mouth." Deborah Warner, directing *Titus* for the RSC in 1987, wrapped Lavinia's stumps, coated her with mud, and allowed "but a trickle" of blood to escape her mouth. Both stylized and naturalistic representations of the mutilation seem to have been effective.

18   For diverse readings of Lavinia's writing, along with essays by Green and Fawcett, see Hulse (1979) who views it as *fellatio* and a reenactment of her violation; Danson (1974), as figuring the frustrated human need to speak and be understood; Calderwood (1971), as part of Shakespeare's protest at being forced to abandon "the chaste poetic word" in his lyric and narrative poems and turn to the barbaric language of the popular theatre.

19   See chapter 1, pp. 20–1, on the work of Jed (1989), Joplin (1984, 1990), and Newman (1994) on gender bias in the appropriation of classical materials by Renaissance authors.

20   Barbara Mowat traces the suggestive parallels between Titus and Hecuba; her article (cited in note 1) first showed me the pertinence of that Ovidian story to the play.

21   This and other quotations from the *Metamorphoses* are taken from the translation by Rolfe Humphries (Bloomington: Indiana University Press, 1961).

22   Jonathan Bate astutely notes that this line conflates two Senecan passages, one from "a moment of appalling sexual knowledge in the *Hippolytus*" and one from the *Epistulae Morales* "on accepting death and enduring whatever nature throws at you"; thus tragic recognition is combined with "the idea of submission to the will of the universe" (1995: 30). I would add that such a fusion serves the basically patriarchal structure of this revenge play by implying that a father has no choice but to revenge a daughter's defilement and die defending his investment in her chastity.

23   See for example *Lucrece* 1079–80, 1128–49; *Cymbeline* 2.2.12–14, 44–6.

24   For an extended argument on this point, see Kahn (1976).

25   Titus still has, significantly, his right hand, for at 3.2.7–8 he comments, "This poor right hand of mine / Is left to tyrannize upon my breast."

'And Wash the Ethiop White': Femininity and the Monstrous in *Othello*

Karen Newman

Extracted from her book Fashioning Femininity and English Renaissance Drama, *this essay on* Othello *exemplifies Newman's call for 'a promiscuous conversation of many texts, early modern elite and non elite, historical records and ideological discourses, contemporary theory and popular culture' (p. 146). Drawing on a range of critical interventions into the contested categories of race and gender in the period, she also asks methodological questions about the status of different readings and material. Her open-ended essay includes diverse texts, from* Othello *to travel and economic literature to Thomas Rymer's scornful critique (see pp. 10–11), to discuss the play's complexities.*

Karen Newman, 'And wash the Ethiop white': Femininity and the Monstrous in *Othello*', in *Fashioning Femininity and English Renaissance Drama*. Chicago; London: University of Chicago Press, 1991.

Shakespear, who is accountable both to the Eyes *and to the* Ears, *And to convince the very heart of an Audience, shows that* Desdemona *was won by hearing* Othello *talk. . . . This was the Charm, this was the philtre, the love-powder, that took the Daughter of this Noble Venetian. This was sufficient to make the Black-amoor White, and reconcile all, tho' there had been a Cloven-foot into the bargain.*

Rymer, "*Short View of Tragedy*" *(1693)*[1]

It would be something monstrous to conceive this beautiful Venetian girl falling in love with a veritable negro.

Coleridge, *Lectures and Notes on Shakespeare*[2]

To a great many people the word "negro" suggests at once the picture of what they would call a "nigger," the wooly hair, thick lips, round skull, blunt features, and burnt-cork blackness of the traditional nigger minstrel. Their subconscious generalization is as silly as that implied in Miss Preston's "the African race" or Coleridge's "veritable negro." There are more races than one in Africa, and that a man is black in colour is no reason why he should, even to European eyes, look sub-human. One of the finest heads I have ever seen on any human being was that of a negro conductor on an American Pullman car. He had lips slightly thicker than an ordinary European's, and he had somewhat curly hair; for the rest he had a long head, a magnificent forehead, a keenly chiselled nose, rather sunken cheeks, and his expression was grave, dignified, and a trifle melancholy. He was coalblack, but he might have sat to a sculptor for a statue of Caesar . . .

M. R. Ridley, editor, the Arden *Othello* (1977)[3]

Mr Ridley's "they" is troublesome. As scholars and teachers, we use his Arden edition of *Othello* (1958, reprinted 1977) and find ourselves implicated in his comfortable assumptions about "a great many people." In answer to the long critical history that sought to refute Othello's blackness, Ridley affirms that Othello was black, but he hastens to add an adversative "but." Othello was not a "veritable negro," he assures us – a type from vaudeville and the minstrel show, a figure of ridicule unworthy of tragedy who would evidently appear "sub-human" to European eyes – but a black who looks white and might have represented the most renowned general of the western tradition, Caesar. What are we to make of a widely used scholarly edition of Shakespeare, which, in the very act of debunking, canonizes the prejudices of Rymer and Coleridge?[4] Can we shrug our shoulders, certain that Ridley's viewpoint represents a long-ago past of American pullman cars and dignified black conductors? Are such prejudices dismantled by the most recent reprint, which represents on its cover a "veritable negro" of exactly the physiognomy Ridley assures us "a great many people" are wrong in imagining?

Much of the disgust Rymer, Coleridge, and other critics betray comes not from the fact of Othello's individual blackness but from the *relation* of that blackness to Desdemona's fair purity. Coleridge calls it "monstrous." Embedded in commentaries on the play that seek to ward off Othello's blackness is the fear of miscegenation, and particularly the white man's fear of the union of black man with white woman. Such commentators occupy the rhetorical position of Roderigo, Brabantio, and Iago, who view the marriage of Othello and Desdemona as against all sense and nature: "I'll refer me to all things of sense, . . . Whether a maid, so tender, fair, and happy, . . . Would ever have (to incur a general mock) / Run from her guardage to the sooty bosom / Of such a thing as thou?" (I, ii, 64, 66, 69–71).

In *Othello*, the black Moor and the fair Desdemona are united in a marriage all the other characters view as unthinkable. Shakespeare uses their assumption to generate the plot itself: Iago's ploy to string Roderigo along is his assurance that Desdemona could not, contrary to nature, long love a black man. Even his manipulation of Othello depends on the Moor's own prejudices against his blackness and belief that the fair Desdemona would prefer the white Cassio.

Miscegenation is an issue not only on the level of plot but also of language; for linked oppositions, especially of black and white and their cultural associations, characterize the play's discourse.[5] "Black ram" tups "white ewe"; "fair" Desdemona runs to Othello's "sooty bosom." The Duke mollifies Brabantio with "Your son-in-law is far more fair than black." Desdemona is described, in what for the Renaissance would have been an oxymoron, as a "fair devil" and as "fair paper" and a "goodly book" across the white pages of which Othello fears is written "whore." In the final scene Emilia exclaims in response to Othello's confession that he has killed Desdemona, "O, the more angell she, / And you the blacker devil!" Like the expression "to wash an Ethiop white," Emilia's lines exemplify what I will term rhetorical miscegenation, for despite the semantics of antithesis, the chiasmus allies the opposing terms rhetorically.

In the Renaissance no other colors so clearly implied opposition nor were so frequently used to denote polarization. As Winthrop Jordan points out in his monumental study, *White over Black*, the meaning of *black* even before the sixteenth century, according to the *Oxford English Dictionary*, included "deeply stained with dirt; soiled, dirty, foul; Having dark or deadly purposes, malignant; pertaining to or involving death, deadly, baneful, disastrous, sinister; . . . iniquitous, atrocious, horribly wicked; . . . indicating disgrace, censure, liability to punishment, etc."[6] In Jonson's *Masque of Blacknesse*, a preeminent example of the black / white opposition in the period, Stephen Orgel observes that it is "only necessary that the 'twelve *Nymphs, Negro's*' be revealed – that we *see* them – for the 'antimasque' to have taken place."[7] White represented the opposite. In *Othello*, the emphasis on Desdemona's fairness and purity, "that whiter skin of hers than snow / And smooth as monumental alabaster" (V, ii,

4–5), and the idealization of fair female beauty it implies, the entire apparatus of Petrarchanism, is usually said to point up the contrast between Desdemona and Othello. But I want to argue the contrary: femininity is not opposed
to blackness and monstrosity, as are the binary opposites black and white, but
identified with the monstrous in an identification that makes miscegenation
doubly fearful. The play is structured around a cultural aporia, miscegenation.

Femininity interrupts not only the characterological but also the critical
discourse of the play. In his commentary, Ridley continues after the passage
quoted above: "To give an insult any point and barb it must have some
relation to the facts. A woman may call a pale-complexioned rival 'pasty' or
'whey-faced,' but it would be silly to call her swarthy . . . in the same way, 'thick
lips' would lose all its venom if it could not be recognizably applicable to
Othello's mouth" (lii). Ridley's justification of Othello's blackness and his
reading of "thick lips" betray a woefully inadequate sense of irony: literary discourse often works by means of negative example, as in Shakespeare's vaunt
"My mistress' eyes are nothing like the sun." But more important than Ridley's
limitations as a reader of texts is how he illustrates his point about Othello's
blackness: he evokes a cultural prejudice against women, their supposed
cattiness in response to a rival. Femininity interrupts Ridley's commentary on
Othello's blackness; pitting women against women, the critic displaces the
struggle of white against black man onto a cultural femininity.

Miscegenation: Blacks and the Monstrous

Until the late sixteenth century, speculation about the cause of blackness
depended on classical sources rather than experience or observation.[8] In the
myth of Phaeton, for example, and Ptolemy's *Tetrabiblos*, Africans' blackness
was explained by their proximity to the sun. With the publication in 1589 of
the many travel accounts and geographies in Hakluyt's *Principal Navigations*,
however, the rehearsal of this ancient topos, though often quoted, was usually
countered by the observation that many peoples living equally close to the sun
in the Indies and other parts of the New World were of olive complexion and
thus disproved the ancients' latitudinal etiology. Myth and empirical observation collided.

In his *Discourse* (1578), George Best, an English traveler, gives an early
account of miscegenation and the causes of blackness:

> I my selfe have seene an Ethiopian as blacke as a cole brought into England,
> who taking a faire English woman to wife, begat a sonne in all respects as blacke
> as the father was, although England were his native countrey, and an English
> woman his mother: whereby it seemeth this blacknes proceedeth rather of some

natural infection of that man, which was so strong, that neither the nature of the Clime, neither the good complexion of the mother concurring, coulde any thing alter.[9]

Best's account of miscegenation is designed to refute the conventional latitudinal explanation, but it does much more. Not only does it emphasize the contrariety of black and white, "blacke as a cole" and "faire English woman";[10] Best's repetitions also betray the Englishman's ethnocentric preoccupation with his native isle.[11]

Best also proffers an alternative explanation of blackness, which he substitutes for the ancients' geographical theory: "this blackness proceedeth rather of some natural infection of that man." Best's claim is more radical than his metaphor of disease implies, because to assert that black and white were "naturally" different also posed a theological problem. If the union of black and white always results in black offspring, "in all respects as blacke as the father," then how can we account for the origin of black or for that matter white, from our first parents? And so Best goes on to explain his claim by referring to scripture and the story in Genesis of Noah and his three sons,

who all three being white, and their wives also, by course of nature should have begotten and brought foorth white children. But the envie of our great and continuall enemie the wicked Spirite is such, that as hee coulde not suffer our olde father Adam to live in the felicitie and Angelike state wherein hee was first created, but tempting him, sought and procured his ruine and fall: so againe, finding at this flood none but a father and three sonnes living, hee so caused one of them to transgresse and disobey his father's commaundement, that after him all his posteritie shoulde bee accursed. The fact of disobedience was this: When Noe at the commandement of God had made the Arke and entered therein . . . hee straitely commaunded his sonnes and their wives, that they . . . should use continencie, and abstaine from carnall copulation with their wives. . . . Which good instructions and exhortations notwithstanding his wicked sonne Cham disobeyed, and being perswaded that the first childe borne after the flood (by right and Lawe of nature) should inherite and possesse all the dominions of the earth, hee contrary to his fathers commaundement while they were yet in the Arke, used company with his wife, and craftily went about thereby to dis-inherite the off-spring of his other two brethren: for the which wicked and detestable fact, as an example for contempt of Almightie God, and disobedience of parents, God would a sonne should bee borne whose name was Chus, who not onely it selfe, but all his posteritie after him should bee so blacke and lothsome, that it might remaine a spectacle of disobedience to all the worlde. And of this blacke and cursed Chus came all these blacke Moores which are in Africa.[12]

Best's myth of a second fall is an extraordinarily rich rehearsal of early English social attitudes. In it are revealed the stock prejudices against blacks in

Elizabethan and Jacobean culture: the link between blackness and the devil, the myth of black sexuality, the problem of black subjection to authority, here displaced onto obedience owed to the father and to God. Best's story passes "segregation off as natural – and as the very law of the origin." Derrida's words written about apartheid are suggestive for understanding not only Best's *Discourse* but travel writing more generally: "There's no racism without a language. The point is not that acts of racial violence are only words but rather that they have to have a word. Even though it offers the excuse of blood, color, birth – or, rather, *because* it uses this naturalist and sometimes creationist discourse – racism always betrays the perversion of man, the 'talking animal'."[13]

But Best's account also represents the effects of a specifically Tudor and Stuart economic and social crisis. Noe's son Cham disobeys his father's will because he is ambitious; he seeks to displace his older brothers in the hierarchy of inheritance. Best's account texualizes the problem of social mobility in early modern England; and ironically, given Best's conservatism, it challenges definitions of social identity based on birth. Best betrays a disquieted fear of the social changes taking place in Elizabethan England, of "masterless men" and the challenge to traditional notions of order and degree. At a time when "elite identity gradually came to depend not on inherited or god-given absolute attributes, but on characteristics which could be acquired by human efforts,"[14] Best's account stands in an interesting transitional relation to such changes in the social formation. Cham recognizes the authority of birthright, as does Best's own anxious parenthesis "(by righte and Lawe of nature)," but he seeks to enact the "Lawe of nature" through human effort, an effort duly punished by the ultimate authority, God.

Similarly Best's nationalism and fear of difference are attitudes characteristic of the period. Even by 1578 the English had a considerable material investment in Africa: English explorers had begun to compete with Portuguese traders, and John Hawkins had organized the first successful slave trading venture between Africa and the West Indies in 1563. Best's is not just a fantasy about Africa and blackness but an enabling discourse that sustains a series of material and economic practices and interests. In England by 1596, blacks were numerous enough to generate alarm: Elizabeth wrote to the Lord Mayor of London and to other towns and observed, "there are of late divers blackmoores brought into this realme, of which kinde of people there are allready to manie, consideringe howe God hath blessed this land with great increase of people of our own nation." A week later she observed that "those kinde of people may be well spared in this realme, being so populous" and licensed a certain Casper van Senden, a merchant of Lubeck who had freed eighty-nine Englishmen imprisoned in Spain and Portugal, "to take up so much blackamoores here in this realme and to transport them into Spain and Portugal" for his expenses.[15] Five years later, van Senden was again licensed, this time to deport "the said kind of people . . . with all speed . . . out of this her majesty's realms" (January 1601).[16]

Other travel accounts of the period display the intersection between ancient legends and myths about black Africa and contemporary experience, observation, and prejudice. Interspersed with descriptions of African tribal customs, language, and landscape were the legendary stories from Pliny and other classical sources (probably via Mandeville, whose popular *Travels* were included in the 1589 edition of Hakluyt) of the Anthropophagi who wore skins and ate human flesh, of people without heads or speech, of satyrs and Troglodytes who lived in caves and dens.[17] The African landscape was presented descriptively in terms of safe harbors, intense heat, and gigantic waterfalls, but also mythically, as traversed by flames and fire that reached as high as the moon, as ringing with the sound of pipes, trumpets, and drums.[18] Always we find the link between blackness and the monstrous, and particularly a monstrous sexuality. Early travelers describe women held in common and men "furnisht with such members as are after a sort burthensome unto them."[19] These accounts often bore no relation to African sexual habits, but they did confirm earlier discourses and representations of African sexuality found in Herodotus, Diodorus, and other classical authors.

The prejudices of the ancients were preserved into the fifteenth and sixteenth centuries. Early cartographers ornamented maps with representations of naked black men bearing enormous sexual organs. Leo Africanus's *Historie of Africa* (1526), widely available in Latin in England and translated in 1600 by John Pory, claimed "negros" were prone to venery. In Jean Bodin's widely read work of political philosophy *The Six Bookes of a Commonweale* he argues against slavery but nevertheless betrays the conventional prejudice about black sexuality when he claims, "there be in mans bodie some members, I may not call them filthie (for that nothing can so be which is naturall) but yet so shamefull, as that no man except he be past all shame, can without blushing reveale or discover the same: and doe they [blacks] for that cease to be members of the whole bodie?"[20] Because of his organic conception of the state, Bodin's political theory does not permit a dualism, slavery for some, freedom for others. But he is so shamed by those members, and the Africans custom of exposing them, he dresses his prose in a series of parentheses and clauses that effectively obscure its meaning.

Such attitudes, both inherited from the past and reconstructed by contemporary historiographers, humanists, and travelers, were quickly assimilated into the drama and culture of early modern England.[21] In *Titus Andronicus*, for example, the lustful union of Aaron and Tamor resulted in a black baby called "a devil" in the play. Similarly, Volpone's copulations that result in monstrous offspring – the fool, dwarf, and hermaphrodite – are accomplished with "beggars, gipseys and Jewes, and black moores." In Bacon's *New Atlantis*

(1624), a holy hermit "desired to see the Spirit of Fornication; and there appeared to him a foul little Aethiop." Treatises on witchcraft and trials of the period often reported that the devil appeared to the possessed as a black man.[22] Finally, contemporary ballads and broadsides, the Renaissance equivalent of news stories, popularized monstrous births such as one recorded by the Stationers' Register (1580): a monstrous child, born at Fenstanton in Huntingdonshire, was described as "a monster with a black face, the Mouth and Eyes like a Lyon which was both Male and Female."[23]

Monstrous Desire in *Othello*

In *Renaissance Self-Fashioning*, Stephen Greenblatt has argued persuasively that Othello submits to narrative self-fashioning, his own and Iago's. He demonstrates the congruence between their narratives and the ideological narratives of Renaissance culture – most powerfully, the orthodox Christian attitude toward sexuality. Iago and Othello, he observes, are linked by shared, if dialectically opposed, cultural values about women and sexuality. Greenblatt quotes Kenneth Burke's claim that they are "consubstantial":

> Iago, to arouse Othello, must talk a language that Othello knows as well as he, a language implicit in the nature of Othello's love as the idealization of his private property in Desdemona. This language is the dialectical opposite of Othello's; but it so thoroughly shares a common ground with Othello's language that its insinuations are never for one moment irrelevant to Othello's thinking. Iago must be cautious in leading Othello to believe them as true: but Othello never for a moment doubts them as *values*.[24]

For Greenblatt, Othello's "identity depends upon a constant performance, as we have seen, of his story, a loss of his own origins, an embrace and perpetual reiteration of the norms of another culture."[25]

What are Othello's lost origins? Greenblatt implies as somehow anterior to identity-as-performance an essential self, and ontological subjectivity, an Edenic moment of black identity prior to discourse, outside, in Derrida's phrase quoted earlier, "the perversion of man, the 'talking animal'." Derrida's words about racism are pertinent to a discussion of origins as well and permit the substitution of ontology for race: "there are no origins without a language." Othello doesn't lose "his own origins"; his only access to those "origins" are the exotic ascriptions of European colonial discourse. Othello's stories of slavery and adventure are *precisely* a rehearsal of his origins, from his exotic tales of monstrous races to the story of the handkerchief's genealogy in witchcraft and sibylline prophecy. Othello charms by reiterating his origins even as he

submits and embraces the dominant values of Venetian culture. His successful courtship of Desdemona suggests that those origins are not simply repres-
sive but also enabling. Greenblatt is moving in his representation of Othello's
submission to such cultural plots, but by focusing on Othello's ideological complicity, Greenblatt effectively erases the other that is constituted discursively
in the play as both woman and black. Othello is both a speaking subject, a
kind of George Best recounting his tales of conquest, and at the same time
the object of his "traveler's history" by virtue of his blackness, which originates
with the very monstrous races he describes.[26]

Similarly he is both the representative and upholder of a rigorous sexual
code that prohibits desire and defines it even within marriage as adulterous,
as Greenblatt claims, and yet also the sign of a different, unbridled sexuality.
Greenblatt effaces the profound paradox of the black Othello's embrace
of Christian sexual mores: Othello is both monster and hero, and his own
sexuality is appropriately indecipherable.[27] As champion of Christian cultural
codes, he assures the senators his wish to take his bride with him to Cyprus
is not "to please the palate of my appetite, / Nor to comply with heat, the
young affects / In my defunct, and proper satisfaction" (I, iii, 262–64). He loves
Desdemona "but to be free and bounteous of her mind" (265). Like Brabantio, Iago, and Roderigo, Othello perceives of his love and indeed his human –
as opposed to bestial – identity as depending on property rights, on absolute
ownership:

> O curse of marriage,
> That we can call these delicate creatures ours,
> And not their appetites! I had rather be a toad,
> And live upon the vapour in a dungeon,
> Than keep a corner in a thing I love,
> For others' uses.
>
> (III, iii, 271–76)

But opposed to the representation of Othello's participation in the play's
dominant sex / gender system is a conventional representation of black sexuality evoked by other characters and by Othello himself in his traveler's tales and
through his passionate action. The textual allusions to bestiality, lubricity, and
the demonic have been often noted. Iago rouses Brabantio with "an old black
ram / Is tupping your white ewe . . . the devil will make a grandsire of you" (I,
i, 88–89, 91), and "you'll have your daughter cover'd with a Barbary horse;
you'll have your nephews neigh to you; you'll have coursers for cousins, and
gennets for germans" (110–13). "Your daughter and the Moor, are now making
the beast with two backs" (115–16); and Desdemona is transported, according to Roderigo, "to the gross clasps of a lascivious Moor" (I, i, 126). Not until

the third scene is the Moor named, and the delay undoubtedly dramatizes Othello's blackness and the audience's shared prejudices vividly conjured up by Iago's pictorial visions of carnal knowledge. To read Othello as congruent with the attitudes toward sexuality and femininity expressed in the play by the Venetians, Iago, Brabantio, Roderigo, and Cassio – and opposed to Desdemona's desire – is to ignore the threatening sexuality of the other, which divides the representation of Othello's character.[28] Othello internalizes alien cultural values, but the otherness that divides him from that culture and links him to the play's other marginality, femininity, remains in visual and verbal allusion.

For the white male characters of the play, the black man's power resides in his sexual difference. Their preoccupation with black sexuality is not the eruption of a normally repressed animal sexuality in the "civilized" white male but of the feared power and potency of a different and monstrous sexuality, which threatens the white male sexual norm represented in the play most emphatically by Iago. For however evil Iago reveals himself to be, as Spivak pointed out, like the Vice in the medieval morality – or we could add, the trickster-slave of Latin comedy – Iago enjoys a privileged relation with the audience.[29] He possesses what can be termed the discourse of knowledge in *Othello* and annexes not only the other characters but the resisting spectator as well into his world and its perspective. By virtue of his manipulative power and his superior knowledge and control over the action, which we share, we are implicated in his machinations and the cultural values they imply.[30] Iago is a cultural hyperbole; he does not oppose cultural norms so much as hyperbolize them.[31]

Before the English had wide experience of miscegenation, they seem to have believed, as George Best recounts, that the black man had the power to subjugate his partner's whiteness, to make both his "victim" and her offspring resemble him, by making them both black – a literal blackness in the case of a child, a metaphorical blackness in the case of a sexual partner. So in *Othello* Desdemona becomes "thou black weed" (IV, iii, 69), and the white pages of her "goodly book" are blackened by writing when Othello imagines "whore" inscribed across them. At IV, iii, she explicitly identifies herself with her mother's maid Barbary, whose name indicates blackness. The union of Desdemona and Othello represents a sympathetic identification between femininity and the monstrous that offers a potentially subversive recognition of sexual and racial difference.[32]

Both the male-dominated Venetian world of *Othello* and the criticism the play has generated have been dominated by a scopic economy that privileges sight, from the spectacular opposition of black and white to Othello's demands for ocular proof of Desdemona's infidelity. But Desdemona *hears* Othello and loves him, awed by his traveler's tales of the dangers he had endured, dangers that emphasize his link with monsters and marvels. Her responses to his tales are perceived as voracious: she "devours" his speech with a "greedy ear," a conflation of the oral and aural; and his language betrays a masculine fear of a cultural femininity envisioned as a greedy insatiable mouth, always seeking increase – a point of view reinforced by Desdemona's response to their reunion at Cyprus.[33] Desdemona is presented in the play as a sexual subject who hears and desires, and that desire is punished because the nonspecular, or nonphallic, sexuality it displays is frightening and dangerous.[34] Instead of a specular imaginary, Desdemona's desire is represented in terms of an aural-oral libidinal economy that generates anxiety in Othello, as his account to the Senate of his courtship via fiction betrays.[35] Othello fears Desdemona's desire because it invokes his monstrous difference from the sex / race code he has adopted and implicates him in femininity, allying him with witchcraft and an imagined monstrous sexual appetite.

Thomas Rymer, a kind of critical Iago, claims the moral of *Othello* is first, "a caution to all Maidens of Quality how, without their parents consent, they run away with Blackamoors," an instruction he follows with the Italian source's version: "Di non si accompagnare con huomo cui la natura & il cielo & il modo della vita disgiunge da noi."[36] Both Rymer and Cinthio reveal how Desdemona is punished for her desire: she hears Othello and desires him, and is punished because she threatens a white male hegemony in which women cannot be desiring subjects. When Desdemona comes to tell her version of their wooing, she says: "I saw Othello's visage in his mind." The allusion here is certainly to her audience's prejudice against the black "visage" both the senators and Shakespeare's audience see in *Othello*, but Desdemona "saw" his visage by hearing the tales he tells of his past, tales that, far from washing the Moor white as her line seems to imply, emphatically affirm Othello's link with Africa and its legendary monstrous creatures. Rymer's moral points up the patriarchal and scopic assumptions of his culture that are assumed as well in the play and most pointedly summed up by Brabantio's often quoted lines: "Look to her, Moor, have a quick eye to see: / She has deceiv'd her father, may do thee" (I, iii, 292–93). Fathers have the right to dispose of their daughters as they see fit, to whom they see fit; and disobedience against the father's law is merely a prelude to the descent into hell and blackness the play enacts – a fall, we might recall, Best's tale uncannily predicts. Desdemona's desire threatens the patriarchal privilege of disposing daughters, and in the play world it signals sexual duplicity and lust.

The irony, of course, is that Othello himself is the instrument of punishment. He enacts the moral Rymer and Cinthio point, both confirming cultural prejudice by his monstrous murder of Desdemona and punishing her desire that transgresses the norms of the Elizabethan sex / race system. Both Othello and Desdemona deviate from the norms of the sex / race system in which they participate from the margins.[37] Othello is not, in Cinthio's words, "da noi," one of "us," nor is Desdemona. Women depend for their class status on their affiliation with men – fathers, husbands, sons – and Desdemona forfeits that status and the protection it affords when she marries outside the categories her culture allows. For her transgression, her desire of difference, she is punished not only by a loss of status but even of life. The woman's desire is punished, and ultimately its monstrous inspiration as well. As the object of Desdemona's illegitimate passion, Othello both figures monstrosity and fem-ininity *and* at the same time represents the white male norms the play encodes through Iago, Roderigo, and Brabantio.[38] Not surprisingly, Othello reveals at last a complicitous self-loathing, for blackness is as loathsome to him as to George Best, or any male character in the play, or ostensibly the audience.

At IV, i, Iago constructs a drama in which Othello is instructed to inter-pret a scene rich in its figurations of desire and the monstrous. Cast as eaves-dropper and voyeur by Iago, Othello imagines and thus constitutes a sexual encounter and pleasure that excludes him and a Desdemona as whore instead of fair angel. Cassio's mocking rehearsal of Bianca's love is not the sight / site of Desdemona's transgression, as Othello believes, but its representation; ironically this theatrical representation directed by Iago functions as effectively as would the real. Representation for Othello is transparent. The male gaze is privileged; it constructs a world that the drama plays out. The aptly and iron-ically named Bianca is a cypher for Desdemona whose "blackened whiteness" she embodies. Plots of desire conventionally figure woman as the erotic object, but in *Othello* the iconic center of the spectacle is shifted from the woman to the monstrous Othello, whose blackness charms *and* threatens but ultimately fulfills the cultural prejudices it represents. Othello is both hero and outsider because he embodies not only the norms of male power and privilege repre-sented by the white male hegemony ruling Venice, a world of prejudice, ambi-tion, jealousy, and the denial of difference, but also the threatening power of the alien: Othello is a monster in the Renaissance sense of the word, a deformed creature like the hermaphrodites and other strange spectacles so fas-cinating to the early modern period. And *monstrum*, the word itself, figures both the creature and its movement into representation, for it meant as well a showing or demonstration, a *representation*.

Historical Contingency: Rereading *Othello*

> The position which a text occupies within the ideological relations of class strug-gle at its originating moment of production is . . . no necessary indication of the positions which it may subsequently come to occupy in different historical and political contexts.
>
> Tony Bennett, *"Text and History"*[39]

His nose was rising and *Roman*, instead of *African* and flat: His Mouth the finest shaped that could be seen; far from those great turn'd Lips, which are so natural to the rest of the Negroes. The whole Proportion and air of his face was so nobly and exactly form'd, that bating his colour, there could be nothing in Nature more beautiful, agreeable and handsome.

Aphra Behn, *Oroonoko* (1688)[40]

Behn's description of her black protagonist Oroonoko is startling in its congruence with Ridley's portrait of the black Othello with which we began. A black tragic hero of Othello's proportions, or Behn's noble Oroonoko, is only possible if black is really white, if features are "classical" – that is, European – and color is merely an unfortunate accident. By the late seventeenth century, the role and status of blacks in English society has changed, and the discourse of racism is fully established. No longer "spectacles of strangeness" and monstrosity who occupied unstable, exotic, and mythic ideological roles; they were now slaves, situated in a growing capitalist economy, which their exploited labor sustained. In the sixteenth and early seventeenth centuries, the slave trade in England had been desultory and the status of blacks liminal rather than fixed. As Best's *Discourse* and the accounts of early voyagers illustrate, blacks occupied mythic roles rather than positions as mere chattel or economic linchpins. In Elizabethan and Jacobean England, blacks were not only servants; they owned property, paid taxes, and went to church.[41] But with the establishment of the sugar industry in the Caribbean and the tobacco and cotton industries in America, the position of blacks changed, and their value as slave labor was fully recognized and exploited. The Royal African Company, chartered in 1672, monopolized the African trade until 1698 when the expansion of the colonies dependent on slave labor was so great that it was deprived of its exclusive rights and the market opened to competition. Newspapers of the late seventeenth century testify to a changed view of blacks, with advertisements of slaves for sale and, more importantly, Hue and Cry notices seeking runaways often described as wearing collars emblazoned with their owner's arms or with inscriptions such as one reported in *The London Gazette* (1688): "The Lady Bromfield's black, in Lincoln's Inn Fields."

By the late seventeenth century, Englishmen had come to recognize the significance of the slave trade to the British economy. In 1746 Postlethwayt put that recognition forcefully into words: "The most approved Judges of the commercial Interests of these Kingdoms have ever been of Opinion, that our West-Indian and African trades are the most nationally beneficial of any we carry on . . . and the daily Bread of the most considerable Part of our British Manufacturers, [is] owing primarily to the Labour of Negroes."[42] By the mid-eighteenth century, the *Gentleman's Magazine* claimed there were some twenty

thousand blacks in London. Their increasing numbers led to growing prejudice and fear that they threatened the position of white working people. In
pamphlets and the popular press, blacks were represented increasingly in car-
icatures as bestial, ape-like, inhuman, and stripped of the exotic or mythic
dimensions that characterized sixteenth- and early seventeenth-century
discourse.

By the time of Rymer's attack on *Othello*, Shakespeare's heroic and tragic
representation of a black man seemed unthinkable. In his "Short View of
Tragedy," (1693), Rymer found Shakespeare's choice reprehensible, a transgression both of tragic and social decorum.[43] Rymer's attitude toward the
"blackmoor" is historically predictable; more surprising, perhaps, is his critical
slippage, like Ridley's some two hundred and fifty years later, from blackness
to femininity.[44]

In ridiculing *Othello*, Rymer notoriously claimed that the play's moral was
"a warning to all good Wives that they look well to their Linnen."[45] He devotes
the last pages of his sardonic attack to the "Tragedy of the Handkerchief,"
claiming that "had it been Desdemona's Garter, the Sagacious Moor might
have smelt a Rat; but the handkerchief is so remote a trifle, no Booby on this
side of *Mauritania* cou'd make any consequence from it. . . . Yet we find it
entered into our Poets head to make a Tragedy of this *Trifle*."[46] Rymer takes
issue with Shakespeare's presentation of the handkerchief because he finds it
too trifling a detail to sustain tragedy. His comment here reflects not only the
changed generic expectations of neoclassicism but also Rymer's cultural prejudices against women, their supposed materiality and preoccupation with the
trivial.[47] In the early modern period, the handkerchief was in fact a sign of
wealth and status; by the early eighteenth century, however, it had become
commonplace.[48] In cinquecento Venice, possession of a lady's handkerchief was
considered proof of adultery and led to stringent punishments. In 1416, for
example, a certain Tomaso Querini received a stiff sentence of eighteen months
in jail and a fine of five hundred lire di piccoli for carrying out "many dishonesties" with Maria, wife of Roberto Bono. Records from the time describe
Tomaso's crime as having "presumed to follow the said lady and on this public
street took from her hands a handkerchief, carrying it off with him. As a result
of this deed the said Tomaso entered the home of Roberto many times during
the day and night and committed many dishonesties with this lady with the
highest dishonor for ser Roberto."[49]

Many critics and readers of the play have sought to save Shakespeare's
handkerchief from Rymer's harsh judgment by demonstrating not its historical significance as a sign of adultery but its symbolic significance and meaning.
Their efforts have been limited by their own historical boundaries and by
reigning critical preoccupations and practices that too often seek to work out
equations that restrict the richness of handkerchief as signifier. The handker-

chief in *Othello* is what we might term a snowballing signifier, for, as it passes from hand to hand, both literal and critical, it accumulates myriad associations and meanings.[50] It first appears simply as a love token given by Othello to Desdemona and therefore treasured by her; only later do we learn the details of its provenance and design. In the Renaissance, strawberries signified virtue and goodness, but also hypocritical virtue as symbolized by the frequently occurring design and emblem of a strawberry plant with an adder hiding beneath its leaves.[51] This doubleness is, of course, appropriate for Othello's perception of Desdemona; for when the handkerchief is first given, it represents her virtue and their chaste love, but it later becomes a sign, indeed a proof, of her unfaithfulness. Iago's description of the napkin as "spotted" constitutes a new meaning for Othello: the strawberries become signs of Desdemona's deceit.[52]

In psychoanalytic terms, the handkerchief Othello inherits from his mother and then gives to Desdemona has been read symptomatically as the fetishist's substitution for the mother's missing phallus. Like the shoe Freud's young boy substitutes "for the woman's (mother's) phallus which the little boy once believed in and does not wish to forego," the handkerchief is the fetish that endows "women with the attribute which makes them acceptable as sexual objects" – that is, makes them like men.[53] For Othello, it both conceals and reveals Desdemona's imperfection, her lack. But the psychoanalytic scenario is problematic because it privileges a male scopic drama, casting the woman as other, as a failed man, thereby effacing her difference and concealing her sexual specificity behind the fetish. The handkerchief in *Othello* does indeed figure a lack, but ironically it figures not simply the missing penis but the lack around which the play's dramatic action is structured, a feminine desire that is described in the play as aberrant and "monstrous" or a "monster."[54] The handkerchief, associated with the mother, witchcraft, and the marvelous, represents the link between femininity and the monstrous, which Othello and Desdemona's union figures in the play. It figures a female sexual topography that is more than a sign of male possession, violated virginity, or even deceit, and more than the fetishist's beloved object. It figures not only Desdemona's lack, as in the traditional psychoanalytic reading, but also her own sexual parts: the nipples, – sometimes, incidentally, represented in the courtly love *blason* as strawberries – lips, and even perhaps, the clitoris, the berry of sexual pleasure nestled within its flanged leaves.[55]

The handkerchief, therefore, is significant not only historically, as an indicator of class and / or transgression, and psychologically, because it signifies male fears of duplicity, consummation, and castration, but also politically, precisely because it has become a *feminine* trifle. *Othello*'s tragic action is structured not around an heroic act or even object – a battle as in *Antony and Cleopatra* or kingship as in *Macbeth* and *King Lear* – but around a trifle, a feminine toy. Instead of relegating *Othello* to the critical category of domestic tragedy, always implicitly or explicitly pejorative bacause of its focus on woman, jealousy, and a triangle, we can reread *Othello* from another perspective, also admittedly historically bound, that seeks to displace conventional interpretations by exposing the extraordinary fascination and fear of racial and sexual difference in Elizabethan and Jacobean culture. Desdemona and Othello, woman and black man, are represented by discourses about femininity and blackness that managed and produced difference in early modern England.

Colonialism and Sexual Difference

Was Shakespeare a racist who condoned the negative image of blacks in his culture? Is Desdemona somehow guilty in her stubborn defense of Cassio and her admiring remark "Ludovico is a proper man.";[56] Or guilty in a newer critical vocabulary, in her "erotic submission, [which,] conjoined with Iago's murderous cunning, far more effectively, if unintentionally, subverts her husband's carefully fashioned identity."[57] Readers preoccupied with formal dramatic features claim such questions are moot, that the questions themselves expose the limits of moral or political readings of texts because they raise the spectres of intention or ignore art's touted transcendence of history. But as much recent poststructuralist and / or political criticism has demonstrated, even highly formalist readings are political, inscribed in the discourse both of the period in which the work was produced and that in which it is consumed.

The task of a political criticism is not merely to expose or demystify the ideological discourses that organize literary texts but to *reconstitute* those texts, to reread canonical texts in noncanonical ways that reveal the contingency of so-called canonical readings, that disturb conventional interpretations and discover them as partisan, constructed, made rather than given, natural and inevitable. Such strategies of reading are particularly necessary in drama because the dramatic immediacy of theatrical representation obscures the fact that the audience is watching a highly artificial enactment – in the case of *Othello*, of what a non-African and a man has made into a vision of blackness and femininity, of passion and desire in the other, the marginal, outside culture yet simultaneously within it.

Shakespeare was certainly subject to the racist, sexist, and colonialist discourses of his time; but by making the black Othello a hero, and by making Desdemona's love for Othello and her transgression of her society's norms for women in choosing him sympathetic, Shakespeare's play stands in a contestatory relation to the hegemonic ideologies of race and gender in early modern England. Othello is, of course, the play's hero only within the terms of a white, elitist male ethos, and he suffers the generic "punishment" of tragedy; but he is nevertheless represented as heroic and tragic at an historical moment when the only role blacks played onstage was that of a villain of low status. The case of Desdemona is more complex because the fate she suffers is the conventional fate assigned to the desiring woman. Nevertheless, Shakespeare's representation of her as at once virtuous and desiring, and of her choice in love as heroic rather than demonic, dislocates the conventional ideology of gender the play also enacts.

Notes

1   Thomas Rymer, "A Short View of Tragedy," *Critical Essays of the Seventeenth Century*, ed. J. E. Spingarn (Bloomington, Indiana University Press, 1957), II, 221–22.

2   S. T. Coleridge, *Shakespearean Criticism*, ed. Thomas M. Raysor (London, 1960), 42.

3   M. R. Ridley, ed., *Othello* (London: Methuen, 1958, rpt. 1984), li. All references are to this edition.

4   On the racism of commentators, see Martin Orkin, "*Othello* and the 'plain face' of Racism," *Shakespeare Quarterly* 38 (1987): 166–88. Orkin points out that Ridley's edition is the preferred text in South Africa.

5   For a useful general discussion of black and white and their cultural associations, see the opening chapter of Harry Levin, *The Power of Blackness* (New York: Vintage, 1958). On *Othello*, see Doris Adler, "The Rhetoric of *Black* and *White* in *Othello*," *Shakespeare Quarterly* 25 (1974): 248–57.

6   Winthrop Jordan, *White over Black* (Chapel Hill: University of North Carolina Press, 1968), 7.

7   Stephen Orgel, *The Jonsonian Masque* (Cambridge: Harvard University Press, 1967; rpt. New York: Columbia University Press, 1981), 120.

   (a) Whitney chose the woodcuts from a collection of Christopher Plantyn, the well-known printer whose shop published *A Choice of Emblemes;* see Charles H. Lyons, *To Wash an Aethiop White: British Ideas about African Educability 1530–1960* (New York: Teacher's College Press, 1975), iv–v.

   (b) For references to this phrase in Elizabethan and Jacobean drama, see Robert R. Cawley, *The Voyages and Elizabethan Drama* (Boston: D. C. Heath, 1938), 85 ff.

   (c) E. V. Lucas, *Highways and Byways in Sussex* (London, 1904), my emphasis; I am grateful to Peter Stallybrass for this reference.

8   For a general account of the classical materials, see Frank M. Snowden, Jr., *Before Color Prejudice* (Cambridge: Harvard University Press, 1983).

9   All the passages quoted appear in R. Hakluyt, *The Principal Navigations, Voyages Traffiques & Discoveries of the English Nation* (1600), ed. Walter Raleigh (Glasgow, 1903–5), VII, 262. Best's *Discourse* was reprinted in a substantially cut version. The story of the origins of blackness in Noah's son Cham is also found in Leo Africanus's popular *Historie of Africa* (1526).

10   Jordan observes that "English experience was markedly different from that of the Spanish and Portuguese who, for centuries, had been in close contact with North Africa and had actually been invaded and subjected by people both darker and more highly civilized than themselves. . . . One of the fairest skinned nations suddenly came face to face with one of the darkest peoples on earth" (6).

11   Hakluyt's book is said to have been a prime motivator of English colonial expansion and to have increased the profits of the East India Company by some twenty thousand pounds; see Walter Raleigh's introductory essay, I, 92.

12   Talmudic and Midrashic commentaries, which inspired interest in the humanist sixteenth century, seem to have been the source for the link between blackness and the curse on Cham; see Jordan, 17–20; 35–39.

13   Jacques Derrida, "Racism's Last Word," trans. Peggy Kamuf, *Critical Inquiry* 12 (1985): 290–99.

14   Frank Whigham, "Courtesy as a Social Code," *Spenser Encyclopedia*, ed. A. C. Hamilton (Toronto: University of Toronto Press, 1990) and also his *Ambition and Privilege* (Berkeley: University of California Press, 1984).

15   *Acts of the Privy Council*, ed. John Roche Dasent (London, 1902), 11 and 18 July, 1596; new series, XXVI, 16, 20). These proclamations must be read in light of the similar dislike and resentment, based on economic distinctions, between the English and the Fleming and Huguenot clothworkers who fled religious persecution and immigrated to England. The clothworkers, however, not only brought needed skills, they were also European, more like the English than the African could ever be; and though they generated hostility, there is no evidence of similar legislation to oust them from England. See C. W. Chitty, "Aliens in England in the Sixteenth Century," *Race* 8 (1966): 129–145, and Anthony Barker, *The African Link* (London: F. Cass, 1978), 30.

16   Paul L. Hughes and James F. Larkin, eds., *Tudor Royal Proclamations* (New Haven: Yale University Press, 1969), III, 221.

17   Rudolph Wittkower, "Marvels of the East: A Study in the History of Monsters," *Journal of the Warburg and Courtauld Institutes* 5 (1942): 159–97, provides a thorough review, particularly of the visual material. Mary Louise Pratt, "Scratches on the Face of the Country; or, What Mr. Barrow Saw in the Land of the Bushmen," *Critical Inquiry* 12 (1985): 119–43, analyzes two modes of travel writing, the scientific-informational and the subject-centered, experiential, that are suggestive not only for her nineteenth-century texts but for earlier examples that already manifest signs of the distinctions she draws.

18   Though these accounts are strikingly similar to discourses about the New World, comparison would require another study.

19   See among others, John Lok's *Second Voyage to Guinea* (1554), in Hakluyt, VI, 154–77; William Towerson's voyage, 1556–57, Hakluyt, VI, 177–212; George Fenner's voyage, 1556, Hakluyt, VI, 266–84; and finally Richard Jobson, *The Golden Trade* (1623), ed. Walter Rodney (London: Dawsons, 1968), 65–67. Lok's long and interesting account also appeared in the 1589 edition of Hakluyt as Robert Gainsh's voyage.

20   This passage appears only in the Latin *De Repubica libri sex* (1601); the translation is Richard Knolles's (London, 1606), available in a facsimile edition, J. Bodin, *The Six Books of a Commonweale*, ed. Kenneth Douglas McRae (Cambridge: Harvard University Press, 1962), Bk. III, viii, 387). The Latin, though somewhat more readable than Knolles's prose, includes both parenthesis and extended subordination (J. Bodini, 1601, L1, 8). Knolles is quoted in David B. Davis, *The Problem of Slavery in Western Culture* (Ithaca: Cornell University Press, 1966), 112.

21   For a review of Portuguese and Spanish sources, see Katherine George, "The Civilized West Looks at Primitive Africa: 1400–1800," *Isis* 49 (1958): 62–72. For a general view of Elizabethans and foreigners, see G. K. Hunter, "Elizabethans and Foreigners," *Shakespeare Survey* 17 (1964): 37–52. On the representation of blacks on the English stage, see Eldred Jones, *Othello's Countrymen: The African in English Renaissance Drama* (London: Oxford University Press, 1965); G. K. Hunter, "*Othello* and Colour Prejudice," *Proceedings of the British Academy* 53 (1967): 139–63; and more recently, Elliot H. Tokson, *The Popular Image of the Black Man in English Drama 1588–1688* (Boston: G. K. Hall, 1982).

22   Keith Thomas, *Religion and the Decline of Magic* (London: Weidenfeld & Nicolson, 1971), 129.

23   Quoted from R. Burton, *Admirable Curiosities* (1703) in Hyder Rollins, "An Analytical Index of the Ballad Entries in the Registers of the Stationers of London," *Studies in Philology* 21 (1924): 53. Teratological treatises often attributed monstrous births to the maternal imagination and desire, linking femininity to the production of monsters. As Marie-Hélène Huet observes, the "monster publicly signals all aberrant desire, reproves all excessive passion and all illegitimate fantasy"; "Living Images: Monstrosity and Representation," *Representations* 4 (1983): 74. A contemporary English source specifically for the link between the maternal imagination and blackness is Sir Thomas Browne's *Pseudodoxia Epidemica* (1646). Ernest Martin, *Histoires des monstres* (Paris: C. Reinwald, 1880), traces the theory of monstrosity and the maternal imagination, 266–94.

24   Kenneth Burke, *A Grammar of Motives* (Berkeley: University of California Press, 1969) quoted by Stephen Greenblatt in *Renaissance Self-Fashioning* (Chicago: University of Chicago Press, 1980), 306. Recently, Eve Kosofsky Sedgwick has deconstructed for an Anglo-American audience such versions of "consubstantiality" by showing how the female body, at once desired object and subject of discourse, becomes the territory across which male bonds she terms homosocial are forged between men; see *Between Men: English Literature and Homosocial Desire* (New York: Columbia University Press), 1985.

25   Greenblatt, 245.

26   The Folio reading "traveler's history," with its generic implication, as Greenblatt notes, seems more convincing than "travel's history," since the tale Othello tells is drawn from accounts such as Mandeville's and repeated by the early Elizabethan travelers recorded in Hakluyt.

27   Linda Williams's essay on the horror film motivated a part of this discussion; "When the Woman Looks," *Re-vision: Essays in Feminist Film Criticism*, ed. Mary

Ann Doane, Patricia Mellencamp and Linda Williams (Frederick, MD: University Publications of America, 1984).

28   Homi Bhabha's notion of hybridity, which he defines as "the revaluation of the assumption of colonial identity through the repetition of discriminatory identity effects," is suggestive for my reading of *Othello*; "Signs Taken for Wonders: Questions of Ambivalence and Authority Under a Tree Outside Delhi, May 1817," *Critical Inquiry* 12 (1985): 154. See also his discussion of the colonial subject and mimicry in "Of Mimicry and Man: The Ambivalence of Colonial Discourse," *October* 25 (1983): 125–33, particularly observations about the ambivalence of mimicry as "almost the same, *but not quite*," 127.

29   Bernard Spivack, *The Allegory of Evil* (New York: Columbia University Press, 1958), 415ff.

30   Casual assumptions about the Shakespearean audience are problematic and the "we" of my own critical discourse equally so. Shakespeare's audience was not a classless, genderless monolith. The female spectators at a Globe performance, both the whores in the pit and the good English wives Stephen Gosson chastises for their attendance at the theatre in *The Schoole of Abuse*, view the play from different perspectives from that of a white male audience of whatever social and economic station. As women, if we are implicated in Iago's perspective and Othello's tragedy, we are unsexed, positioned as men; if we identify with Desdemona, we are punished. See the interesting work on female spectatorship in film theory by Laura Mulvey, "Visual Pleasure and Narrative Cinema," *Screen* 16 (1975): 6–18, and Mary Ann Doane, "Film and the Masquerade: Theorizing Female Spectatorship," *Screen* 23 (1983): 74–87.

31   In Leo Africanus's *Historie of Africa* (1526), the "Portugals" are most often singled out as the destroyers of Africa and her peoples. From this perspective, the Iberian of Iago's name suggest that his destruction of Othello / Africa can be read as an allegory colonialism. For detailed, if occasionally dubious, parallels between Leo's *Historie* and *Othello*, see Rosalind Johnson, "African Presence in Shakespearean Drama: *Othello* and Leo Africanus's *Historie of Africa*," *African Presence in Early Europe*, special issue of the *Journal of African Civilizations* 7 (1985): 267–287.

32   For a recent attempt to look at both race and gender in *Othello*, see Ania Loomba, *Gender, Race, Renaissance Drama* (Manchester: Manchester University Press, 1989), chap. 2.

33   Compare Thomas Becon's lively description of the whore in his "Catechisme". Becon makes explicit what is only implied in *Othello*, the link between female orifices – ear, mouth, genitals – as well as their perceived voraciousness.

34   This alternative sexual economy suggests another trajectory of desire in *Othello* between Iago and Othello, which cannot be explored further here other than to note Iago's repeated au / oral seduction, as for example when he pours "pestilence into his [Othello's] ear" (II, iii, 347). For an interesting discussion of *Othello* and the "pathological male animus toward sexuality," particularly Desdemona's, see Edward A. Snow, "Sexual Anxiety and the Male Order of Things in *Othello*," *English Literary Renaissance* 10 (1980): 388.

35   I am grateful to Rey Chow and the other members of the Brown Seminar "Cultural Constructions of Gender" (1988) at the Pembroke Center for Teaching and Research on Women for valuable discussion of the play's sexual economies.

36   Quoted by Rymer (1963), ed. Spingarn, 221. On the status of blacks and moors in Renaissance Venice, see Giorgio Fedalto, "Stranieri a Venezia e a Padova," *Storia del cultura veneta dal primo quattrocento al concilio di Trento*, ed. Arnaldi and M. P. Stocchi (Vicenza, 1976), 499–535.

37   For an excellent discussion of gender and class in *Othello*, see Peter Stallybrass, "Patriarchal Territories: The Body Enclosed," *Rewriting the Renaissance*, eds. Margaret Ferguson, Maureen Quilligan, and Nancy Vickers (Chicago: University of Chicago Press, 1986).

38   For a psychoanalytic reading of Othello's relation to "the voice of the father," see Snow, 409–10, cited above.

39   Tony Bennett, "Text and History," *Re-reading English*, ed. Peter Widdowson (London: Methuen, 1982), 229.

40   Quoted in Jordan, 28.

41   James Walvin, *The Black Presence* (New York: Schocken Books, 1972), 13, and Folarin Shyllon, *Black People in Britain 1555–1833* (London: Oxford University Press, 1977). It is worth noting that slavery between Europe and Africa was reciprocal. W. E. B. DuBois points out that during the sixteenth century "the [black] Mohammaden rulers of Egypt were buying white slaves by the tens of thousands in Europe and Asia"; *The World and Africa* (New York: International Publishers, 1972), 111. Blonde women were apparently in special demand. See also Wayne B. Chandler, who points out that "moors" were black, and historians' efforts to claim their tawniness represent racial prejudice; "The Moor: Light of Europe's Dark Age," *African Presence in Early Europe*, special issue of *Journal of African Civilizations* 7 (1985): 144–75.

42   Postlethwayt writes in order to justify the Royal African Company's attempts to regain its monopoly; his pamphlet is exemplary, but many others could also be cited. Quoted in Walvin, 51–52.

43   Rymer's attack on Shakespeare in an age of growing Shakespeare idolatry prompted other critics to a different tack, to dispute Othello's blackness altogether rather than reprehend it.

44   This same slippage from blackness to femininity is implicit in the commonly believed notion that apes and negroes copulated and especially that "apes were inclined wantonly to attack Negro women," Jordan, 31.

45   Rymer, ed. Spingarn, 221.

46   Rymer, ed. Spingarn, 251, 254.

47   Rymer's characterization of Emilia as "the meanest woman in the Play" (254) requires comment. The moralism of the "Short View" might lead most readers to award Bianca that superlative, but predictably Rymer cannot forgive Emilia her spunky cynicism toward men and her defense of women.

48   Norbert Elias, *The Civilizing Process: The History of Manners*, trans. Edmund Jephcott (New York: Urizen Press, 1978), 143–52.

49   Guido Ruggiero, *The Boundaries of Eros: Sex Crimes in Renaissance Venice* (New York: Oxford University Press, 1985), 61–62. I am grateful to Jonathan Goldberg for this reference.

50   See also Stallybrass, cited above.

51   Lawrence Ross, "The Meaning of Strawberries in Shakespeare," *Studies in the Renaissance* 7 (1960): 225–40.

52   Lynda Boose argues that the handkerchief represents the lovers' consummated marriage and wedding sheets stained with blood, a sign of Desdemona's sexual innocence. She links the handkerchief to the folk custom of displaying the spotted wedding sheets as a proof of the bride's virginity; "Othello's Handkerchief: The Recognizance and Pledge of Love," *English Literary Renaissance* 5 (1975): 360–74.

53   Sigmund Freud, "Fetishism" (1927), in *Sexuality and the Psychology of Love*, ed. Phillip Rieff (New York: Macmillan, 1963, rpt. 1978), 215, 216.

54   See, for example, *Othello* I, iii, 402; III, iii, 111, 433.

55   Snow associates the spotted "napkin" not only with Desdemona's stained wedding sheets but also with menstrual blood. He argues that the handkerchief is therefore "a nexus for three aspects of woman – chaste bride, sexual object, and maternal threat" (392).

56   For a discussion of critical attitudes toward Desdemona, and particularly this line, see S. N. Garner, "Shakespeare's Desdemona," *Shakespeare Studies* 9 (1976): 232–52.

57   Greenblatt, 244.

10

History and Politics: An Overview

Walter Cohen's essay on 'Political Criticism of Shakespeare' discusses the politicization of literary studies in North America during the 1980s. Cohen usefully identifies 'two main strategies in British Marxist studies of Shakespeare: a revisionist historical analysis of the plays in their own time and a radical account of their ideological function in the present' (Cohen, 1987, p. 27). It is a distinction which animates the broad topic of 'history and politics' in Shakespeare criticism: whose history and whose politics? Writing in 1952, R. W. Babcock could write that 'probably the most important type of modern criticism is historical criticism' (Babcock, 1952, p. 6): 'Basically, historical criticism enhances the aesthetic value of a piece of early literary art by increasing its intellectual appeal' (p. 8). Babcock notes that such archaeological research is likely to be undertaken cooperatively, rather than the individual and individualistic work of Romantic critics 'each interpreting Hamlet, for example, in his own likeness' (p. 9), and he reviews current criticism by Stoll, Tillyard and Lily Campbell, among others. Forty years later, Lisa Jardine argues for the importance of *Reading Shakespeare Historically* (1996) as a way of gaining 'a fresh understanding of the rootedness of our present uncertainties, derived by some kind of engaging dialogue with the textual residue of history' (Jardine, 1996, p. 1). For Babcock, historical criticism of Shakespeare was about the past; for Jardine, it is about the present, and this dual focus can be seen through the historical and political approaches to Shakespeare in the twentieth century. As Peter Brook puts it in his introduction to Jan Kott's *Shakespeare our Contemporary* (1946), 'Shakespeare is a contemporary of Kott, Kott is a contemporary of Shakespeare' (Kott, 1946, p. x).

L. C. Knights' British Academy Shakespeare Lecture, *Shakespeare's Politics* (1957), argued that Shakespeare had 'a clear perception of the actualities of political situations' (Knights, 1957, p. 117). Knights suggested that *King Lear* 'has marked political implications' (p. 119) and that 'Shakespeare's political

meanings – the things he tells us about politics – are inherent in and inseparable from his method, his way of presenting his political material' (p. 112).
Few critics have, however, wanted to try and identify the writer's politics from
his writing, although arguments for Shakespeare, as well as 'Shakespeare', as
either conservative or radical have been fierce ones. Many critics declare their
own hand as part of their readings. Derek Cohen's *The Politics of Shakespeare*
(1993) clearly declares at the outset its 'socialist bias' as a response to the 'liberal
assumptions [which] have limited the kinds of scrutiny to which the plays have
been subjected' (Cohen, 1993, p. 1). Cohen describes Othello's suicide as 'the
complete triumph of the white world's ethos of individualism'; he discusses
the monetary and moral connotations of value in *King Lear*, proposing that
moderation is 'a value likelier to find sympathy in a *Lear* audience than is the
value of excess' (p. 74), and develops this theme in a discussion of *Timon of
Athens*. The tragic worlds of the plays are driven by 'the lonely and relentless
hunger for self-definition that is the motive force of individualism' (p. 87).
Terry Eagleton's conclusion to his 1986 book *William Shakespeare* delights in
breaking the 'bad news' to Shakespeare: the fallibility of a liberal belief in 'a
way of harnessing what is most productive about bourgeois transgression to
the old polity, grafting upon that settled structure fertile strains of dynamic
energy and individual self-development' (Eagleton, 1986, p. 99). He admits,
though, that Shakespeare 'may well have suspected as much himself', as a man
who seems, ironically, to have been 'almost certainly familiar with the writings
of Hegel, Marx, Nietzsche, Freud, Wittgenstein and Derrida' (pp. ix–x).

In their introduction to the volume *Political Shakespeare*, Jonathan
Dollimore and Alan Sinfield claim cultural materialism's attentiveness to the
political and ideological significance of all cultural productions. Rather than
trying to mystify this dimension, 'it registers its commitment to the transformation of a social order which exploits people on the grounds of race,
gender and class' (Dollimore, 1985, p. viii). Victor Kiernan's *Eight Tragedies of
Shakespeare: A Marxist Study* (1996) discusses the plays as expressions of
'approaching crisis':

> The tragic climax is the funeral pyre of an old order doomed to perish in order
> to make room for a new and worthier one. It burns away in its conflagration
> thick clouds of human incomprehension, painfully yet healingly. In a few indi-
> vidual fates it seems to teach the historical lesson that nothing short of a cata-
> clysm of some kind can jolt sluggish humanity out of its customary unthinking
> grooves. In this can be recognised the affinity between tragedy and revolution.
> (Kiernan, 1996, p. 40)

David Margolies, in his *Monsters of the Deep* (1992) argues against proposing
that 'an abstract structure of causation' (Margolies, 1992, p. 9) such as the

notion of a 'tragic flaw' precipitates the tragedy. Rather he proposes that Shakespeare's tragedies 'can reasonably be seen as provoking a coherent emotional response to the world in their contemporary audience' and that 'the subject of the plays is the same contradictory, evolving society'. While the subject matter of the plays change, they share a common thematic structure as 'metaphors of social disintegration. Each succeeding tragedy, in a different play-world, shows a world at a further stage of decline' (p. 11). Margolies devotes a chapter to exploring this thesis in each play, except for *Othello*, which he designates a 'Problem Tragedy' which 'maximises conflict of content and form' (p. 13).

Many critics have worked by historicizing Shakespeare's plays. Blair Worden's essay 'Shakespeare and Politics' in a volume of *Shakespeare Survey* devoted to the theme argues that if Shakespeare's plays reveal little about their author, 'they leave little doubt about when they were written' (Worden, 1990, p. 9). The 'new historicism' associated with Stephen Greenblatt is discussed in Dutton and Wilson (1992) and in Veeser (1989 and 1994). Greenblatt's own discussion of Shakespeare can be found in his *Renaissance Self-Fashioning* (1980) and *Shakespearean Negotiations* (1988), where he argues for a 'study of the collective making of distinct cultural practices and inquiry into the relations among these practices – a poetics of culture' (Greenblatt, 1988, p. 5). His chapter on *King Lear* reads the play alongside contemporary Jesuit exorcisms to discuss its self-conscious deployment of spectacular impostures. David Aers and Gunther Kress's 'The Language of Social Order: Individual, Society and Historical Process in *King Lear*' in Aers (1981) argues that different modes of perceiving the self in the play – individual identity versus social identity – reflect a historical shift away from the old social order of Lear's disintegrating reign. Jonathan Goldberg's 'study of the relationships between authority and its representations in the Jacobean period' (Goldberg, 1983, p. xi) in *James I and the Politics of Literature* (1983) includes a discussion of the Roman plays of the early seventeenth century. Placing *Julius Caesar* and *Coriolanus* alongside Jonson's *Sejanus* and *Catiline* and Massinger's *The Roman Actor* enables Goldberg to draw out common and topical themes of power, language and theatricality. In *Power on Display: The Politics of Shakespeare's Genres* (1986), Leonard Tennenhouse argues that Shakespeare's work belongs to 'a situation where literature and political discourse had not yet been differentiated' (Tennenhouse, 1986, p. 2). Tennenhouse argues that in the tragedies of the 1590s, Shakespeare shows the 'transfer of dynastic power' and displays 'the destruction incurred when the state goes to war against itself', whereas the Jacobean tragedies 'focus on the restoration and consolidation of political power' (p. 4). Elizabeth's control of her own and her court's sexuality throws into relief the depiction of aristocratic women on the stage, explored through the association of Lavinia's body with the Roman polis in *Titus Andronicus*, through the 'meaning and disposition of Gertrude's body' (p. 112) in the disrupted accession of Claudius to the Danish throne, in the murder of Desdemona, and in the elegiac Elizabethanism of the death of 'the desiring and desired woman' (p. 146), Cleopatra. Aristocratic women in Jacobean tragedy are introduced in order to be mutilated as the embodiment of male desire: they figure dislocated patrilineal succession and the indivisibility of sexual and political relations.

In her *Shakespeare and the Popular Voice* (1989) Annabel Patterson argues against the generally held view that Shakespeare's plays demonstrate contempt for the 'common' people. By discussing the plays in their immediate context, she is able to activate Shakespeare's commentary on professional theatrical rivalries in *Hamlet*; the presence of the Midlands revolt in 1607 within *Coriolanus* gives the play a more populist focus than much criticism has allowed; and *A Midsummer Night's Dream*, *The Tempest* and *Henry V* are also historicized to reveal a Shakespeare closer in sympathy to Caliban, Trinculo and Stephano than to Prospero. David Scott Kastan's 'Is There a Class in This (Shakespearean) Text?' (1993) also picks up the question of social relations, arguing that the theatre transgresses class and gender lines in social as well as sexual cross-dressing. He discusses Edgar's disguise as Poor Tom in *King Lear* in the context of rogue literature and the attitudes of the bourgeois theatre audience. Richard Wilson's *Will Power: Essays on Shakespearean Authority* (1993) includes close historical readings of, for example, the Annesley case behind *King Lear*, and Leah Marcus argues for 'localization' as an idea which needs to be applied to readers and to texts in order to tease out interpretative specificity (*Puzzling Shakespeare*, 1988). Important interpretations of Shakespeare and racial politics are offered by Smith (1998), Adelman (1997), Callaghan (1999) and Alexander (2000).

The debates about these kind of historicist readings were the subject of an issue of the journal *New Literary History* in 1990. Richard Levin's 'Unthinkable Thoughts in the New Historicizing of English Renaissance Drama' (pp. 433–47) develops some of the contentions of his *New Readings vs. Old Plays* (1979). His article proposes that new historicist shibboleths about self-conscious theatre, about the constructedness of gender, about changing concepts of selfhood and subjectivity are guilty of the failing they identify in the historicism of Tillyard and Campbell: 'they homogenize Renaissance thought' (Levin, 1990, p. 437). He also goes on to counter the claims with opposing evidence. A number of scholars replied in the journal. Catherine Belsey's 'Richard Levin and In-Different Reading' (pp. 449–56) defends a criticism which 'deliberately seeks out the moments of difference within the text, looks out for the formal breaks and disruptions which draw attention to discontinuities of meaning' (Belsey, 1990, p. 445). Jonathan Dollimore's contribution, 'Shakespeare, Cultural Materialism, Feminism and Marxist Humanism' (pp. 471–93) stresses the specificity of materialist criticism through a critique of writing by Lynda E. Boose (1987), Carol Thomas Neely (1988), and Kiernan Ryan (1989). Another collection of essays, Ivo Kamps' *Shakespeare Left and Right* (1991), includes contributions by Levin and his critics, including Gayle Greene and Michael Bristol, and again makes explicit the ground of the debate about political or ideological approaches to Shakespeare. Graham Bradshaw's *Misrepresentations: Shakespeare and the Materialists* (1993) takes issue with new historicism, taking *Henry V* and *Othello* as 'test cases . . . from which to appraise our present critical situation' (Bradshaw, 1993, p. 2). Bradshaw's critical debate with Dollimore (1984), Sinfield (1992), Hawkes (1986), Evans (1986) and Greenblatt (1980 and 1988) among others concludes with an association of Iago as a new historicist, opposing idealism with materialism. Bradshaw accuses his critical adversaries of a 'failure to engage seriously with Shakespeare's irreducibly complex designs' and consequently the failure 'to engage seriously with their professed belief . . . that values are culturally and historically specific' (p. 18). He cites as fallacious the 'new historicist E-effect, or estrangement effect': 'whatever separates "us" from Shakespeare and the Renaissance is more important than what joins us, so that anybody who thinks Shakespeare is our contemporary is showing how little he or she understands' (pp. 28–9). 'As for the argument that there is no Shakespeare, only "Shakespeare's," this book presents a lengthy reply,' Bradshaw proposes. 'A short answer would be that "Shakespeares" is interesting but Shakespeare are better' (p. 33). James Cunningham's *Shakespeare's Tragedies and Modern Critical Theory* (1997) discusses, as a 'practical advocate of critical pluralism' (Cunningham, 1997, p. 208), how the plays have been reinterpreted by feminist, poststructuralist and new historicist criticism.

Further Reading

Adelman, Janet. 'Iago's Alter Ego: Race as Projection in Othello'. *Shakespeare Quarterly* 48 (1997): 125–44.

Aers, David, Hodge, Bob, and Kress, Gunther R. *Literature, Language, and Society in England, 1580–1680*. Dublin: Barnes & Noble, 1981.

Alexander, Catherine M. S., and Wells, Stanley W. *Shakespeare and Race*. Cambridge: Cambridge University Press, 2000.

Babcock, R. W. 'Historical Criticism of Shakespeare'. *Modern Language Quarterly* 13 (1952): 6–20.

Belsey, Catherine. 'Richard Levin and In-Different Reading'. *New Literary History* 21 (1990): 449–56.

Boose, Lynda. 'The Family in Shakespeare Studies; or – Studies in the Family of Shakespeareans; or – The Politics of Politics'. *Renaissance Quarterly* 40 (1987): 707–42.

Bradshaw, Graham. *Misrepresentations: Shakespeare and the Materialists*. Ithaca; London: Cornell University Press, 1993.

Callaghan, Dympna. *Shakespeare without Women: Representing Gender and Race on the Renaissance Stage.* London: Routledge, 1999.

Cohen, Derek. *The Politics of Shakespeare.* Basingstoke: Macmillan, 1993.

Cohen, Walter. 'Political Criticism of Shakespeare'. *Shakespeare Reproduced: The Text in History and Ideology,* eds Jean Howard and Marion O'Connor. London; New York: Methuen, 1987.

Cunningham, James. *Shakespeare's Tragedies and Modern Critical Theory.* Madison, NJ; London: Associated University Presses, 1997.

Dollimore, Jonathan. *Radical Tragedy: Religion, Ideology and Power in the Drama of Shakespeare and his Contemporaries.* London: Harvester Wheatsheaf, 1984.

—— 'Shakespeare, Cultural Materialism, Feminism and Marxist Humanism'. *New Literary History* 21 (1990): 471–93.

——, and Sinfield, Alan. *Political Shakespeare: New Essays in Cultural Materialism.* Manchester: Manchester University Press, 1985.

Dutton, Richard, and Wilson, Richard. *New Historicism and Renaissance Drama.* London: Longman, 1992.

Eagleton, Terry. *William Shakespeare.* Oxford: Blackwell, 1986.

Evans, Malcolm. *Signifying Nothing: Truth's True Contents in Shakespeare's Text.* London: Harvester Wheatsheaf, 1989.

Goldberg, Jonathan. *James I and the Politics of Literature: Jonson, Shakespeare, Donne, and their Contemporaries.* Baltimore: Johns Hopkins University Press, 1983.

Greenblatt, Stephen. *Renaissance Self-fashioning: From More to Shakespeare.* Chicago: University of Chicago Press, 1980.

—— *Shakespearean Negotiations: The Circulation of Social Energy in Renaissance England.* Berkeley: University of California Press, 1988.

Hawkes, Terence. *That Shakespeherian Rag: Essays on a Critical Process.* London: Methuen, 1986.

Jardine, Lisa. *Reading Shakespeare Historically.* London: Routledge, 1996.

Kamps, Ivo. *Shakespeare Left and Right.* New York; London: Routledge, 1991.

Kastan, David Scott. 'Is There a Class in This (Shakespearean) Text?'. *Renaissance Drama* 24 (1993): 101–22.

—— *Shakespeare after Theory.* New York: Routledge, 1999.

Kiernan, V. G. *Eight Tragedies of Shakespeare: A Marxist Study.* London: Verso, 1996.

Knights, L. C. *Shakespeare's Politics: With some Reflections on the Nature of Tradition.* London: Oxford University Press, 1957.

Kott, Jan. *Shakespeare our Contemporary.* London: Methuen, 1964.

Levin, Richard. *New Readings vs. Old Plays: Recent Trends in the Reinterpretation of English Renaissance Drama.* Chicago; London: University of Chicago Press, 1979.

—— 'Unthinkable Thoughts in the New Historicizing of English Renaissance Drama'. *New Literary History* 21 (1990): 433–47.

Marcus, Leah S. *Puzzling Shakespeare: Local Reading and its Discontents.* Berkeley; London: University of California Press, 1988.

Margolies, David. *Monsters of the Deep: Social Dissolution in Shakespeare's Tragedies.* Manchester: Manchester University Press, 1992.

Neely, Carol Thomas. 'Constructing the Subject: Feminist Practice and the New Renaissance Discourses'. *English Literary Renaissance* 18 (1988): 5–18.

Patterson, Annabel M. *Shakespeare and the Popular Voice.* Oxford: Basil Blackwell, 1989.

Ryan, Kiernan. *Shakespeare.* New York; London: Harvester Wheatsheaf, 1989.

Sinfield, Alan. *Faultlines: Cultural Materialism and the Politics of Dissident Reading.* Oxford: Clarendon Press, 1992.

Smith, Ian. 'Barbarian Errors: Performing Race in Early Modern England'. *Shakespeare Quarterly* 49 (1998): 168–86.

Tennenhouse, Leonard. *Power on Display: The Politics of Shakespeare's Genres.* New York; London: Methuen, 1986.

Veeser, H. Aram. *The New Historicism.* New York; London: Routledge, 1989.

—— *The New Historicism Reader.* New York; London: Routledge, 1994.

Wilson, Richard. *Will Power: Essays on Shakespearean Authority.* New York; London: Harvester Wheatsheaf, 1993.

Worden, Blair. 'Shakespeare and Politics'. *Shakespeare Survey* 44 (1991): 1–15.

11

History and Politics: Critical Extracts

Macbeth and the 'Name of King'

David Scott Kastan

Kastan's book, Shakespeare after Theory, *aims to "examine Shakespeare's plays as they appeared and circulated both as drama and as texts. Such a focus would see the plays no less as social facts than as aesthetic forms, their meanings products of the density of intentions that saturate them" (p. 18). In this chapter on* Macbeth, *Kastan discusses the play's inscription of Stuart rule in terms of legitimacy and absolutism. He builds on previous criticism and develops a compelling and politicized account of the play's characteristic doubling, which, as he concludes, needs to be 'understood in historical terms, not least of which are our own'.*

David Scott Kastan, 'Macbeth and the "Name of King"', in Shakespeare after Theory. London: Routledge, 1999.

> The political dimension of tragedy does not consist in illuminating the displacements of power, as happens in the long procession of sovereigns in the histories and even in *Julius Caesar*; it lies rather in posing the question of whether a *cultural foundation* of power is still possible, and in answering in the negative.
>
> Franco Moretti

Macbeth is at one the most violent of the major tragedies and the one whose violence has been most securely recuperated by criticism, if not by the text itself. Macbeth's savage tyranny is powerfully envisioned by the play but is seen to exist, in De Quincey's phrase, as "an awful parenthesis" in nature, a hideous aberration that at once opposes and legitimizes the moral order. Duncan's gracious sovereignty is shattered and replaced by Macbeth's increasingly gratuitous brutality, but Scotland is eventually released from the nightmare of Macbeth's rule by an army of English troops and disaffected Scottish nobles who come "to dew the sovereign flower, and drown the weeds" (5.2.30). With

Malcolm's restoration of the line of Duncan, the forms of power are returned to legitimate hands and legitimate uses, the royal house and sovereignty itself successfully renewed. After a monstrous intrerregnum, authority is again natural and benign. Thus, critics characteristically hold that "the form of the play triumphantly asserts its thematic, moral resolution,"[1] reestablishing "the natural relationship between sovereign and subject,"[2] and, in affirming "the moral and natural legitimacy of rule through primogeniture,"[3] healing the breach in nature rent by Macbeth's violent usurpation and complimenting the absolutism of King James.

What, however, prevents this now familiar account of the moral reflex traced by the plot from being an entirely adequate description of the action of *Macbeth* is that it reduces the play to its confident moral assertions, reproducing rather than analyzing the construction of difference that underwrites them. It accepts as both normative and unassailable the moral oppositions produced (and dissolved) in the densities of the text. Legitimate is, of course, set against illegitimate, loyal against rebellious, natural against unnatural, good against evil. Indeed, Hazlitt observed that the play "is done upon a stronger and more systematic principle of contrast than any other of Shakespear's plays."[4] But the play is more disturbing than this would suggest. This insistent principle of moral contrast, wonderfully unconditional and reassuring, is not stable but is unnervingly unsettled by the text's compelling strategies of repetition and resemblance.

Like Lady Macbeth's hospitality, the play itself appears, with its two invasions, its two thanes of Cawdor, its two feasts, two doctors, two kings, and two kingdoms, "in every point twice done, and then done double" (1.6.15). These mirroring effects, what Jonathan Goldberg has incisively called the play's "specular contamination,"[5] insist that the radical difference asserted by its fierce moral oppositions is both tendentious and insecure. As a recent group of critics has argued, apparent opposites are discovered to be dismayingly similar, and, more dismaying still, even implicated in one another.[6] If the play does produce the almost inescapable binaries of its criticism, it reveals as well that the moral hierarchy they define is achieved and sustained only by denying the radical dependence of the dominant term upon its demonized contrary.

Duncan's benign sovereignty is no doubt set in opposition to Macbeth's willful brutality, but Duncan's rule depends upon — indeed demands — Macbeth's violence. The unexplained revolt that begins the play is put down by Macbeth's brutal defense of Duncan's authority. Violent disruption is violently repaired. Certainly we are to distinguish Macbeth's killing *for* the king from Macbeth's killing *of* the king: in the service of Duncan, killing marks Macbeth as "valiant," a "worthy gentleman" (1.2.24); in the service of his own ambitions, killing marks Macbeth as monstrous, and "abhorred tyrant"

(5.7.11). But if from the first the play asserts the absolute difference between loyal and rebellious action, it no less resolutely disrupts if not denies that difference, not merely in Macbeth's merciless treatment of "the merciless Macdonwald" (1.2.9), but in the unanchored pronouns that literally confuse the two: Macbeth carves "out his passage"

> Till he fac'd the slave
> Which ne'er shook hands, nor bade farewell to him,
> Till he unseam'd him from the have to th' chops,
> And fix'd his head upon our battlements.
>
> (1.2.20–23)

Only "*our* battlements" is clearly differentiated; the referents of the third person singular pronouns are as "doubtful" (1.2.7) as the battle itself that the captain reports. All that is "fixed" is the head of a rebel.

Macbeth's violent defense of the King at once confirms Duncan's rule and collapses the distinctions upon which it rests. Difference dissolves into disruptive similarity. Hero and villain, as Harry Berger has ingeniously demonstrated,[7] are disturbingly intertwined and indistinguishable, as in the captian's image of the rebel forces and Duncan's troops as "two spent swimmers, that do cling together" (1.2.8). In the battle Macbeth fights bravely, but textual density and syntactic ambiguity uncannily dislocate his loyalties. Duncan "reads / [Macbeth's] personal venture in the rebels' fight" (1.3.91); the Scottish King "finds [Macbeth] in the stout Norweyan ranks" (1.3.95). Macbeth confronts the invading King of Norway, who is "assisted by that most disloyal traitor, / The Thane of Cawdor" (1.2.53–54), not with Duncan's certain authority but, disturbingly, only with "self-comparisons, / point against point, rebellious arm 'gainst arm" (1.2.56–57).

Yet it might well be objected that the subtle reading gives too much away, that the legitimacy of Duncan, "clear in his great office" (1.7.18), itself stands as an absolute value that locates and fixes moral positions, necessitating and validating precisely the stark moral and political contrasts that textually, or rather *only* textually, blur. Duncan's unambiguous right demands and legitimates Macbeth's violent service as it later repudiates and demonizes Macbeth's violent ambition. Perhaps such a reading would have been James's own, and the play has regularly been seen as a compliment to the King ("a topick the most likely to conciliate the favour of the court,"[8] as Malone said), not merely in the vivid "show" of the Stewart kings, with their "two-fold balls and treble sceptres" (4.1.11sd, 121), envisioning precisely the imperial claim of James's monarchy,[9] but also in the play's reproduction of the absolutist logic of James's own political theorizing. In spite of the murderous violation of "the Lord's anointed temple" (2.3.68), sovereign authority is here wondrously compelling and resilient, both worthy and capable of being defended and restored. "Things . . . climb upward to what they were before" (4.2.24–5); the usurper is purged, and natural hierarchy and lineal descent are reestablished. Even in the face of Macbeth's savage criminality, "Shakespeare makes it seem," writes Leonard Tennenhouse, "as if nothing can disrupt the progress of the crown from Banquo to James; all the elements of nature, like those of the theater, join to put Malcolm on the throne."[10]

But if Tennenhouse correctly recognizes the genealogical telos of Shakespeare's *Macbeth*, his formulation unwittingly reveals the impossibility of appealing to an absolute notion of sovereignty to authorize the play's oppositions, for Tennenhouse has in fact identified *two* dynastic genealogies, an embarrassing surplus that must unsettle the claim to legitimacy for either. If the Stewart line is seen to derive from Banquo, then Malcolm's claim to the throne and James's own seem to conflict. The play offers two seemingly incompatible sources of legitimacy: it is Banquo who will plant the "seeds of kings" (3.1.69) that will flower into the Stewart dynasty, but the play asserts as well that Malcolm's restoration of the line of Duncan reestablishes legitimate rule in Scotland.

Macbeth thus makes evident that Stewart legitimacy rests on something less certain than patrilineal descent, though the play is oddly silent about the contradiction that it makes visible. Historically (and that may be the wrong word since "Fleance" seems to be an invention of Hector Boece in 1572[11]), the dynastic lines eventually merge some six generations after the events of the play, when Walter, putatively the descendant of Fleance, marries Marjory, the daughter of Robert I. Their son, Robert II, is the first of the Stewart kings, claiming, however, his throne from his mother (and, ironically, given the later Stuarts' commitment to the Union, succeeding only after an effort by David Bruce to have the king of England or his son "undertake the Kingdom"[12]). The play's emphasis upon Banquo as "father to a line of kings" (3.1.59) rather than Duncan has, then, the effect of avoiding the vexed problem of inheritance through the female, comfortably locating authority in the male body. But if this is appropriate for a play, if not a culture, that consistently demonizes female power, a play in which to be not "of woman born" (4.1.80) is to be invulnerable and to be "unknown to woman" (4.3.126) is to be virtuous, it leaves unmistakable the fault line in the play's, if not the culture's, understanding of legitimacy – and not least because James inherits his Scottish crown through the female, a fact at issue in the Witches' "show of eight kings," as the eighth monarch of the Stewart line was in fact James's mother, Mary, whose presence in, no less than her absence from the pageant must necessarily trouble its putative assertion of patrilineal succession.[13]

The plot's strenuous efforts to reestablish sovereign authority by restoring the line of Duncan always exists uncomfortably, that is, too obviously, with its parallel insistence that "Banquo's issue" will "ever / Reign in this kingdom" (4.1.102–3), making it impossible to see "the progress of the crown" as inevitable and undeviating. With Malcolm's investiture the crown is returned to legitimate hands, but the Stuart future, stretching "out to th'crack of doom" (4.1.117), clearly has its source elsewhere. Though James was proud of "the continued line of lawfull discent, as therin he exceedeth all the Kings that the world now knoweth," as Ellesmere wrote,[14] Shakespeare's play at once demonizes the disruption of "lawfull discent" and seemingly insists upon it, valorizes the concept of legitimacy and discloses its instability.

Renaissance absolutism,[15] of course, usually attempted to stabilize the concept theoretically, if not historically, by insisting upon sovereignty's divine authorization. Thus, Henry VIII strove to establish "the surety of both his title and succession" by appealing to the "grants of jurisdiction given by God immediately to Emperors, kings and princes in succession to their heirs."[16] James claimed his throne on similar grounds, Coke arguing on his behalf that "the kinges's matie, in his lawful, juste and lineall title to the Crowne of Englaunde, comes not by succession onelye, or by election, but from God onelye . . . by reason of lineall discente."[17] And James spectacularly extended the implications of occupying "the office giuen him by God": "For Kings are not onely GODS Lieutenants vpon earth, and sit vpon GODS throne, but euen by GOD himselfe they are called Gods."[18]

Scripture commanded the Israelites: "set him a king over thee, whom the Lord thy God shall choose" (Deut. 17:15), but exactly how God's choice was to be known and established in rule was uncertain. The crown may well insist upon its origins in an absolute and direct grant of authority from God, but it cannot escape the evidence of its heavily mediated existence in a world of historical agency. Though authority usually seeks to occlude the fact, imagining itself always both sanctified and permanent, it characteristically originates, and usually maintains itself, in violent action. Trotsky, of course, provocatively claimed that "every state is founded on force,"[19] but even conservative Renaissance political thinkers usually understood that what came to be known as "divine right" did not solve the question of authority: it mystified it. Even while insisting that kingship is divinely sanctioned, they saw that its origins were decidedly more mundane and compromised. In 1595, William Covell, in his *Polimanteia*, admitted that most "common wealths had their beginnings by violent Tyrannies."[20] In 1604, Sir Henry Saville concurred, holding that of the kingdoms now in existence "all of them and perhaps all that ever were . . . [were] first purchased by conquest."[21] As Marchamont Nedham would say in later years, when the complex issue of legitimating a regime founded on violence had become apparent to all, "the power of the sword is, and ever hath been, the foundation of all titles to government."[22]

On the other hand, though the identification of authority's origins in power was commonplace, many recognized the political danger in acknowledging the fact, a danger uncannily admitted, in the folio orthography, in Macbeth's somatic response to the mere thought of the murder of sovereignty: the "horrid Image doth unfixe my Heire" (1.3.135; TLN 246). Both hairs and heirs may well be unfixed by the knowledge of sovereignty's violent origins, as the Presbyterian divine, Richard Baxter understood. Writing in prison in 1686, he argued that monarchs must suppress such knowledge, not because the truth was otherwise but for fear it would "encourage Rebels" or invasion from without: "while France is stronger than England, Holland or other Kings, I dare not say that if that Kingdom conquer them he is their rightfull monarch, lest such doctrine entice him to attempt it."

What had provoked Baxter's consideration and rejection of conquest theory was "a little book written by a namelesse Scot 1603, called the Law of free Monarchies" that "foundeth the originall right of Monarchy uppon *strugle* and *Conquest* by which only Kings are made Kings."[23] Baxter's "namelesse Scot," however, was King James himself, and in his *True Law of Free Monarchies* (which was originally published in 1598 with the pseudonym "C. Philopatris"), even James admitted the inevitable coercion in "the first maner of establishing the Lawes and forme of gouernement among vs."[24] In part to escape the dangerous implications of the view that monarchy begins with a transfer of power from the people, James was forced to concede that Scottish monarchical authority derived directly from the conquest of Scotland by the Irish King Fergus, "making himself master of the countrey, by his owne friendship, and force," just as English monarchical authority derived from the conquest of England by "the Bastard of *Normandie*" who "made himselfe king . . . by force, and with a mighty army."[25]

But once authority admits its customary origins in force and violence the question of legitimacy becomes complex. What king is then not a usurper, or at least a usurper's heir? While King James assumed that "the trew difference betwixt a lawful good King and an vsurping Tyran"[26] was absolute and unassailable, the distinction cannot be rigidly maintained, logically collapsing in the discussion of authority's origin (a collapse interestingly enacted in an anxious sentence in Bodin's *Six Bookes of a Commonweale* deploring interpreters "ioyning these two incompatible words together, *a King a Tyrant*,"[27] where Bodin hysterically performs at the level of syntax the very "ioyning" he seeks to prevent). If the crown is claimed by right of conquest, even if carefully designating it a second cause animated and validated by providence, the difference between lawful authority and usurped power must blur if not be completely erased.

The problem was a crucial one for Renaissance political theorists who increasingly recognized the difficulty posed by coercive origination for the theory of absolutism. The Book of Homilies had confidently asserted that "we be taught by experience, how Almighty God never suffereth the third heir to enjoy his father's wrong possessions,"[28] but, in fact, experience often taught otherwise, history regularly testifying to the successful legitimation of usurped authority. Indeed, in 1643, Henry Ferne maintained that "If this Answerer should looke through all Christendomne, he would scarce find a Kingdom that descends by inheritance, but had a beginning in Armes, and yet I thinke he will not say the Titles of these Kings are no better then of Plunderers; for though it may be unjust at first in him that invades and Conquers, yet in the succession, which is from him, that providence which translates Kingdomes, manifests it selfe and the will of God; and there are *momenta temporum* for the justnesse of such Titles, though we cannot fixe them."[29]

Though Pocock has claimed that "conquest struck few roots in royalist thought,"[30] obviously a conquest theory had developed and taken hold by the end of the sixteenth century and, perhaps surprisingly, precisely among those most committed to royalism. King James himself had articulated it in his appeal to Fergus's conquest to authorize Scottish kingship, though James attempted to defuse the potentially subversive implications of grounding authority in power by insisting, improbably, that the "people willingly fell to him" and that, in any case, the country was "scantly inhabited.[31] Others, who recognized the impossibility of escaping the contradiction James attempted to evade, worried more about forging a political distinction that could rational- ize the process by which power is converted into authority, fixing the *momenta temporum* that Ferne had invoked. William Barret, chaplain of Cambridge's Gonville and Caius College, reversed the claim of the Elizabethan homilist, insisting that several generations (*nonnulla secula*) of possession would validate and legitimize a usurped crown;[32] Thomas Preston similarly argued that tyrants and usurpers "with their progenie doe by prescription get a lawfull right to the souereigntie by possessing it a hundred yeeres of more";[33] and the Canons passed by the clergy in 1606, which King James significantly refused to endorse, were even more liberal: "new forms of government," the clergy held, even those "begun by rebellion," became legitimate as soon as they are "thor- oughly settled."[34]

For *Macbeth*, of course, the problem is further complicated by the fact that in Scotland, unlike England, patrilineal succession to the crown was itself a "new" form of government, an innovation introduced at the end of the tenth century by Kenneth III. The traditional mode of transferring sovereignty in Scotland had been a quasi-elective system of succession within an extended royal family, consciously devised to prevent both the succession of a minor and the perpetuation of tyrannical rule. But Kenneth III (grandfather of the play's Duncan), "greeuing not a little," as Holinshed reports following Boece, "for that thereby his sonnes should be kept from inioieng the crowne," poisoned the prince who "ought to have succeeded in the rule of the kingdom," appointing his own eldest son, Malcolm, as heir and persuading the nobles to abrogate the old law of tanistry. The nobility, "perceiuing it was in vaine to denie that which would be had by violence," reluctantly agreed to the designation of Kenneth's son as Prince of Cumberland and to the institution of a system whereby "the sonne should without anie contradiction succeed the father in the heritage of the crowne and kinglie estate."[35]

Though scholars have questioned how well Shakespeare actually knew or understood the intricacies of Scottish political history,[36] he could not but be aware of this aspect of Scotland's past, which, as republican historians like George Buchanan made clear, exposes the mutable, historical (and hence contestable) nature of hereditary kingship. For *Macbeth*, which combines materials from several reigns, Shakespeare obviously read widely in Holinshed's *Historie of Scotland*, and so would certainly have encountered evidence and discussion of Scotland's earlier dependence for the transfer of authority upon the traditional system of collateral inheritance. But even in Holinshed's account of Macbeth's reign the procedures and principles by which authority is transmitted are prominent; indeed they are precisely what provokes Macbeth to act to obtain the crown. The chronicle notes not only that Macbeth had many qualities necessary for rule but also that by "the old lawes of the realme" he had a credible claim to the throne. Following Duncan's nomination of his son Malcolm as his successor, Holinshed (or rather Francis Thynne) writes, Macbeth "began to take counsell how he might usurpe the kingdome by force, having a just quarell so to doo (as he took the matter) for that Duncane did what in him lay to defraude him of all maner of title and claime, which he might in time to come, pretend unto the crowne."[37]

Shakespeare's play, of course, does nothing to question Duncan's right or assert Macbeth's own, and many critics have noted how Shakespeare selects and shapes his source material in writing *Macbeth* to clarify if not produce its sharp oppositions. Among other changes, the history's account of "the feeble and slothful administration of Duncane"[38] is unmentioned in the play, along with Macbeth's ten years of humane and effective rule, as Shakespeare erases the equivocations of the source material, transforming, as Peter Stallybrass has said, "dialectic into antithesis."[39] What has less often been considered is why Shakespeare's attention should be drawn to a reign that demanded such substantial alteration and erasure. No doubt he was attracted to the story because the chronicle account includes an extended digression tracing the origins of the Stuart dynasty back to Fleance.[40] Nonetheless, if the subject was chosen because of its relation to King James, Shakespeare has chosen historical matter determinedly resistant to the story he apparently wants to tell – and certainly incompatible with the absolutist politics of his sovereign. The Scottish history not only complicates, if not contests, the right of Duncan but presents patrilineal succession itself, which the play idealizes and naturalizes, as an innovation brought about by an ambitious and murderous tyrant. That is, Shakespeare's sources disturbingly suggest that the hereditary kingship that Macbeth assails – and that King James champions – originates with a king who is, in fact, Macbeth's double rather than his opposite.

But Shakespeare's own story is profoundly a story of doubles, doubles, as Jonathan Goldberg has said, that render "determinate difference indeterminate,"[41] reinstating, that is, the complexities of the source material apparently banished by the insistent antitheses of the Shakespearean plot. Everywhere the play palters "with us in a double sense" (5.8.20), offering both an orthodox version of events and one disturbingly heterodox: a moral play "that maketh Kings feare to be Tyrants,"[42] in Sidney's phrase, and a subversive one that uncannily collapses the distinction between them. The ending may be seen either to restore the legitimate line of Duncan, redeeming the murderous interlude of Macbeth's tyranny, or merely to repeat the pattern of violent action that Macbeth initiates. The play both begins and ends with an attack upon established rule, with a loyal nobility rewarded with new titles, and with the execution of a rebellious thane of Cawdor. Malcolm is three times hailed as king exactly as Macbeth has been by the witches, and Malcolm's coronation at Scone either returns the nation to health and order or provides the conditions for a new round of temptation and disorder (as in Roman Polanski's 1971 film of the play, which ends with Donalbain going off to seek the witches and his own crown, or, indeed, as in the chronicles themselves, where the historical Donald Bane turned rebel, allying himself with the King of Norway, killing Malcolm's son and successfully claiming the throne).

The play's insistent doubling, then, insures that it cannot simply be seen as an orthodox demonstration, designed to delight and praise King James, of the inevitable recoil of the moral world, successfully purging sin and reestablishing right. But that is, however, exactly how the troops accompanying Malcolm understand the action. "March we on," says Caithness, "To give obedience where 'tis truly ow'd: / Meet we the med'cine of the sickly weal; / and with him pour we, in our country's purge, / Each drop of us" (5.2.25–29). Malcolm may well be the "med'cine of the sickly weal," but if the moral alignments are certain and secure the political ones are significantly less so. The play makes it difficult to discover exactly where obedience is "truly owed." Macduff calls Macbeth an "untitled tyrant bloody-scepter'd" (4.3.104), but in fact, however bloody his scepter, he certainly is, as Macduff well knows, *titled*. Although Macbeth is undeniably a murderer, he lawfully succeeds and is crowned. "'Tis most like / The sovereignty will fall upon Macbeth," observes Ross; and Macduff responds: "He is already nam'd, and gone to Scone / To be invested" (2.4.29–32). "Named" and legally enthroned, Macbeth is king and arguably truly owed the obedience of his countrymen.

The difficulty of maintaining the distinction between a "lawful" king and a "usurping" tyrant is not only articulated by Macduff's contradictory judgments but registered structurally by his role in the play. He is obviously a loyal version of the ambitious Macbeth. Macbeth kills both a rebel then a king, exactly as does Macduff, but, as Alan Sinfield has shrewdly noted, Macduff's rebel and king are the same man.[43] Macbeth's acts, of course, are clearly differentiated: one is a heroic defense of the nation and its king, the other a murderous attack upon them; but Macduff's single act at once defends and attacks sovereignty. It is a liberation and a regicide, one more thing that is "fair and foul" in the "hurly-burly" of the play. While apparently an unproblematic reassertion of right and reason, it should be perhaps only as "welcome and unwelcome" (4.3.138) as his first impression of Malcolm.

If Macduff has rescued Scotland, freeing the time from the tyrant, avenging "crimes against the family and against the state,"[44] in David Norbrook's phrase, we should note also that Macduff is himself charged with "crimes against the family and the state," charged, that is, with being the "traitor" (4.2.81, 45) that both the first murderer and Lady Macduff term him. For the first murderer, Macduff is a "traitor" simply because he opposes the king of Scotland that has suborned the murderer's services. For Lady Macduff, of course, the charge is not that her husband has betrayed a political allegiance but that he betrayed his family precisely *in* his political allegiance: "He loves us not: / He wants the natural touch" (4.2.8–9). In a change from the source, where Macduff goes to England "to reuenge the slaughter so cruellie executed on his wife, his children, and other friends,"[45] Shakespeare's Macduff chooses the state over his family as his primary loyalty, in the process leaving his family vulnerable to the murderous "firstlings" (4.1.147) of Macbeth's heart as he seeks aid for his country.

Norbrook argues that "Shakespeare invents the scene of the murder of Lady Macduff and her son in order to bring home the 'natural' links between the public and the private."[46] But it seems to me possible to argue exactly the reverse: the episode reveals that the homology that absolutism characteristically posited between state and family is false. Kinship and kingship are not necessarily mutually reinforcing, as the ideological efforts to naturalize domination would insist, but here revealed as conflicting spheres of existence, distributing power and demanding service in ways that are incompatible and contradictory. "What is a traitor?" innocently asks Macduff's young son, but the play prevents an easy answer; "Why, one that swears and lies" (4.2.46–47), bitterly answers Lady Macduff, resentful of her husband's betrayal of his familial obligations (and in words no doubt alluding to the equivocations of the Jesuit Henry Garnet in the Gunpowder trial in March of 1606). Yet in this play where it often seems that "nothing is, but what is not." (1.3.142), the first murderer's charge of treason is as true – and admittedly as false – as Lady Macduff's, and both charges speak that profound instability in the discourse of authority that was expected to rationalize and guarantee all social relations.

If considering Macduff a "traitor" seems hard justice for one who means so well and loses so much, it does reveal the difficulty of articulating persuasively and coherently a theory of resistance without at the same time admitting the conditional and contingent nature of political power. The Huguenot Theodore Beza, for example, attempted to discover a legitimate place for political opposition by distinguishing between tyranny by those who "by force or fraud" have "usurped a power that does not belong to them by law" (against whom "each private citizen" has the right to "exert all his strength to defend the legitimate institutions of his country") and a "sovereign magistrate" who is "otherwise legitimate" against whom the people "have no other remedy" than "penitance and patience joined by prayers."[47] Macbeth's case, however, doesn't precisely fit either circumstance. Certainly he has proceeded by "force and fraud" but the crown may indeed be said "to belong to [him] by law." Not only has he right, but he achieves his kingship by proper election and investiture. And yet, although he is therefore a "sovereign magistrate," unquestionably he has compromised the "legitimate institutions of his country." Is he, then, owed obedience or not?

The conventional political answer was clear; though ironically it is not the one conventional readings of the play presume. William Sclater, a Protestant clergyman, asserted that neither the means by which a king assumed power nor his behavior in office affected his authority as king: "the persons are sometimes intruders, as in the case of vsurpation; sometimes abusers of their authoritie, as when they tyrannize: but the powers themselues haue God as their author."[48] Similarly, King James argued that a lawfully enthroned king no matter how monstrous must not be opposed. Determined to resist both Catholic and Calvinist resistance theories, King James insisted that even a murderous tyrant was to be patiently suffered, for the king was to be judged by God alone. "It is casten vp by diuers that employ their pennes vpon Apologies for rebellions and treasons," wrote James, "that euery man is borne to carry such a naturall zeale and duety to his common-wealth, as to his mother; that seeing it so rent and deadlie wounded, as whiles it will be by wicked and tyrannous Kings, good Citizens will be forced, for the naturall zeale and duety they owe to their owne natiue countrey, to put their hand to worke for freeing their common-wealth from such a pest."[49]

But this apparently natural and patriotic course, which exactly anticipates the moral claims and rhetorical strategies of the avenging Scots in the play, is, in fact, condemned by James, held to be both blasphemous and ineffective: first, it violates, he says, "a sure Axiome in *Theologie*, that evil should not be done, that good may come of it: The wickednesse therefore of the King shall never make them that are ordained to be iudged by him, to become his Iudges." Rebellion is "evil" in every circumstance; the behavior of the king in no way affects the fact that those "that are ordained to be iudged" must always stay so and support the status quo. And, second, James is certain that "in place of relieuing the common-wealth out of distresse (which is their onely excuse and colour) they shall heape double distresse and desolation vpon it; and so their rebellion should procure the contrary effercts they pretend it for."[50] Instead of improving the situation, their principled opposition only makes it worse.

Neither pragmatically nor theologically can any effort to oppose the "wickednesse . . . of the King" be justified. Indeed, writes James, a ruler might be "a Tyrant, and vsurper of their liberties; yet in respect that they had once received and acknowledged him for their king, he not only commandeth them to obey him, but euen to pray for his prosperitie. . . ."[51] Thus, strangely, in the play the orthodox moral position is at odds with the orthodox political position; the inevitable moral revulsion at Macbeth's brutal criminality produces a political reflex that must itself be condemned. As Macbeth's rule is lawful (having been "received and acknowleged"), the English troops and Scottish nobles that arrive as saviors of Scotland become exact doubles of the Norwegian troops and rebellious nobles that distress Duncan's lawful reign at the play's beginning.

In each case an indigenous force combines with a foreign power to assail the security of a Scottish monarch, the very neatness of the parallel undoing the overdetermined difference the play asserts. The repair of violated patrilineal succession (though it is perhaps worth noting that the play has not very clearly established the principle of patrilineal succession, "the due of birth," since Malcolm's right to the Scottish crown seems to originate in Duncan's nomination of his son), as well as the insistent Englishness of the resources that repair it, works, of course, to differentiate the recoil against Macbeth from the Norwegian-supported revolt against Duncan. Macbeth's savagery demands and legitimates any and all savagery in the campaign to dethrone him, and the English invasion is not merely *English* but is endowed with a unique spiritual authority, evident in Edward's "most pious" kingship (3.6.27), which, remarkably, keeps itself discretely aloof from the military action necessary to activate its moral charge.[52] Yet, for all the efforts to insure the sanctity of the restorative violence, it is nonetheless and inescapably violence, and almost uniquely visible on stage. Though the play would see Macbeth's violence as aberrative and blasphemous, as that which assails sovereign authority and must be repudiated, it offers no obvious alternative to that violence as that which is necessary to construct and defend sovereignty.

The spectacular sight of Macbeth's head fixed upon a pole, which might be seen as evidence of the inevitable triumph of moral order and political right, cannot, then, be easily used to stabilize the play's politics. Though the traitor's fate may be intended to signal "the terrible magnificence of sovereign power," like virtually all signs in the play it is equivocal, providing, as Karin Coddon argues, testimony only to "the inefficacy of symbolic closure."[53] "Behold, where stands / Th'usurper's cursed head" (5.9.20–21), proudly proclaims Macduff, but the visual image that in its spectacular assertion of legitimate power would resolve the political instability produced by the play's violence in fact reanimates the problematic. If it marks the end of Macbeth's savage tyranny, it marks as well the vulnerability of sacred kingship.

The image of the severed head certainly recalls the heads of traitors fixed on Tower Bridge, but, alternatively, it resonates as well with the crucial term of James's absolutism, characteristically articulated in the anthropomorphizing metaphor of the body politic. James, of course, conceived of the king as "the head of a body composed of diuers members,"[54] and the similitude produces a clear, if predictable, political logic. Quoting Gerson, James wrote that the people have no right to resist "the head" of the civil body even if the "deadlie poyson of tyrannie" infect it, and James finds that Gerson's arguments "doe make very strongly and expresly against butchering euen of Tyrannical Kings."[55] The head cut off, the body must wither. "It may very well fall out that the head will be forced to garre cut off some rotten members . . . to keep the rest of the body in integritie," James wrote, "but what state the body can be in, if the head, for any infirmitie that can fall to it, be cut off, I leaue to the readers iudgement."[56] Strictly within the context of James's own political thought, then, Macduff's entrance with "the usurper's cursed head" can only be seen less as a "tribute to James"[57] than as a challenge to his "iudgement," the image of unlawful resistance rather than of lawful rule. The severed head of Macbeth would, at least for James, mark not the restoration of legitimate authority but its violation: the unwarranted and blasphemous "butchery" of a "tyrannical King." It could not be a sign of renewed sovereignty but must appear as a "breach in nature" (2.3.11) no less awful than the "gashed stabs" in Duncan's sacred body, a breach that within a generation would find its form in the severed head of James's son shockingly displayed upon another "bloody stage" (2.4.6).

My point, however, is obviously not that the play demands to be read in the context of James's own political thought or ambitions, though this has been a familiar critical assertion; it is more to show the impossibility of any such reading, to see the way the play inscribes not merely the contradictions present in the source material but in the absolutist logic itself. One could, of course, find in the English invasion that frees Scotland from Macbeth's murderousness tactful reference to James's profound hopes for the union of England and

Scotland, and, indeed, George Buc had in 1605 used the alliance of Malcolm and the English Edward as an anticipation of and argument for ("a slight shadow of") the Union.[58] But if *Macbeth*'s emphasis on Englishness is designed to legitimize the Union of the Kingdoms (and one might wonder how neatly a view of England as physician to a diseased Scotland would fit with James's understanding of the Union project), ironically it was, as Holinshed reports, precisely this Englishness that left Scotland vulnerable to the depredations of Malcolm's rebellious brother:

> manie of the people abhorring the riotous maners and superfluous gormandiz-ing brought in among them by the Englishmen were willing inough to recieve this Donald for their King, trusting (because he had beene broght up in the Iles with the old customes and maners of their ancient nation, without tast of the English likerous delicats) they should by his severe order in gouernement recouer againe the former temperance of their old progenitors.[59]

Shakespeare's play is silent about Donalbain's revolt, its possibility only dimly suggested by Lennox's reply to Caithness's question, "Who knows if Donalbain be with his brother?": "For certain, sir, he is not" (5.2.7–8). And Macbeth alone articulates the "severe" Scottish view of the English, in his bitter response to his disloyal nobles: "fly, false Thanes / And mingle with the English epicures" (5.3.7–8).

Shakespeare, unsurprisingly, writes Englishness differently. His English are hardly rioters and epicures, though their social practices, perhaps ominously, do indeed influence Scottish custom, in Malcolm's introduction of English titles for his nobility: "Earls, the first that ever Scotland / In such an honour nam'd" (5.9.29–30). These new forms of honor are obviously, like those titles Duncan gave his followers, at once generous and instrumental, rewards for loyal service and opportunities to articulate the social order that would create and reflect the monarch's power. But the innovative English titles can also be read, as the English manners adopted by Malcolm's court were by both Boece and Buchanan, less benignly within this royal economy: not as "signs of noble-ness" designed to "shine / On all deservers" (1.4.41–42) but as marks of cor-ruption and catalysts for decline, less an argument for the Union than a motive for revolt.[60]

English-Scottish relations in the play do not, then, seem to promise or promote the joyful Union that James imagined. The corporate fantasy of "One King, one people, one law, and, as it was in the beginning, one land of Albion"[61] that underwrote the Union project is belied by *Macbeth*'s insistent doubles and inescapable double-talk. The very "name of king" is neither univocal nor fixed but is dislocated and destabilized in the recursive plot of the play no less than it was in the volatile political thought that the play engages. And "the name of king" was not merely an abstractly controversial focus for the ongoing Renaissance discussions about the nature and limits of sovereignty but was explicitly a contested term in the Union debates, as the English Commons in 1604 worried about the effects of conceiving of Britain as a single geopolitical entity. James's desire to "discontinue the divided names of England and Scotland" and unite the two kingdoms "under one Imperiall Crown,"[62] was anxiously discussed, and the Commons expressed their discomfort with this new "imperial theme" (1.3.129) that seemed to threaten England and Englishness. "The Name of Emperour is impossible," they declared; "The name of King a sweet name: – Plenitude of Power in it: – A Name, which God taketh upon him."[63]

Certainly, in *Macbeth* "the name of King" has a "Plenitude of Power in it," though not a power inhering in the word itself but in the social relations its speaking defines. Acknowledged "king," the monarch can effectively mobilize the institutions and agencies of power that define and defend his sovereignty. For Malcolm, Edward the Confessor, the English king, is the type of sacred and efficacious majesty: "sundry blessings hang about his throne, / That speak him full of grace" (4.3.158–59). But what "speaks" his plenitude are less the "blessings" that "hang about his throne" than the loyalty of the "ten thousand warlike men" (4.3.134) who will fight to uphold it. And if the name of king activates the power of the state that constitutes and maintains the crown, it also works to naturalize that power, sanctioning violence, converting it into valor. Thus Malcolm and the avenging nobles insistently deny the name to Macbeth. He is always the "tyrant," whose violent acts make him unworthy of loyalty; Duncan and Malcolm alone are called "King of Scotland" (1.2.28; 5.9.25), a name that turns the acts of violence done on their behalf into loyal and heroic action.

Indeed, though Macbeth enters "*as King*" at the beginning of act three, and is lawfully "named" before he goes "to Scone / To be invested" (2.4.31–32), the word "King" seems to stick even in his own mouth. He speaks it only five times, on three occasions referring to the witches' prophecy (1.3.73; 1.3.144; 3.1.57), once to the apparition of a "child crowned" (4.1.87), and once to Duncan: "Let us toward the King" (1.3.153). Many critics have remarked on the euphemisms Macbeth used to describe the murders he plans and commits, but "the name of king" is subject to exactly the same verbal displacements. "When 'tis, / It shall make honor for you," he says to Banquo (2.1.25–26), exactly like the pronominal evasions of "If it were done, when 'tis done, then 'twere well / It were done quickly" (1.7.1–2). Even Lady Macbeth cannot fully articulate his prophesied progress to the throne: "Glamis thou art, and Cawdor; and shalt be / What thou art promis'd" (1.5.14–15), not "King," as the witches' three-fold prophecy demands, but merely the paraphrastic "What thou art promised." The name of king, with its plenitude of power, is not so easily spoken, not quite so "sweet," when one admits the fearsome agency necessary to achieve and defend it.

I hope it is clear that my purpose here is neither to set the play in the context of Jacobean absolutist fantasies, nor to find in its doublings and dislocations mere indeterminacy, a hall of mirrors, endlessly reflecting and ultimately "signifying nothing" (5.5.28). "The name of king" that the witches first "put . . . upon" (3.1.57) Macbeth, like all their imperfect speaking, is, of course, equivocal, but it is, in fact, no more stable when Macbeth is "named" (2.4.31) by the nobles, or as it functions in the diverse political discourses that circulate around and through the play. In all its iterations, the name of king is unnervingly labile, but no less potent for being so. It would define itself as the opposite of the blasphemous savagery the play calls "Macbeth," imagining itself, stable and singular, as a benign principle of plenitude; but, in the play's doublings and dislocations, it is revealed instead to be the name of the agency able to command and legitimate the very savagery it demonizes – not, then, the opposite of Macbeth but at least potentially, and unnervingly so, Macbeth himself.[64] It is he who most thoroughly reveals the plenitude in "the name of king," reveals it to be neither an empty signifier nor a transcendental signified, but a name assuming meaning always and only in history and demanding to be understood in historical terms, not least of which are our own.

Notes

1 Lawrence Danson, *Tragic Alphabet: Shakespeare's Drama of Language* (New Haven: Yale Univ. Press, 1974), p. 141.

2 Leonard Tennenhouse, *Power on Display: The Politics of Shakespeare's Genres* (New York and London: Methuen, 1986), p. 132.

3 Marilyn L. Williamson, "Violence and Gender Ideology in *Coriolanus* and *Macbeth*," in *Shakespeare Left and Right,* ed. Ivo Kamps (New York and London: Routledge, 1991), p. 150.

4 *Characters of Shakespear's Plays* (1817; rpr. London: Dent, 1969), p. 191.

5 "Speculations: *Macbeth* and Source," in *Reproducing Shakespeare,* ed. Jean E. Howard and Marion F. O'Connor (London: Methuen, 1987), p. 249.

6 Jonathan Goldberg, "Speculations: *Macbeth* and Source"; Harry Berger, Jr., "The Early Scenes of *Macbeth*: Preface to a New Interpretation," *ELH* 47 (1980): 1–31; rpt. in *Making Trifles of Terrors: Redistributing Complicities in Shakespeare* (Stanford: Stanford Univ. Press, 1997), pp. 70–97; Alan Sinfield, "*Macbeth*: History, Ideology and Intellectuals," *Critical Quarterly* 28 (1986); rpt. in *Faultlines: Cultural Materialism and the Politics of Dissident Reading* (Berkeley: Univ. of California Press, 1992), pp. 95–108; David Norbrook, "*Macbeth* and the Politics of Historiography," in *Politics of Discourse: The Literature and History of Seventeenth-Century England,* ed. Kevin Sharpe and Stephen N. Zwicker (Berkeley and Los Angeles: Univ. of California Press, 1987), pp. 78–116.

7   Berger, "The Early Scenes of *Macbeth*: Preface to a New Interpretation"; see also Stephen Booth, *King Lear, Macbeth, Indefinition, and Tragedy* (New Haven and London: Yale Univ. Press, 1983), pp. 96–101.

8   Edmund Malone, "An Attempt to Ascertain the Order in which the Plays of Shakespeare were Written," in *The Plays of William Shakespeare* (London, 1778), vol. 1, p. 324.

9   E. B. Lyle, "The 'Twofold Balls and Treble Scepters' in *Macbeth*," *Shakespeare Quarterly* 28 (1977): 516–19.

10   *Power on Display*, p. 131.

11   See *The Chronicles of Scotland, compiled by Hector Boece*, trans. into Scots by John Bellendon (1531) and ed. Edith C. Batho and H. Winifred Husbands (Edinburgh: William Blackwood and Sons, 1941), vol. 2. pp. 154–5. On the use of fictional "history" to underpin the Scottish monarchy, see Colin Kidd, *Subverting Scotland's Past: Scottish Whig Historians and the Creation of an Anglo-British Identity, 1689–c. 1830* (Cambridge: Cambridge Univ. Press, 1993), esp. pp. 18–23.

12   George Buchanan, *The History of Scotland* (London, 1690), sig. Qq3^r.

13   Arthur Kinney, in one of several interesting essays on the historical contexts of the play, discusses this show, though he assumes that the eighth "King" must have been James himself, remarking this "singularly striking moment . . . when . . . suddenly the representation of the audience's own king appears on stage." It is unlikely that the eighth monarch in the show would be explicitly identified as James; such representation would be prohibited, and, in any case, James was the ninth of the Stewarts. It is, of course, possible that Mary, actually the eighth monarch in the Stewart line, was excluded as she was not a *king* but a queen, but if so her exclusion is no less unsettling. See Arthur F. Kinney's "Scottish History, The Union of the Crowns, and the Issue of Right Rule: The Case of Shakespeare's *Macbeth*," in *Renaissance Culture in Context*, ed. Jean R. Brink and William F. Gentrup (Aldershot: Scolar Press, 1993), p. 21.

14   Louis Knafla, *Law and Politics in Jacobean England: The Tracts of Lord Chancellor Ellesmere* (Cambridge: Cambridge Univ. Press, 1972), p. 22. James was the ninth consecutive Stuart monarch to rule in Scotland; the longest unbroken post-Conquest English reign lasted only five generations.

15   No doubt this is a contested term and is often used imprecisely. Nonetheless, the claim of a number of recent historians of seventeenth-century England that the Stuarts ruled within and through the law and cannot therefore be thought of as "absolutist" seems to run the risk of losing a useful distinction in considering not only the centralization of power in the crown but more crucially how the monarchy conceived of the sources and sanctions of its authority. James, for example, saw himself sitting "in the Throne of God," and if he ruled within the law clearly thought himself "above the law, as both the author and giver of strength thereto" (*The Political Works of James I*, ed. Charles Howard McIlwain [Cambridge, Mass: Harvard Univ. Press, 1918], pp. 326, 63). Charles I also could be said to have ruled through the law (though that, of course, is not an uncomplicated claim), but he had no doubt that the court that tried him for treason in 1649 had no right to sit in judgment on a king. For important considerations of the concept, see

Nicholas Henshall, *The Myth of Absolutism: Change and Continuity in Early Modern European Monarchy* (London: Longman, 1992); *Absolutism in Seventeenth-Century Europe*, ed. John Miller (London: Macmillan, 1990), esp. the essay by J. H. Burns, "The Idea of Absolutism," pp. 21–42; Howard Nenner, *By Colour of Law: Legal Culture and Constitutional Politics in England 1660–1689* (Chicago: Univ. of Chicago Press, 1977); and Glenn Burgess, *Absolute Monarchy and the Stuart Constitution* (New Haven: Yale Univ. Press, 1996); but see also Perry Anderson's *Lineages of the Absolutist State* (London: Verso, 1974).

16   "An Act for the establishment of the King's succession" (1534; 25 Henr. VIII, c. 22). Rpt. in *Tudor Constitutional Documents, A.D. 1485–1603, with Historical Commentary*, ed. J. R. Tanner (Cambridge: Cambridge Univ. Press, 1930), pp. 382–85.

17   *Les Reportes del Cases in Camera Stellata, 1593–1609*, ed. William Paley Baildon (London: privately printed, 1894), pp. 163–64.

18   "A Speach to the Lords and Commons of the Parliament at White-Hall" (21 March 1609), in *The Political Works of James I*, p. 307.

19   Quoted in Max Weber, *From Max Weber: Essays in Sociology*, trans. and ed. H. H. Gerth and C. Wright Mills (1946; rpt. New York: Oxford Univ. Press, 1958), p. 78. Weber is here arguing about the state's "monopoly" on legitimate violence.

20   [William Covell], *Polimanteia* (London, 1595), sig. C4ʳ.

21   *The Jacobean Union: Six Tracts of 1604*, ed. Bruce R. Galloway and Brian P. Levack (Edinburgh: Scottish History Society, 1985), p. 196.

22   *The Case of the Commonwealth of England, Stated*, ed. Philip. A. Knachel (Charlottesville: Univ. of Virginia Press, 1969), p. 15.

23   Quoted in William M. Lamont, *Richard Baxter and the Millennium* (London: Croom Helm, 1979), p. 97.

24   *The Trew Law of Free Monarchies*, in *Political Works of James I*, p. 61.

25   Ibid., 62–63.

26   *Basilikon Doron*, in *Political Works of James I*, p. 18. A Scottish coin of 1591, the silver helf merk, had as its motto on the reverse, *his differet rege tyrannus*. See Adam R. Richardson, *Catalogue of Scottish Coins in the National Museum of Antiquities* (Edinburgh: Society of Antiquaries, 1905), p. 253. Alan Sinfield, in *Faultlines*, similarly observes the theoretical polarization of tyrant and legitimate king that is demanded to legitimize the state's monopoly on violence (pp. 95–108).

27   Jean Bodin, *The Six Bookes of a Commonweale*, trans. Richard Knolles (London, 1606), sig. V2ᵛ.

28   "The Fourth Part of the Sermon for Rogation Week," in *Certain Sermons and Homilies* (London: Society for Promoting Christian Knowledge, 1908), p. 530. See also the proverbial "Ill-gotten goods thrive not to the third heir," in Morris Palmer Tilly's *Dictionary of Proverbs in England in the Sixteenth and Seventeenth Century* (Ann Arbor: Univ. of Michigan Press, 1950), p. 267.

29   *Conscience Satisfied* (London, 1643), sig. D4ᵛ.

30   J. G. A. Pocock, *The Ancient Constitution and the Feudal Law: A Study of English Historical Thought in the Seventeenth Century* (1957; rpt. Cambridge: Cambridge Univ. Press, 1987), p. 149.

31   *The Trew Law of Free Monarchies*, in *Political Works of James I*, pp. 62–63.

32   *Ius Regis* (London, 1612), sig. Ff8^v.

33   Roger Widdrington [i.e., Thomas Preston], *Last Reioynder to Mr Thomas Fitz-Herberts Reply* . . . (London, 1619), sig. L4^r.

34   Ecclesiastical Canons of 1606, in *Synodalia*, ed. Edward Cardwell (Oxford: Oxford Univ. Press, 1842), vol. l, p. 346. On the political theory of absolutism, see n. 15, as well as J. P. Sommerville, *Politics and Ideology in England, 1603–1640* (London: Longman, 1986), esp, pp. 9–56; and James Daly, *Sir Robert Filmer and English Political Thought* (Toronto: Univ. of Toronto Press, 1979).

35   Raphael Holinshed, "The Historie of Scotland," *Chronicles of England, and Ireland* (London, Scotland 1587), vol. 2, sig. O1^r.

36   See, for example, Henry N. Paul, *The Royal Play of "Macbeth"* (New York: Macmillan, 1950): "He might have learned it from Buchanan's history, with which he certainly had some acquaintance; but this seems unlikely because of the meagerness of what Buchanan says on the subject. Or – and this is more likely – he may have sought the aid of some well informed Scot to keep him from falling into errors about the history of Scotland" (p. 155).

37   Holinshed, *Chronicles*, vol. 2, sig. P2^r.

38   Ibid.

39   "*Macbeth* and Witchcraft," in *Foucus on "Macbeth,"* ed. John Russell Brown (London: Routledge and Kegan Paul, 1982), p. 193.

40   See Arthur F. Kinney, "Scottish History, the Union of the Crowns and the Issue of Right Rule: The Case of Shakespeare's *Macbeth*," in *Renaissance Culture in Context*, esp. pp. 18–20.

41   "Speculations: *Macbeth* and Source," p. 242.

42   Philip Sidney, *The Defence of Poesie* (London, 1595), sig. E4^v.

43   Sinfield, "*Macbeth*: History, Ideology and Intellectuals," p. 100.

44   Norbrook, "*Macbeth* and the Politics of Historiography," p. 104.

45   Holinshed, *Chronicles*, vol. 2, sig. P3^v.

46   Norbrook, "*Macbeth* and the Politics of Historiography," p. 104.

47   *The Right of Magistrates*, in *Constitutionalism and Resistance in the Sixteenth Century*, ed. and trans, Julian Franklin (New York: Pegasus, 1969), pp. 105, 107, 129.

48   *A sermon preached at the last general assize holden for the county of Sommerset at Taunton* (London, 1612), sig. A4^v.

49   *The Trew Law of Free Monarchies*, in *Political Works of James I*, p. 66.

50   Ibid.

51   Ibid., 60.

52   See Francis Barker, *The Culture of Violence: Essays on Tragedy and History* (Chicago: Univ. of Chicago Press, 1993), p. 66.

53   Karin S. Coddon, "'Unreal Mockery': Unreason and the Problem of Spectacle in *Macbeth*," *ELH* 56 (1989): 499.

54   *The Trew Law of Free Monarchies*, in *Political Works of James I*, p. 64.

55   *A Remonstrance for the Right of Kings*, in *Political Works of James I*, p. 206.

56   *The Trew Law of Free Monarchies*, in *Political Works of James I*, p. 65.

57   Tennenhouse, *Power on Display*, p. 132.

58   *Daphnis Polystephanus* (London, 1605), sig. A3r.

59   Holinshed, *Chronicles*, vol. 2, sig. P8ᵛ.

60   Boece remarks that Malcolm's introduction of the "maners, langage, and super-flew chere of Inglishmen" was felt by many to contribute to the "perdicioun of his pepill" (p. 172); and Buchanan similarly comments on the unfortunate "reforming of the publick Manners" and notes that Donald Bane felt that English values were "corrupting the Discipline of his Ancestry" (sig. Ee3ᵛ–4ʳ) and were what led to his revolt.

61   *The Progresses, Processions, and Magnificent Festivities of James I*, ed. John Nichols (London, 1828), 1, 331.

62   *Stuart Royal Proclamations*, ed. J. F. Larkin and L. P. Hughes (Oxford: Clarendon Press, 1973), vol. 1, pp. 95–9.

63   *Journals of the House of Commons* (London, 1803), vol. 1, p. 183. On the idea of the *plenitudo potestatis*, see J. H. Burns, "The Idea of Absolutism," in *Absolutism in Seventeenth-Century Europe*, ed. John Miller, pp. 21–42.

64   This is, of course, not to say that there is no difference between a humane ruler and a brutal one, or, as the play writes this difference, between Duncan and Macbeth. Such a claim would be silly at best. It is, however, to say that the significant differences that do exist in the political relations that their kingship structures should not be sought in an idea of legitimacy, which works, I have argued, to mystify rather than clarify the distinction that would be made, and is a mystification that itself functions insidiously to make the effective power relations ever more invisible and beyond remedy.

'Is This a Holiday?': Shakespeare's Roman Carnival

Richard Wilson

Published in the journal English Literary History, *Wilson's discussion of* Julius Caesar *draws on its depiction of the onstage audience in relation to the context of its first performances. Wilson sees the play endorsing bourgeois forms of control, power and subjectivity within the city-state of Rome / London. By staging its own subversive elements, and reflecting consciously on modes of control, the play dramatizes the theatre's complex relation to the emerging dominant ideology.*

Richard Wilson, 'Is This a Holiday from Shakespeare's Roman Carnival?', *English Literary History* 54. Baltimore: Johns Hopkins University Press, 1987.

Julius Caesar was the first Shakespearean play we know to have been acted at the Globe and was perhaps performed for the opening of the new

Bankside playhouse in 1599. The Swiss tourist Thomas Platter saw it on September 21, and his impressions locate the work within the different cultural practices that went to make the playhouse. To our minds, accustomed to a decorous image of both Shakespeare and ancient Rome, it is just this collision of codes and voices which makes the traveller's report seem so jarring and bizarre:

> After lunch, at about two o'clock, I and my party crossed the river, and there in the house with the thatched roof we saw an excellent performance of the tragedy of the first emperor, Julius Caesar, with about fifteen characters; and after the play, according to their custom, they did a most elegant and curious dance, two dressed in men's clothes and two in women's.[1]

Along with the chimney-pots, feather hats and chiming clocks in the play itself, we can absorb the shock of 'the house with the thatched roof,' but the elegant jig of Caesar and the boy dressed as Caesar's wife is too alienating a mixture for us of the 'merry and tragical.' Even the Swiss visitor thought it a curious local custom, and he was lucky to see it, because by 1612 'all Jigs, Rhymes and Dances after Plays' had been 'utterly abolished,' to prevent the 'tumults and outrages whereby His Majesty's peace is often broke,' alleged to be caused by the 'cut-purses and other lewd and ill-disposed persons' who were attracted by them into the auditorium in droves at the close of each performance.[2] Platter was an observer of a theatre already expelling gatecrashers and purging itself of the popular customs that had legitimized their unwelcome intrusion. He was witnessing what Francis Barker admits were 'the seeds of an incipient naturalism growing up' inside the Elizabethan theatre, and the inauguration of a new kind of drama in England, where clowns would learn to 'speak no more than is set down for them,' and laughter – as Hamlet prescribes – would be conditional on the 'necessary question of the play.' Authority in this theatre would come to be concentrated in 'the speech' written in what Hamlet proprietorially tells the players are 'my lines' (3.2.1–45), and the mastery of the author as producer would be founded on the suppression of just those practices which Platter thought so picturesque: the unwritten scenario of the mummers' dance, transvestite mockery, Dick Tarlton's 'villainous' comic improvisation, and the raucous collective gesture of disrespect for 'His Majesty's peace.' Elite and popular traditions coexist in embarrassed tension in Platter's travel diary, where the excellence of the classical tragedy consorts so oddly with the curiosity of the antic hay. The diarist did not realize, of course, that the sequence he recorded represented the scission between two cultures and for one of them the literal final fling, nor that 'the house with the thatched roof' was the scene, even as he applauded the performance, of bitter social separation.[3]

The opening words of *Julius Caesar* seem to know themselves, nevertheless, as a declaration of company policy towards the theatre audience. They are addressed by the Roman Tribune Flavius to 'certain Commoners' who have entered 'over the stage,' and they are a rebuke to their temerity: 'Hence! home, you idle creatures, get you home / Is this a holiday?' Dressed in their festive 'best apparel,' these 'mechanical' men have mistaken the occasion for a 'holiday,' and to the rhetorical question 'Is this a holiday?' they are now given the firm answer that for them, at least, it is an ordinary 'labouring day' (1.1.1–60). This is an encounter, then, that situates what follows explicitly within the contemporary debate about the value or 'idleness' of popular culture, a debate in which, as Christopher Hill has written, 'two modes of life, with their different needs and standards, are in conflict as England moves out of the agricultural Middle Ages into the modern industrial world.'[4] And as Flavius and his colleague Marullus order the plebeians back to work, it is a confrontation that confirms Hill's thesis that the Puritan attack on popular festivity was a strategy to control the emerging manufacturing workforce. The Tribunes oppose 'holiday' because it blurs distinctions between the 'industrious' and the 'idle,' just as their counterparts the London Aldermen complained the theatres lured 'the prentices and servants of the City from their works.' In fact, the Tribunes' speeches echo *The Anatomy of Abuses* (1583) by the merchants' censor Philip Stubbes, and in so doing the actors of the Globe were disarming one of the most powerful, because pragmatic, objections to their trade. As Thomas Nashe protested when the first playhouse was opened on the South Bank in 1592, professional players were not to be confused with 'squirting bawdy comedians'; they were distinct from 'the pantaloon, whore and zany' of street theatre. Their patrons were 'Gentlemen of the Court, and the Inns of Court, and captains and soldiers' (a clientele corroborated by the 1602 police raid on the playhouses), and the citizens could rest assured that 'they heartily wish they might be troubled with none of their youth nor their prentices.' So theatre-owners such as Philip Henslowe were careful to obey the ban on 'interludes and plays on the Sabbath,' closing their doors on city workers (as James I complained) on the only afternoon when they were regularly free. If working men were present to hear the beginning of *Julius Caesar* and stayed despite it, the implication is clear that they had no business to be there. Theatre, we infer, is now itself a legitimate business with no room for the 'idle.'[5]

The first scene acted at the Globe can be interpreted, then, as a manouevre in the campaign to legitimize the Shakespearean stage and dissociate it from the subversiveness of artisanal culture. As historians such as Peter Burke have demonstrated, revelry and rebellion were entangled in Renaissance popular entertainments, and it was no coincidence that insurrections such as the Peasants' Revolts of 1381 and 1450, the Evil May Day riot of 1517, or Kett's Rebellion of 1549 should have been sparked off at seasonal plays or have had vivid carnivalesque features. The juridical function of folk drama had been to cement the ties and obligations of an agrarian community, and when these were threatened in the transition to capitalist social relations, it was through the 'rough music' of folk customs – mummings, wakes and charivaris – that the new masters were called to ritual account. The world of carnival, with its travesty and inversion, was a standing pretext for protest; but if, as happened increasingly in the early modern period, rulers chose to ignore the 'wild justice' of festivity, there could be what Burke calls 'a "switching" of codes, from the language of ritual to the language of rebellion,' when 'the wine barrel blew its top.'[6] This is what happened spectacularly in the bloody Carnival at Romans in 1580, and it was what happened less explosively in London during the crisis years of the 1590s, when hunger and unemployment drove 'disordered people of the common sort' (in the Aldermanic phrase) 'to assemble themselves and make matches for their lewd ungodly practices' at Shrovetide, May Day or Midsummer: festivals when, like the workers in *Julius Caesar*, they could still 'cull out a holiday' from the industrial week. Associating all revels with rebellion, the authorities were instinctively sure that riotous 'apprentices and servants drew their infection' from the playhouses where people also caught the plague; but, as Nashe insisted, this analogy was a kind of category mistake, which miscalculated the new theatres' social role. If the playhouse was, as coroners reported, the site of 'frays and bloodshed,' it was as the target of violence, not the origin, as when apprentices rampaged traditionally on Shrove Tuesday to 'put play houses to the sack and bawdy houses to the spoil' (in 1617 wrecking the Cockpit Theatre with the loss of several lives). The rough music of charivari was hollered in anger from outside the playhouse walls.[7]

'The disorders of the 1590s were the most serious to menace the metropolis in the decades up to the Civil War,' writes the urban historian Peter Clark in a recent essay, and what concerns him is how this unprecedented metropolitan crisis was contained.[8] The answer must lie at least partly in the success with which the language of carnival as a discourse of legitimation was commandeered by the commercial players and then tamed. For as scenes like the opening of *Julius Caesar* remind us, and as history, in Foucault's words, 'constantly teaches us, discourse is not simply that which translates struggles or systems of domination, but is the thing for which struggle takes place.'[9] It was no mere evasion of authority, therefore, which led to the theatre being situated on the criminalized southern bank of The Thames, where Platter and his party rowed to unbrace and recreate themselves after lunch. In the complex zoning of the metropolis that dates precisely from this time, Southwark was to occupy the position of a policed and segregated annex to the business and residential districts on the river's northern side. Within its licensed liberties, the Bankside was to have the status of a permanent but strictly circumscribed carnival in the city's economy of repression and indulgence, a disposal-valve in its regulation of productivity and waste. Suspect and sinistral, until the final suppression of Hogarth's Southwark Fair in 1762, the South Bank was to function as the unconscious of the capital of trade. Nor, in this geography of desire, was it accidental that the Globe was built beside those very institutions that, in Foucault's analysis, shaped the discourses of modern subjectivity. Ringed by reconstructed prisons such as The Marshalsea and The Clink, and flanked by the newly refounded St. Thomas's Hospital, the playhouse meshed with a chain of buildings charged with those dividing practices whereby the productive subject was defined by isolation from its negative in the sick, the mad, the aged, the criminal, the bankrupt, and the unemployed: separated, as Flavius urges and the 1569 Charter of St. Thomas's decreed, from 'all Idle, Begging people.'[10] The wooden operating theatre of St. Thomas's survives as the celebrated arena where the body was cut into diseased and healthy parts. The 'Wooden O' of the Globe next door, which must have resembled it in design so much, operated in analogous ways on the body politic to divide and control the visceral language of carnival, separating out productive revelry (or art) from the idleness and infection of rebellion.

If Thomas Platter was a naive theatre critic, as a sociologist he was shrewder. 'England,' he observed, 'is the servants' prison, because their masters and mistresses are so severe.' The foreign visitor could see what has been confirmed in detail by Lee Beier in his study of masterless men and the vagrancy problem in Shakespearean England, that the public order system which Foucault dated from the founding of the Paris General Hospital in 1656 was already being established in London by 1599.[11] It was a system based, however, less on crude severity than on the strategy of self-regimentation and surveillance which Brutus proposes in *Julius Caesar* when he argues for a controlled and strictly rational rebellion:

> And let our hearts, as subtle masters do,
> Stir up their servants to an act of rage,
> And after seem to chide 'em. This shall make
> Our purpose necessary, and not envious.
>   (2.1.175–78)

The Shakespearean text belongs to a historical moment when a revolutionary bourgeois politics has not naturalized its own productive processes, and Brutus's realpolitik is a complete statement of the technique of the modern state whereby subversion is produced in both consciousness and society to legitimize the order that subjects it. Unruly passions and apprentices are both checked in this regime, as Hal also demonstrates in his career as agent provocateur in Eastcheap, by being known and hated: incited to be rejected. This is a system of discipline whose subtlety, as Brutus recognizes, depends not on how it obstructs but on how it manipulates desire, so that sexuality, for example, will no longer be so much forbidden as the very ground through which power controls the community and the individual. And it is just this 'subtle, calculated technology of subjection,' as analyzed by Foucault, operating in the new factory, hospital or school of Elizabethan London, which surely explains why Bakhtin says so little in his work on the subversiveness of carnival about either Shakespeare or England. His ideas were recently applied to Elizabethan drama by Michael Bristol, who argues for what he terms the 'carnivalization' of Shakespearean literature. The argument is not convincing because, as Umberto Eco has remarked, what Bakhtinians crucially forget in their idealization of carnival is precisely the revenge of Lent: that is to say, the confinement of desire within a dialectic of transgression and containment. If carnival were always so emancipatory, Eco adds, 'it would be impossible to explain why power uses circuses.'[12]

The conditions of modern subjectivity are inscribed within the Shakespearean text. Thus, when Portia tries to persuade her husband to share 'the secrets of [his] heart' by divulging the plot she calls the 'sick offence within your mind,' she challenges him: 'Dwell I but in the suburbs / Of your good pleasure? If it be no more, / Portia is Brutus' harlot' (2.1.268–306). Body, language and thought are all held in ideological subjection in the bourgeois order Brutus represents, but when he succumbs to Portia's emotional blackmail he destroys himself by failing to quarantine desire in the suburbs of his self, where it should have been confined like the brothels of the Bankside. In *Julius Caesar* carnival – the language of desire and the flesh – is a discourse that is always mastered by the dominant. Thus, the opening scenes take place on the Roman 'feast of Lupercal:' February 14, St. Valentine's Day and the approximate date of Mardi Gras. So Shakespeare's revelling artisans connect with those 'bands of prentices, 3,000 or 4,000 strong, who on Shrove Tuesday do outrages in all directions, especially in the suburbs,' in contemporary accounts, and whose Kingdoms and Abbeys of Misrule have been researched, in their European manifestations, by Natalie Zemon Davis.[13] In the play their carnival ceremonies have been appropriated by Caesar to legitimize his intended coronation. Antony therefore runs in the 'holy chase' to 'touch' Calphurnia for fertility (1.2.7–8), while Caesar himself performs in the Shroving game by pretending to give 'the rabblement' the freedom that they shout for. This would be the tactic of King James's *Book of Sports* (1618), of royalist propagandists such as Herrick, and ultimately of the Restoration, when (contrary to Bakhtin's thesis) the rituals 'of May-poles, Hock-carts, Wassails, Wakes' could be harnessed to the legitimation of a program of social conservatism. It belongs to the world of what Hill calls 'synthetic monarchy,' of Elizabeth's Accession Day anniversary and the Stuart revival of 'touching.' And by this appropriation of the discourse of festival Caesar turns politics into theatre as 'the tag-rag people clap and hiss him, according as he pleas'd and displeas'd them, as they do the players' (1.2.255). He is the Carnival King, a Lord of Misrule who governs by exploiting his subjects' desires with his 'foolery' (1.2.232), manipulating 'fat, Sleek-headed men' (1.2.190), as he indulges Antony in plays and music when he 'revels long a'nights' (2.2.116). Provoking them 'to sports, to wildness, and much company' (2.1.189), Caesar is the master of revels who knows that 'danger' belongs to the 'lean and hungry' who can discipline the body to their purposes. So his Roman carnival becomes a model of authoritarian populism, the true regimen of bread and circuses.[14]

According to Anne Barton the theatre image in *Julius Caesar* is uniquely positive and 'the actors are no longer shadowy figures: they are the creators of history.'[15] This may be true, but it over-simplifies the process that the play rehearses whereby discourses, which are the means of struggle, are themselves shaped by that struggle as it unfolds. It unfolds in the Shakespearean text like carnival itself, as a masquerade in which successive ideologies which had seemed to be authoritative are 'discovered' and discarded as power is displaced. On Mardi Gras the aim is to see without being seen behind the carnival mask; and here the eye of power strips the mask of discourse from its antagonist, revealing – as Cassius demonstrates with his satirical broadsheets 'wherein Caesar's ambition shall be glanced at' – the naked drives discursive practices hide (1.2.315). Thus the plebeians who are masterless in their holiday guise are exposed by the Tribune's Puritan analysis as Caesar's 'idle creatures'; but Puritan discourse is itself 'put to silence' when it tries to 'pull the scarfs' from Caesar's images (1.2.282). That demystification belongs to the knives of the aristocratic fraction, whose mask of constitutionalism – with its common law reverence for ancient custom and contempt for the absolutist yoke – is worn 'like Roman actors do' (2.1.226), until Antony seizes the pulpit / stage in turn and reveals the carnivorous butchery their Lenten rhetoric conceals. This is the radical potentiality of Renaissance tragedy that Jonathan Dollimore and others would mobilize as a critical weapon: the revelry with which one discourse decodes the authority of another, as Antony deconstructs the discursivity of the 'honourable men' (3.2.120–230). With 'their hats pluck'd about their ears, / And half their faces buried in their cloaks' (2.1.73–74) or masked by handkerchiefs (2.1.315), the plotters who meet in Pompey's theatre assume the anonymity of carnival and arrogate its dispensation to kill a scapegoat in their coup against Caesar, just as the real rebels of the Dutch Revolt had started their uprising against the Spanish governor at Carnival in 1563 dressed in motley and jester's cap and bells. In the Renaissance, as Stephen Greenblatt contends, 'theatricality is one of power's essential modes'; so when their 'antic disposition' is ripped from these revellers, it is fittingly by the consummate theatricality and power of speech of a champion gamesman and seasoned masker. 'A masque is treason's licence' in Jacobean drama, but the incremental logic of this revelry will be to strip all power, including that of rebels, of its legitimacy, exposing the face of bare ambition beneath the 'veil'd look' (1.2.36) of rites and ceremonies (3.1.241).[16]

The Carnival at Romans in 1580 described by Emmanuel Le Roy Ladurie provides a paradigm of Renaissance festival as a 'psychological drama or ballet' whose players danced or acted out class struggle through the 'symbolic grammar' of processions and masquerades. There the poor had celebrated a mock funeral of the rich whose flesh they pretended to eat on Mardi Gras, until the law and order party had organized a massacre in retaliation, arraying themselves for the ambush in carnival costume and carrying carnival torches.[17] The Roman carnival in *Julius Caesar* follows a similar timetable and pattern through the cannibalistic feast of Caesar's assassination and the mock-trial of the conspirators at the funeral, to the counterrevolution of a revanchist repression. In Shakespearean Rome, as in actual Romans, the symbolic discourse of public festival is a system whose social significance will be dictated by the strongest. Likewise, poems, plays, letters, music, names, dreams, prophecies, clouds, storms, stars, entrails and flights of birds are all discredited as 'idle ceremonies' (2.1.197) in *Julius Caesar*, the random signifiers on which praxis enforces meaning. This is a deconstructive carnival that leads ineluctably to the burlesque textuality of Caesar's blood-stained 'vesture' as interpreted by Antony in the Forum through its gaps and 'wounded' tears, and finally, when the corpse is divested of even that last tattered shred of discursivity, to the exposure of Caesar's naked 'will': the 'bleeding piece of earth' which is metonymic of all desire and power (3.2.130–160). Twenty-seven times in thirty lines the favourite Shakespearean phallic pun is repeated through all its libidinous connotations as it is taken up by Antony and passed around the crowd, to substantiate in a riot of polysemy that at the point where text and body fuse, discourse and power are one. Caesar had offered his murderers wine on the Ides of March. Now his carved meat becomes with cannibalistic literalism the carnival sacrament of a festive fraternity of blood.

Power constructs its own discursivity in Shakespearean tragedy by appropriating the radical subversiveness of carnival, and a text such as *Julius Caesar* seems knowingly to meditate upon its participation in this process of sublimation and control. Thus, Caesar's will, which is his butchered flesh, is also by etymological extension his testament – his will power disseminated through his signed and written text – where the potency denied him in his sterile marriage and abortive reign is regenerated from his posthumous stimulation of the desires of the crowd he makes his heir. Where there's a will, in the modern state, there is also a way for power to make its own, and Caesarism works here through a system of license and surveillance that exactly parallels the real dividing practices of Shakespearean London. Sequestered in the suburb of the city, desire can henceforth be partitioned and canalized in the interests of the governing group:

> ANTONY.   Moreover, he hath left you all his walks,
>   His private arbours, and new-planted orchards,
>   On this side Tiber: he hath left them you,
>   And to your heirs for ever: common pleasures,
>   To walk abroad and recreate yourselves.
>   Here was a Caesar! When comes such another?
> PLEBEIAN. Never, never! Come away, away!
>   We'll burn his body in the holy place,
>   And with the brands fire the traitors' houses.
>   Take up the body.
>   (3.2.249–58)

So the incendiary brands of carnival are transformed into instruments of counterrevolution (as in London the Corpus Christi and Midsummer cressets became the flambeaux for the Lord Mayor's Show and the stolen fire of Halloween illuminated the thanksgiving for Stuart deliverance from the Gunpowder Plot). Caesar's authoritarian paternalism deflects the *vox populi* towards the institution of the monarchy by the invigilation of the people's private desires. Likewise, the sexual license of the Bankside funfair would prove the conduit through which power would recreate itself by the regulation of the public's common pleasures in the impending bourgeois age. The corpse exhibited by Antony stands in something of the same relation to the organization of modern subjectivity, therefore, as the exemplary cadaver in Rembrandt's picture of *The Anatomy Lesson of Dr. Tulp* discussed by Francis Barker. It is the material ground, the 'earth' (3.1.254), on which bourgeois ideology will proceed to write its own interpretation of society and human life, inscribing a discourse of reason and morality on a scene of lust and blood that 'else were a savage spectacle' (3.1.223). This is quite literally how Antony uses the body for demonstration, when he effaces his own discursive practice in the interpellation of the members of the crowd as obedient subjects of the revived monarchic state:

> For I have neither wit, nor words, nor worth,
> Action, nor utterance, nor the power of speech
> To stir men's blood; I only speak right on.
> I tell you that which you yourselves do know,
> Show you sweet Caesar's wounds, poor poor dumb mouths,
> And bid them speak for me.
>   (3.2.233–28)

Like Tulp's dissection, Antony's anatomy lesson – to be repeated with the body of Brutus – reproduces the spectacular corporeality of the carnivalesque in the service of the new power of the disciplinary society, forcing the corpse to signify 'that which you yourselves do know' about what it is to say 'This was a man!' (5.5.75). And as Antony turns desire in the mob to authoritarian ends, this is also the manoeuvre of the Shakespearean text, which reworks the ceremonies of an older kind of ritual – 'to execute, to dismember, to eat' – not simply to erase them but, as Barker notes of Rembrandt's painting, 'to take them over, to appropriate the ancient vengeful motifs and to rearticulate them for its own new purposes.' Text and picture belong to a moment, that is to say, when the bourgeoisie still has need of the energies of 'the earlier pageant of sacramental violence,' and when its 'image fashions an aesthetic which is ratio-nalistic, classical, realistic, but one to which the iconography of a previous mode of representation is not completely alien.' As Barker goes on to explain, 'if it continues to evoke the signs of a punitive corporeality,' bourgeois repre-sentation 'also aims to draw off and reorganise the charge of these potent residues, and to invest them, transformed,' in the name of the rational spirit of capitalism, 'which will soon free itself entirely from the old body, even if it trades at first on the mystique and the terror of that abandoned materiality.'[18] So Antony must yoke 'mischief' to his politics and 'let it work' for the restora-tion of the social status quo (3.2.262). By syphoning the subversiveness of popular festivity in the representation of a deflected and contained rebellion, the Shakespearean text anticipates the counter-revolution of the Cromwellian Commonwealth and faithfully enacts the coercive strategy of those subtle London masters who 'stir up servants at an act of rage' (2.1.176) the better to control them. Located on the threshold of revolutionary upheaval, *Julius Caesar* is the image of bourgeois ascendency as 'necessary, and not envious,' (2.1.178) separated from popular or sectarian movements, and the natural issue of 'a general honest thought' – as Antony claims over the body of Brutus – 'and common good to all' (5.5.71–72).

Julius Caesar is the representation of a world turned upside-down to be restored, where citizens' houses are set alight by the mob in order that prop-erty values should be upheld. The question that it seems to address in this paradoxical operation is the one which would become, according to Christo-pher Hill, the critical dilemma of the Commonwealth, posed eventually by a pamphleteer of 1660: 'Can you at once suppress the sectaries and keep out the King?'[19] Because it arises from a historical juncture when the English bour-geoisie was engaged in a reorganization of the absolutist state to effect this end, it is a text that discloses the materiality of power with self-important openness. In particular, this early Globe play reflects candidly on the process whereby hegemony is obtained through the control of discourse, a process in which the inauguration of the playhouse was itself a major intervention.

Victory in *Julius Caesar* goes to those who administer and distribute the access to discourse, and the conspirators lose possession of the initiative in the action the moment that they concede Antony permission to 'speak in the order of [the] funeral' (3.1.230–50). Inserting his own demagogic rhetoric into Brutus's idealistic scenario, Antony disrupts that order of discourse, rearranges the 'true rites and lawful ceremonies' (3.1.241) of the republic to facilitate his counter-coup, and imposes his domination through the populist device of Caesar's will. Censorship, Barker insists, was 'a constitutive experience' in the seventeenth-century construction of both the bourgeois subject and the modern state, and one which predicated the very possibility of bourgeois enunciation.[20] This text proclaims that fact when Antony revises the clauses of the will to finance his army, cuts off Cicero's Greek irony with the orator's 'silver hairs' (2.1.144), and 'damns' his enemies 'with a spot' when 'their names are prick'd out' on his proscription list (4.1.1–10). The murder by the mob of the poet Cinna for his 'bad verses' (3.3.30) and mistaken name merely confirms what Cassius and Brutus learn to their cost, that power goes with those who command the materiality of signs (3.3.30–35). Tzvetan Todorov proposes that the Incas and Aztecs fell victim to the Spanish Conquistadors because of their inferior system of signification, defeated, he believes, by Cortez's capacity to decipher their semiotic conduct whilst baffling them with his own.[21] Likewise, the republicans fail in *Julius Caesar* when they lose control of signs. Quarrelling over the meaning of their correspondence and at cross-purposes in their reading of the 'signs of battle' (5.1.14–24), Brutus and Cassius become deaf even to Homer's textual warning when they hear *The Iliad* read (4.3.129–37), while the words of Caesar that the Romans record when they 'mark him and write his speeches in their books' (1.2.125) come back to haunt the assassins at the end in the form of the Ghost, which appears the instant Brutus finds 'the leaf turn'd down' in his book and opens it to read, presumably, the aveng-ing text: '*Veni, vidi, vici*' (4.3.251–75). 'Words before blows' (5.1.27) is the battle-order in this play, which rehearses the English Revolution by enacting the Gramscian doctrine that the iron fist is preceded by the velvet glove, and that power is first enthroned in pulpits, poetry and plays.

Carnival, *Julius Caesar* reminds us, was never a single, unitary discourse in the Renaissance, but a symbolic system over which continuous struggle to wrest its meaning was waged by competing ideologies. It is the pretense of the Shakespearean text, however, that the masquerade of false appearances comes to its end in bourgeois realism, as Antony closes the action and announces his domination when he discounts all 'objects, arts, and imitations' as 'out of use and stal'd by other men' (4.1.37–38), learning to separate the idleness of drama from the business of politics. Thus the rupture forced by holiday in history would be sealed during the course of the seventeenth century as the English bourgeoisie elided its own revolutionary past. To make this representation of tragic acquiescence possible, nonetheless, the playhouse had been made the bloody site of contestation between social groups. 'The Triumph of Lent' is what Peter Burke calls the seventeenth-century suppression of the carnivalesque 'World Turned Upside Down.' It was a triumph achieved only after many eruptions into the Shakespearean space of festive rout, and to grasp the operation of the new theatre as an institution of division it is only necessary to recall those intrusions from outside the enclosure of the 'Wooden O': interruptions like the episode at Shrewsbury in 1627 when the actors of the Globe were driven out of town in the middle of a performance by fairground revellers with flaming brands, or the one that recurred on Shrove Tuesday in the capital itself, according to reports, when players half-way through an 'excellent tragedy' were 'forc'd to undress and put off their tragic habits' by the holiday crowd, and made to 'conclude the day with *The Merry Milkmaids*. And unless this were done, and the popular humour satisfied (as sometimes it so fortun'd that the players were refractory), the benches, the tiles, the laths, the stones, oranges, apples, nuts, flew about most liberally; and as there were mechanics of all professions there upon these festivals, every one fell to his trade and dissolved the house in an instant, and that made the ruin of a stately fabric.'[22] The floor of the new playhouse was not yet quite an arena which the dominant ideology could call its own, and excluded or enclosed the festive melee still found the means on occasion to deconstruct – or transvalue – the sign system of the imposing 'house with the thatched roof'.

Notes

A version of this paper was given to the 1986 Higher Education Teachers of English Conference at the University of Sussex.

1 Quoted in T. S. Dorsch, ed., The Arden Shakespeare: *Julius Caesar* (London: Methuen, 1955), vii. All citations of *Julius Caesar* are to this edition and will be included parenthetically in the text.
2 E. K. Chambers, *The Elizabethan Stage* (Oxford: Oxford Univ. Press, 1923), 4:340–41 (Order of the Middlesex Sessions, October 1, 1612).
3 Francis Barker, *The Tremulous Private Body: Essays on Subjection* (London: Methuen, 1984), 18; The Arden Shakespeare: *Hamlet*, ed. Harold Jenkins (London: Methuen, 1982).
4 Christopher Hill, *Society and Puritanism in Pre-Revolutionary England* (Harmondsworth: Penguin, 1986), 163.
5 Thomas Nashe, 'Pierce Penniless' in *The Unfortunate Traveller and other Works*, ed. J. B. Steane (Harmondsworth: Penguin, 1972), 114–15; Chambers, 4:307 (Privy Council Minute, July 25, 1591); L. A. Govett, ed., *The King's Book of Sports* (London, 1890), 30.

6   Peter Burke, *Popular Culture in Early Modern Europe* (London: Temple Smith, 1978), 203.

7   Chambers, 1:264–65.

8   Peter Clark, *The European Crisis of the 1590s: essays in comparative history* (London: Allen and Unwin, 1985), 54.

9   Michel Foucault, 'The Order of Discourse,' trans. I. McLeod, in Robert Young, ed., *Untying the Text: A Post-Structuralist Reader* (London: Routledge, 1981), 52–53.

10 R. E. McGraw, *Encyclopaedia of Medical History* (London: Macmillan, 1985), 138.

11 A. L. Beier, *Masterless Men: The vagrancy problem in England, 1560–1640* (London: Methuen, 1985). For Platter's comment, see 164.

12 Foucault, *Discipline and Punish: The Birth of the Prison*, trans. A. Sheridan (Harmondsworth: Penguin, 1979), 221; Umberto Eco, 'The Frames of Comic Freedom,' in Thomas Sebeok, ed., *Carnival!* (New York: Mouton, 1984), 3. Mikhail Bakhtin's influential account of carnival is in *Rabelais and his World*, trans. H. Iswolsky (Bloomington: Indiana Univ. Press, 1984). See also Michael Bristol, *Carnival and Theatre* (London: Methuen, 1985); Chambers, 1:265.

13 Natalie Zemon Davis, 'The Reasons of Misrule,' in *Society and Culture in Early Modern France* (Stanford: Stanford Univ. Press, 1975).

14 Robert Herrick, *The Poems of Robert Herrick,* ed. L. C. Martin (Oxford: Oxford Univ. Press, 1965), 5. Hill, *The World Turned Upside Down: Radical Ideas During the English Revolution* (Harmondsworth: Penguin, 1975), 353–54.

15 Anne Barton, *Shakespeare and the Idea of the Play* (Harmondsworth: Penguin, 1967), 141.

16 Jonathan Dollimore, *Radical Tragedy: Religion, Ideology and Power in the Drama of Shakespeare and His Contemporaries* (Brighton: Harvester, 1984); Stephen Greenblatt, 'Invisible Bullets: Renaissance authority and its subversion, *Henry IV* and *Henry V*,' in Jonathan Dollimore and Alan Sinfield, eds. *Political Shakespeare: New Essays in Cultural Materialism* (Manchester, Manchester Univ. Press, 1985), 33; Cyril Tourneur, *The Revenger's Tragedy*, ed. R. A. Foakes (London, 1966), 5.1.181.

17 E. Le Roy Ladurie, *Carnival in Romans: A People's Uprising in Romans, 1579–1580* (Harmondsworth: Penguin, 1981), 192–215; for cannibalistic symbolism see 173, 198.

18 Barker, 76.

19 Hill, *The World Turned Upside Down*, 347.

20 Barker, 51.

21 Tzvetan Todorov, *The Conquest of America: The Question of The Other* (New York: Harper and Row, 1984).

22 E. Gayton, 'Festivous Notes Upon Don Quixote' (1654), in Chambers, 1:265.

12

Texts: An Overview

Questions about the status of the different Shakespeare texts we have, their presumed likeness to the lost Shakespearean manuscripts we wish we had, and of the editions in which we ought to read and study Shakespeare have long been part of the plays' critical history. In the twentieth century, textual bibliography has been one of the most lively, and fundamental, areas of disagreement in Shakespeare criticism.

Bibliographic study of Shakespeare's texts was a dominant theme of early twentieth-century criticism. In a lecture entitled 'What is Bibliography?' delivered in 1912, W. W. Greg argued for its crucial role in the understanding and appreciation of the plays: 'it is only by the application of a rigorous bibliographical method that the last drop of information can be squeezed out of a literary document. Thus in spite of my interest in bibliography it is as the handmaid of literature that I still regard it' (Greg, 1911–13, p. 47). Like his nineteenth-century predecessors, Greg drew on the language of science: 'Critical bibliography is the science of the material transmission of literary texts, the investigation of the textual tradition as it is called, in so far as that investigation is possible without extraneous aids. It aims at the construction of a calculus for the determination of textual problems' (p. 48). In his British Academy Lecture of 1923, Alfred Pollard spoke on 'The Foundations of Shakespeare's Text'. Pollard identified eighteen 'first quarto' texts and the folio as 'the twin Foundations of Shakespeare's text' (Pollard, 1933, p. 5), and influentially grouped together the 1597 *Romeo and Juliet*, the 1600 *Henry V*, the 1602 *Merry Wives of Windsor* and the 1603 *Hamlet* as 'the Bad Quartos [. . .] The other fourteen Quartos it is convenient to call, equally sweepingly the Good Quartos, although the goodness of some of them is painfully obscured by defects' (pp. 5–6). Pollard argues that the Bad quartos are pirated texts, the Good ones are texts authorized for publication by the playhouse. Many of the imperfections are to be attributed to Shakespeare himself, rather than blamed on intermediaries such as printers.

In his exhaustive study *The Manuscript of Shakespeare's 'Hamlet' and the Problems of its Transmission: An Essay in Critical Bibliography* (1934) J. Dover Wilson argued that textual matters are intrinsic to any reading of the play:

> It is impossible, for example, to be certain that we have justly estimated Hamlet's character, until we know the meaning of everything that he says and that other characters say about him, while it is equally impossible to be certain what the speakers say until we have made up our minds exactly what Shakespeare intended to write. The textual problems are therefore fundamental. (Wilson, 1934, pp. xi–xii)

Through the speculative reconstruction of the particular styles of two scribes, the original promptbook, and the activities of the print collector, Dover Wilson was able to elucidate his 'increasing certainty that in the Second Quarto we possess what may, without undue presumption, be described as a typographical facsimile, however vilely printed, of the autograph manuscript of the greatest play in the world' (p. xiii). W. W. Greg identified the particular characteristics of one scrivener, Ralph Crane, in his *The Shakespeare First Folio* (1955). The search for Shakespeare's lost manuscripts continued as the new bibliography continued to develop and refine its analytical techniques. F. P. Wilson and Helen Louise Gardner's *Shakespeare and the New Bibliography* (1970) gives a thorough account of the achievements of the new bibliographers. On these bibliographic methods, see also Duthie (1941 and 1964) and Greg (1911, 1954 and 1955).

Surveying the field of 'Today's Shakespeare Texts and Tomorrow's' in 1966 Fredson Bowers reviewed existing editions and their shortcomings. He announced that 'we await [...] the authoritative critical edition of Shakespeare' (Bowers, 1966, p. 58), and certain problems remained to be resolved before such an edition could be completed. Bowers suggested the need 'to evolve a more scientific and logically rigorous method to govern the critical choice of alternatives in respect to the words of the text' (p. 58), 'to indicate the degree of confidence that a reader can feel in the various critical choices that have been made' (p. 61), and 'to bring some order and authority into the preparation of the accidentals of a text, especially those that share directly in the communication of meaning' (p. 62). Such methods would ensure that 'that unique instrument of Shakespeare's language in all its Elizabethan vigor and subtlety will have its eighteenth- and nineteenth-century tarnish rubbed off and will gain some new glints that cumulatively will strike all but the dullest eyes and ears' (p. 64). 'The sole function,' Bowers argued, 'of linguistic analysis and of textual bibliography, with all its mechanical aids, is to guide an editor's critical intelligence to the truth' (p. 65).

But that singular truth was becoming harder to identify. In *The Stability of Shakespeare's Text* (1965), E. A. J. Honigmann argued that textual differences could be explained by accepting that Shakespeare revised his plays, and other bibliographers developed this argument to suggest that the practice of conflation was therefore inadequate. On these theories of revising, see Ioppolo (1991), Honigmann (1965 and 1996), Taylor and Warren (1983), and Taylor and Jowett (1993). Jones (1995) discusses the critical and dramatic significance of Shakespeare's revisions. In addition, more detailed accounts of Elizabethan and Jacobean printing houses were undertaken, including, for example, Peter Blayney's *The Texts of 'King Lear' and their Origins* (1982), and the whole field of bibliography was influenced by D. F. McKenzie's (1986) significant concept of the 'sociology of texts', arguing that the material form of texts crucially determines their meanings. There are other influences on this new approach to textual criticism, as Leah Marcus points out in her essay on the state of Renaissance studies published in 1992: 'One of the most interesting recent developments in the field of Renaissance / early modern studies has been an adaptation of postmodernist ideas about textual indeterminacy that cuts across the Barthian distinction between "text" and "work" [Roland Barthes, 'From "Text" to "Work"' (1971), in Waugh and Rice (1996)] to explore forms of textual instability related to modes of textual production specific to the period' (p. 51). Historical research alongside post-structuralist reconceptualizations of the categories 'author' and 'text' stimulated new bibliographic questions in Shakespeare studies (McGann, 1983). On the questions of the integrity of the early texts, and arguments against conflation and for the specific materiality of the printed text are de Grazia and Stallybrass (1993), McLeod [Cloud] (1982), Charney (1988), Holderness and Loughrey (1992) and Holderness, Loughrey and Murphy (1995). The quarto texts have now begun to get more investigation in their own right, and the idea that textual bibliography was aiming at a single definitive text for each play in the canon has itself been placed under scrutiny. Michael Warren's influential essay on *King Lear* is reprinted in chapter 13 as an early intervention into debate.

In *The Division of the Kingdoms*, a collection of essays edited by Gary Taylor and Michael Warren in 1983, a number of contributors offered essays on the two texts of *King Lear*. These explored aspects of the hypothesis that 'both texts represent independent Shakesperian versions of *King Lear*', and also attempted to reintegrate textual and literary scholarship (Taylor and Warren, 1983, p. v). For example, John Kerrigan discussed the significance of the different role for the Fool in the two texts ('Revision, Adaptation, and the Fool in *King Lear*'), Michael Warren 'The Diminution of Kent' and Roger Warren 'The Folio Omission of the Mock Trial: Motives and Consequences'. In his article in the journal *Shakespeare Quarterly* (1982) Randall McLeod, writing as 'Random Cloud', argued for 'The Marriage of Good and Bad Quartos': 'the real problem with good and bad quartos is not what the words denote, but why we use terminology that has such overt and prejudicial connotations'. Drawing on examples from *Romeo and Juliet*, Cloud argued for an 'infinite text' (McLeod, 1982, p. 421) which preserves multiplicity rather than trying to adjudicate between readings, and this theoretical idea may have its actual counterpart in editions such as Warren's *The Complete 'King Lear'* (1989) or Bernice W. Kliman's hypertext published on the internet as 'The Enfolded *Hamlet*' (1986) [http://www.global-language.com/enfolded.html]. Other texts have emerged from this reassessment of traditional bibliographical principles. The 'Shakespearean Originals' series has published a series of annotated, modern-spelling editions of quarto texts as a challenge to established editorial practice:

> It seems to us that there is in fact no philosophical justification for emendation, which foregrounds the editor at the expense of the text. The distortions introduced by this process are all too readily incorporated into the text as holy writ. Macbeth's famous lines, for example, 'I dare do all that may become a man / Who dares do more is none,' on closer inspection turns out to be Rowe's. The Folio reads 'I dare do all that may become a man / Who dares no more is none.' (Holderness and Loughrey, 1992, p. 9)

Discussing their edition of the 1603 'bad' quarto of *Hamlet*, Graham Holderness and Bryan Loughrey identify the text's particular theatrical energy with reference to a production in 1985, which 'found the text of Q1 resisting the conventional interiorisation of action within the tragic subject: the problems of the play became less psychological, more circumstantial and contingent [. . .] the accelerated narrative produc[ed] a particular emphasis on the political rather than the psychological dimension' (pp. 24–5). There are more articles on the textual criticism and performance history of *Hamlet* Q1 in Clayton (1992), and the textual history of *Hamlet* has also been discussed by Urkowitz (1986), Loughrey (1992), Campbell (1991): *King Lear* by Patterson (1989), Taylor and Warren (1983), Urkowitz (1980); *Othello* by Honigmann (1996); and *Romeo and Juliet* by Cloud (1982) and Levenson (1998). This new direction in bibliographic studies, however, was not uncontroversial. Something of these disagreements can be seen in a series of 'Letters to the Editor' in *The Times Literary Supplement* during 1994, following Brian Vickers' review, entitled '*Hamlet* by Dogberry: a perverse reading of the Bad Quarto' (24 December 1993), of Holderness and Loughrey's edition of *Hamlet* Q1. Vickers argued that the text was presented 'in an ideologically predetermined frame, denying editorial responsibilities while performing some of them sloppily': '[the editors] latch on to a recent trend in Shakespeare textual criticism which has leapt from the recognition that the plays existed as theatre-scripts, subject to cutting and expansion, to the deduction that therefore there can be no authentic edition'. Holderness and Loughrey responded to Vickers' review – 'a sufficiently contemptuous anathematisation of the series' – as 'a staunch defence of traditional scholarship and a clear attempt to inhibit, by the deployment and invocation of a traditionalist academic authority, certain new developments in textual theory and bibliographical practice' (4 February 1994). Brian Vickers reiterated that 'as for the 1603 *Hamlet*, its inferiority to the authentic texts is an issue that cannot be settled by purely new textual theories, since it depends on literary critical judgments, which depend in turn on sensitivity' (4 March 1994); Holderness accused the Shakespearean establishment of excluding him from seminars on editing, ending his letter 'I prefer to leave the cheap jibes – such as his suggestion that I might never have clapped eyes on an early edition of Shakespeare – to Brian Vickers' (8 April 1994). As a case-study in violently opposed bibliographic principles and the vehemence with which they are held, the exchange of letters is a valuable document in the recent history of textual criticism.

The theatrical provenance of the texts has become a more prominent feature of recent editing, as Stanley Wells and Gary Taylor's introduction to the influential *Oxford Shakespeare* (1986) identifies: 'It is in performance that the plays lived and had their being. Performance is the end to which they were created, and in this edition we have devoted our efforts to recovering and presenting texts of Shakespeare's plays as they were acted' (Shakespeare, 1986, p. xxxvii). The question of how the quartos reached publication has continued. Kathleen Irace, in her study of six quarto texts in *Reforming the 'Bad' Quartos* (1994), argues that

> performance features as well as other clues in these six texts suggest that they were deliberately adapted and abridged [. . .] The reporters' apparently deliberate alterations affect plot structure and tempo, character development, staging, tone, and even poetic language, as in some cases the shortened texts seem to preserve coherent alternate versions, different from Shakespeare's longer scripts, but often with their own internal logic. (Irace, 1994, p. 160)

Her conclusions fix the quartos to the theatrical practices of the Shakespearean period, though she is also interested in how their particular theatrical qualities are endorsed in unexpected ways, discussing, for example, similarities between Franco Zeffirelli's film of *Hamlet* (1991) with the text of Q1. Bate (1991) also argues for the theatrical provenance of the quartos. By contrast, Laurie Maguire in her *Shakespearean Suspect Texts* (1996), argues that the memorial reconstruction theory had enjoyed particular popularity because of its apparent flexibility at once to explain textual accuracy, perceived inaccuracy and inconsistency. After exhaustively tabulating analyses of forty quartos, not just Shakespearean texts, Maguire concludes that memorial reconstruction is only a possibility, not a fact, and that this hypothesis may distort our understanding of the quarto texts.

Kathleen Irace imagines an ideal Shakespearean text

> projected on a flickering computer screen, simultaneously flashing alternate readings before our eyes – the perfect text for the ideal postmodern poststructuralist. A more modest (and user-friendly) format might be a carefully prepared modern edition that would present these valuable early quartos in a form suited to critics and students alike, allowing further investigations in to the special features of these intriguing and important Renaissance texts. (Irace, 1994, p. 170)

In recent years Cambridge University Press has begun just such a series, with editions of *The First Quarto of King Henry V*, edited by Andrew Gurr (2000), Jay Halio's edition of *The First Quarto of King Lear* (1994), Kathleen Irace's *The First Quarto of Hamlet* (1998) and Scott McMillin's *The First Quarto of Othello* (2001). Thompson's *Which Shakespeare?* (1992) gives advice to consumers about which edition of Shakespeare they might prefer, and although the volume has been superseded by additional new editions, the general points about different purposes and different consumers are still relevant. These new editorial developments are also informed by renewed interest in the history of editing, in, for example, Margreta de Grazia's discussion of Malone (1991), work by Walsh (1997) and Jarvis (1995) on the assumptions and achievements of eighteenth-century textual scholarship, Grady's account (1991) of late Victorian and modernist editing, Franklin's (1991) discussion of Victorian scholarship and Dobson's (1992) account of the invention of Shakespeare as national poet by various means, including editorial, in the post-Restoration period. West (2001) gives an account of the fortunes of the First Folio as an object bought and sold, changing in value, across four centuries.

Further Reading

Barthes, Roland. 'From "Text" to "Work"'. *Modern Literary Theory: A Reader*, Philip Rice and Patricia Waugh (eds). London: Arnold, 1996, 191–7.

Bate, Jonathan. 'Shakespeare's Tragedies as Working Scripts'. *Critical Survey* 3 (1991): 118–27.

Blayney, Peter W. M. *The Texts of 'King Lear' and their Origins*. New Cambridge Shakespeare studies and supplementary texts series. Cambridge: Cambridge University Press, 1982.

Bowers, Fredson. 'Today's Shakespeare Texts and Tomorrow's'. *Studies in Bibliography* 19 (1966): 39–66.

Campbell, Kathleen. 'Zeffirelli's Hamlet – Q1 in Performance' *Shakespeare on Film Newsletter* 16 (1991): 7–8.

Charney, Maurice, and Shakespeare Association of America. *'Bad' Shakespeare: Revaluations of the Shakespeare Canon*. Rutherford NJ: Fairleigh Dickinson University Press, 1988.

Clayton, Thomas. *The Hamlet First Published (Q1, 1603): Origins, Form, Intertextualities*. Newark; London: University of Delaware Press; Associated University Presses, 1992.

de Grazia, Margreta. *Shakespeare Verbatim: The Reproduction of Authenticity and the 1790 Apparatus*. Oxford: Clarendon Press, 1991.

——, and Stallybrass, Peter. 'The Materiality of the Shakespearean Text'. *Shakespeare Quarterly* 44 (1993): 255–83.

Dobson, Michael. *The Making of the National Poet: Shakespeare, Adaptation and Authorship, 1660–1769*. Oxford: Clarendon Press, 1992.

Duthie, George Ian. *The 'Bad' Quarto of Hamlet: A Critical Study*. Cambridge: Cambridge University Press, 1941.

——*Papers: Mainly Shakespearean*. Edinburgh: Oliver and Boyd, 1964.

Franklin, Colin. *Shakespeare Domesticated: The Eighteenth-century Editions*. Aldershot: Scolar, 1991.

Grady, Hugh. *The Modernist Shakespeare: Critical Texts in a Material World*. Oxford: Clarendon Press, 1991.

Greg, W. W. 'What is Bibliography?' *Transactions of the Bibliographical Society* 12 (1911–13): 39–54.

——*The Editorial Problem in Shakespeare: A Survey of the Foundations of the Text*. The Clark lectures, 1939. Oxford: Clarendon Press, 1954.

——*The Shakespeare First Folio: Its Bibliographical and Textual History*. Oxford: Clarendon Press, 1955.

Gurr, Andrew. *The First Quarto of King Henry V*. Cambridge: Cambridge University Press, 2000.

Halio, Jay L. *The First Quarto of King Lear*. Cambridge: Cambridge University Press, 1994.

Holderness, Graham, and Loughrey, Bryan. *The Tragicall Historie of Hamlet Prince of Denmark*. Hemel Hempstead: Harvester Wheatsheaf, 1992.

——, Loughrey, Bryan, and Murphy, Andrew. '"What's the Matter?" Shakespeare and Textual Theory'. *Textual Practice* (1995): 93–119.

Honigmann, E. A. J. *The Stability of Shakespeare's Text*. London: Arnold, 1965.

——*The Texts of 'Othello' and Shakespearian Revision*. London: Routledge, 1996.

Ioppolo, Grace. *Revising Shakespeare*. Cambridge, Mass; London: Harvard University Press, 1991.

Irace, Kathleen O. *Reforming the 'Bad' Quartos: Performance and Provenance of Six Shakespearean First Editions*. Newark; London: Associated University Presses, 1994.

——*The First Quarto of Hamlet*. Cambridge: Cambridge University Press, 1998.

Jarvis, Simon. *Scholars and Gentlemen: Shakespearean Textual Criticism and Representations of Scholarly Labour, 1725–1765*. Oxford: Clarendon Press, 1995.

Jones, John. *Shakespeare at Work*. Oxford: Clarendon Press, 1995.

Levenson, Jill. 'Editing Romeo and Juliet: "A Challenge(,) on My Life".' *New Ways of Looking at Old Texts*, ed. W. Hill Speed, vol. 2. Tempe: MRTS, 1998. 61–70.

Loughrey, Bryan. 'Q1 in recent performance: an interview'. *The Hamlet First Published*, ed. Thomas Clayton, 1992.

Maguire, Laurie E. *Shakespearean Suspect Texts: The 'Bad' Quartos and their Contexts*. Cambridge: Cambridge University Press, 1996.

Marcus, Leah. 'Renaissance / Early Modern Studies'. *Redrawing the Boundaries: The Transformation of English and American Literary Studies*, eds Stephen Greenblatt and Giles Gunn, New York: Modern Language Association of America, 1992, pp. 41–63.

——*Unediting the Renaissance: Shakespeare, Marlowe, Milton*. London: Routledge, 1996.

McGann, Jerome J. *A Critique of Modern Textual Criticism*. Chicago: University of Chicago Press, 1983.

——*Textual Criticism and Literary Interpretation*. Chicago: University of Chicago Press, 1985.

McKenzie, D. F., and British Library. *Bibliography and the Sociology of Texts*. 1985. London: British Library, 1986.

McKerrow, Ronald Brunlees. *Prolegomena for the Oxford Shakespeare: A Study in Editorial Method*. Oxford: Clarendon Press, 1939.

McLeod, Randall [Random Cloud]. 'The Marriage of Good and Bad Quartos'. *Shakespeare Quarterly* 33 (1982): 421–31.

——*Crisis in Editing: Texts of the English Renaissance Papers Given at the Twenty-Fourth Annual Conference on Editorial Problems, University of Toronto, 4–5 November 1988*. New York: AMS Press, 1994.

McMillin, Scott. *The First Quarto of Othello*. New Cambridge Shakespeare. Early quartos. Cambridge: Cambridge University Press, 2001.

Patterson, Annabel M. *Shakespeare and the Popular Voice*. Oxford: Basil Blackwell, 1989.

Pollard, Alfred. 'The Foundations of Shakespeare's Text'. *Aspects of Shakespeare: Being British Academy Lectures* (1933): 1–22.

Rice, Philip, and Waugh, Patricia. *Modern Literary Theory: A Reader*, 3rd edn. London: Arnold, 1996.

Shakespeare, William, *The Complete Works*. Oxford: Clarendon Press, 1986.

——, Hinman, Charlton, and Hooker, Richard. *The First Folio of Shakespeare*. London: Hamlyn, 1968.

Taylor, Gary, and Jowett, John. *Shakespeare Reshaped, 1606–1623*. Oxford: Clarendon Press, 1993.

——, and Warren, Michael. *The Division of the Kingdoms: Shakespeare's Two Versions of King Lear*. Oxford; New York: Clarendon Press; Oxford University Press, 1983.

Thompson, Ann. *Which Shakespeare? A User's Guide to Editions*. Milton Keynes: Open University Press, 1992.

Urkowitz, Steven. *Shakespeare's Revision of King Lear*. Princeton; Guildford: Princeton University Press, 1980.

——'"Well-sayd olde Mole": Burying three *Hamlets* in modern editions'. *Shakespeare Study Today*, ed. Georgianna Ziegler. New York: AMS Press, 1986, pp. 37–70.

—— 'Five Women Eleven Ways: Changing Images of Shakespearean Characters in the Earliest Texts'. *Images of Shakespeare*, ed. Werner Habicht. Newark: University of Delaware Press, 1988.

Walsh, Marcus. *Shakespeare, Milton, and Eighteenth-century Literary Editing: The Beginnings of Interpretative Scholarship*. Cambridge: Cambridge University Press, 1997.

Warren, Michael. *The Complete King Lear, 1608–1623*. Berkeley: University of California Press, 1989.

Wells, Stanley, and Taylor, Gary. Introduction, *Oxford Shakespeare*. Oxford: Oxford University Press, 1986.

West, Anthony James. *The Shakespeare First Folio: The History of the Book – Volume I: An Account of the First Folio Based on its Sales and Prices*. Oxford: Oxford University Press, 2001.

Wilson, F. P., and Gardner, Helen Louise. *Shakespeare and the New Bibliography*. Oxford: Clarendon Press, 1970.

Wilson, John Dover. *The Manuscript of Shakespeare's 'Hamlet' and the Problems of its Transmission: An essay in critical bibliography*. Cambridge: Cambridge University Press, 1934.

13

Texts: Critical Extracts

Quarto and Folio *King Lear* and the Interpretation of Albany and Edgar

Michael Warren

Warren's essay is historically significant for its careful description of the two texts of King Lear *– the quarto text 'The History of King Lear' (1608) and the Folio text 'The Tragedy of King Lear' (1623). His argument that both texts have authority and that therefore conflating them is to produce an amalgam with no intrinsic validity except as an editorial creation is forwarded by way of three brief examples: the characters of Albany and Edgar, and the dialogue in 2.4 between Lear and Kent. Warren's conclusion is delivered without fanfare, but it is a radical one: 'all further work on the play [needs to] be based on either Q or F'. It is significant that Warren does not confine himself to textual criticism. It is implicit in his closing sentence that the differences between the early texts of* King Lear *are not only a matter for bibliographers, but for all readers, performers and critics of Shakespeare.*

Michael Warren, 'Quarto and Folio *King Lear* and the Interpretation of Albany and Edgar', in *Shakespeare: Pattern of Excelling Nature*, David Bevington and Jay L. Halio (eds). Newark; London: Associated University Presses, 1978.

I

The two texts of *King Lear* present obvious editorial and critical problems. The Quarto of 1608 prints about 283 lines that are not printed in the 1623 Folio; the Folio prints about 100 that are not printed in the Quarto.[1] A variation of nearly 400 lines in a text of around 3,300 lines is significant;[2] in addition, there are also a very large number of variant substantive readings. However, far from alarming editors and critics to the delicate problems involved in printing and discussing a single play called *King Lear*, this wealth of material has been treated as an ample blessing from which a "best text" of Shakespeare's *King Lear* may be evolved. Indeed, the standard methods of bibliography and editing – the application of critical principles "to the textual raw material of the authoritative preserved documents in order to approach as nearly as may be to the ideal of the authorial fair copy by whatever necessary process of recovery, independent emendation, or conflation of authorities"[3] – such methods and the accepted assumptions of the origins of each text have led to the editorial habit of establishing and publishing a *King Lear* text that is produced by a process of conflation, by the exercise of a moderate and quasi-scientific eclecticism, and by a studied disregard for the perils of intentionalism.[4] In a recent article Kenneth Muir writes:

> This paper is an enlarged version of that delivered at the International Shake-speare Association Congress in Washington. D. C. in April 1976. As a consequence of delivering the paper I have become aware that three scholars are currently writing dissertations arguing for the distinctness of the Quarto and Folio texts of *King Lear*: Steven Urkowitz of University of Chicago, Georgia Peters Burton of Bryn Mawr College, and Peter W. M. Blayney of Cambridge University; each of us has arrived at the same major conclusion independently of the others. I would like to thank my colleague Professor John M. Ellis for his helpful advice and criticism with respect to the argument of the first part of this paper.
>
> Until the work of bibliographers and textual critics in the present century, editors chose readings from either text, according to taste. It is now generally agreed that, whatever the basis of the Quarto text, the Folio text of *King Lear* is nearer to what Shakespeare wrote; but, even so, editors are still bound to accept a number of readings from the inferior text and, since there were cuts in the prompt-book from which the Folio text was derived, a number of long passages.[5]

This statement reveals certain clear attitudes of editors to their task. It is assumed that there is one primal lost text, an "ideal *King Lear*" that Shakespeare wrote, and that we have two corrupted copies of it. It is hypothesized that F is a less corrupt version of the ideal text than Q though both preserve features of the ideal original; and that while there is more corruption in Q some uncorrupted elements remain that can mitigate the admittedly lesser corruption of F. The concept of the "ideal *King Lear*" is problematic here, first, because its existence cannot be known, and second, because in the absence of such knowledge it is nevertheless further assumed that all alterations of any nature from that imaginary text are by hands other than Shakespeare's. Such an assumption is based on no evidence, and is counter to our experience of authors and their habits – for example, the modification of texts after first publication by Jonson, Pope, Yeats, James, and Pinter. Of course, it is conceivable that this standard hypothesis may indeed be true, but the confidence with which it is assumed is unwarranted, and the lack of a constant awareness that it is an assumption leads to poorly founded judgments. For instance, a statement such as "editors are still bound to accept a number of readings from the inferior text" is merely an editor's justification of the right to be eclectic; although editors may well be advised at times to adopt readings where comparison of texts indicates simple misprints or nonsensical readings, circumspection and wariness are always necessary, for nonsense may merely be sense we do not yet understand, and further we cannot know that alterations between Q and F are not authorial in origin. Most editors admit that the examination of the two texts leads to the conclusion that editing has taken place, and yet they are generally reluctant to take that editing seriously.

Having asserted the necessity of a decent skepticism in relation to the concept of the "ideal" text, I wish to argue that in a situation where statements about textual status are never more than hypotheses based upon the current models of thought about textual recension, it is not demonstrably erroneous to work with the possibility (a) that there may be no single "ideal play" of *King Lear* (all of "what Shakespeare wrote"), that there may never have been one, and that what we create by conflating both texts is merely an invention of editors and scholars; (b) that for all its problems Q is an authoritative version of the play of *King Lear*; and (c) that F may indeed be a revised version of the play, that its additions and omissions may constitute Shakespeare's considered modification of the earlier text, and that we certainly cannot know that they are not.[6]

Of course, I am once more introducing, after over fifty years of relative quiescence, the specter of "continuous copy": not, I would hope, in the confident, fantastic, and disintegrationist mode of Robertson and Dover Wilson, but in a skeptical and conservative way. In his famous lecture *The Disintegration of Shakespeare*, E. K. Chambers dismissed the excesses of his contemporaries as much by the force of ironic rhetoric and an attractive appeal to common sense as by any real proof; but he nowhere succeeded in denying the possibility of authorial reworking. He instanced the few cases of recorded extensive revision as indicative that revision of any kind was rare; and he asserted as follows: "That any substantial revision, as distinct perhaps from a mere abridgement, would entail a fresh application for the Master's allowance must, I think, be taken for granted. The rule was that his hand must be 'at the latter end of the booke they doe play'; and in London, at least, any company seriously departing from the allowed book would run a considerable risk."[7] Which is an interesting hypothesis; but what in this connection would constitute "substantial revision" or "serious departure"? Chambers to the contrary, that same common sense which leads me to praise him in his rejection of disintegrationist excesses leads me nevertheless to believe that a play like *King Lear* may have undergone revision beyond "mere abridgement" – what Chambers, following

Henslowe, might classify as "altering" – without the necessity of resubmission to the Master of the Revels.

In putting forward this argument I have ignored many of the complexities of relation that have been the stuff of textual debate for many years. I have done so because they are merely the current working hypotheses of the editing world, and because they are not immediately relevant to my contention. I would maintain that Q and F *King Lear* are sufficiently dissimilar that they should not be conflated, but should be treated as two versions of a single play, both having authority. To substantiate my argument I wish to present three brief studies. In the first I will deal with a short exchange of dialogue to illustrate the impact of conflation on the text as script for the theater; in the second and third I will discuss the varying presentations of Albany and Edgar in Q and F.

II

In Act 2 Lear discovers Kent in the stocks; the two texts present the following dialogue (2.4.12–23):[8] first Q:

LEAR.	Whats he, that hath so much thy place mistooke to set thee here?		
KENT.	It is both he and shee, your sonne & daugter.		
LEAR.	No.	KENT.	Yes.
LEAR.	No I say,	KENT.	I say yea.
LEAR.	No no, they would not.	KENT.	Yes they haue.
LEAR.	By Iupiter I sweare no, they durst not do't,		

They would not, could not do't, . . .

then F:

LEAR.   What's he,
That hath so much thy place mistooke
To set thee heere?
KENT.   It is both he and she,
Your Son, and Daughter.
LEAR.   No.
KENT.   Yes.
LEAR.   No I say.
KENT.   I say yea.
LEAR.   By Iupiter I sweare no.
KENT.   By Iuuo, I sweare I.
LEAR.   They durst not do't:
They could not, would not do't: . . .

Editors here customarily conflate these texts so that both "No no, they would not / Yes they haue," and Kent's "By Iuuo, I sweare I" are retained; in consequence four exchanges are produced where three exist in each of the original texts. Muir's note in the Arden text (p. 83) is concerned with the integrity of the Q lines and critics' opinions of their quality. But the more important issue is that his text (like most others) presents us with a reading that has *no* authority. If F was printed from a copy of Q as is widely and reasonably accepted, then one ought to assume that any omission may have had a purpose: but that assumption is doubly imperative when new material is included in F that appears to make up for the omission. However, even if one ignores the standard theory concerning the recension, there is still no case for four exchanges. In each text the climax on the third exchange is powerful, and sufficient; neither can be proved to be un-Shakespearean – they are both probably "what Shakespeare wrote"; and so respect for the theatrical proportions of the play dictates that conflation cannot be other than textual tinkering, distortion. Either Q or F: *not* both together.

III

As the above passage indicates, the editor, like any other reader of Shakespeare, must always be conscious that play texts are scripts for performance; when they are realized on the stage, presence, absence, action, inaction, speech, and silence have far more impact than when they are noted on the printed page. With this observation in mind I wish to argue that Q and F reveal significant differences in the roles of Albany and Edgar, differences sufficiently great that one is obliged to interpret their characters differently in each, and, especially in relation to the alterations in the last scene, to appreciate a notable contrast in the tone and meaning of the close of each text. These differences go beyond those which may be expected when two texts descend in corrupted form from a common original; they indicate that a substantial and consistent recasting of certain aspects of the play has taken place. In brief, the part of Albany is more developed in Q than in F, and in Q he closes the play a mature and victorious duke assuming responsibility for the kingdom; in F he is a weaker character, avoiding responsibility. The part of Edgar is shorter in F than in Q; however, whereas in Q he ends the play a young man overwhelmed by his experience, in F he is a young man who has learned a great deal, and who is emerging as the new leader of the ravaged society.

In both texts Albany speaks little in the first act. Neither Albany nor Cornwall speaks in the first scene in Q; their joint exclamation "Deare Sir forbeare" (1.1.162) appears in F only. In the fourth scene, which Goneril dominates in both texts, Q lacks two of the eight brief speeches that F assigns to Albany, and a phrase that completes a third. Missing are "Pray Sir be patient" (1.4.270) and "Well, you may feare too farre" (1.4.338), and the phrase "Of what hath moued you" (1.4.283), which in F succeeds "My Lord, I am guilt-lesse, as I am ignorant." Albany, who is bewildered and ineffectual in either text, is more patently so in Q, where he is given no opportunity to urge patience in response to Lear's question – "is it your will that wee prepare any horses" (F "Is it your will, speake Sir? Prepare my Horses") (1.4.267) – and no opportunity to warn Goneril of the unwisdom of her acts. Goneril's part also is smaller in Q than in F – she lacks 1.4.322–43 – but she dominates the scene nevertheless.

However, when Albany enters in the fourth act after a period in which he does not ride to Gloucester's house with Goneril and is mentioned only in the context of the always incipient conflict between himself and Cornwall, his reappearance is different in quality in each text. In both texts the scene begins with Oswald reporting Albany's disaffection (4.2.3–11) while Goneril scorns "the Cowish terror of his spirit" (4.2.12). In F Albany's speech on entering is very brief:

> Oh *Gonerill*,
> You are not worth the dust which the rude winde
> Blowes in your face.
>
> (4.2.29–31)

However, Q continues:

> I feare your disposition
> That nature which contemnes ith origin
> Cannot be bordered certaine in it selfe,
> She that her selfe will sliuer and disbranch
> From her materiall sap, perforce must wither,
> And come to deadly vse.
>
> (4.2.31–36)

And Goneril's prompt dismissal "No more, the text is foolish" leads to a longer speech of powerful moral reproach, likening the sisters to tigers, and reaching its climax in the pious pronouncement that

> If that the heauens doe not their visible spirits
> Send quickly downe to tame this vild offences, it will come
> Humanity must perforce pray on it self like monsters of the deepe.
>
> (4.2.46–50)

The speeches that follow in Q are much reduced in F, and both Albany and Goneril lose lines. The cuts in Goneril's part are largely references to Albany as a "morall foole," statements critical of his mild response to the invasion of France; her stature is not notably diminished by the loss. The reduction of Albany's part, by contrast, severely reduces his theatrical impact. In F he is left with barely six lines between his entrance and that of the messenger, and there is no sense of the new strong position that lines such as the following, even allowing for Goneril's belittling rejection, establish in Q:

> ALB. Thou changed, and selfe-couerd thing for shame
> Be-monster not thy feature, wer't my fitnes
> To let these hands obay my bloud,
> They are apt enough to dislecate and teare
> Thy flesh and bones, how ere thou art a fiend,
> A womans shape doth shield thee.
> GON. Marry your manhood mew . . .
>
> (4.2.62–68)

In Q the succeeding lines of moral outrage at the news of the blinding of Gloucester present Albany as a man of righteous wrath, outraged by injustice; the same sequence in F presents Albany as equally outraged, but because of the brevity of his previous rebukes he appears more futile in context, less obviously a man capable of action. The cutting diminishes his stature.

Although Albany does assert himself in the fifth act in both texts, he is much stronger in Q by virtue of the presence of three passages that are not his in F. At his entrance he asserts control over the situation in both texts with his first speech; Q reads:

> Our very louing sister well be-met
> For this I heare the King is come to his daughter
> With others, whome the rigour of our state
> Forst to crie out, . . .
>
> (5.1.20–23)[9]

The speech continues in Q, but not in F:

> where I could not be honest
> I neuer yet was valiant, for this busines
> It touches vs. as France inuades our land
> Not bolds the King, with others whome I feare,
> Most iust and heauy causes make oppose.
>
> (5.1.23–27)

The inclusion of this passage in Q gives immediate prominence to the complexity and scrupulousness of Albany's understanding of the political and moral issues. More important, however, are the two alterations in the closing moments of the play: at 5.3.251 Q assigns to Albany the order "Hast thee for thy life," which F gives to Edgar; and Q assigns the final four lines to Albany, which again F gives to Edgar. I shall discuss these changes more fully as I deal with Edgar, but it is sufficient to point out at this stage that Albany is in command throughout the last scene in Q, while in F he is considerably effaced at the close.

IV

In both Q and F Edgar presents far more complex problems than Albany, not least because he is intrinsically a more complex and difficult character even before textual variations are considered. Edgar's part, which in conflated texts is second only to that of Lear in length,[10] is reduced in size in F, but unlike Albany, Edgar receives some new material which, however it is interpreted, tends to focus attention more precisely upon him.

The differences in Edgar's role between Q and F in the first act are not of major significance: at 1.2.98–100 Q includes and F omits an exchange between Edmund and Gloucester about Edgar that reveals more about Gloucester's character than Edgar's; F omits Edmund's imitative discourse upon the current crisis and Edgar's ironic reply "How long haue you been a sectary Astronomicall?" (1.2.151–57); and F includes a passage not in Q in which Edmund proposes concealing Edgar in his lodging, and recommends going armed, to the surprise of his brother (1.2.172–79). More important variations appear in the third act. At 3.4.37–38 in F (after a stage direction "*Enter Edgar, and Foole*," which contradicts Kent's speech a few lines later "What art thou that dost grumble there i'th' straw? Come forth"), Edgar utters a line that Q lacks: "Fathom, and halfe, Fathom and halfe; poore *Tom*"; this offstage cry makes a chilling theatrical introduction to Edgar-as-Tom, and it is moreover the event that, coupled with his entrance, appears to propel Lear finally into madness. Later in the third act F omits material that Q includes. F lacks the trial of Goneril that Lear conducts with the support of Edgar and the Fool (3.6.17–56). While F provides the Fool with a new last line in the play "And Ile go to bed at noone"(3.6.88), it omits Kent's tender speech over Lear in Q, which begins "Oppressed nature sleepes" (3.6.100–104). However, very important alterations in this middle section of the play follow immediately; they are F's omission of the soliloquy with which Edgar closes 3.6 in Q and F's minor amplification of Edgar's first speech in the fourth act, two speeches that provide the transitions to and from the climactic scene of the blinding of Gloucester. These alterations need to be discussed in the larger context of the character and function of Edgar in the play.

In recent years serious challenges have been made to the traditional conception of Edgar as the good, devoted, abused but patient, loving son. Some of this examination has led to the formulation of extreme positions in which Edgar has appeared as almost as culpable and vicious as Edmund, dedication to an ideal of selfless virtuous support being interpreted as an unconscious psychic violence, a dangerous self-righteousness that must exercise itself on others.[11] It is unnecessary, however, to censure Edgar so strongly to accommodate some of the distance that one frequently feels from him; one may allow him his virtue while still seeing its weakness. Speaking much in aside and soliloquy, Edgar is distanced theatrically from many of the events of the play. However, despite his involvement with Lear in the mad scenes, he also appears at times to be distanced emotionally from the events around him; his moral commentary reflects his response to the events, his assessment of his philosophical position in their light. The problem is that his response is frequently inadequate. As the play proceeds Edgar is obliged to confront the shallowness of his rationalizations, and yet much of the time he nevertheless appears impervious to the new knowledge that is being forced upon him. He possesses a naively pious and optimistic faith in the goodness of the world and the justice of the gods, and in his own youthful, romantic vision of his role in this world of conflict. In his mind his father's despair will be conquered by his endless encouragement; the triumphant climax will be the restoration to Gloucester of the knowledge of his son's existence and readiness to go off to recover his dukedom for him. The mode of Edgar's thought is Christian romantic-heroic, in which virtue usually triumphs splendidly. That it bears little relation to the realities of the universe in which the play takes place is evident; but it does save Gloucester from abject misery, and provides incidentally a happy, well-deceived death for him. We can appreciate Edgar's love and concern for his father, while doubting the maturity of many of his judgments.

It is in the context of this conception of Edgar, which is appropriate to either text, that I wish to demonstrate the major alterations in the role. When the soliloquy beginning "When we our betters see bearing our woes" is spoken at the close of 3.6. in Q (3.6.105–18), we are aware of Edgar's ability to comment upon the king's suffering, the power of fellowship, and his capacity to endure; in F, which lacks these meditations, Edgar has played a very small part in a rather brief scene, and the play rushes to the blinding of Gloucester. But F compensates for these cuts by expanding the speech with which Edgar opens the fourth act in both texts by adding an extra sentence. The speech reads:

> Yet better thus, and knowne to be contemn'd,
> Then still contemn'd and flatter'd, to be worst:
> The lowest, and most deiected thing of Fortune,
> Stands still in esperance, liues not in feare:
> The lamentable change is from the best,
> The worst returnes to laughter.
>
> (4.1.1–6)[12]

But F continues:

> Welcome then,
> Thou vnsubstantiall ayre that I embrace:
> The Wretch that thou hast blowne vnto the worst,
> Owes nothing to thy blasts.
>
> (4.1.6–9)

And then Gloucester enters. In both texts Edgar expresses the philosophic confidence of the man who has reached the bottom, but in F Edgar speaks still more facilely courageous lines of resolution against fortune just prior to having the inadequacy of his vision exposed by the terrible entrance of his father. What the revision in F achieves is this. The play is shortened and speeded by the loss from 3.6 and the opening of 4.1 of about 54 lines (three minutes of playing time at least). The absence of Edgar's moral meditation from the end of 3.6 brings the speech at 4.1.1 into sharp focus, isolating it more obviously between the blinding and the entrance of Gloucester; in F the two servants do not remain onstage after Cornwall's exit. The additional lines at this point emphasize the hollowness of Edgar's assertions; while the quantity of sententiousness is reduced, its nature is made more emphatically evident. Edgar gains in prominence, ironically enough, by the loss of a speech, and the audience becomes more sharply aware of his character.

The last act reveals major alterations that surpass those briefly described in the discussion of Albany. In both texts Edgar describes the death of his father with rhetorical fullness and elaborate emotional dramatization (5.3.181–99). In Q, however, he is given an additional speech of seventeen lines (5.3.204–21) only briefly interrupted by Albany, in which he reports his meeting with Kent. The removal of this speech not only speeds the last act by the elimination of material of no immediate importance to the plot, but also reduces the length of the delay between Edmund's "This speech of yours hath mou'd me, / And shall perchance do good" (5.3.199–200) and the sending of an officer to Lear. It also diminishes the sense of Edgar as the immature, indulgent man displaying his heroic tale of woe, for in F Albany's command "If there be more, more wofull, hold it in" (5.3.202) is obeyed; in Q by contrast Edgar nevertheless continues:

> This would haue seemd a periode to such
> As loue not sorow, but another to amplifie too much,
> Would make much more, and top extreamitie . . .
>
> (5.3.204–7)

and the speech reveals Edgar's regard for his own dramatic role in the recent history:

> Whil'st I was big in clamor, came there in a man,
> Who hauing seene me in my worst estate,
> Shund my abhord society, but then finding
> Who twas that so indur'd . . .
>
> (5.3.208–11)

F, then, maintains the fundamental nature of Edgar as philosophical agent through the play, but in the last act reduces somewhat his callowness, his easy indulgence of his sensibility in viewing the events through which he is living. In so doing F develops Edgar into a man worthy to stand with the dukes at the close of the play, capable of assuming power.

The elevation of Edgar at the close and relative reduction of Albany that distinguish F from Q can be documented from three other places. At 5.3.229[13] in Q Edgar says to Albany "Here comes Kent sir," but "Here comes Kent" in F. The transfer of the command "Hast thee for thy life" (5.3.251) from Albany in Q to Edgar in F gives Edgar a more active role in the urgent events; indeed, Q may indicate that it is Edgar who is to run. All Edgar's lines after "Hast thee for thy life" are shared by Q and F apart from the last four, which Q assigns to Albany. Though they are partial lines at most, they are susceptible of quite different interpretations according to whether Edgar speaks the last lines or not. If one considers Edgar's behavior in Q in the light of his lachrymose speech about Kent and his apparently subordinate role to Albany, he appears to be silenced by Lear's death: initially in Q he cries out "He faints my Lord, my Lord" (5.3.311), then appeals to Lear "Look vp my Lord" (312), only to say after Kent has assured him of the death "O he is gone indeed"(315), and to fall silent for the rest of the play. By contrast, F omits the "O" in this last statement, and then gives Edgar the last lines. In Q, then, Edgar concludes the play stunned to silence by the reality of Lear's death, a very young man who does not even answer Albany's appeal "Friends of my soule, you twaine, / Rule in this Realme" (5.3.319–20), so that Albany reluctantly but resolutely accepts the obligation to rule: "The waight of this sad time we must obey" (323). This characterization of Edgar is a far cry from the Edgar of F who comes forward as a future ruler when he enables Albany to achieve his objective of not ruling; F's Edgar is a young man of limited perceptions concerning the truth of the world's harsh realities, but one who has borne some of the burdens and appears capable of handling (better than anybody else) the responsibilities that face the survivors.[14]

In summary, Q and F embody two different artistic visions, In Q Edgar remains an immature young man and ends the play devastated by his experience, while Albany stands as the modest, diffident, but strong and morally upright man. In F Edgar grows into a potential ruler, a well-intentioned, resolute man in a harsh world, while Albany, a weaker man, abdicates his responsibilities. In neither text is the prospect for the country a matter of great optimism, but the vision seems bleaker and darker in F, where the young Edgar, inexperienced in rule, faces the future with little support.

V

In discussing these two texts I have focused on what seem to me to be the two major issues of the revision; I have not attended to the absence of 4.3 from F, nor to the relatively minor but nevertheless significant differences in the speeches of Lear, the Fool, and Kent. However, I submit that this examination of the texts and the implications of their differences for interpretation and for performance make it clear that they must be treated as separate versions of *King Lear*, and that eclecticism cannot be a valid principle in deciding readings. Conflated texts such as are commonly printed are invalid, and should not be used either for production or for interpretation. Though they may give their readers all of "What Shakespeare wrote," they do not give them Shakespeare's play of *King Lear*, but a play created by the craft and imagination of learned scholars, a work that has no justification for its existence. The principle that more is better, that all is good, has no foundation. What we as scholars, editors, interpreters, and servants of the theatrical craft have to accept and learn to live by is the knowledge that we have two plays of *King Lear* sufficiently different to require that all further work on the play be based on either Q or F, but not the conflation of both.

Notes

1 I am using the figures cited by Alfred Harbage on p. 1104 of his appendix to his text of *King Lear* published in *The Pelican Shakespeare* (Baltimore, 1969), pp. 1104–6.

2 *The Pelican Shakespeare* states that *King Lear* is 3,195 lines long; *The Norton Facsimile: The First Folio of Shakespeare*, ed. Charlton Hinman (New York, 1968), gives *King Lear* 3,301 lines.

3 Fredson Bowers, *Textual and Literary Criticism* (Cambridge, 1966), p. 120.

4 Harbage, "Note on the Text": "In 1608 a version of *King Lear* appeared in a Quarto volume sold by Nathaniel Butter at his shop at the Pied Bull. Its text was reproduced in 1619 in a quarto falsely dated 1608. Various theories have been offered to explain the nature of the Pied Bull text, the most recent being that it represents Shakespeare's rough draft carelessly copied, and corrupted by the faulty memories of actors who were party to the copying. In 1623 a greatly improved though 'cut' version of the play appeared in the first folio, evidently printed from the quarto after it had been carefully collated with the official playhouse manuscript. The present edition follows the folio text, and although it adds in square brackets the passages appearing only in the quarto, and accepts fifty-three quarto readings, it follows the chosen text more closely than do most recent editions. However, deference to the quarto is paid in an appendix, where its alternative readings, both those accepted and those rejected, are listed. Few editorial emendations have been retained, but see. . . ." (p. 1064). See also G. Blakemore Evans, "Note on the Text" of *King Lear*, in *The Riverside Shakespeare* (Boston, 1974), pp. 1295–96, and Kenneth Muir, "Introduction" to *King Lear* (Arden Shakespeare) (Cambridge, Mass., 1959), pp. xix–xx.

5. Kenneth Muir, "King Lear," in Stanley Wells, ed., *Shakespeare: Select Bibliographical Guides* (Oxford, 1973), p. 171.

6. Nor, of course, can we know with absolute confidence that they are, though that is my suspicion. The views of four other scholars are notable on this subject of revision. Dr. Johnson remarked that "I believe the Folio is printed from Shakespeare's last revision, carelessly and hastily performed, with more thought of shortening the scenes than of continuing the action," quoted by H. H. Furness. ed., *King Lear* (New Variorum Edition), 9th ed. (London, 1880), p. 215. In *The Pictorial Edition of the Works of Shakespeare*, ed. Charles Knight, 8 vols, (London, [1839]–1843), Knight argued vigorously that the Folio represents an authorial revision of the play (VI, 391–93); but he nevertheless included the passages that derive from Q alone in brackets in his published text. In *The Stability of Shakespeare's Texts* (Lincoln, Neb., 1965), E. A. J. Honigmann regards the differences in the texts of *King Lear* as authorial in origin (pp. 121–28), but conceives of them as cases of "authorial 'second thoughts' *before* its [the play's] delivery to the actors. I envisage, in short, two copies of a play, each in the author's hand, disagreeing in both substantive and indifferent readings: the play being regarded as 'finished' by Shakespeare in each version though not therefore beyond the reach of afterthoughts" (p. 2). By contrast, Peter W. M. Blayney (see the extract on p. 290 of

this essay) informs me in a letter that he believes that Shakespeare's was not the only hand involved in the revision that led to F.

7. E. K. Chambers, *The Disintegration of Shakespeare* ([London], 1924), p. 17.

8. For convenience I shall cite line numberings based on Muir's Arden edition throughout this essay; apparent inconsistencies occasionally result from the Arden relineation. All quotations from Q are from *King Lear, 1608 (Pied Bull Quarto): Shakespeare Quarto Facsimiles No. 1*, ed. W. W. Greg (Oxford, 1939); all quotations from F are from *The Norton Facsimile: The First Folio of Shakespeare*, ed. Charlton B. Hinman (New York, 1968). The text will normally make clear whether Q or F is being quoted: on occasions when the text is not specified and the lines under discussion appear in both Q and F with only insignificant differences in spelling and punctuation, I quote from F alone.

9. At 5.1.21 F reads "Sir, this I heard," for "For this I heare."

10. See *Pelican Shakespeare*, p. 31.

11. For sympathetic readings of Edgar, see (among others) R. B. Heilman, *This Great Stage* (Baton Rouge, La., 1948), and William R. Elton, *King Lear and the Gods* (San Marino, 1966). For more unsympathetic interpretations, see William Empson, "Fool in Lear," in *The Structure of Complex Words* (London, 1951); Nicholas Brooke, *Shakespeare: King Lear* (London, 1963); Stanley Cavell, "The Avoidance of Love," in *Must We Mean What We Say?* (New York, 1969); Marvin Rosenberg, *The Masks of King Lear* (Berkeley, Calif., 1972); S. L. Goldberg, *An Essay on King Lear* (Cambridge, 1974). However, there are signs of a restoration of honor and respect to Edgar; see, for instance, F. T. Flahiff, "Edgar: Once and Future King," in Rosalie L. Colie and F. T. Flahiff, eds, *Some Facets of King Lear: Essays in Prismatic Criticism* (Toronto, 1974), pp. 221–37, and Barbara A. Kathe, rsm, "The Development of the Myth of the Birth of the Hero in the Role of Edgar," a paper delivered at the International Shakespeare Association Congress in Washington, D. C., in April 1976.

12. At 4.1.4 Q reads "experience" for "esperance."

13 This is the Arden placing that follows F; Q places this line in the middle of Albany's next speech at 5.3.232.

14 If this distinction between the presentations of Edgar in the two texts is made, the subtitle of Q makes more than merely conventional sense in its place: *"With the unfortunate life of Edgar, sonne and heire to the Earle of Gloster, and his sullen and assumed humor of TOM of Bedlam."*

Bad Taste and Bad *Hamlet*

Leah Marcus

This piece is an extract from Marcus' book Unediting the Renaissance: Shakespeare, Marlowe, Milton *(1996). The project of 'unediting' is defined as a 'temporary abandonment of modern editions in favour of Renaissance editions that have not gathered centuries of editorial accretion around them' (p. 5) in order to become more aware of editorial shaping and convention. In this section on* Hamlet, *Marcus offers three anecdotal scenarios to explain the proliferation of texts, implicitly preferring multiple possibilities over the apparent monolithic certainty of earlier bibliographic scholarship. In setting out these possibilities she also reviews much of the textual criticism of the play / s.*

Leah S. Marcus, 'Bad Taste and Bad *Hamlet*', in *Unediting the Renaissance*. London: Routledge, 1996.

We are apt to call *barbarous* whatever departs widely from our own taste and apprehension, but soon find the epithet of reproach retorted on us.

David Hume

The centuries-old ritual is about to begin anew. In a small theater, Hamlet nears his most famous soliloquy, the immortal language of which has remained relatively stable over time, even as other elements of the play have altered. The audience shift in their seats and become still with concentration. The house lights seem to dim and the stage lights, to brighten. How will this actor's delivery measure up to that of the thousands who have preceded him in the role? What new nuances, new emphases, will he (or occasionally she, as in the case of Sarah Bernhardt's Hamlet and more recent female Hamlets) bring to the performance? In what way will this Hamlet mark the soliloquy as his own? He begins traditionally enough, but then something goes radically wrong:

> To be or not to be – aye, there's the point.
> To die, to sleep – is that all? Aye, all.
> No!
> To sleep, to dream – aye, marry, there it goes.
> For in that dream of death, when we awake –
> And borne before an everlasting judge –
> From whence no passanger ever returned –
> The undiscovered country, at whose sight
> The happy smile, and the accursed, damned –
> But for this, the joyful hope of this,
> Who'd bear the scorns and flattery of the world:
> Scorned by the right rich, the rich cursed of the poor,
> The widow being oppressed, the orphan wronged,
> The taste of hunger, or a tyrant's reign,
> And thousand more calamities besides,
> To grunt and sweat under this weary life,

> When that he may his full quietus make
> With a bare bodkin? Who would this endure,
> But for a hope of something after death,
> Which puzzles the brain and doth confound the sense,
> Which makes us rather bear those evils we have
> Than fly to others that we know not of?
> Aye, that!
> O this consciènce makes cowards of us all.[1]

The Hamlet uttering these lines will, needless to say, forfeit his opportunity to measure up to the long tradition of great Hamlets, since his lines will not be perceived as *Hamlet*. So deeply engrained in our cultural expectations is the established text of "To be or not to be" that any deviation from it is likely to be greeted as parody, and the audience on this theatrical occasion is no exception. Hamlet's first wrong turn of language meets with polite titters, but as the mistakes multiply, the titters quickly expand into guffaws. While some laugh at the apparent burlesque, others sit in uneasy silence, not sure how to react. Still others quicken to intellectual alertness: this is not the usual soliloquy, but something strange and heterodox, too close to the received version to be effective parody, yet too distant to communicate the same message. What is the meaning of this speech, the message of this strangely altered *Hamlet*?

The scene being described is a hypothetical reconstruction of events that have actually occurred in recent productions of the first quarto of *Hamlet*, yet another of our "bad" quartos, but one that has aroused extraordinarily strong interest during the past decade, particularly in theatrical circles.[2] My reconstruction is in one major way fallacious: during performances of Q1 *Hamlet*, it would be an uneducated audience indeed that would fail to recognize before the moment of "To be or not to be" that they were watching a radically different *Hamlet* than the usual one – different not only in terms of its brevity, since many productions prune the play down almost to bare bones, but in terms of its choice of words and altered syntax – its consistent debasement, bastardization, or (to adopt a more neutral term) simplification of the refined, poetic language of the play as we expect to find it.

The textual situation of *Hamlet* is more complex than any treated so far in the present study in that, since 1823, when the first of two extant copies of Q1 *Hamlet* was discovered, the play has existed for us not in two, but in three early versions: the first and second quartos (1603 and 1604–05 respectively), and the First Folio (1623). All three texts are interrelated: the folio version resembles Q1 more closely in some respects, Q2 more closely in others. Each has significant pieces of dialogue that exist in no other version. As Philip Edwards has acutely noted, our sense of the deep ambiguity of the play is closely connected with its lack of a clear text: "Both the prince and his play come down to us in more shapes than one. If the prince were not so mercurial the text would be more stable."[3]

Of the three early *Hamlet* texts, the second quarto has most often served as the copytext for modern editions, although G. R. Hibbard, Stanley Wells, and Gary Taylor adopt the folio for substantives in their recent Oxford editions on the grounds that the folio version represents Shakespeare's own revision of the play.[4] But in their attempts to establish a stable text for *Hamlet*, those who have constructed the major twentieth-century editions have ransacked all three early versions and related plays (the German *Der bestrafte Brudermord*, *The Spanish Tragedy*, *Antonio's Revenge*) for recurring configurations that would lead them to Shakespeare's intent. *Hamlet* as we usually read it is an elaborate mosaic of readings culled from early quartos, folios, and a long tradition of editorial emendation whereby the irregularities and grotesqueries of the early printed texts are smoothed over. Having made use of Q1 and other contemporary plays, however, most recent editors have gone on to suppress them as possible influences on Shakespeare, according to elaborate versions of the "Purity and Danger" ritual analyzed above in chapter 3. Indeed, in Harold Jenkins' Arden edition, the ritual is enacted twice: first to protect the editor's preferred *Hamlet* against John Marston's *Antonio's Revenge*, which includes many similar incidents and which older editors had regarded as the earlier play and therefore an influence on Shakespeare, and second to protect Q2 against the marauding energies of Q1. To the extent that they adopt readings from Q1 or confirmed by Q1, editors tend to avoid mentioning that text in their notes.[5] Q1 is an embarrassment, a potential blot on the reputation of Shakespeare.

In general, the fortunes of Q1 *Hamlet* have altered along with that of the other "bad" quartos considered in previous chapters. After its discovery in the 1820s, most scholars regarded it as Shakespeare's earliest sketch for the play, albeit probably marred by corruptions. Charles Knight described it as a "vigorous sapling" that grew luxuriantly over time to become the "monarch of the forest."[6] After 1900, more and more editors regarded it as a corrupt adaptation or memorial reconstruction of the "real" *Hamlet*, even though they conceded that Shakespeare's *Hamlet* could not have been the first play of that name. For A. C. Bradley in 1904, Q1 *Hamlet* was still the "original form" of Shakespeare's play; in textual matters, as in many others, Bradley was heir and culmination of a long nineteenth-century tradition. By the time of John Dover Wilson's *What Happens in Hamlet* (1935), Q2 was the obvious choice for copytext and Q1 could be confidently dismissed even by Wilson, who had earlier posited it as Shakespeare's source play somewhat touched up by Shakespeare. For the later Wilson, Q1 was a "garbled text based upon notes got together by someone, whether actor or spectator, present at original performances of the play, as all critics are now agreed."[7] Editors after Wilson still acknowledged that there must have been some sort of "Ur-*Hamlet*" a pre Shakespearean play of the same name. But they posited the Ur-*Hamlet* as unrecoverable and thereby created an unbridgeable gulf between it and Shakespeare's version of the play: the Ur-*Hamlet* receded into a mythic past and Shakespeare's *Hamlet* magically achieved the status of a charismatic original independent of any forebears.

The modernist consensus still holds firm in terms of editorial practice in mainstream editions of *Hamlet* despite a strong movement recently afoot in other circles to rehabilitate Q1.[8] Most recent editors continue to assert that Q1 is a memorial reconstruction – even Gary Taylor and Stanley Wells, who have done so much to rehabilitate Q *King Lear*.[9] But in their attempts to sort out the echoes and transformations from one early printed text to another, modern editors have been driven almost to a version of Hamlet's madness: which textual ghost speaks the truth of Shakespeare's meaning? Or do all of them bear treacherous false witness to the author's intent?

In the present chapter, I will not reenter the vast, disorienting labyrinth of conflicting evidence that has had to be negotiated by every modern editor of the play, but will confine myself for the most part to a small corner of it – to a reexamination of the early quarto versions of the play, the first of which is "bad" and the second of which is "good." Q1 *Hamlet* is indeed "bad" *Hamlet*, and will continue to be bad so long as we rank the early texts of the play on the basis of their adherence to culturally predetermined standards of literary excellence. Given that "To be or not to be" in its traditional form is itself generally regarded as a touchstone for rarefied, discriminating taste – a pinnacle of literary artistry – any attempt to assert the value of an alternative version of the immortal lines is automatically defined as evidence of a tin ear, an inability to appreciate the sublimity of Shakespeare. The matter is therefore unarguable within the established limits of the inquiry: "To be or not to be" in its traditional form is quintessential Shakespeare. Either you grasp its inexpressible excellence or you don't, and if you don't, God help you. As Samuel Taylor Coleridge put the matter long since, "O heaven! words are wasted to those that feel and to those who do not feel the exquisite judgement of Shakespeare."[10]

But the soliloquy has served as a powerful cultural shibboleth in part because it is uttered by an attractive, strongly-drawn, noble character who himself posits a hierarchy of taste by which the "judicious" are sequestered off from the "general" on the basis of their ability to see the world – and human artifacts – with the same discriminating taste that Hamlet himself does. We need to remind ourselves of the almost overpowering degree to which literate culture in general and professors of literature in particular are invested in an appreciation of literary excellence as a guarantor of their membership in an intellectual elite. *Hamlet* in its high cultural form is "caviary to the general," and we who have the ability to savor it earn inclusion in a select circle that Hamlet himself – and through him, Shakespeare – has defined.

As Barbara Herrnstein Smith and others have argued, literary value is contingent: the degree and kind of artistry we attribute to a given play or poem will depend not only on the particular era we inhabit, but also on our specific situation within that era – the cultural group we come from, belong to, aspire towards.[11] Indeed, as we have already noted earlier, much of the power of traditional editorial practice has derived from the editor's ability to call upon and reinforce seemingly unquestionable standards of taste shared with the more enlightened members of his or her readership. These standards, and the editions that both reflect and promulgate them, can alter markedly over time. For I. A. Richards, anyone who liked a sonnet by Ellen Wheeler Wilcox was "incapable of surviving in a complex environment and therefore biologically unfit" (cited in Smith, p. 37). Feminist scholars operating successfully in the yet more complex environment of the 1990s may question the critical assumptions behind Richards' assessment. Alexander Pope's Shakespeare would scarcely serve the present age, any more than our Shakespeare would serve his.

Moreover, the existence of shared standards of taste is much easier to document in broad matters than in instances of textual detail: literary scholars and other informed readers may agree in general about the authors to be included in an established canon, and about the basic shape of the works attributed to those authors, but when it comes to minute discriminations of language, the apparent consensus breaks down into wrangling and petty difference. *Hamlet* itself supplies an excellent case in point: for much of our century, at least before the new Oxford Shakespeares, editors were in substantial agreement about the broad shape of the play, thereby cementing an elite community with each other and with their discriminating readers. But when it comes to choosing or amending the precise wording of individual passages, the consensus falls into fragments and the text remains in flux, with no two editors precisely in accord. One famous example is the array of suggested language for the famous crux in 4.2 – Hamlet's sarcastic reference to Claudius and his creatures in terms of (variously) apes, apples, nuts and jaws, depending on the edition that we happen to consult.

The proliferation of readings here and elsewhere in *Hamlet* derives in part from each editor's need to document that she or he has perused the early materials independently of previous editors. But that need is itself driven by a strong urge to make "progress" against the insidious and intractable textual problems of the play. "Advancement in perfectness" has been one of the chief goals of *Hamlet* editors at least since that goal was articulated by Edward Capell in the late eighteenth century.[12] "To be or not to be" in its traditional form has been important for nineteenth- and twentieth-century culture in part because it is, unlike much of the rest of the play, a passage upon which (with the exception of two or three words) there has long been strong unanimity. Here, at least, is immortal language that exists precisely as Shakespeare intended it. And here, at last, is Shakespeare disclosing his deepest thoughts about the human condition. The soliloquy is difficult and subject to a variety of interpretations, but the words themselves can be relied on. They are woven deeply into the fabric of our culture and their static, monolithic power serves the useful function of helping to keep the community of good taste intact and deflecting attention away from textual variations elsewhere in the play that might destabilize the apparent consensus.

It will not be the business of this chapter to attack the hierarchy of taste by which "To be or not to be, that is the question" is defined as high, refined, and Shakespearean, and "To be or not to be, aye, there's the point," as low, vulgar, and fraudulent. The theoretical bases for such an argument have been clearly set out by others already cited in my notes, and the argument itself, although easily made, will not convince anyone who is not already willing to admit the fallibility of his or her own judgment. Rather, I will seek to recast the discussion about Q1 *Hamlet* entirely by considering that text and its "betters" in terms of the differing expectations created by orality and writing as competing forms of communication within the Renaissance playhouse. Was Shakespeare's theater as literate as modern editorial practice, with its insistence on the sovereign authority of Shakespeare's manuscripts and acts of writing, assumes it was? How did actors in the Elizabethan and early Jacobean playhouses learn their lines? How did they conceptualize the plays they worked on – as written "text," as oral discourse, or as a complicated mixture of both? And finally, how might recent studies of memory and mnemonics in early modern and earlier culture alter our received notions about the role of memory in the early modern theater?

For advocates of the theory of memorial reconstruction, memory is inherently contaminated and texts generated by that means, by definition untrustworthy. According to W. W. Greg, memorial reconstruction denotes "any process of transmission which involves the memory no matter at what stage or in what manner."[13] By such a definition, as I shall argue later, nearly all Renaissance playtexts are culpable in one degree or another. Over and over again within Shakespeare's plays, but particularly in *Hamlet*, bad taste is associated with an outmoded oral theatrical culture. Similarly, for twentieth-century adherents of the theory of memorial reconstruction, "bad" Shakespeare is the product of defective memory and insufficient literacy. Modern readers and critics have, quite understandably, recapitulated Shakespeare's own apparent assumptions about the relative value of oral and literate culture: good taste is associated with writing as opposed to orality; and "good" Shakespeare, with the creation of a theater that is specifically literary.

These matters are obviously highly speculative, but as we shall see, the cultural authority that defines the first quarto as "bad" *Hamlet* derives in large part from Hamlet himself, and from the new, more self-contained literary theater that he favors. When the ghost commands Hamlet to "Remember me" the prince does not trust to his memory, but writes the words down, except that he doesn't record them quite accurately: in both Q1 and Q2, the ghost thrice cries "adiew" before the command "remember." Hamlet writes down only two adieus. Modern editors follow the folio in having the ghost utter only two adieus, so that Hamlet's writing has the precision we expect of a "copy." Just as in this instance the folio version is more "literate" in its reproduction of language than either quarto version, Q2 is regularly more literary and literate than Q1 in terms of formalized criteria of difference between primarily oral and primarily literate cultures.[14] Insofar as Q2 participates more fully in our own profoundly literate assumptions about the proper shaping and complexity of art, Q2 and F (which resembles Q2 much more closely than it does Q1 in terms of language) will remain a standard against which Q1 is found wanting. But Q1 will remain like a beckoning ghost who does not write but intones, urging us to remember that the theatrical culture of the Elizabethan playhouse may have been profoundly different from the literary cultures within which *Hamlet* has been edited.

Hamlet, Q1 and Q2

The textual mystery of *Hamlet* begins with the peculiar circumstances of its early publication. The first quarto appeared in 1630 with a title page that reads in full:

THE / Tragicall Historie of / HAMLET / *Prince of Denmarke* / By William Shake-speare. / As it hath beene diuerse times acted by his Highnesse ser- / uants in the Cittie of London: as also in the two V- / niuersities of Cambridge and Oxford, and else-where / At London printed for N.L. and Iohn Trundell. / 1603.

The printer of this edition has been identified as Valentine Simmes. As has frequently been noted, there was an irregularity in the publication, in that "A booke called the Revenge of Hamlett Prince [of] Denmarke as yt was latelie Acted by the Lord Chamberleyne his servantes" had already been registered in 1602 to another printer, James Roberts.[15]

The plot thickens with the appearance of the second quarto in late 1604 and early 1605. Its title page reads:

THE / Tragicall Historie of / HAMLET, / *Prince of Denmarke.* / By William Shakespeare. / Newly imprinted and enlarged to almost as much / againe as it was, according to the true and perfect / Coppie. / AT LONDON. / Printed by I.R. for N. L. and are to be sold at his / shoppe vnder Saint Dunstons Church in / Fleetstreet. 1604 [or 1605].

This time, James Roberts, to whom *Hamlet* was registered, was the printer. For many twentieth-century editors, the second title page has seemed actively to supplant the first, so that a narration of the publication history of the play might read rather like this: some low character, probably John Trundell (who was mentioned as co-publisher on the Q1 title page, and who was known for his sponsorship of base, popular printed materials – ballads, marvellous narratives, and the like) illegally acquired a corrupt copy of the play. Rather than suffer such a debased text to be promulgated under his name, Shakespeare hastened to put the "true" play in print the very next year with the printer whom he had previously authorized to publish *Hamlet*, so that Q2 would be based on the author's genuine papers and not on a pirated copy.[16]

Recent research has somewhat diminished the cloak-and-dagger drama of this narrative: Roberts regularly printed for the publisher Nicholas Ling, whose device appears on both title pages, and Ling made a practice of acquiring texts from others in the trade. Since Roberts and Ling worked together un-interruptedly both before and after the first quarto was published in 1603, it is likely that the two reached some understanding about Q1 and that it was published with Roberts' consent.[17] Nevertheless, the two title pages, with their double and conflicting guarantees of authenticity to performance (in the case of Q1) and to the written copy (in the case of Q2), have helped to generate a strict dualism in our understanding of the two texts: Q1 was a performance text of some kind, or a debased copy thereof, with all of the corruption that such a suspect origin suggests; Q2, on the other hand, was a literary text based on the author's own manuscript "Coppie," with the promise of genuineness that such provenance implies. I am less interested in disputing this differentiation of the two quartos for descriptive purposes than in probing into the subtle moral and evidentiary valuation that causes one text to rank very high and the other, very low. Why such privilege for the literary over the theatrical?

Before delving further into the matter of provenance, however, we need to look more closely at differences between the two quarto versions. As usual with the bad quartos, the specific scapegoat function to which Q1 has been put has caused it to appear a disjointed heap of fragments rather than a respectable work of literature possessing its own claim to unity. In fact, Wilson charac-terized it as a thing "of shreds and patches," adapting Hamlet's closet scene description of Claudius as a way of rendering it both morally bad and uninterpretable.[18] To prefer Q1 over Q2 would be to demonstrate the same base perversity of taste that has caused Gertrude to prefer loathsome Claudius over fidelity to the memory of King Hamlet. Ironically, however, it is only in Q1 that the ragtag language is unequivocally applied to Claudius. In that version, Hamlet demands to know how his mother could "leaue him that bare a Monarkes minde, / For a king of clowts, of very shreads" (H 168 [G2]v),[19] and the ghost enters only after twelve more lines of dialogue. In both Q2 and F, however, the equivalent phrase does not occur until after the entrance of the ghost – a timing that makes Hamlet's meaning more problematic:

GER. No more.

                Enter Ghost

HAM. A King of shreds and patches,
     Saue me and houer ore me with your wings
     You heauenly gards: what would your gracious figure?

                            (H 170 [I3]v)

In both Q2 and F (but not in Q1) it is possible that the "King of shreds and patches" Hamlet describes is the ghost whose entrance has been recorded immediately before. In Q1 the stage directions call for the ghost to enter "*in his night gowne*" but his attire is unspecified in the alternative texts: might he be wearing a cerecloth or some other strange and irregular apparel?

Only by reference to Q1 can editors achieve certainty as to Hamlet's meaning and thereby keep intact the hierarchy of taste by which Hamlet Sr is associated with the "good" quarto and Claudius, with the "bad." Indeed, one of the defining marks of Q1 is that it is usually clearer and more straightforward than the other early texts – not only in terms of language, but also, preeminently, in terms of action. It is not a "thing of shreds and patches" if considered in its own terms, but shows the same pattern of consistent difference that we have already observed in the other "bad" quartos.

In Q1, Polonius is named Corambis, and some other names vary slightly: Ophelia is spelled Ofelia, Laertes becomes Leartes, Q2's *Gertrard* is Gertred in Q1, and *Guyldersterne* and *Rosencraus* (Q2) have the more sinister names of Gilderstone and Rossencraft. Their behavior in Q1 matches the more foreboding nomenclature. In Q2, Hamlet greets them as "good friends," refers to them later as "deare friends," and several times alludes to his love for them and theirs for him; moreover, his mother confirms that he has "much talkt" of them. In Q1, she makes no such claim and the relationship is more distant: he greets them only as "kinde Schoole-fellowes" (H 96, 98) and engages in none of the affectionate badinage with them that he does at least initially in Q2. Indeed, in Q1 their primary allegiance appears to be to Claudius – he, not Hamlet, calls them "friends" and protests his "great loue" for them (H 76). Fittingly, in

Q1, unlike Q2, Horatio expresses not the slightest regret over their death: they were Claudius's creatures from the start.

Other characters' roles are also subtly but significantly altered in the first quarto so that the line between good and evil is sharper. In Q1 Claudius is a more thoroughly villainous character than he is in Q2: he lacks the unctuous surface geniality he often displays in Q2, and works less in concord with the queen. In Q1, it is he, not Leartes [Laertes], who suggests the stratagem of the poisoned sword to ensure Hamlet's death. If Claudius is more clearly nefarious in Q1, however, Gertred is more clearly innocent of at least the worst crimes of which she stands accused.[20] She acts less in concord with Claudius, and swears to her son in the closet scene that she was unaware Claudius had dispatched her first husband: "But as I haue a soule, I sweare by heauen, / I neuer knew of this most horride murder" (H 172 G3r). Moreover, in Q1 only, at the end of the scene she hastens to promise her help in Hamlet's revenge:

> I vow by that maiesty,
> That knowes our thoughts, and lookes into our hearts,
> I will conceale, consent, and doe my best,
> What stratagem soe're thou shalt deuise.
>
> (H 176 G3)

Later on, in a scene unique to Q1, Horatio reveals to Gertred Hamlet's successful evasion of Claudius's plot for his execution in England and she responds by renewing her allegiance to her son, remarking of Claudius, "I perceiue there's treason in his lookes / That seem'd to sugar o're his villanie" and assuring Horatio that she will cover up her true feelings, "soothe and please" Claudius "for a time" only to allay his suspicions, "For murderous mindes are alwayes jealous" (H 208 [H2]v).

Hamlet, too, is less unfathomable in Q1 than in Q2, but also more "healthy minded" in the conventional meaning of the phrase. Nearly all of his language of sexual loathing is absent from Q1. To be sure, in the soliloquy parallel to Q2's more famous "O that this too too sallied flesh would melt," he exclaims in Q1, "O that this too much grieu'd and sallied flesh / Would melt to nothing," and later on in the same speech he notes (as in Q2) his mother's sexual hunger for Claudius: "Why she would hang on him, as if increase / Of appetite had growne by what it looked on" (H 32 [B4]r). But that speech is almost the only point in the first quarto version at which Hamlet seems to dwell on his mother's sexual frailty and his own "sallied flesh," and even there, the idea of his mother's gaining appetite by "looking" on Claudius lacks some of the grotesqueness of Q2's conflation of the sexual and the alimentary: "As if increase of appetite had growne / By what it fed on" (H 32).

Similarly, in the stage direction describing the dumbshow, Q1 is empty of most of the sexualization that is so prominent in Q2 and F. The Q1 stage directions read:

Enter in a Dumbe Shew, the King and the Queene, he sits downe in an Arbor, she leaues him: Then enters Lucianus with poyson in a Viall, and powres it in his eares, and goes away: Then the Queene commeth and findes him dead: and goes away with the other.

(H 140 F3r)

In this version from Q1, it is never stated on what terms she "*goes away with the other*." In Q2, by contrast, her behavior with both men is explicitly sexualized by the stage directions – the queen embraces the king and he, her; he "*declines his head vpon her necke*"; finding him dead she "*makes passionate action*" and allows herself to be wooed by the poisoner: "*shee seemes harsh awhile, but in the end accepts loue*" (H 140 [H1]v). In the Q1 version of the actual play, the murder takes place in "*guyana*" rather than "*Vienna*" and the Duke's name is *Albertus* rather than *Gonzago*. But a more crucial difference is that in the Q1 "Mouse trap" the pair has been married for "full fortie yeares" rather than thirty, as in Q2; appropriately, the husband in Q1 is more seriously burdened with age and loss of sexual potency: the "blood" that filled his "youthfull veines" now "Runnes weakely in their pipes" (H 142). In Q2 the parallel passage is, for once, less graphic than Q1: "My operant powers their functions leaue to do" (H 142).

There is a similar contrast in the two closet scenes: the Hamlet of Q2 dwells yet again on his mother's appetites: the "ranck sweat of an inseemed bed / Stewed in corruption, honying, and making loue / Ouer the nasty stie" (H 168 I3r). In Q1, his language is far less voyeuristically graphic: "Who'le chide hote blood within a Virgins heart, / When lust shall dwell within a matrons breast?" (H 168 [G2]v). For a broad stream of Freudian critics beginning with Freud himself and his disciple Ernest Jones, Hamlet is the English Oedipus – unable to kill Claudius because of his own repressed desire for his mother and covert identification with Claudius as the man who has won her away from his father.[21] That interpretation is far less available in Q1, in which most of Hamlet's "diseased" language is not present and in which most of his sexual anguish seems to relate to the breach with Ofelia rather than repressed desire for his mother. Indeed, in the speech cited above, he seems to regard "hote blood" as (relatively speaking) appropriate for a "Virgin" – perhaps for a virgin like Ofelia?

Q1 also "lacks" Hamlet's wonderfully ambiguous lines from the final soliloquy that exists only in the second quarto ". . . how stand I then / That haue a father kild, a mother staind, / Excytements of my reason, and my blood, /

And let all sleepe" (H 190 [K3]v). A Freudian reading of the passage would take its lack of clarity over agency as an unwitting confession of Hamlet's unconscious desire to possess his mother and dispose of his father – is it he who, in the labyrinthine world of his own repressed fantasies, has killed his father and stained his mother? By failing to include most of Hamlet's incestuous preoccupation with his mother's sexuality, Q1 fails to confirm one of the master discourses of the twentieth century. Given that the Freudian reading of Hamlet's relationship to Gertrude has been prominent in screen and stage versions of the play since Laurence Olivier's classic film version a half century ago, it is understandable that Q1 *Hamlet* has seemed during the same period to lack authenticity in terms of its psychodynamics.

Q1 is also more "healthy minded" than Q2 in terms of the philosophical and religious attitudes it articulates, at least to the extent that adherence to mainstream opinion can be defined as healthier than deviance. Q1 is a short, strangely powerful revenge play in which Hamlet almost entirely "lacks" the crippling melancholy or weakness or depression that many critics have found central to his character. In his conversation with Rossencraft and Gilderstone, for example, the Hamlet of Q1 is decidedly less melancholy than in the Q2 version of the speech, which confesses a pervasive heaviness of disposition that has caused Hamlet's world to lose light, color, and meaning to the point that it appears but a "pestilent congregation of vapoures" (H 100). In Q1, he complains merely "No nor the spangled heauens, nor earth nor sea, / No nor Man that is so glorious a creature, / Contents not me" (H 100 [E2]v).

Similarly, at the end of the encounter with Polonius / Corambis in which Hamlet taunts him as a "Fishmonger," Q2 has Hamlet respond to Polonius's announcement that he will take his leave with the arresting speech, "You cannot take from mee any thing that I will not more willingly part withall: except my life, except my life, except my life" (H 94 [F1]v). Q1 omits the world-weary repetition and Hamlet offers only insult: "You can take nothing from me sir, / I will more willingly part with all, / Olde doating foole" (H 94 [E2]v). In Q1's version of "O what a rogue and pesant slaue am I," by contrast, Hamlet's opening appears to display a more vehement self-contempt than in the standard version. The first line of the soliloquy in Q1 reads "Why what a dunghill idiote slaue am I?" Further on in the same soliloquy, moreover, Hamlet refers, as in Q2, to "my weakenesse and my melancholy." But in Q1 those passions have a clearer "objective correlative" in that, as part of the same speech, he articulates (in Q1 only) his bitterness at his loss of the throne: "His father murdred, and a Crowne bereft him" (H 114–18 [E4]v–F[1]r).

"To be or not to be" is also vastly different in the two quarto versions. Whatever we may think of the nervous, staccato, almost catechetical questions and answers, interspersed with disjointed speculations, that constitute the soliloquy in its Q1 form [. . .], we will note that its argument is considerably altered.

To put the matter in the baldest possible terms, in Q2, Hamlet contemplates suicide, but rejects it on account of some unknown terror in the afterlife: ills "we know not of". In Q1, he contemplates suicide but rejects it on more conventional religious grounds: not out of dread of something after death, but "for a hope of something after death" – the hope of being numbered among the "happy" rather than the "accursed." In Q2, the "vndiscouer'd country" of the afterlife is totally mysterious and unknown, despite the earlier testimony of the ghost (perhaps a sign, as W. W. Greg suggested long since, that the ghost is not to be trusted?). In Q1, the afterlife bears a familiar, more comforting shape: conscience makes men cowards in the very direct sense that he who takes revenge risks damnation. Conversely, however, he who does not take revenge can console himself with hope for the life to come. Hamlet's reservations about the revenge in Q1 are rationally arrived at, for all of the seeming dislocation of his language. Q2 is much darker and more paralyzing, in that he cannot perceive any of his alternatives as clearly preferable to the others: indeed, they all seem to converge upon the same stalemating uncertainty about an afterlife that, if he adhered to standard Christian teaching, would have a much more definable shape. Q1 Hamlet's questioning takes place against a ground of basic epistemological stability. Q2 Hamlet, at least as the play is usually interpreted, inhabits a more inhospitable, unfathomable universe – one more closely in tune with the deep skepticism of twentieth-century modernism.

In Q2, similarly, Hamlet dies uttering the enigmatic line, "the rest is silence." It is left to Horatio to provide the hope of "flights of Angels" that may (or may not) sing the dead prince to his "rest." In Q1, it is Hamlet himself who clothes his death in orthodoxy: his last words are "heauen receiue my soule" (H 266). Yet once more, good and evil are more easily distinguished than in Q2. Despite the blood he has shed, the prince dies in the hope that he has not irrevocably jeopardized his place among the righteous. Much is obviously lost in the first quarto of *Hamlet* through the absence of the moral stalemating and wide-ranging interrogation that is such an important part of most twentieth-century audiences' experience of *Hamlet* in performance and of *Hamlet* in the standard editions. Q1 Hamlet carries little of the existential angst that has endeared the play to modernists; indeed, the young prince in Q1 is scarce recognizable as the "melancholy Dane." But what is lost in terms of Hamlet's relentless, nearly manic probing of the dark borders of human existence is partly gained back by his increased capacity for action.

Q1 *Hamlet*, if recent testimony by actors, directors, and audiences is any guide, can work wonderfully well in the theater. Its rhythms are entirely different from those of Q2: what it lacks in terms of philosophic range and refinement of language, it compensates for through an abundance of theatrical energy. Q1 is "*Hamlet* with the brakes off."[22] While Q2 frequently doubles back upon itself and slows down the action with long meditative speeches, Q1 *Hamlet* has no time for prolonged meditation and very little time for soliloquies. The play moves relentlessly and powerfully from the first, horrifying encounter with the ghost to Hamlet's bloody end. The differing language of "To be or not to be" correlates with larger structure: in Q2 the ontological alternatives constitute a "question" with no obvious answer; in Q1, Hamlet's posing the alternatives instead constitutes a "point," a step along the way to a decisive conclusion: "To be or not to be – aye there's the point!"

As has frequently been noted, Q1 "straightens out" the action of the play so that Hamlet's actions follow logically one from another.[23] The two main soliloquies in the middle of the play are reversed, as they often are in modern productions: Corambis [Polonius] reads Claudius the letter in which Hamlet professes his love to Ofelia, and they decide to eavesdrop on a conversation between the two. That plan is put immediately into effect. Hamlet enters upon the lines "To be or not to be" and then launches into the Nunnery scene with Ofelia. Shortly after, the players enter and, at Hamlet's request, offer the Priam and Hecuba speech (much curtailed); Hamlet asks them to perform the "murder of *Gonsago*" with a few added lines, they exit, he launches into the soliloquy ending "The play's the thing, / Wherein I'le catch the conscience of the King" (H 118 F[1]r) and, after a brief scene between Claudius, Gertred, Rossencraft and Gilderstone, the "play within a play" commences. Hamlet moves effectively from thought to action, his every decision ironically pushing him closer to his doom. His final major soliloquy, "How all occasions doe informe against me," is "missing" from Q1, as it is from the folio version of the play.

In Q2 and modern edited versions, by contrast, Hamlet's every action is blocked or its energies "turned awry." He draws the seemingly decisive conclusion, "the play's the thing / Wherein Ile catch the conscience of the King," early on, before the encounter with Ophelia. But then his resolve is deflected: we find him brooding on suicide in "To be, or not to be," which had appeared much earlier in Q1. Well after *The Mousetrap* was supposed to settle the matter of Claudius's guilt, in Q2 (and that version only) we find Hamlet reengaging the same knotty questions as earlier, albeit from a new perspective, in his final soliloquy, "How all occasions doe informe against me." Only in Q2 is he, at this late point in the action, continuing to castigate himself for delaying the revenge.

The switchback pattern of Q2 has its own considerable fascination – Bradley thought it a Shakespearean revision that was one of the most brilliant coups of the play in terms of revelation of character.[24] But Q2 Hamlet's self-reversals do slow the play down in the theater – a major reason why directors frequently adopt the somewhat streamlined pattern of F or even the greatly increased pace of Q1 for performance. If the two quarto versions of *Hamlet* are considered intertextually, Q2 can safely be described as slow, meditative, and introspective. Q1, rather like the *Faustus* A text, is fast, powerful, and iconoclastic and offers some of the pleasures of iconoclasm: it brutally excises "idle" verbiage and strips away impediments to action. That is not to say that Q1 is to be preferred over Q2: in the absence of the icon, the power of iconoclasm is lost. And Q2, in any case, offers at the thematic level its own pleasures for the iconoclast – its restless philosophical searching can be seen as undercutting the relative orthodoxy of Q1.

Moreover, there is a fascinating correlation in the two quartos between the pacing of the action and the putative age of the prince, at least if we are willing to accept the data by which Hamlet's age has traditionally been calculated. In Q1, he is a young man of about twenty: Yorick's skull has lain in the ground "this dozen yeare," and Hamlet's memories of him are those of a child: "A fellow of infinite mirth, he hath caried mee twenty times vpon his backe, here hung those lippes that I haue Kissed a hundred times . . ." (H 234 I[1]r). In Q2, he has the same memories of Yorick, but the jester's skull "hath lyen you i'th earth 23. yeeres" (H 234 [M3]v). Q2 Hamlet has to be thirty because the sexton, who has kept his trade "man and boy thirty yeeres," began it in the year of young Hamlet's birth. (Interestingly enough, Hamlet Sr's victory over Fortinbras is also more recent in Q1: it happened a mere dozen years before, not thirty, as in Q2, which means that Hamlet is considerably younger at the time of the play than his father was at the time he conquered Fortinbras.) Q1's Hamlet has some of the breakneck impetuosity associated elsewhere in Shakespeare, as in the Renaissance generally, with youth: like the young lovers of *Romeo and Juliet*, he hastens to meet his end. By comparison, Q2 Hamlet, although capable of precipitate action, is more cautious and deliberative, perhaps even jaded, as is appropriate for a somewhat older man. Indeed, in Renaissance terms, a man of thirty was on the threshold of middle age. We would not wish to push the contrast too far: there are slow youths in Shakespeare (like Slender in *The Merry Wives of Windsor*) and plenty of rash men a decade or so older. But in both quartos of *Hamlet*, the hero's age is curiously apt in terms of the structure and language of the play.

To what are we to attribute the profound differences between Q1 and Q2? We can easily generate narratives of origin to place in competition with the theory of memorial reconstruction and its wholesale rejection of Q1.

Narrative A

> In which Shakespeare, newly arrived in London,
> tries his inexperienced hand at a play

We know that there was a *Hamlet* play extant as early as 1589, as referred to in Nashe's preface to Greene's *Menaphon* (1589). Nashe describes a new and uneducated type of playwright, "shifting companions" who can scarcely claim literacy but "will affoord you whole Hamlets, I should say handfuls of Tragicall speeches." As noted in the previous chapter, a *Hamlet* was played at Newington Butts on June 9, 1594, as part of the same run as *Titus Andronicus* and some version of *The Taming of the/a Shrew*. Thomas Lodge saw a *Hamlet* performed at the Theatre by the Lord Chamberlain's Men in or shortly before 1596: he refers in his *Wit's Misery and the World's Madness* to the pale "Visard of the ghost which cried so miserably at the Theatre, like an oister-wife, Hamlet, revenge."[25] All of these *Hamlets* but the first were specifically associated with Shakespeare's company, but none was specifically attributed to Shakespeare. Indeed, *Hamlet* was not included in Francis Meres' list of Shakespeare's plays as of 1598, although we have no reason to suppose that his list was meant to be exhaustive.

Eric Sams has recently made a spirited case for Q1 *Hamlet* as the "Ur-*Hamlet*," written by Shakespeare in 1589 or earlier. Shakespeare *could* have been in London early enough for such a feat: we have no sure evidence as to the year of his arrival. As Sams suggestively notes, the specific name Hamlet derives from none of the earlier tales of Amleth, but is closely associated with Shakespeare, who remembered "Hamlett Sadler" in his will along with Heminge and Condell and named his own son Hamlet or Hamnet Shakespeare. Another Hamlett – Katherine Hamlett – drowned in the Avon near Stratford in 1579 and was, like Ophelia, the object of a "coroner's quest."[26] Sams' theory should have elements of attractiveness for Shakespeareans in that it gives over the whole field of *Hamlet* to Shakespearean authorship. There is no longer a mysterious, lost Ur-*Hamlet* to muddy the waters of Shakespeare's dramatic creativity.

On the other hand, Sams' theory puts the Bard in rather disreputable company – among the rough and ready, semi-literate dramatists ridiculed by Nashe, and (worse yet) among oyster wives. Given the persistent tradition that Shakespeare himself played the part of the ghost, we are offered the unsavory spectacle of the Bard managing his part so "miserably" that he can be likened to a fishwife bawling her wares. Most nineteenth-century editors were able to imagine Shakespeare in his early days as part of just such a rough and tumble world, but in the mainstream twentieth-century editorial tradition, he cannot be associated with the *Hamlet* of the 1590s, either as actor or author, because the play is described by contemporaries in such low and contemptuous terms. Hence the editorial energy that has gone into separating Q2 *Hamlet* altogether from the mysterious, vanished Ur-text. However, Robert Greene himself disparaged Shakespeare by name in or before 1592 as

> an vpstart Crow, beautified with our feathers, that with his *Tygers heart wrapt in a Players hide*, supposes he is as well able to bumbast out a blanke verse as the

best of you: and being an absolute *Iohannes factotum,* is in his owne conceit the onely Shake-scene in a countrie.[27]

Despite the best efforts of editors and others, there appears to be no way around the uncomfortable fact that Shakespeare, in the early years of his career, was considered by some as *arriviste* and even, if Greene means what he appears to mean, a plagiarist, or at least a habitual borrower of more learned people's work.

My own main difficulty with Sams' argument lies in his assertion of a perfect homology between Q1 and the Ur-*Hamlet*. As editors have noted, there is no point in Q1 at which the ghost utters the precise words, "Hamlet, revenge." He addresses his son as "Hamlet" and cries for "revenge" a few lines later, but the two words are not quite juxtaposed. If the phrase in question became well enough known in the theater to inspire ridicule (we find it again in *Satiro-mastix* (1601) "my name's Hamlet reuenge: thou hast been at Paris garden hast not?"),[28] then that notoriety is perhaps sufficient reason for it to have been excised (if it was) from the play as published in 1603. But given what we know about the instability of Elizabethan playtexts in general and the marked differences among printed *Hamlet*s in particular, is it likely that *Hamlet* would have remained the same play on stage from 1589 to 1599 or even later? Q1 may well have derived from the same "corrupt" line of descent as one or more other *Hamlet*s from the 1590s. Those involved in recent productions of Q1 have sometimes noted that it seems to have the raw, inchoate energy of a work in progress.[29] But we are unlikely ever to know at what stage Shakespeare entered the process. Was he the originator of *Hamlet*, a joint originator working with other dramatists, or the reviser of an earlier play of the same name, to which he was drawn, perhaps, by the many reverberations between its title and his own earlier life in Stratford?

Narrative B

In which Shakespeare becomes dissatisfied
with his first *Hamlet* and revises it
(May be used along with Narrative A, above)

Since nearly everyone prefers Q2 over Q1 in terms of polish and poetic refinement, it is easy to generate narratives to explain Shakespeare's hypothesized revision of Q1 into Q2. We have reached the late 1590s, possibly as late as 1603. As Shakespeare matures as an artist and his company becomes increasingly prosperous, the old *Hamlet* begins to look shabby. The players call upon him to create a fuller, more polished version in much the same way that the King's Company was later to call upon Thomas Middleton to expand *A Game at Chess* from the short and inferior version he initially offered them.[30] Moreover, Richard Burbage, who has long played the title role with great success, is becoming too senior to be happy in the part of a twenty-year-old. Then too, the temper of the nation is changing: stage melancholy is becoming increasingly fashionable and the optimism of an earlier era is giving way to Jacobean gloom. Revenge plays in the ranting old Senecan mode are becoming passé and the old, relatively upbeat *Hamlet* too closely resembles the traditional pattern. It is too conventional in its ideas to suit the emerging mood of the new century.

To these public, institutional considerations may be added a host of speculations about Shakespeare's private sentiments. It is 1601 and Shakespeare has fallen into a depression, possibly brought on by the double blow of his only son Hamnet's death in 1596 and his father's death in 1601, which has re-awakened all the pain of the earlier loss. As James Joyce's Stephen Daedalus suggested in his *Hamlet* lecture (*Ulysses*, chap. [9]), Shakespeare maps his own experience of loss onto the play, reviving both of the departed. He is simultaneously father and son: the ghost, father of Hamlet, come back as from the grave to tell of horrors; the son, who of all of Shakespeare's tragic heroes, is the one most immersed in the theater, the one most like Shakespeare himself. He now finds his earlier *Hamlet* to be utterly inadequate to the mystery of the human condition, in which good and evil are so inextricably mixed as to be inseparable.

To this hypothetical narrative may be added still others. In 1601 or thereabouts, possibly as late as 1603, Shakespeare becomes despondent over the recurrence of the plague, or over the unsettled state of the nation and the obvious decline of the reigning monarch, who was to die in 1603. And indeed, as Eric Mallin has suggested, Q2 *Hamlet*, by comparison with Q1, suffers from a pall of disease like that affecting London in 1603 and other plague years: it is sicklied over not only with the pale cast of thought, but also with physical contagion.[31] The list of plausible reasons why Shakespeare should have wanted to portray the world of *Hamlet* more darkly than before is long, intriguing, and also, alas, almost entirely speculative. But there is yet another possibility.

Narrative C

In which Shakespeare,
Having written the true and perfect Copy later published as Q2, cuts down
Hamlet for performance.
(Can be used as a substitute for A and B above)

According to this scenario, Q2 precedes Q1, as in the theory of memorial reconstruction, but Q1's origins are more respectable. Shakespeare brings his new play in for reading to the company; all acknowledge that he has produced a masterpiece, but suggest that the stage version needs to be much shorter, simpler, and less philosophically complex to be accessible to the usual audience. Shakespeare, possibly with the assistance of other members of the company, obligingly constructs Q1, which, as its defenders regularly note, skillfully manages to include every significant plot element of the play in its long form, but honed into an effective piece of theater in its own right.

This narrative can be modified in a number of ways. Perhaps Shakespeare and / or the company decide that the play is too long and / or daring for a particular audience, and modify the text for a specific performance or series of performances, possibly for production on tour during one of the London plague times or earlier. Modern companies have performed Q1 *Hamlet* with as few as nine actors by using clever doubling. For Shakespeare's company, the same number would have been possible if a man (rather than a boy) played the role of the Player Queen. Although boys regularly played young women in the Elizabethan theater, men frequently played older women, and the Q1 player queen, having been married a full forty years, scarcely qualifies as young.[32]

To suppose that Shakespeare did the cutting is, of course, to attribute the monstrous brutalization of the major soliloquies to the Bard himself. It goes against the grain for us to imagine an artist deliberately lowering the level of his work's refinement; indeed, most twentieth-century advocates of the theory of authorial or authorized abridgement for Q1 have still felt the need to posit some form of playhouse corruption to account for "To be or not to be" in its Q1 form. The most noteworthy of these advocates has been Hardin Craig: although he was highly respected as a critic, his defense of the "bad" quartos fell on deaf ears in the heyday of the New Bibliography during the 1960s.[33] The sad fact is that we don't know that Shakespeare was at all committed to having his dramatic art appear only in its most polished possible form (he appears to have cared considerably more about the long lyric poems). The Q2 title page has seemed to most twentieth-century readers and editors to fall clearly into the familiar Renaissance category of a published author's lament for the theft and mutilation of his work as a result of unsupervised printing. But as we have already seen in the case of John Day and *Gorboduc*, printers and publishers could make similar laments about previous and "corrupt" printings, perhaps in part to convince the public that the new edition was an essential purchase even for buyers who already possessed the old. Nicholas Ling, the publisher of both quarto *Hamlets*, was a canny entrepreneur, and certainly capable of such a marketing gesture, as were Heminge and Condell later on in their preface to the First Folio, which similarly dismissed earlier editions of the plays as "stolne and surreptitious."

Then too, we have concrete evidence that at least one other Renaissance playwright – and one who appears to have taken more care over the publication of his dramatic work than Shakespeare did – was inclined to lengthen, shorten, and otherwise "mutilate" his own copy. Trevor Howard-Hill has demonstrated, to his own considerable dismay, that the authorial manuscripts of Thomas Middleton's *A Game at Chess* show the playwright altering his own play seemingly at will.[34] As I shall theorize later on, we may have misconceived the way in which playwrights of the period went about the business of making plays even in cases when they worked alone rather than collaboratively – they may have conceptualized them more in terms of malleable rhetorical "places" (*topoi*) than in terms of fixed language. Given the parallel case of Middleton, it would be hazardous to rule out the possibility that Shakespeare himself created the "short" *Hamlet* out of a longer version resembling Q2, quite possibly for performance before provincial audiences who might have been put off by the intellectual adventurousness of Q2.

Indeed, in Q1 the ending of the play can be interpreted as alluding metadramatically to just such performance conditions. Rather than ordering the bodies to be placed "high on a stage," according to Horatio's petition in the Q2 version, Q1 Fortinbrass orders the captains to carry "*Hamlet* like a souldier to his graue." Horatio is the one who will occupy the scaffold:

> Content your selues, Ile shew to all, the ground,
> The first beginning of this Tragedy:
> Let there a scaffold be rearde vp in the market place,
> And let the State of the world be there:
> Where you shall heare such a sad story tolde,
> That neuer mortall man could more vnfolde.
>
> (H 268 [14]r)

Horatio's public, theatrical telling of the tale in the marketplace mimetically recapitulates some of the actual performance conditions of *Hamlet* on tour, so that the "sad story" he will "vnfolde" becomes the very production of *Hamlet* in which he is performing. By 1603 the staging of a play on a scaffold erected in the marketplace would have appeared, perhaps, anachronistic, since even on tour the actors usually performed indoors or in inn yards. But the ending of Q1 *Hamlet* strongly evokes the conditions of popular performance in the absence of a fixed theater.

Our evidence, yet once more, is far from conclusive as to the chronological order of the two quarto *Hamlet*s: the Q1 ending that puts Horatio on a scaffold-stage can just as easily be interpreted as confirmation of Narrative A above, in which Shakespeare, in his "lost" early years in London during the 1580s, a time of flux and confusion for English dramatic companies generally, finds himself writing for a company as yet without a reliable permanent abode. And there are other possible scenarios: at least one scholar has argued that Q2 postdates both Q1 and F.[35] The mystery generated by the 1603 and 1604–05 title pages remains a mystery. Our admittedly hasty survey of possible narratives as to the origins and chronology of Q1 in relation to Q2 has left us with too many plausible answers, too little conclusive evidence.

Notes

1 For the purpose of this anecdote, I offer my own edited version of the first quarto of *Hamlet*, with modernized spelling and punctuation; see also Albert B. Weiner, ed., *Hamlet: The First Quarto 1603* (Great Neck, New York: Barron's Educational Series, 1962), pp. 104–05.

2 The most electrifying recent production has been Sam Walter's 1985 Q1 *Hamlet* for the Orange Tree Theatre, Richmond, which several reviewers considered the theatrical highpoint of the year in the London area. For descriptions of that and other recent productions, see the accounts in Thomas Clayton, ed., *The* Hamlet *First Published (Q1, 1603): Origins, Form, Intertextualities* (Newark: University of Delaware Press; London and Toronto: Associated University Presses, 1992), pp. 59–60 and 123–36; and Graham Holderness and Bryan Loughrey, eds, *The Tragicall Historie of Hamlet Prince of Denmarke*, Shakespearean Originals: First Editions (Hemel Hempstead, UK: Harvester Wheatsheaf, 1992), pp. 13–29. Q1 has also aroused interest on the Polish stage: see Clayton's introduction, p. 18 and n. 2. See also Marvin Rosenberg's "The First Modern English Staging of *Hamlet* Q1," in Clayton, ed., pp. 241–48, for William Poel's less successful effort in 1881.

3 New Cambridge *Hamlet*, ed. Philip Edwards (Cambridge and New York: Cambridge University Press, 1985), p. 8. See also two important recent articles: Paul Werstine, "The Textual Mystery of *Hamlet*," *Shakespeare Quarterly* 39 (1988): 1–26; and Barbara Mowat, "The Form of *Hamlet's* Fortunes," *Renaissance Drama*, n.s. 19 (1988): 97–126.

4 See Stanley Wells and Gary Taylor, *William Shakespeare: A Textual Companion* (Oxford: Clarendon Press, 1987), p. 402; and G. R. Hibbard's single-volume *Hamlet* for the Oxford Shakespeare (Oxford: Clarendon Press, 1987). As usual, for all my disagreements with them, my own thinking is strongly indebted to recent editions of the play, in particular Wells and Taylor's Oxford Shakespeare (*Textual Companion*); Edwards' New Cambridge *Hamlet* (n. 3); G. R. Hibbard's *Hamlet*; and Harold Jenkins Arden edition, *Hamlet* (London and New York: Routledge, 1982; reprinted 1987 and 1989). For readers interested in working with the second quarto and the first folio versions concurrently in a convenient pocket edition, the New Folger Library *Hamlet*, ed. Barbara Mowat and Paul Werstine (New York and London: Washington Square Press, 1992), which conflates the two texts but marks all passages unique to Q2 and all passages unique to F1, is particularly valuable. There is also a useful discussion of Q1 variants in Grace

Ioppolo, *Revising Shakespeare* (Cambridge and London: Harvard University Press, 1991), pp. 134–46, which vacillates between memorial reconstruction and authorial revision as explanations for the origins of Q1.

5 See in particular, Jenkins, ed. (n. 4); and Marga Munkelt's analysis of editorial practice, "Traditions of Emendation in *Hamlet*: The Handling of the First Quarto," in Clayton, ed. (n. 2), pp. 211–40.

6 See Charles Knight, *William Shakspere: A Biography*, 3rd edition (London: Routledge & Sons, 1867), p. 361. The theory of Q1 as an inept reconstruction of some sort was articulated during the nineteenth century, most notably by John Payne Collier, but was not dominant then. See the surveys of opinion in Hibbard, ed. (n. 4), pp. 75–76; and in George Ian Duthie, *The "Bad" Quarto of Hamlet: A Critical Study*, Shakespeare Problems VI (Cambridge: Cambridge University Press, 1941), pp. 90–91.

7 See A. C. Bradley, *Shakespearean Tragedy* (1904; reprinted New York: Meridian, 1955), p. 111, n. 2; and John Dover Wilson, *What Happens in Hamlet* (1935; reprinted Cambridge and New York: Cambridge University Press, 1990), p. 120. For Wilson's earlier views of Q1, see his "The Copy for 'Hamlet,' 1603," *Library*, 3rd series 9 (1918): 153–85; and "The 'Hamlet' Transcript, 1593" in the same volume, pp. 217–47. See also the discussion of his theories in Duthie (n. 6).

In 1919 T. S. Eliot notoriously agreed with the "disintegrator" J. M. Robertson that *Hamlet* was a palimpsest and an artistic failure – a philosophical tragedy uneasily grafted upon a much simpler and cruder revenge play closely resembling Q1. But in the case of *Hamlet*, yet once more, E. K. Chambers and the anti-disintegrationists won the day during the 1920s; thereafter, the image of the Bard "as a patcher of other men's plays" became intolerable for the twentieth-century critical mainstream. See J. M. Robertson, *The Problem of "Hamlet"* (London: George Allen & Unwin, 1919); T. S. Eliot, *The Sacred Wood* (1920; reprinted London: Methuen, 1972), pp. 95–103; his *Selected Essays, 1917–1932* (New York: Harcourt, Brace, 1932), pp. 121–26, and the contextualization of Eliot's opinion in William H. Quillian, *Hamlet and the New Poetic: James Joyce and T. S. Eliot*, Studies in Modern Literature, no. 13 (Ann Arbor, Michigan: UMI Research Press, 1983, 1975), pp. 49–77; Terence Hawkes, *Meaning by Shakespeare* (London and New York: Routledge, 1992), pp. 93–96; and his *That Shakespeherian Rag: Essays on a Critical Process* (London and New York: Methuen, 1986), pp. 92–119.

8 One recent exception is Holderness and Loughrey's edition (n. 2) an early copy of which was kindly supplied by Bryan Loughrey. For other recent work "rehabilitating" Q1 *Hamlet*, see especially Steven Urkowitz, "'Well-sayd olde Mole': Burying Three *Hamlets* in Modern Editions," in Georgianna Ziegler, ed., *Shakespeare Study Today* (New York: AMS Press, 1986), pp. 37–70; his "Good News about 'Bad' Quartos," in Maurice Charney, ed., *"Bad" Shakespeare: Revaluations of the Shakespeare Canon* (Rutherford: Farleigh Dickinson University Press, 1988), pp. 189–206; and "Back to Basics: Thinking about the *Hamlet* First Quarto," in Clayton, ed. (n. 2), pp. 257–91. See also Philip C. McGuire's essay in the same volume, "Which Fortinbras, Which *Hamlet*?" pp. 151–78, which the author kindly sent me in manuscript; and Kathleen O. Irace's discussion in *Reform-*

ing the "Bad" Quartos: Performance and Provenance of Six Shakespearean First Editions
(Newark: University of Delaware Press; London: Associated University Presses,
1994), which argues for Q1 as memorially reconstructed but still worthy of perusal.

9 See in particular their *Textual Companion* (n. 4), pp. 23–31 and 398. The Norton
Shakespeare currently in preparation will, in using the Oxford text, presumably
keep its hypothesis of memorial reconstruction for Q1; similarly, Kathleen Irace's
forthcoming Cambridge edition of Q1 will posit it as memorially reconstructed.
But the critical landscape is gradually changing. See, in addition to Holderness
and Loughrey's edition of Q1 (n. 2), two recent editions that leave open the matter
of Q1's origins: the Folger edition, ed. Mowat and Werstine (n. 4), and the new
Three-Text Hamlet, ed. Paul Bertram and Bernice W. Kliman (New York: AMS
Press, 1991), cited in the present study as H. The *New Variorum Hamlet*, ed.
Bernice Kliman and William Hutchings with anticipated completion in 2001, will
appear in both computerized hyper-text and in print format, and will enormously
facilitate textual work on the play.

10 Cited from T. M. Raysor, ed., *Coleridge's Shakespearean Criticism* (London:
Constable, 1930), 1:21.

11 See Barbara Herrnstein Smith, *Contingencies of Value: Alternative Perspectives for
Critical Theory* (Cambridge and London: Harvard University Press, 1988); Pierre
Bourdieu, *Distinction: A Social Critique of the Judgment of Taste*, trans. Richard Nice
(Cambridge and London: Harvard University Press, 1984); and Terry Eagleton,
The Ideology of the Aesthetic (Oxford: Basil Blackwell, 1990).

12 Cited from Boswell's *Malone's Shakespeare* 1: 134–35, in J. D. Wilson, *The
Manuscript of Shakespeare's Hamlet, and the Problems of Its Transmission: An Essay
in Critical Bibliography*, 2 vols (New York: Macmillan; Cambridge: Cambridge
University Press, 1934), 1:2.

13 W. W. Greg, *Two Elizabethan Stage Abridgements: The Battle of Alcazar & Orlando
Furioso*, Malone Society Extra Volume, 1922 (Oxford: Frederick Hall, 1923),
p. 256.

14 Although I am skeptical about the technological determinism of some of the arguments in the first two authors in the following list, my speculations in this chapter
are strongly indebted to: Walter J. Ong, *Orality and Literacy: The Technologizing
of the Word* (London and New York: Methuen, 1982); Jack Goody, *The Interface
between the Written and the Oral*, Studies in Literacy, Family, Culture and the State
(Cambridge and New York: Cambridge University Press, 1987); his earlier book
in the same series, *The Logic of Writing and the Organization of Society* (Cambridge
and New York: Cambridge University Press, 1986); and Ruth Finnegan's extension and critique in *Literacy and Orality: Studies in the Technology of Communication* (Oxford: Basil Blackwell, 1988).

15 Cited from Jenkins, ed. (n. 4), p. 13.

16 For recent editorial discussion and attenuation of this hypothetical scenario, see
Jenkins, ed. (n. 4), pp. 13–18, Hibbard, ed. (n. 4), pp. 67–71; and Edwards, ed.
(n. 3), pp. 9–10.

17 See Gerald D. Johnson, "Nicholas Ling, Publisher 1580–1607," *Studies in
Bibliography* 38 (1985): 203–14, and his "John Trundle and the Book-Trade

1603–1626," *Studies in Bibliography* 39 (1986): 177–99. Despite Trundle's poor reputation among modern editors, some of his publications were highly interesting. He was, for example, the publisher of *Hic Mulier* and *Haec-Vir*.

18 Wilson (n. 12), 1:20; other scholars (also with Claudius in mind?) refer to the play as a patchwork: see in particular Duthie's definitive dismissal of Q1 (n. 6).

19 Here and throughout, the *Hamlet* texts are cited from *The Three-Text Hamlet*. I have also checked all Q1 citations either against the Huntington Library copy of Q1 or against Q, and have checked Q2 citations against Q. For the convenience of readers not in possession of the parallel-text edition, my citations include signature numbers for substantive quotations in addition to the page numbers from H.

20 For recent readings of Q1 Gertred, see, for example, Steven Urkowitz, "Five Women Eleven Ways: Changing Images of Shakespearean Characters in the Earliest Texts," in *Images of Shakespeare*, Proceedings of the Third Congress of the International Shakespeare Association, 1986, ed. Werner Habicht, D. J. Palmer, and Roger Pringle (Newark: University of Delaware Press; London and Toronto: Associated University Presses, 1988), pp. 292–304; Kathleen Irace, "Adapting *Hamlet* Q1 to Zeffirelli," paper presented at the Shakespeare Association of America seminar on text, 1992; and Dorothea Kehler, "The First Quarto of *Hamlet*: Reforming the Lusty Widow," paper presented at the SAA seminar on text, 1994.

21 Ernest Jones, *Hamlet and Oedipus* (1949; reprinted New York: Norton, 1976), written, according to Jones, "as an exposition of a footnote in Freud's 'Traumdeutung' (1900), p. 9."

22 Quoted from Peter Guinness in Brian Loughrey, "Q1 in Recent Performance: An Interview," Clayton, ed. (n. 2), p. 128.

23 See Loughrey (n. 22) and the current of minority opinion represented in Frank G. Hubbard, ed., *The First Quarto Edition of Shakespeare's Hamlet*, University of Wisconsin Studies in Language and Literature no. 8 (Madison: [University of Wisconsin], 1920), pp. 32–35; Weiner, ed. (n. 1); Maxwell E. Foster, *The Play behind the Play*: Hamlet *and Quarto One*, ed. Anne Shiras (Pittsburgh: Privately published by the Foster Executors, 1991); Hardin Craig, *A New Look at Shakespeare's Quartos* (Stanford: Stanford University Press, 1961), pp. 78–82; Urkowitz (n. 20); and Holderness and Loughrey, eds (n. 2), pp. 13–29.

24 Bradley (n. 7), pp. 112–13, nn.

25 Nashe and Lodge are cited from Geoffrey Bullough, ed., *Narrative and Dramatic Sources of Shakespeare*, vol. 7 (London: Routledge & Kegan Paul; New York: Columbia University Press, 1973), pp. 15, 24.

26 Eric Sams, "Taboo or Not Taboo? The Text, Dating and Authorship of *Hamlet*, 1589–1623," *Hamlet Studies* 10 (1988): 12–46.

27 Robert Greene, *Groats-worth of Wit* . . . (London: for Richard Oliue, 1596), [E3]v–[E4]r.

28 *The Dramatic Works of Thomas Dekker*, 4 vols, ed. Fredson Bowers (Cambridge: Cambridge University Press, 1953), 1:351.

29 See in particular Peter Guinness's comments on Q1 in Loughrey (n. 22), p. 124.

30 See Trevor Howard-Hill's speculation in "The Author as Scribe or Reviser? Middleton's Intentions in *A Game at Chess*," *TEXT* 3 (1987): 305–18.

31 Eric S. Mallin, *Inscribing the Time: Shakespeare and the End of Elizabethan England* (Berkeley, Los Angeles, and London: University of California Press, 1995). The hypothesis that Shakespeare wrote Q2 while the theaters were closed during plaguetime conflicts with Leeds Barroll's stimulating recent argument that he tended to do his writing for the stage when the theaters were open, and also with my speculations below about the orality of the Shakespearean theater. See Barroll's *Politics, Plague, and Shakespeare's Theater: The Stuart Years* (Ithaca and London: Cornell University Press, 1991).

32 For the doubling of roles, see Loughrey (n. 22), p. 127, and Scott McMillin's differing view in "Casting the *Hamlet* Quartos. The Limit of Eleven," in Clayton, ed. (n. 2), pp. 179–94.

33 See Craig (n. 23), pp. 78–82. His arguments are refined and amplified in Robert E. Burkhart, *Shakespeare's Bad Quartos* (The Hague and Paris: Mouton, 1975), pp. 96–113.

34 Howard-Hill (n. 30); see also Ioppolo (n. 4), pp. 70–76.

35 See David Ward, "The King and *Hamlet*," *Shakespeare Quarterly* 43 (1992): 280–302; and, for a sense of the continuing malleability of the chronological arrangement of the texts, G. R. Hibbard's revision of the argument made in his Oxford Shakespeare *Hamlet* edition, "The Chronology of the Three Substantive Texts of Shakespeare's *Hamlet*," in Clayton, ed. (n. 2), pp. 79–89.

14

Performance: An Overview

The history of modern performance criticism is usually traced to the work of Arthur Colby Sprague. In his *Shakespeare and the Actors* (1944), Sprague traced the accumulated stage business of the plays' theatrical history from the Restoration to the beginning of the nineteenth century, arguing that 'Shakespeare's plays were written for performance, and surely, through performance, light has been shed on many dark places in them' (Sprague, 1944, p. xxv). Since Sprague, approaches to Shakespeare in performance have diverged to include accounts by theatre practitioners, theoretical discussions of the dynamics of theatre and, latterly, film, stage histories showing how individual plays have changed over a long period of productions, reviews and interpretations of current individual performances or productions, reconstructions of the contexts of historical productions, speculative accounts of theatrical possibilities, and theories of intention and reception. There is as much fruitful debate in this as in any other approach to Shakespeare.

In *Moment by Moment by Shakespeare* (1985), Gary Taylor attempts to analyse Shakespeare in performance from the perspective of the spectator and to investigate the pleasure of theatre-going through a sophisticated 'study of response' (Taylor, 1985, p. 3). Taylor argues that plays in performance unfold as a series of moments, not a static whole. He examines the assassination of Julius Caesar, describing how the movements on stage and the different characters add to the unease and confusion. Taylor's other chapters take *Twelfth Night*, *Henry V* and *King Lear* as examples, concluding:

> The dramatist's manipulation of emphasis might therefore be described in terms of his control of the direction, distance, velocity, mass, and impact of a hypothesis moving through a very particular kind of space. At least, any adequate description of how an audience responds to particular moments in that movement must take account of all these factors, and must at the same time resist all

of the associated occupational prejudices of the academic reader. I believe that anyone who could achieve such a description would indeed have succeeded in catching Shakespeare 'in the act of greatness'. (p. 236)

In *The Shakespeare Revolution* – the title refers to his argument that 'the initiative in recovering Shakespeare has shifted to the theatre' (Styan, 1977, p. 232) – J. L. Styan argues that both page and stage are needed for the fullest appreciation: 'the scholar will modify the actor's illumination, the actor will modify the scholar's, a process of infinite adjustment' (p. 237). The book discusses different eras in twentieth-century Shakespearean production. In his *Perspectives on Shakespeare in Performance* (2000), however, Styan proposes a more antithetical relationship between criticism and theatre:

> Criticism is inevitably a generalizing activity, whereas the theatre experience is always particular; criticism is reflective and docile, whereas perceptions in the theatre are wild and immediate and alive. Yet by performance, notions and theories can at least be tested, and the ultimate question can be asked – 'Does it work?' (Styan, 2000, pp. 5–6)

H. R. Coursen's *Shakespearean Performance as Interpretation* (1992) sides with this approach:

> A Shakespearean script exists only in performance. Period. Performance sharpens 'the text' necessarily in this or that direction. We are free to debate or enjoy the choices a director and his actors make. But the debate has relevancy only as it responds to performance. Otherwise, 'the text' becomes a spaceship filled with tinkerers and dial-watchers, but with no destination. (Coursen, 1992, p. 15)

Harry Berger's *Imaginary Audition: Shakespeare on Stage and Page* (1989) takes issue with the proponents of what he dubs 'New Histrionicism': 'that reading is irresponsible unless it imitates playgoing' (Berger, 1989, p. xii). Instead, through a critique of the limited methodology of current performance criticism, including Taylor (1985) and Styan (1977), he proposes the practice of 'imaginary audition' as

> an attempt to reconstruct text-centered reading in a way that incorporates the perspective of imaginary audition and playgoing; an attempt to put into play an approach that remains text-centered but focuses on the interlocutionary politics and theatrical features of performed drama so as to make them impinge at every point on the most suspicious and antitheatrical of readings. (p. xiv)

Richard Levin's 'Performance-Critics *vs* Close Readers in the Study of English Renaissance Drama' (1986) also proposes that both schools of criticism can learn from each other: 'one of the most valuable contributions that performance-criticism might make would be to curb the excesses of the close readers of the thematic and ironic schools, whose interpretations of the plays of this period are often so far removed from theatrical experience that they could not be conveyed in any performance' (Levin, 1986, p. 545). 'Once we acknowledge that the plays of Shakespeare and his fellow dramatists were written for the stage, then it necessarily follows that any interpretation of them that cannot be conveyed on the stage could not have been intended by the author and so must be rejected' (p. 547).

Opposed to such deference to the theatre, Martin Buzacott, in his *The Death of the Actor*, questions the 'current social and aesthetic supremacy of *actors* in general' (p. 7). Following Barthes' proleptic declaration of 'the death of the author', Buzacott announces the death of the actor as 'a body devoid of any cultural authority', instead arguing that 'Shakespearean texts speak regardless of the individual who presumes to be their mouthpiece' (Buzacott, 1991, p. 142). *Shakespeare Quarterly* 36 (1985) includes a special issue 'Reviewing Shakespeare', with essays by Cary Mazer, Alan Dessen, Robert Speaight and H. R. Coursen. Thompson and Thompson (1989) gather a collection of essays on performance criticism which review its methodology and practice, including a useful bibliography (pp. 252–6). W. B. Worthen's discussion of performance criticism (1989) usefully reviews a number of different positions, arguing for the need to locate the claims of these approaches as criticism, and to integrate performance with other theoretical and methodological enquiries. Alan Sinfield's essay in Dollimore and Sinfield's *Political Shakespeare: New Essays in Cultural Materialism* (1985; 2nd edn, 1994) offers one example of this integration: in 'Royal Shakespeare: Theatre and the Making of Ideology', Sinfield discusses the ideological work of the Royal Shakespeare Company in Britain since the 1960s and argues for a more incisive critique of that '*Shakespeare* – the whole aura of elusive genius and institutionalised profundity' (Sinfield, 1985, p. 178) which is sustained through theatrical means. In 'Thatcher's Shakespeare?' (1989), Isobel Armstrong extends Sinfield's analysis in her discussion of the relationship between 'radical academic critique and the performing arts', and in his Afterword to Holderness (ed.), *The Shakespeare Myth* (1988), Terry Eagleton criticizes the theatre practitioners represented in the volume, including Jonathan Miller and Sam Wanamaker, for failing to take up the challenge of radical Shakespeare critics: their 'bland Hampstead bohemianism' promotes 'depressing' 'liberal pluralism' and 'depoliticising eclecticism', and their 'dismally regressive opinions' are at odds with avant-garde political scholarship (Holderness, 1988, pp. 206–7).

A recent growth in performance criticism has been in published diary accounts by actors of particular roles or productions, giving the practitioners' perspective. Brian Cox, for example, in his *The Lear Diaries* (1992), discusses his performance in Deborah Warner's National Theatre production of *King Lear*, giving an insight into its logistics as well as interpretative aspects, including the Fool's use of a clown's red nose, which was finally placed on the body of the dead Cordelia, and the party with which the production began. A production of *Titus Andronicus* in a South Africa emerging from the apartheid era is the subject of Antony Sher and Gregory Doran's *Woza Shakespeare!* (1996). Janet Suzman discusses a South African *Othello* in Bate, Levenson and Mehl (1998). In *Clamorous Voices: Shakespeare's Women Today* (1988), Carol Rutter mediates interviews with a number of Shakespearean actors. In the chapter on *Macbeth*, Sinead Cusack gives a detailed account of her performance in the production co-starring Jonathan Pryce and directed by Adrian Noble (1986), describing her attempts to break out of a stereotypical 'black widow spider of theatre tradition' (Rutter and Evans, 1988, p. 57) and to uncover the domestic tragedy of what the production imagined as the Macbeths' lost child. Other actors talk about their roles in the four volumes of the *Players of Shakespeare* series edited by Philip Brockbank (volume 1, 1985), which includes essays on the Nurse in *Romeo and Juliet*, Timon, Hamlet and Polonius; by Jackson and Smallwood (volume 2, 1988) including Mercutio, Ophelia, the Fool in *King Lear*, Othello and Iago; in volume 3 (1993), Hamlet and Titus Andronicus (reproduced on pp. 337–49); and in volume 4 (1998, ed. Smallwood), Menenius in *Coriolanus*, Brutus, Macbeth, and Friar Lawrence of *Romeo and Juliet*. Michael Pennington's *Hamlet: A User's Guide* (1997) combines autobiography and textual analysis from the actor's viewpoint. In her *Modern Hamlets and Their Soliloquies* (1992), Mary Z. Maher discusses performances by Hamlets from Gielgud to Kevin Kline. Barton's 1984 volume *Playing Shakespeare* reports on workshops in which actors discuss and experiment with different readings of Shakespeare's language.

John Russell Brown, another pioneer of performance approaches, discusses *Shakespeare's Plays in Performance* (1966), in which he combines a speculative discussion of the plays' theatrical potential through careful attention to matters of structure, plotting, grouping and movement, with an account of specific recent performances including Franco Zeffirelli's *Romeo and Juliet* (1960–2). Ralph Berry's *Shakespeare in Performance* (1993) gives an account of how casting and doubling make theatrical meaning. In addition to chapters on *King Lear*, *Coriolanus* and *Measure for Measure*, Berry discusses a number of productions of *Hamlet* and the different effects of doubling, for example, Ghost / Fortinbras, Ghost / Claudius, Ghost / Laertes, Polonius / Gravedigger, or Ghost / Hamlet. Virginia Vaughan's *Othello, a Contextual History* (1994) discusses the different theatrical contexts, from the Restoration to the 1990s, in which aspects of Shakespeare's text have been emphasized or repressed. Carol Rutter's *Enter the Body* (2001) focuses on the material bodies of women on the stage: Ophelia's body in the grave in four film *Hamlet*s,

Cordelia's corpse at the end of *King Lear*, the whitening of Cleopatra in performance, the specifics of costumed female bodies in *Troilus and Cressida* and Zoe Wanamaker's performance of Emilia in Trevor Nunn's 1989 Stratford production.

A number of series offer longitudinal stage histories of specific plays. Marvin Rosenberg's *The Masks of Othello* (1961) synthesizes critical approaches with theatrical conceptions and works through the play scene by scene. The same method is used in his volumes on *King Lear* (1972), *Macbeth* (1978), and *Hamlet* (1992). The *Shakespeare in Performance* series includes a number of volumes on individual tragedies, including Alexander Leggatt on *King Lear* (1991), which covers stage performances by Gielgud, Scofield, Gambon, Sher and Hordern, and film versions directed by Brook, Kozintsev and Olivier; Bernice Kliman on *Macbeth* (1992) includes stage pairings of McKellan and Dench, Olivier and Leigh, three different television versions and the films by Welles and Polanski; Alan Dessen on *Titus Andronicus* gives particular emphasis to Peter Brook's landmark performance and the production by Deborah Warner (also described by Brian Cox, pp. 337–49); Jill Levenson on *Romeo and Juliet* (1987) considers the play from its Elizabethan performances to Zeffirelli's film of 1968. Another series, *Shakespeare in Production*, covers performances of individual plays with a substantial introduction outlining the stage history, and a text of the play annotated with performance examples. Titles in the series include Robert Hapgood on *Hamlet* (1999), Hankey on *Othello* (1987), Bratton on *King Lear* (1987) and Madelaine on *Antony and Cleopatra* (1998). Dennis Kennedy's *Looking at Shakespeare: A Visual History of Twentieth-Century Performance* (1993) combines methodological and descriptive commentary, and the contributions to his collection *Foreign Shakespeare: Contemporary Performance* (1993) shifts the focus away from British theatre.

By contrast with these studies, which usually favour culturally central productions in Stratford-upon-Avon, London and Hollywood, John Russell Brown's polemic *Free Shakespeare* (1997) argues that 'seeing the usual kinds of Shakespeare production will not help the reader to advance further' (Brown, 1997, p. 3). Brown suggests that directors may impose 'a confinement, a cutting down of a work founded on something other than an intellectual idea' (p. 14), and advocates 'radical experiment' (p. 83), much of it based on Elizabethan staging practices such as cue-scripts for actors, the same lighting for stage and audience and stressing 'the explorative and fluid engagement for which they were written' (p. 82). The most developed account of recreated Elizabethan staging is Pauline Kiernan's *Staging Shakespeare at the New Globe* (1999), which reflects on the early findings of the rebuilt Globe theatre. Standard works on the Shakespearean theatre are by Gurr (3rd edn, 1992) and Thomson (2nd edn, 1992). Gurr's work on *Playgoing in Shakespeare's London*

(2nd edn, 1996) and *The Shakespearian Playing Companies* (1996) develop this field.

The discussion of Shakespeare in recent performance has flourished in the area of film and television productions of the plays. Pioneering studies by Manvell (1971) and Hamilton Ball on silent versions (1968) were followed by Jorgens (1979), who usefully divided Shakespearean film into the 'theatrical' – in which film is used to record a performance designed for theatrical representation, as in the Broadway production of *Hamlet* directed by John Gielgud and starring Richard Burton (1964); the 'realist' – which uses film's mimetic qualities to situate the play in a realist context, such as the film of *Hamlet* by Kenneth Branagh (1996); and the 'filmic' – where the director is a 'film poet, whose works bear the same relation to the surfaces of reality as poems do to ordinary conversation' (Jorgens, 1979, p. 10), and here an example might be the Russian Grigori Kozintsev's version of *Hamlet* (1964). Anthony Davies' *Filming Shakespeare's Plays* (1988) focuses on film adaptations by Olivier, Welles, Brook and Kurosawa, bringing a particular awareness of spatial dynamics and arguing that the success of Shakespearean films 'depends ultimately on the extent to which their spatial strategies accommodate essential theatricality within a dramatic framework which is filmic' (Davies, 1988, p. 25). Also concerned with the distinctions between stage and film is H. R. Coursen's *Shakespeare: The Two Traditions* (1999) which attempts to identify the differences between the two media in terms of the relative importance of language and image. Deborah Cartmell in *Interpreting Shakespeare on Screen* (2000) has chapters on *Hamlet*, *Othello* and *Romeo and Juliet* and is particularly alert to the pedagogical context of Shakespearean films. John Collick's *Shakespeare, Cinema and Society* (1989) stresses the Victorian antecedents of silent Shakespeare films, and the cultural diversity of the genre as practised by Kozintzev and Kurosawa. *Watching Shakespeare on Television* (1993) by H. R. Coursen develops some of the specifics and the implications of the reduced format of Shakespearean film on video and small screen. Susan Willis (1991) discusses the BBC television Shakespeare series. Coursen's *Shakespeare in Production: Whose History?* (1996) discusses and contextualizes a number of productions of the 1990s and earlier. Contributors to Russell Jackson (ed.), *The Cambridge Companion to Shakespeare on Film* (2000) consider specific genres and plays, including J. Lawrence Guntner on '*Hamlet*, *Macbeth* and *King Lear* on Film' (pp. 117–34) and Harry Keyishian's account of 'Shakespeare and Movie Genre: The Case of *Hamlet*' (pp. 72–84), as well as assessments of Olivier, Welles, Kozintsev, Zeffirelli and Branagh, and a section on 'critical issues' including Carol Chillington Rutter, 'Looking at Shakespeare's Women on Film' (pp. 241–60), and Neil Forsyth's 'Shakespeare the Illusionist: Filming the Supernatural' (p. 274).

Further Reading

Armstrong, Isobel. 'Thatcher's Shakespeare?' *Textual Practice* 3 (1989): 1–14.

Ball, Robert Hamilton. *Shakespeare on Silent Film: A Strange Eventful History*. London: Allen & Unwin, 1968.

Barton, John. *Playing Shakespeare*. London: Methuen, 1984.

Bate, Jonathan, Levenson, Jill L., and Mehl, Dieter. *Shakespeare and the Twentieth Century: The Selected Proceedings of the International Shakespeare Association World Congress, Los Angeles, 1996*. Newark; London: University of Delaware Press; Associated University Presses, 1998.

Berger, Harry. *Imaginary Audition: Shakespeare on Stage and Page*. Berkeley: University of California Press, 1989.

Berry, Ralph. *On Directing Shakespeare: Interviews with Contemporary Directors*. London: Hamish Hamilton, 1989.

—*Shakespeare in Performance: Castings and Metamorphoses*. Basingstoke: Macmillan, 1993.

Bratton, J. S. *King Lear*. Plays in Performance. Bristol: Bristol Classical Press, 1987.

Brockbank, Philip, et al. *Players of Shakespeare: Essays in Shakespearian Performance by Players with the Royal Shakespeare Company*, vol. 1. Cambridge: Cambridge University Press, 1985.

Brown, John Russell. *Shakespeare's Plays in Performance*. London: Edward Arnold, 1966.

—*Free Shakespeare*. London: Applause, 1997.

Buchman, Lorne M. *Still in Movement: Shakespeare on Screen*. New York; Oxford: Oxford University Press, 1991.

Burnett, Mark Thornton, and Wray, Ramona. *Shakespeare, Film, Fin de Siècle*. Basingstoke: Macmillan, 2000.

Buzacott, Martin. *The Death of the Actor: Shakespeare on Page and Stage*. London: Routledge, 1991.

Cartmell, Deborah. *Interpreting Shakespeare on Screen*. Basingstoke: Macmillan, 2000.

Collick, John. *Shakespeare, Cinema and Society*. Manchester: Manchester University Press, 1989.

Coursen, Herbert R. *Shakespearean Performance as Interpretation*. Newark; London: University of Delaware Press; Associated University Presses, 1992.

—*Watching Shakespeare on Television*. Rutherford NJ; London; Cranbury, NJ: Fairleigh Dickinson University Press; Associated University Presses, 1993.

—*Shakespeare in Production: Whose History?* Athens: Ohio University Press, 1996.

—*Shakespeare: The Two Traditions*. Madison NJ; Associated University Presses, 1999.

Cox, C. B. *The Lear Diaries: The Story of the Royal National Theatre's Productions of Shakespeare's Richard III and King Lear*. London: Methuen, 1992.

Davies, Anthony. *Filming Shakespeare's Plays: The Adaptations of Laurence Olivier, Orson Wells, Peter Brook and Akira Kurosawa*. Cambridge: Cambridge University Press, 1988.

Dawson, Anthony B. *Watching Shakespeare: A Playgoers' Guide*. Basingstoke: Macmillan, 1988.

Dollimore, Jonathan, and Sinfield, Alan. *Political Shakespeare: New Essays in Cultural Materialism*. Manchester: Manchester University Press, 1985; 2nd edn, 1994.

Gurr, Andrew. *The Shakespearean Stage 1574–1642*, 3rd edn. Cambridge: Cambridge University Press, 1992.

— *Playgoing in Shakespeare's London*, 2nd edn. Cambridge: Cambridge University Press, 1996.

— *The Shakespearian Playing Companies*. Oxford: Clarendon Press, 1996.

Hankey, Julie. *Othello*. Plays in Performance. Bristol: Bristol Classical Press, 1987.

Hapgood, Robert. *Hamlet, Prince of Denmark*. Cambridge: Cambridge University Press, 1999.

Holderness, Graham. *The Shakespeare Myth*. Manchester: Manchester University Press, 1988.

Jackson, Russell. *The Cambridge Companion to Shakespeare on Film*. Cambridge: Cambridge University Press, 2000.

—, and R. L. Smallwood. *Players of Shakespeare 2: Further Essays in Shakespearean Performance*. Cambridge: Cambridge University Press, 1988.

— *Players of Shakespeare 3: Further Essays in Shakespearian [sic] Performance*. Cambridge: Cambridge University Press, 1993.

Jorgens, Jack J. *Shakespeare on Film*. A Midland Book. Bloomington; London: Indiana University Press, 1979.

Kennedy, Dennis. *Foreign Shakespeare: Contemporary Performance*. Cambridge: Cambridge University Press, 1993.

— *Looking at Shakespeare: A Visual History of Twentieth-century Performance*. Cambridge: Cambridge University Press, 1993.

Kiernan, Pauline. *Staging Shakespeare at the New Globe*. Basingstoke: Macmillan, 1999.

Kliman, Bernice W. *Hamlet: Film, Television, and Audio Performance*. Rutherford NJ; London: Fairleigh Dickinson University Press; Associated University Presses, 1988.

— *Macbeth*. Manchester: Manchester University Press, 1992.

Kozintsev, Grigori. *King Lear: The Space of Tragedy: The Diary of a Film Director*. London: Heinemann, 1977.

Leggatt, Alexander. *King Lear*. Manchester: Manchester University Press, 1991.

Levenson, Jill L. *Romeo and Juliet*. Manchester: Manchester University Press, 1987.

Levin, Richard. 'Performance-Critics *vs* Close Readers in the Study of English Renaissance Drama'. *Modern Language Review* 81 (1986): 545–59.

McKernan, Luke, and Terris, Olwen. *Walking Shadows: Shakespeare in the National Film and Television Archive*. London: British Film Institute, 1994.

Madelaine, Richard. *Antony and Cleopatra*. Cambridge: Cambridge University Press, 1998.

Maher, Mary Zenet. *Modern Hamlets and their Soliloquies*. Iowa City: University of Iowa Press, 1992.

Manvell, Roger. *Shakespeare and the Film*. London: Dent, 1971.

Mazer, Cary M. 'Shakespeare, the Reviewer, and the Theatre Historian'. *Shakespeare Quarterly* 36 (1985): 648–61.

Pennington, Michael. *Hamlet: A User's Guide*. London: Nick Hern, 1997.

Rosenberg, Marvin. *The Masks of Othello: The Search for the Identity of Othello, Iago, and Desdemona by Three Centuries of Actors and Critics*. Berkeley: University of California Press, 1961.

— *The Masks of King Lear*. Berkeley: University of California Press, 1972.

— *The Masks of Macbeth*. Berkeley: University of California Press, 1978.

— *The Masks of Hamlet*; Newark; London: University of Delaware Press; Associated University Presses, 1992.

Rutter, Carol Chillington. *Enter the Body: Women and Representation on Shakespeare's Stage*. London: Routledge, 2001.

—, and Evans, Faith. *Clamorous Voices: Shakespeare's Women Today*. London: Women's Press, 1988.

Sher, Antony, and Doran, Gregory. *Woza Shakespeare!: Titus Andronicus in South Africa*. London: Methuen Drama, 1996.

Smallwood, R. L. *Players of Shakespeare 4: Further Essays in Shakespearian [sic] Performance*. Cambridge: Cambridge University Press, 1998.

Sprague, Arthur Colby. *Shakespeare and the Actors: The Stage Business in his Plays (1660–1905)*. Cambridge, Mass: Harvard University Press, 1944.

Styan, J. L. *The Shakespeare Revolution: Criticism and Performance in the Twentieth Century*. Cambridge: Cambridge University Press, 1977.

— *Perspectives on Shakespeare in Performance*. Studies in Shakespeare, vol. 11. New York; Canterbury: P. Lang, 2000.

Suzman, Janet. 'South Africa in *Othello*'. *Shakespeare and the Twentieth Century*, eds Jonathan Bate and Jill Levenson, 1998. 23–40.

Taylor, Gary. *Moment by Moment by Shakespeare*. London: Macmillan, 1985.

Thompson, Marvin, and Thompson, Ruth. *Shakespeare and the Sense of Performance: Essays in the Tradition of Performance Criticism in Honor of Bernard Beckerman*. Newark; London: University of Delaware Press; Associated University Presses, 1989.

Thomson, Peter. *Shakespeare's Theatre*. London: Routledge, 2nd edn, 1992.

Vaughan, Virginia Mason. *Othello: A Contextual History*. Cambridge: Cambridge University Press, 1994.

Willis, Susan. *The BBC Shakespeare Plays: Making the Televised Canon*. Chapel Hill; London: University of North Carolina Press, 1991.

Worthen, W. B. 'Deeper Meanings and Theatrical Technique: The Rhetoric of Performance Criticism'. *Shakespeare Quarterly* 40 (1989): 441–455.

15

Performance: Critical Extracts

Titus Andronicus

Brian Cox

Brian Cox's essay is an account of his portrayal of Titus in Deborah Warner's acclaimed production of the play for the Royal Shakespeare Company in 1987. Cox approaches the play from an actor's, rather than a scholar's, point of view, and this is both the strength and the limitation of this piece. It is revealing about the tone of the play, and the discovery of its macabre humour, and more generally about the way productions make sense of difficult texts. Its paraphrases of Titus' mood show how an actor gets into role and understands a character, rather than the way in which motive and plot might be understood through literary analysis.

Brian Cox, '*Titus Andronicus*', in *Players of Shakespeare 3*, Russell Jackson and Robert Smallwood (eds). Cambridge: Cambridge University Press, 1993.

Brian Cox played the title role in Deborah Warner's production of *Titus Andronicus* at the Swan Theatre, Stratford, in 1987, and the following year in the Pit Theatre at the Barbican; the performance won him the Olivier 'Best Actor in a revival' award. It was his first season in Stratford and his other roles that year were Petruccio in *The Taming of the Shrew* and Paul Cash in *Fashion*, with Vershinin in *Three Sisters* added in the Barbican season. Earlier roles for the RSC in London had been Danton in *The Danton Affair*, John Tarleton in *Misalliance*, and Timothy Bellboys in *A Penny for a Song*. A wide range of earlier work in Edinburgh, Nottingham, Birmingham, Manchester, for the National Theatre, and elsewhere had included Iago in *Othello*, De Flores in *The Changeling*, Orlando in *As You Like It*, Brutus in *Julius Caesar*, the title roles in *Macbeth* and in *Peer Gynt*, Gregers Werle in *The Wild Duck*, Eilert Lovborg in *Hedda Gabler*, as well as many modern plays. More recently he played Buckingham in *Richard III* and the title role in *King Lear* for the National Theatre (London and world tour, 1990–91). A great range of television work includes *Rat in the Skull*, *The Devil's Crown*, *The Cloning of Joanna May*, *Redfox*, *Six Characters in Search of an Author*, and *Inspector Morse*. His more recent films have been *Hidden Agenda*, *Secret Weapon*, and *Shadow in the Sun*. His autobiography (and account of his teaching experiences with students of the Moscow Arts Theatre School) *Salem to Moscow: An Actor's Odyssey* was published in 1991.

Titus Andronicus – the most berated of Shakespeare's tragedies. All the debates of scholarship come into play whenever the authorship and value of this apprentice masterpiece are discussed. In this essay I shall not attempt further to grace this debate except to state that in my view *Titus Andronicus* was most assuredly written by William Shakespeare and by William Shakespeare alone.

I describe the play as an 'apprentice masterpiece' in this respect: just as an apprentice carpenter of the period would prepare and create for himself a test piece, thereby attaining his final articles before becoming a fully fledged practitioner of his craft, so in much the same way *Titus Andronicus* was Shakespeare's test piece, a test piece and template for all the great tragedies that were to follow – *Lear*, *Othello*, *Hamlet*, and *Macbeth*. Just as the apprentice would create a formula piece, such as an infant's high chair, so Shakespeare's formula was to write within the style and structure of the revenge drama of the time. Performing within this structure one becomes increasingly aware of the genius of the writer. The apprentice carpenter serves his master, but Shakespeare is his own apprentice and his own master. The disciplines he has created for himself are the disciplines which will exercise, and, paradoxically, exorcise, the spirit of his art and the ultimate meaning of the story he wants to tell, the story of Titus Andronicus.

As the apprentice works to create his test piece, his idiosyncratic nature and ability become fused with the practical necessities of the piece itself. So Shakespeare allows each individual scene of *Titus Andronicus* an idiosyncratic movement that beats through from scene to scene, act to act, and adheres quite carefully to the discipline he has imposed upon himself. After all, there are thirteen murders, four mutilations, and one rape during the course of the play. Shakespeare has created a very slender, but strong, tightrope of absurdity between comedy and tragedy – and the performer has to be very careful how he traverses that tightrope.

This understructure to the play seems to me the reason for writing it in the first place. What is it about, what are the deeper implications for the author? *Titus Andronicus* was written when Shakespeare was in his late twenties. The themes are honour, family, chauvinism, justice, cruelty, revenge, rape, and murder – a fairly bilious diet denoting an acute visceral sensibility, the work, I believe, of a very angry young man, a young man disaffected with the society of which he is a member, a young man with a killingly clear grasp of nihilism before the word 'nihilism' was ever thought of.

Titus Andronicus has survived grudgingly for four centuries because of the effect on its audiences within any given historical context during those four centuries. The absurdity of the play mirrors the absurdity of man's existence within systems he creates for himself to maintain that existence, and how those systems become a tyranny by which man traps and imprisons himself and which he finally rebels against and destroys; but the replacement systems in time also become a tyranny and thereby a never-ending cycle is created which becomes impossible to break.

In our century the context for this play has never been more powerful. When Peter Brook produced it in 1951 the shadow of totalitarianism was very much upon us: Stalinism and the purges of the thirties, Hitler's Germany and the subsequent revelations of the Nuremburg trials. And now we have the rise of Islamic fundamentalism, the breakdown of social units, the mindless violence of soccer hooliganism, the sectarian violence of Northern Ireland, the disaffection of individuals within society resulting in mass murder sprees, not to mention the ever-increasing rise in rape crimes over the last forty years.

This may seem an over-generalized spectrum of events relating to just one play by Shakespeare, but every one of those incidents has its parallel in *Titus Andronicus*. The nature of barbarous and civilized behaviour is extremely double-edged in the play. The conquered enemy, the Goths, are described as barbarous, yet the first questionable action of a barbarous nature comes from the allegedly civilized Romans, the ritual slaughter of Alarbus, the eldest of Tamora's sons, killed because of his nobility as a warrior. In Titus's view this is a religious sacrifice; in Tamora's it is cruel and irreligious. The parallel is with Irish Catholic versus Irish Protestant, perhaps – one man's civilized behaviour becomes another man's barbarity. This becomes the central question of *Titus Andronicus*: why does man lose his organic connection with his own life-force? I had a letter from someone during our run of the play saying what a chronicle of our age it is, and I know a lot of people felt this. This is why I think the play is so extraordinary now, why it so caught audiences. This was only the third significant production of it in half a century, and perhaps it caught the right moment when we can respond to its terrible laughter without diminishing its horror.

Playing Titus was a unique experience in that the part was relatively uncharted. Actors over the years have put their stamp on many Shakespearian roles, which for each succeeding generation of players then present a new challenge. Olivier marked Richard III's card for a very long time – until Tony Sher came along and invented a wholly new image – as did Gielgud with Richard II and Hamlet. Of course, Titus was successful for Olivier too in Brook's sumptuous production, but the text was cut and reworked and the humour of the play studiously rationalized.

When I was asked to play the role in the 1987–88 season at Stratford I was initially uneasy, before I'd read the play, because of its blood-and-guts reputation – the death-wish of its generation and yet one of the most popular plays of the period – but when I started work on it I began to realize its many hidden values. Its post-war history in Stratford has been a chequered one. After Peter Brook's production in 1951 it was not seen again until 1972 when Trevor Nunn directed a fairly full Roman-pomp production with the late, great, Colin Blakely (who was, I believe, magnificent). Then John Barton directed a heavily cut production which made up part of an ill-conceived double bill with *The Two Gentlemen of Verona* in 1981. In discussions with Terry Hands, the Artistic Director of the RSC, it seemed important that whoever was to direct *Titus Andronicus* this time around needed not to be forced into preconceptual judgements of the play, and that it required someone fresh and fearless who would allow the play its own identity. Such a director was Deborah Warner. In more than twenty years of working in the theatre I have never witnessed such an auspicious beginning. The coolness and authority with which she allowed the play to grow were awesome. Deborah's methods are egalitarian, thereby harnessing the total input of the whole cast. The process is extremely tiring, as democracy can be, but effective, since it creates a responsibility within the ensemble towards the play as a totality and not just to the individual characters, with the result that a lot of the staging ideas came very quickly in rehearsal.

The most significant example of this was the discovery of how to kill Lavinia, which happened at the first read-through. We were sitting in chairs to read and we didn't put a chair out for Lavinia because (obviously) she doesn't have any lines in the later part of the play. But she is supposed to be in the scenes so, naturally, dutifully, the actress playing Lavinia (Sonia Ritter) came in – and found nowhere to sit. So I asked her to sit on my knee and as she was sitting there I realized that this image, this classic image of parent and child, was also an image of vulnerability and of potential brutality. You could do incredible damage, you could poke somebody's eyes out, when they are that close, trusting you as a little child, a little animal, might trust you. It suddenly occurred to me that this would be perfect for breaking her neck, this close and this intimate. There was something about the image that was tender but at the same time ultimately brutal, and I started really from that point. The whole of the creation of Titus came from that one image of a man sitting in a chef's outfit with a little girl on his knee, about to break her neck like a chicken. It contained the world of tragedy and comedy and the whole middle ground of ludicrousness, of man's ludicrous journey through life which seems to me so important in the play. Because, if you think about it, so much of life is ludicrous: it has its high and low points, its points of passion, romance, comedy, tragedy, but for quite a lot of the time – it's ludicrous. And that image, from so early in rehearsal, seemed to catch that.

The play of *Titus Andronicus* is often described as lacking spiritual depth. One of the main facets of Titus's character, however, is that he is a spiritual bankrupt and his journey through the play is to confront and come to terms with this spiritual bankruptcy. Titus is a general, a warrior, a soldier, a trained killer, trained to kill for Rome. His allegiance to Rome has superseded any domestic, social, or personal affiliations he may have had: Rome is the centre of his life. Twenty-five sons and one daughter he has sired. Twenty-one of these sons are already dead, killed in the service of Rome. Through his overweening pride in the victorious dead of his own house we witness a man who has become brutalized and disconnected from a true sense of parental love. The links to his children, particularly Lavinia, are sentimental. He has destroyed the feminine within himself. His preoccupations are with death, honour, retirement; he is a man who instinctively wants to retire the field while ahead of the game, but who will be forced to pay the price for the self-brutalization of his own nature.

Along with this sense of the brutality and the horror, though, must go that element of the ludicrous. The vaudeville aspect of the part was very important to me, making the character much more accessible than he otherwise would be. He is a consummate actor, putting on, it seems to me, particularly in the early scenes, a wonderful kind of wilful senility: 'O, I'm too old; I don't know' – he does a lot of 'losing the place'. The sense of the vaudevillian in these opening scenes comes largely from the fact that they are played out to the audience, with almost no interplay between characters. It's all addressed out front; the image of Archie Rice is much stronger than the image of Hamlet. The entry to Rome, the great warrior returning, has irresistible undertones of the performer coming back, the famous actor meeting his audience again: 'I'm so tired, and it's so hot, but my public is waiting . . .' – and the public, the audience, is Rome.

Here, at the beginning of the play, we see Titus at the height of his power, the conquering hero returning from a ten-year campaign against the Goths. Born aloft on the yoke of his prisoners, battle-scarred, exhausted, a touch senile, he enters in triumph. For our production this image, too, came from early in the rehearsal process. I felt he should be at his highest point (quite literally) and that the boys, Tamora's boys, his victims, should be trussed up like pieces of meat, so that you didn't know, at first, that they were absolutely debased. Hence that metal ladder on which they carried him in. The process of getting onto that ladder and sitting on it with the boys' heads sticking through immediately made him a kind of grandiose figure but also slightly comic as well. This idea comes, probably, from my own roots, from constantly looking at things through a slightly comic kaleidoscope. Greatness and absurdity are so constantly connected. There is the greatest sailor of all time, Nelson on his column in Trafalgar Square, but the ludicrous thing is that a bird will sit on his head and shit on it and there's nothing at all he can do about it. That idea seems to me relevant to Titus. He has done everything for Rome and now he wants to retire. With twenty-five sons he may not have noticed which ones were dying, but with only four left he knows well enough now. He wants to retire, he feels he's had it, but the play is going to make him pay for the life he has led. One of the first ideas I had was of a statue that had corroded – the face gone, cracked, bits showing through. This was where the mud make-up came from: a man caked in mud, like a miner caked in the grime of his trade, a particular kind of workhouse. Titus has campaigned so much, has spent so much of his life on the road; he is no longer a human personality, he has become a kind of machine. That is what is carried in on that ladder in the first scene. He is weary; done-all, seen-all, just waiting to go out to grass.

There is still, however, a price to be paid. Shakespeare insists on that: as a young writer he was particularly moralistic. This man is not going to be let off the hook, not allowed to go out to grass. This shambling statue, this disintegrating edifice, is only the start. The man who has destroyed the feminine in himself must now try to go through a journey of reconnection, of rediscovery of values. His first value was Rome, but Rome has changed – they have moved the goalposts of Titus's Rome a long time before. And so there we see him, sitting on his ladder, in this incredibly vain entry – for I think he is vain, with a powerful sense of his own achievements. At this point he is monstrously egocentric: 'things are done in this way because *I* say so, and we do it for *Rome*'. He has always been a servant, but, like all servants, all butlers, he actually runs the show, knows more about it than the master does. 'Patience, Prince Saturninus', he says (i.i.203), commanding the future emperor without reflecting on it, but the next moment kneeling to him, vowing service. Like all soldiers (RSMs or generals), he needs to serve.

Because of his popularity, Titus's own name is entered in the lists of contenders for empery. He declines the opportunity, self-mockingly stating his age and feebleness as the reasons for his inadequacy. He is also aware of his limitations. He has been a soldier too long, and a successful one. What is a soldier if not a trained killer? For a moment we have echoes (or, rather, preechoes) of Macbeth. Both Macbeth and Titus are soldiers, soldiers and generals, Macbeth younger and with more ambition to become king. But soldiery is what he is best at, the job most fitting his sensibilities. After his disastrous kingship Macbeth's moment of glory comes when once again he dons the armour of the soldier warrior and goes to his death as the person he really is and was meant to be, a man who excels at what he does best – being a soldier.

The story of Macbeth might be described as that of a man ambitious for the wrong job. So, too, was Titus, but because of his age and experience he avoids taking the wrong job and his path to self-realization is therefore more brutal. Unlike Macbeth he has no aspirations. He is what he is: he knows about campaigning, about the legalized aspects of killing men, for reasons of honour, imperialism, and all the other monstrous values that prompt men to do such things.

Saturninus becomes Emperor and his direct impetuous action is to take Lavinia as his wife, although she is already betrothed to his brother Bassianus. Titus's condition of servile stoicism complies with this action, which he views only too happily as a reward for his service to the state. Without these codes of behaviour and rules of state he would be lost, and in the next few minutes he will frantically invoke these rules, first with the rebuttal of the just claim of Bassianus to Lavinia; then the callous murder of his youngest son Mutius; then Saturninus's rejection of Lavinia in preference for Tamora, Queen of the Goths; and finally Titus's initial refusal and final submission to having Mutius buried in the family vault. In this rapid sequence of events we watch Titus steadfastly holding on to the book of law and that book being tossed aside by Saturninus to suit his own purposes; Titus's being governed by his own preconditioned allegiance to the state in his imperviousness to his daughter's happiness, and that imperviousness even further magnified in the killing of Mutius. He doesn't even notice that he's killed him, he's not aware of it at first. It is only an impediment that must be removed, like an impediment in war: here are five bridges that must be destroyed; it just happens that there are 1,200 people crossing them at the time, but the impediment must still be removed. That is the soldier mentality, and the horror of it is shot through with the ludicrous, the deeply silly.

Titus has seen it all before and he has long since ceased to be affected by it. He is ripe for a fall. His mistake at the start of the play is the mistake of the arch conservative, a refusal to recognize that the role he was so passionately wedded to has atrophied and no longer exists. A wind of change is needed and he refuses to acknowledge it; hence his holding to the idea of succession by primogeniture and his support for the unstable Saturninus. He has retired and quite clearly abdicated responsibility to the edifice he has helped to maintain, the edifice of Rome. In the course of this first scene his loyalty to a vanished idea of Rome, and to the Emperor he has so foolishly created in deference to it, prompts him to give his daughter away to Saturninus:

> Kind Rome, that hast thus lovingly reserv'd
> The cordial of mine age to glad my heart.
> (1.i.165–6)

Thus he greets Lavinia's arrival; and it's all *me* (and Rome), nothing about Lavinia. And the first thing he does is to treat her like a piece of property in a meat market. Even his brother Marcus protests as he takes her from Bassianus. Brutality and absurdity again combine, again storing up debts which have to be expiated. During the rest of the play we watch him trying to rebuild his connection with his daughter. It has to be a real connection and not a sentimental one, for the sentimental always debases real emotion. (One sees this in *King Lear*, where the danger of sentimentalizing the father–daughter relationship is particularly important.) The real relationship between parent and child is never sentimental; it is something far deeper and more mysterious than that. Titus treats his daughter in this first scene like a piece of property because Roman society permits him to do that. In attempting to remake the relationship Titus will find himself having to examine that society. His daughter is for him an idealized image and the society he has put his faith in, the society he has upheld, allows her to be defiled, to be desecrated; and he must try to come to terms with that.

The stone-like edifice that Titus presents to the world, that is carried in on that ladder at the beginning, must be broken into to discover the tenderness encased within that embossed exterior. This is wonderful; this is where the poetic element of the play takes over. But it is only momentary, this inner discovery. Titus is too far gone, too hardened, too wrong. His capacity for tenderness is too unformed, like a chicken still in the egg, not properly incubated. Nothing in his life has incubated. When he opens himself, therefore, in response to Lavinia's pain, it's too much, too shocking. It was not for nothing that audiences could not always take it: when members of the audience left the performance it was not, I think, because of the horrors of the play; they left because of the man's grief. Nobody can bear that – but he must go through it. That is the price he has to pay; and unfortunately it's too late. Like Ibsen's Brand, his self-discovery comes too late. Shakespeare doesn't save him. In the 'fly scene' (iii.ii) there is the hint of a possibility that Titus has found a sort of spiritual communion with Lavinia:

> Speechless complainer, I will learn thy thought;
> In thy dumb action will I be as perfect
> As begging hermits in their holy prayers:
> Thou shalt not sigh, nor hold thy stumps to heaven,
> Nor wink, nor nod, nor kneel, nor make a sign,
> But I of these will wrest an alphabet,
> And by still practice learn to know thy meaning.
> (iii.ii.39–45)

But even here, we decided, he actually misinterprets her simple desire for a drink – 'She says she drinks no other drink but tears' (line 37) – and the moment of possible communion vanishes into pain and horror again. No, no, the play says, you have to come to terms with what you are, and you have nearly done so through this girl, but what has happened has been too much. For what happens to this girl is the consequence of years and years of battering people into the ground; finally someone comes along and batters him. And they get him through his daughter, where he never expected it, and he is pushed over the edge. When he laughs instead of weeping he has gone over the edge and cannot then be saved. 'Why dost thou laugh?', his brother asks him, and he replies:

> Why, I have not another tear to shed:
> Besides, this sorrow is an enemy,
> And would usurp upon my wat'ry eyes,
> And make them blind with tributary tears:
> Then which way shall I find Revenge's cave.
> (iii.i.266–70)

Titus is pushed over the edge and the play becomes a tale of revenge. The horrors have mounted up and up and finally he is totally overwhelmed. There is a sense of him wanting to connect himself with something that is elemental here:

> I am the sea. Hark how her sighs doth blow;
> She is the weeping welkin, I the earth:
> Then must my sea be moved with her sighs;
> Then must my earth with her continual tears
> Become a deluge . . .
> (iii.i.225–9)

Here we are at the edge, and he can't take any more, and suddenly he starts to laugh and that laughter becomes a cue (and a clue) to how the next part of the play should take shape. And you need all your skills as an actor here to turn on a sixpence and change direction from the path you were on and take another, the path of gallows humour, of black, nihilistic humour, very twentieth-century in its mood – for in some ways this is the most modern of plays. Once you've made that turn there are immense new rewards to find in the role. Titus becomes a richly potent figure of nihilism, of destruction, of revenge, who keeps searching, searching for a justice he will never find, for justice has been long dead for him.

To say that he goes mad is to oversimplify. He is obviously on the verge of madness when the play starts, but the line between madness and sanity is a very fine one through all of Shakespeare's plays. For me, playing Titus, the mad state is when he is elevated to the point when he sees quite clearly what he has to do. The end is crystal clear, even though he pretends, and gets others to pretend with him, that other avenues (shooting the arrows, for example) should be tried first. After that laughter, after he has said that he has 'not another tear to shed', when the severed hand and heads are brought on, then he dies – in spirit. And he says to himself: 'Oh, I'm dead. I'm a dead man, and I can do whatever I like – because I'm dead.' That is really the cue. When you decide you're dead, nobody can harm you. He still has his pain, and his tasks to finish, of course, things to tidy, the end to achieve, but he is no longer vulnerable.

The fly scene marks this point of arrival in the play, another crossing-point of the tragic and the ludicrous of which the play presents so much, and which differentiates the part so sharply from the English classical tradition of acting. It is more in the tradition of Scottish vaudeville, of the Glasgow comedians with their sharp sense of reality. How can he kill that fly, that 'had a father and a mother'? (III.ii.60); yet two seconds later he is stabbing viciously at the same fly which has become 'like to the empress' Moor' (line 67). Where do I exist in that? How do I deal with that? This is a good thing, this is a bad thing – they are so easily said, but Titus can no longer deal with them and he sinks back into what he knows, the relentless trying to discover who raped his daughter, the only concrete thing for him to connect with. 'Come, take away' at the end of the scene (line 81) means superficially merely 'clear the table', but for me it means also 'get rid of this thing that's driving me to distraction (and to destruction); take it away, lift this burden from me'. There is only revenge left for him to hang on to. The interval in our production was placed here – at what seems to me a real watershed.

The second half of the play sees an accelerating journey towards the realization of revenge. The mud, the dirt, the crap are more obvious as the man neglects everything in pursuit of his end and more extreme images of the ludicrous emerged – a handkerchief on my head, knotted at the corners, like grandpa at the beach, an old string vest like a navvy. I felt that one had to be merciless in one's presentation of Titus here. I was not going to play him as a dear, hard-done-by, charming old man. There is real harshness here and it must be faced. The man has to be dragged over the coals, seen to be over the edge long before the final scene. One could, I suppose, make that last scene a leap, but I felt that one had to see a progression of images, of a man not caring, rolling around in mud, who hasn't washed, hasn't done anything, who's let himself go, as the household has gone, who's become crazy old Titus, locked up in his house. A man who had admitted, who had deliberately said: 'I am disastrous, therefore I shall be disastrous.' Titus punishes himself and these images of squalor were important for me – not least in the making of the final scene, with his clean, white chef's uniform, a sharp contrast for the celebration of revenge.

Through these scenes of madness and squalor, he tries to make himself concentrate, tries to stay with what he should be doing, discovering the identity of the rapists. It is interesting, however, that he has little to do in the scene where the discovery is made. He is merely an observer there; it is all done by Marcus. Titus takes no control – he's gone, away, contemplating the idea of revenge rather than the identity of its victims. The same seems to me true of the scene with the bows and arrows. In theory vengeance should be sought from the gods, so all right, we'll send the letters, and we'll see what happens. Of course he knows that nothing will happen, because the gods don't exist; he knows that, though he doesn't say it. The scene was funny for the audience, funny, but bleak. These were images I felt strongly committed to – the knotted handkerchief, the string vest, the lack of money to give the clown so he steals some from Marcus – all the little jokes that emphasize the bleakness of it all. For Titus is death-bound now; he knows it, and he's ready.

When he is visited by Tamora disguised as Revenge he is continuing the logic of his course, pursuing vengeance through the approved channels of communion with the gods. He is doing it all by the book – and they say he's mad. Of course he's mad; but society does this, his society did those things. 'Who doth molest my contemplation?' he asks (v.ii.9) and we have the most frightening kind of comically logical point of the play.

When Tamora comes in pretending she is Revenge we felt there was no need for the actress (Estelle Kohler) to be disguised. They all think he's mad, so there's no need to pretend. 'I'm revenge,' she says. 'No, you're not, you're Tamora, Queen of the Goths,' he replies.

> Know thou, sad man, I am not Tamora;
> She is thy enemy, and I thy friend.
> (v.ii.28–9)

And he, supposedly mad, ends up humouring her – 'Art thou Revenge?' – which shows the level of his deviousness and the fact that he can suck people up into his energy even while they think he's mad (as Hamlet does with Polonius). Titus is at one and the same time in the middle of the madness and yet capable of steering it, concentrating his energies to seek his ends, while she pushes him further towards the edge. And that energy and singleness of purpose leave him with the boys as his prisoners at the scene's end. Tamora thinks he's far gone. She doesn't understand what she has done in leaving her sons behind; no more do they; no more, really, does Titus, by this point, as the terrible logic of the play makes possible the achievement of his vengeance.

I was aware, as I played the scene with the boys, that members of the audience were thrilled that I had them, thrilled as I gripped their heads to expose their throats, thrilled at the revenge. The scene plays on certain yearnings in people, which is legitimate, truthful, and honest – and frightening. At a time when we seem to be rediscovering Victorian values in censorship, when television is under attack for its violence, the effect of this scene from this old play is extraordinary. You couldn't get anything more violent. We had held back in the production from showing much blood but here blood was spilled, unstintingly. To the horror, and to the delight, of the audience the blood of Demetrius and Chiron gushed into the bowl held between Lavinia's stumps and we moved into the final scene.

The final scene is a celebration, long anticipated for Titus, and there is something of the priestly about his part in it. This is the end, the last, and he sees himself as host: 'Why art thou thus attir'd?' asks Saturninus (v.iii.30) and Titus replies

> Because I would be sure to have all well
> To entertain your highness and your empress.

We felt it needed something celebratory and toyed at first with the idea of balloons. Because of the general spareness of the production it was clear that that wouldn't work and we then had the idea of using the work-song of Deborah Warner's Kick Theatre Company, the *Snow White* dwarves' song, 'Hi-Ho'. At first we intended to sing the words, but that seemed too much, so it was decided that the company should whistle the tune as the banquet is prepared. It was a risk, but I believe one worth taking – once again for its contribution to the play's sense of the ludicrous. It was also unsettling, and at this point it is important to unsettle the audience, to create something from a different space, a different place, a different genre. People attacked it, some have said it's the only thing they disliked in the production, but I thought it was vital. It unsettled the audience and prepared them for what was coming. And then, in full starched white chef's garb, I came in, leaping over the table, with the pie. The world had gone crazy; the audience's embarrassment about serving the boys in the pie was released in laughter – but laughter from which you could cut them off. You could allow another laugh in the welcome:

> Welcome, my lord; welcome, dread Queen;
> Welcome, ye warlike Goths; welcome, Lucius;
> And welcome, *all* . . .
>
> (v.iii.26–8)

– the last words addressed to the pie. The laugh there, the frisson of it, released the audience, since they immediately started questioning their reactions. The play has constantly walked the borderline between horror and laughter: 'You thought that was funny, well what about this?' – get people to laugh, and then kick them. 'Why, there they are, both baked in this pie; / Whereof their mother daintily hath fed' (v.iii.60). Sometimes that got a laugh, sometimes none at all. And then Tamora laughs in disbelief, and Titus laughs at her disbelief, and the audience is released to laugh again, only to be silenced by the terrible suddenness of the deaths. The real sensation of that was quite extraordinary, the visceral sense of it for the audience. It is so economic, this point of the play, that you have to pull the audience through it, really pull them, as though through the eye of a needle. They're waiting for it, but they don't know when it's going to be. From the greeting to the pie, through the killing of Lavinia, to the astonishing rapidity of the trio of deaths, is all profoundly theatrical, and you've got to go for it and not be afraid of it; be bold and audacious, because you've earned it. You can always be audacious in the theatre if you've earned it. It's as if you know what your cards are, and you've got the best hand, and you keep it, until you finally have the call. That's one of the things I learned from this play; that you can absolutely do that.

Titus Andronicus is a brilliant play. The more I did it, the more I discovered in it, and the more it yielded up. There is no final forgiveness for Titus, no final forgiveness in the play. Its last image is of the casting out of Tamora's body for the birds to peck at. All possibility of progress is destroyed by man's capacity for brutalization. Even poor old Marcus is reduced in the end to a kind of avenging figure. The man of integrity and reason, the man who can deal with the horrors of life if he can find a logic to them, discovers that there is no logic, just as there is no logic to the life of Titus. The play is asking deep, almost existential, questions. It is a very profound piece of work and the more I did it the more I realized that. It offers no philosophical weave to its questioning, as do *Hamlet* or *Lear*; it is spare, to the bone. Shakespeare simply sticks to his brief, and within it unfolds his horrific tale. It out-Bonds Bond. It is a cruel play, deliberately cruel. But, as we know from the history of our own century and the events of our own age, its harshness and horror are not incredible, and its ludicrousness tells a fearful truth. The way human life is prized, the value of man and of his destiny – these things have never been as severely under question as they are now. *Titus Andronicus* examines the values by which we live.

'These Violent Delights Have Violent Ends': Baz Luhrmann's Millennial Shakespeare

James N. Loehlin

James Loehlin's account of Baz Luhrmann's popular and influential 1996 film of Romeo and Juliet *emphasizes its modernity and its nostalgia. By considering the film's production and reception within the generic, non-Shakespearean context of the 'teen movie', Loehlin locates the cinematic text in commercial and aesthetic terms. His account of Luhrmann's 'characteristic technique of replacing or supplementing the verbal text with a cinematic equivalent' engages with a fundamental aspect of filmed Shakespeare: the translation of linguistic metaphors into visual ones.*

James N. Loehlin, '"These Violent Delights Have Violent Ends": Baz Luhrmann's Millennial Shakespeare, in *Shakespeare, Film, Fin de Siècle*, Mark Thornton Burnett and Ramona Wray (eds). London: Macmillan, 2000.

Baz Luhrmann's 1996 film, *William Shakespeare's 'Romeo + Juliet'*, is necessarily a central text for any consideration of Shakespearean film-making at the millennium.[1] Of all the Shakespeare film releases of the 1990s, it is the one most obviously oriented toward the twenty-first century. Along with its effective plundering of youth culture and its aggressive marketing toward a teenage audience, it employs post-modern aesthetic strategies that set it off from the substantial body of teen-star-crossed-lovers films from which it derives. Luhrmann's flashy, eclectic visual style and ultra-hip ironies earmark *William Shakespeare's 'Romeo + Juliet'* as *fin-de-siècle* spectacle; yet the gesture to bardic authority in the film's title, and the watery cocoon in which Luhrmann shelters his young lovers, evince a romantic nostalgia that is a surprising and poignant response to the frenetic excess of late twentieth-century culture.

Luhrmann's resetting of the play is explicitly millennial: 'Verona Beach' is a near-future urban dystopia of guns, drugs, conspicuous consumption and civic breakdown. Filmed in Mexico City, *William Shakespeare's 'Romeo + Juliet'* depicts a multiracial society where lavish wealth exists alongside grinding poverty, and the sensation-crazed, trigger-happy populace are kept in check only by police helicopters and riot squads. Social organization is a strange amalgam of late-model capitalism, Catholicism and feudalism: the smoggy skyline is dominated by a monumental statue of Christ flanked by the skyscrapers of the Capulet and Montague empires. The rival families are powerful factions whose members drive flashy cars with vanity licence plates (CAP 002, MON 005) and carry high-tech sidearms marked with the family crests. Despite this post-millennial setting, Luhrmann's basic approach to the story is not new: teenage lovers resist the corrupt values of their parents and so fall victim to a violent and uncaring society. The generation-gap emphasis of *William Shakespeare's 'Romeo + Juliet'* links it to a whole series of teen films from the 1950s forward.

The teen film was part of the emergence of a distinctive youth culture in the decades following the second world war. Unsupervised teenagers with time on their hands formed both a national social concern and a fertile commercial market. Hollywood responded to this phenomenon with some films that portrayed teens as menacing delinquents (such as *The Blackboard Jungle* and, to some extent, *The Wild One*), but just as often with films that showed them as sensitive idealists misunderstood by their shallow, vain and greedy parents.[2] Films like *Are These Our Parents?*, *Where Are Your Children?* and *Youth Runs Wild* placed much of the blame for teenage tragedies on the older generation, but the most influential of all was Nicholas Ray's 1955 *Rebel Without a Cause*. *Rebel* introduced the archetypes of James Dean as the troubled, brooding youth, Natalie Wood as the neglected daughter who falls for him, and Sal Mineo as his wealthy, emotionally wounded, presumably homosexual friend: a variation on the Romeo / Juliet / Mercutio triangle. Natalie Wood went on to play love-struck tragic teens in *Splendour on the Grass* and the Bernstein / Wise / Robbins musical, *West Side Story*, both in 1961. When Franco Zeffirelli released his immensely popular film of *Romeo and Juliet* in 1968, it joined a flourishing cultural tradition of young love crossed by parental opposition.[3] Historically, Romeo and Juliet had mostly been played by mature actors, as in the 1936 George Cukor film version, with Norma Shearer and Leslie Howard; Zeffirelli's stage and film versions of the play, along with *West Side Story*, redefined them as rebellious adolescents.[4] This tradition of star-crossed love extended beyond the movies to all aspects of youth culture, including rock-and-roll, which produced such tragic hits as 'Teen Angel' and 'Leader of the Pack' ('My folks were always putting him down / They said he came from the wrong side of town').[5]

William Shakespeare's 'Romeo + Juliet' repeatedly associates itself with this tradition. The sweet-faced young leads, Claire Danes and Leonardo DiCaprio, came to the film with established credentials as misunderstood adolescents (*My So-Called Life*, *This Boy's Life*, *The Basketball Diaries*). The Montague and Capulet parents are played as wealthy, status-conscious and stereotypically out of touch with their children. Gloria Capulet (Diane Venora) is a chain-smoking, pill-popping trophy wife with no time for her daughter's problems; Ted Montague (Brian Dennehy) watches Romeo gloomily out of the tinted window of his limousine, unable to speak to his son. Luhrmann conceived Romeo in terms of the teen film archetype: 'In a way, he was the original rebel without a cause, the first James Dean. He is someone who is a young rebel in love with the idea of love itself.'[6] The first shots of DiCaprio in the film, wandering the beach to avoid his parents, replicate the tilted head, hanging forelock and introspective squint of Dean's Jim Stark. DiCaprio's anguished cry – 'Then I defy you, stars!' – perhaps unconsciously, exactly matches the tone and cadences of Dean's trademark outburst, 'You're tearing me apart!'[7] Luhrmann follows *West Side Story* in recasting Shakespeare's feuding families as rival gangs; his Montague and Capulet boys duplicate not only the ethnic affiliations (Anglo and Latino) but also the colour schemes (gold and blue versus black and red) of the Jets and Sharks.[8] Romeo and Tybalt's duel even includes an automotive 'chicken run', recalling that in *Rebel Without a Cause*. Yet Luhrmann's film distances itself from the teen film tradition by virtue of the qualities that mark it as a postmodern production: an aggressively fragmented aesthetic, a highly self-conscious, ironic intertextuality and a cynical fatalism tinged with nostalgia.[9]

The film's frenzied camera movement, staccato editing and pop music score led many critics to compare it to the quintessential postmodern product, MTV.[10] Luhrmann, together with his cinematographer, Donald McAlpine, and editor, Jill Bilcock, uses a whole range of self-conscious cinematic tricks and rock-video flourishes. The film reels with dizzying hand-held shots, slam zooms and swish pans, as well as the changing film speeds, jump cuts and lush, unnatural saturation of colour that made Luhrmann's one previous picture, *Strictly Ballroom*, so visually distinctive. *William Shakespeare's 'Romeo + Juliet'* foregrounds its own status as a mediated representation; it wears its visual bravura on its sleeve, begins and ends as a television broadcast, and sets several scenes in an abandoned cinema, the Sycamore Grove.[11] The film features an elaborate sound design with sophisticated layering and sampling, amplified sound effects and a wide range of musical styles, including many alternative pop songs commissioned especially for the film and incorporating lines from the play, such as the pounding hardcore rap of 'Pretty Piece of Flesh' by One Inch Punch. This sonic and visual flair is needed to balance out weaknesses in the film, notably the vocal shortcomings of the cast. For the most part, the actors speak with toneless naturalism, their reedy voices flattening out the elaborate poetic conceits of one of Shakespeare's most self-consciously verbal plays. In the tradition of innovative Shakespearean filmmakers like Welles and Kurosawa, Luhrmann finds visual and aural replacements for the lost poetry. Claire Danes doesn't do much with Juliet's wish to take Romeo 'and cut him out in little stars' (III.ii.22), but she is backed up by Stina Nordenstam's haunting song, 'Little Star', and the lines recall the film's image of Juliet, in white party dress and angel's wings, standing dreaming on her balcony, with slow-motion fireworks drifting like stars around her head. Leonardo DiCaprio mumbles through Romeo's premonition that 'Some consequence yet hanging in the stars / Shall bitterly begin his fearful date / With this night's revels' (I.iv.107–9), but Luhrmann supports him with a brief, eerie flash-forward to Romeo walking among the shimmering candles and dying flowers of Juliet's tomb. Luhrmann replaces the linguistic complexity of the play with cinematic wit of equivalent virtuosity: his delight in his own medium matches the young Shakespeare's, even while the poetry dies in his teen actors' mouths.

One of the chief aesthetic devices of *William Shakespeare's 'Romeo + Juliet'*, and one of the hallmarks of postmodern cinema, is intertextuality – the reference to other works, genres and styles, whether as homage, parody, simple imitation or even unconscious duplication.[12] Luhrmann's film is a compendium of references to twentieth-century popular culture. His avowed intention in creating this bricolage was simply clarity:

> The idea behind the created world was that it's a made-up world comprised of twentieth-century icons, and these images are there to clarify what's being said ... The idea was to find icons that everybody comprehends, that are crystally, overtly clear. The hope was that by associating the characters and places with those images, then what is being said is freed from its cage of obscurity.[13]

However, the overlapping and intersecting meanings of Luhrmann's allusions actually do much to complicate and enrich the film. *William Shakespeare's 'Romeo + Juliet'* continually and playfully juxtaposes contemporary kitsch with the high-culture world of Shakespeare, classical music and Renaissance art and architecture. In Catherine Martin's Fellini-inspired production design, the phantasmagorical mixes with the social real in a wealth of telling details.[14] The Capulet mansion is a Florentine palazzo, decked out for the masked ball with Christmas lights and metal detectors at the gates. Capulet and his wife host the party costumed as Antony and Cleopatra: grotesque parodies of great Shakespearean lovers, complete with garish makeup, sweaty toga and glittering gold dress. Luhrmann delights in forcing Shakespearean language and ideas into his squalid late capitalist world: the gangs wield flashy handguns with brand names like 'Rapier' and 'Sword 9 mm'; Romeo and his friends hang out at the Globe Theatre pool hall; a billboard advertises Prospero Scotch Whiskey ('Such Stuff as Dreams Are Made On'). Friar Laurence's message fails to reach Romeo in Mantua through the incompetence of an overnight delivery service called 'Post Haste Dispatch'.[15] In spite of these satirical touches, the film is far from being the kind of all-out cynical parody of Lloyd Kaufmann's *Tromeo and Juliet*, discussed elsewhere [in *Shakespeare, Film, Fin de Siècle*] by Margaret Jane Kidnie. Luhrmann's attitude towards its Shakespearean source is often quite reverential. He retains much of the text that Zeffirelli left out, including the Friar's meditation on plants in II.iii, the complex bantering exchanges between Romeo and his friends in I.i and II.iv, and much of Juliet's 'Gallop apace' and potion speeches (III.ii and IV.iii). As Luhrmann's title suggests, the film depends on the cultural authority of Shakespeare even as it playfully undermines it.[16]

The opening sequence of *William Shakespeare's 'Romeo + Juliet'* provides a good instance of the film's intertextual allusiveness: its combination of parody and bardolatry nicely encapsulates Luhrmann's ambivalent attitude towards his sources. Shakespeare's prologue is read by a news anchorwoman on a low-tech, 1970s era television which hangs suspended in darkness, then gradually moves forward until it fills the screen. The anchorwoman (played by a real TV newsreader, Edwina Moore) uses the sympathetic but upbeat, half-smiling style characteristic of local broadcasts, and reads the lines with sincere banality. Over her shoulder is a projected headline icon reading 'Star-Cross'd Lovers' and showing Romeo and Juliet's broken wedding ring. At the line, 'the two hours' traffic of our stage' (Prologue, 12), the film cuts to a montage of urban violence, backed by a bombastic choral piece, a pastiche of Orff's 'O Fortuna' entitled 'O Verona'. Over this, a deep, grave, Shakespearean-sounding male voice repeats the words of the prologue, which now appear on the screen in the film's trademark baroque font (the uncredited voice sounds like that of Pete Postlethwaite, who plays Friar Laurence, an RSC veteran and the most 'authentic' Shakespearean in the cast). As the montage reaches a frenzied climax, the words are again flashed at unreadable speed, followed by the film's title, *William Shakespeare's 'Romeo + Juliet'*. This doubled presentation of the prologue, once in a cheeky pop-culture parody, once with grave seriousness and an earnest bow to textual authority, sums up the film's divided approach to the chaotic world of Verona Beach and the timeless tragedy of the lovers.

The brawl scene that follows continues the postmodern tendency toward pastiche, parody and pop culture. The Capulet / Montague feud is rendered in the style of action-film *auteurs*, Sergio Leone and John Woo. Guitar chords and eerie whistlings evoke Ennio Morricone's trademark western scores, while close-up slow-motion and freeze-frame shots of Tybalt lighting a cheroot, then crushing out the match with the silver heel of his cowboy boot, quote shots of Clint Eastwood in *A Fistful of Dollars* and Charles Bronson in *Once Upon a Time in the West*. The freeze-frame introduction of the characters with onscreen titles ('Tybalt Capulet, Prince of Cats, Juliet's Cousin') recalls the opening of *The Good, the Bad and the Ugly*. Once the showdown starts, the fast editing, changing camera speeds, and especially the slow-motion shots of the leaping Tybalt firing two guns at once, are clearly a parody of, or homage to, the Hong Kong director, John Woo. Luhrmann's use of flashy action-film devices both engages and distances the audience – we vicariously experience the intoxication fun of violence, while being perfectly aware that this is a spectacle staged for our pleasure. The later fight between Mercutio and Tybalt is staged very differently, in *cinéma vérité* style, with a hand-held camera thrust among the awkwardly scuffling combatants – a device Zeffirelli also used in his version of the fatal duel.

The pervasive keynote of hip irony returns again and again throughout the film. Romeo laboriously writes out his Petrarchan conceits in a journal ('O brawling love, O loving hate, / O anything of nothing first create!' [I.i.174–5], then impresses Benvolio with his poetic romanticism by seeming to invent them *extempore*. Gloria Capulet's metaphorical praise of Paris as a book of love – 'Read o'er the volume of young Paris' face' (I.iii.81) – is mocked by a magazine cover showing a smiling Dave Paris as 'Bachelor of the Year'. Romeo and his friends learn of the Capulet ball, not from a servant, but by watching an *Entertainment Tonight*-type TV show, whose garish hostess winks the camera an invitation: 'if you be not of the house of Montagues . . . come and crush a cup of wine' (I.ii.81–2).

Not all of the film has this degree of wit and invention. Sometimes Luhrmann's allusions seem to be merely failures of imagination, simple replications rather than pointed reworkings. His frequent borrowings from Zeffirelli's *Romeo and Juliet* tend to fall in this category. Harold Perrineau's Queen Mab speech, for instance, is a clumsy copy of John McEnery's from the earlier film, though making 'Queen Mab' a hallucinogenic pill on Mercutio's forefinger is an inspired touch. Perrineau builds to misogynistic fury on the account of Mab's nocturnal assaults on maids, then repeats his final 'This is she' (I.iv.95) in rage and confusion, whereupon Romeo's hand on his shoulder causes him to start and wheel towards the camera in startled recollection of his senses. The sequence matches the exchange between John McEnery and Leonard Whiting almost shot for shot, down to the blue light haloing the two young men as Romeo embraces Mercutio to calm him down. The real revelation of Perrineau's Mercutio comes immediately after, in the party scene, where he vogues through a glitzy camp performance of 'Young Hearts Run Free' that combines Busby Berkeley with *Paris is Burning*. This memorable performance, atop a brightly lit staircase, in high heels, spangled bra and Jean Harlow wig, serves the structural function of the Mab speech, encapsulating the brilliancy, imaginative energy and homosocial bonding of Mercutio's world, just before Romeo meets the woman who will draw him away from it. The whole sequence exemplifies Luhrmann's characteristic technique of replacing or supplementing the verbal text with a cinematic equivalent.

The balcony scene begins as a witty parody of Zeffirelli, playing on the audience's conventional expectations for the scene. In mid-long shot, Romeo emerges from the foliage into a dreamy, moonlit Renaissance courtyard; the camera angle, lighting and mood match Zeffirelli's treatment of the scene exactly. Suddenly the courtyard is bathed in searchlights: Romeo has set off the security system's motion detector, and he trips over the poolside furniture in a clumsy panic. Collecting himself, Romeo climbs a trellis toward Juliet's balcony, where a shadowy form appears on the illuminated curtains. No sooner has Romeo intoned, 'It is the east and Juliet is the sun!' (II.ii.3), than the windows are flung open to reveal the portly middle-aged Nurse; meanwhile, Juliet walks out of an elevator next to the swimming pool. Romeo's approach to the startled Juliet ends up tumbling both of them into the pool, where Romeo must hide underwater while Juliet smiles winningly at a bemused security guard who comes to investigate.

The parodic comedy of the first part of the scene frees the young actors from expectations of grand and lyrical passion. Having invoked and discarded the traditional trappings of the famous love duet, Luhrmann can film an appealing scene about two wide-eyed kids in a swimming pool. Whispering and kissing in a tight close-up, Danes and DiCaprio are convincingly love-struck, and the awkwardness and danger of their situation excuse the low-key approach to the poetry. They communicate their desire not with their words but with their eyes, which appear huge and shining in the surreal light from the pool.

This scene forms a crucial part of an ongoing visual metaphor associating the lovers with water. The first image of Juliet in the film, as described here in the screenplay, shows her face underwater: 'INT. JULIET'S BATHROOM. DAY. The still, serene, submerged features of a beautiful young girl. Dark floating hair gently frames the face. Heavy liquid eyes stare up through the water.'[17] A similar shot of Romeo's face submerged in a bathroom sink precedes his initial meeting with Juliet. They first see each other through a huge salt-water aquarium which forms the wall separating the men's and women's guest bathrooms at the Capulet mansion. The blue calm of the water, with its glowing tropical fish, replaces the deafening revelry of the party as the lovers stare at each other, entranced, through the glass. Luhrmann's use of water helps remove the lovers from the noisy and frenetic world of Verona Beach, sheltering their story in a silent element that seems outside of time.

Luhrmann's aquatic insulation of the lovers leans toward sentimentality, but it is actually part of the film's fatalism. Romeo and Juliet's love literally has no place in this world. Luhrmann reminds us of this repeatedly through brutal editing that shatters his lovers' idylls. During the 'Gallop apace' speech (III.ii.1–31), Juliet's enraptured face fills the screen as she calls on the night to bring her Romeo; the image is suddenly replaced by a shocking match cut of Romeo's face, bloody and contorted with hate as he races his car after Tybalt in the 'chicken run' duel. When Romeo shoots Tybalt, Luhrmann intercuts a half-second image of Juliet in her bedroom, as if hearing the shots. This effect is reversed in the morning scene (III.v). The camera glides slowly down on the twined, discreetly nude bodies of the lovers, again recalling Zeffirelli's film; a sudden cut to Tybalt's bullet-riddled body jerks Romeo awake in terror. The lovers' private world is always vulnerable to the sudden intrusion of violent death.

William Shakespeare's 'Romeo + Juliet' is a love story for a generation that can't imagine a future, and this is what sets it off so completely from the teen-star-crossed-lovers films it otherwise resembles. *Rebel Without a Cause* ends with a rehabilitation of the older generation, and a hope for better communication. *West Side Story* ends with Maria's passionate denunciation of the cycle of violence the gangs have been perpetuating. Zeffirelli's film focuses on the final reconciliation of the two households, who walk together in a moving and orderly funeral procession. In all of these films, the Romeo and Juliet characters are ahead of their time; their love points the way to a better future, a new unity beyond the greed, anger and factionalism of their parents' world. But Luhrmann's Romeo and Juliet live after their time. The film repeatedly associates them, not with the future, but with the past. At the Capulets' masked ball, the future is represented by the smiling, smug Dave Paris, the young business school type, who is costumed as an astronaut. Romeo and Juliet, by contrast, are dressed as a knight in shining armour and a Botticelli angel; costumes that look nostalgically back to a cultural past that could embrace their love. Throughout the film they wear simple clothes in blue, silver and white, making them appear watery and spectral amid their gaudy surroundings. It is only in their timeless underwater world that they can shut out the frenetic present of Verona Beach and sustain their love.

Accordingly, the tomb scene is completely isolated and self-contained, intruded upon by neither Paris nor the Friar. Romeo, dodging police helicopters and machine guns, breaks into the church where Juliet's body is laid, and suddenly he is in another world. Hundreds of candles and blue neon crosses give the tomb a shimmering aquatic glow, as if Romeo an Juliet were indeed underwater. This beautiful refuge is the scene of the film's final, cruelly cynical trick on the self-immersed young lovers. Juliet stirs and wakes, smiling to see Romeo with her; too wrapped up in his grief to notice, he drinks the poison just as her hand reaches up to stroke his cheek. The device of having Juliet awake before Romeo dies was common in the eighteenth century, and was apparently used in a 1916 film with Theda Bara.[18] None the less, its effect here is profoundly shocking and painful. For a few tortured seconds the lovers try to cling together in life, staring at each other in horrified realization. Kenneth Rothwell aptly describes these cruel moments as breaking through the romantic isolation Luhrmann has previously afforded his lovers: 'In an ironic way the last scene critiques the narcissism the movie might elsewhere be seeming to uphold.'[19]

Alone with Romeo's corpse, Juliet sobs for a moment, then pulls out his pistol. She fumbles slightly with the hammer, which makes a frighteningly loud click in the silent tomb, then puts the gun to her head and shoots herself. After the double suicide, the watery romantic isolation of the lovers returns for a poignant moment. The last phrases of Wagner's 'Liebestod' from *Tristan und Isolde* play during an overhead shot of the bodies surrounded by a sea of candles. Once again Romeo and Juliet are associated with a mythic medieval past of chivalry and courtly love, rather than the raucous present of the rest of the film. Juliet's violent suicide is washed over by the ecstatic love-death of Isolde, swooning in bliss on the body of her lover: 'ertrinken, versinken – unbewußt – höchste Lust!' ('To drown, to sink – unconscious – highest pleasure!').[20] As the camera floats over the entwined lovers, the film cuts to a brief montage of their happy moments together, concluding with a slow-motion shot of them kissing under water. As the Wagner fades from the soundtrack, the screen whites out, then resolves to a bleak image of two shrouded corpses on hospital gurneys being loaded into an ambulance.

The film ends with this harsh and reductive scene. The Capulet and Montague parents, emerging from their limos in front of the church, look stunned and bleary in the pre-dawn light, but make no move towards each other. Luhrmann's film offers neither the orderly reconciliation of Zeffirelli's ending, nor the distancing irony of Michael Bogdanov's stage version, where the families continued their rivalry in the competing public relations gestures of erecting golden statues of their dead children. The deaths of Luhrmann's Romeo and Juliet bring no resolution; they become merely another lurid image for a media-besotted culture, body-bagged victims in a grainy news video, as the film returns to the newscast framework of the opening. The bland anchor-woman recites the closing words of the epilogue, then moves on to the next story as the TV screen dissolves in static snow.

The grim conclusion of *William Shakespeare's 'Romeo + Juliet'* signals a fatalis-tic acceptance of the triumph of the postmodern world of Verona Beach. There is no refuge for the lovers, even in romantic death; their idyll is interrupted, reduced, commodified, turned into televised spectacle. Yet Luhrmann's final pessimism seems to smack slightly of bad faith, given the film's involve-ment in a whole range of mediated commercial practices. Unlike previous Shakespeare films, *William Shakespeare's 'Romeo + Juliet'* relates not only back to an authorizing text but forward and outward to a whole network of cultural and commercial enterprises: merchandising tie-ins, two soundtrack albums, a screenplay / text edition and an interactive CD-ROM. The official Twentieth-Century Fox website features a 'Verona Beach Visitor's Guide' instructing users on 'what to wear, what to buy, and what to drive', as well as pop-psychology character biographies condemning the older generation: 'Lady Capulet really blew it and got into a co-dependency thing, while her husband abused her daughter, much to his later regret.'[21] At the UK *Romeo + Juliet* website, 'You can choose an alternate future for the star-cross'd lovers or go to Verona Beach school to learn more about the film and the play.'[22] Another website includes 230 'Signs that you are obsessed with *Romeo + Juliet*', among them:

7   You spend hours thinking up R + J merchandise – 'Montague and Capulet guns', 'Romeo and Juliet clothing line', 'The "Fair Verona" play-set (dolls included)' . . .

10   You used to check the Internet everyday to find out when the second soundtrack was coming out.

11   You suddenly have an obsession with angels, Catholic imagery and bright Hawaiian shirts.[23]

The distinctly commercial and materialist aspect of many responses to the film suggests that its young viewers were attracted largely by fashion, as well as by its heart-throb stars. The film was immensely successful with the teen audiences it carefully courted (test-marketers nervously asked young viewers 'whether the Shakespeare language in the film bothered you or not').[24] *William Shakespeare's 'Romeo + Juliet'* did well at the 1997 MTV Movie Awards, with Danes winning for Best Female Performance, along with nominations for Best Male Performance, Best On-Screen Duo, Best Song and Best Kiss. Peter Newman quoted a number of teenage responses in *Shakespeare Bulletin*, and some show a degree of sophistication: 'the scenes flip-flop from extravagance and grace to poverty and despair. Luhrmann uses every opportunity to display the tumult and passion of teenagers' lives'. But many teenagers seemed to approach the film at a lowest common denominator level: 'Orlando DiCaprio [*sic*] is hot!'; 'It was almost like watching an MTV video'; 'I thought it was going to be a girly film, but there was a lot of killing – that was cool'.[25] Needless to say, this response delighted Fox executives. 'From the very first screening, we knew it would attract younger audiences,' said Tom Sherak, head of distribution, after the film grossed a chart-topping $11.6 million in its opening weekend. 'If you don't believe this remains the greatest love story ever told, look at these numbers.'[26]

These somewhat depressing responses to the film do not necessarily invalidate Luhrmann's achievement. *William Shakespeare's 'Romeo + Juliet'* is a flagship Shakespeare film for the new millennium in part because it is able to assimilate and exploit the materials of contemporary culture, while keeping them in a relationship of provocative tension with the Shakespearean source. The lurid contemporary setting and the ageless love story criticize and comment on each other in ways that bring both into sharper relief. Like several of the films discussed in this volume, *William Shakespeare's 'Romeo + Juliet'* reinvents the conventions of Shakespearean filmmaking in a self-consciously postmodern way. Like Adrian Noble's *A Midsummer Night's Dream*, discussed by Mark Thornton Burnett, it interrogates the mythic status of the text by reframing it within a complex network of cultural associations. Like Christine Edzard's *As You Like It*, discussed by Amelia Marriette, it uses a contemporary urban setting to reverse audience expectations of Shakespearean 'prettiness' and to engage, in a limited way, with modern social concerns. Like Richard Loncraine's *Richard III*, discussed by Stephen Buhler, it quotes a range of cinematic styles and genres to create unsettling juxtapositions between different cultural modes.[27] And, as is the case with *Richard III*, I believe that the juxtapositions in *William Shakespeare's 'Romeo + Juliet'* – of teen films, MTV culture, various Hollywood genres and courtly romance – go beyond mere playful pastiche or ahistorical nostalgia.

Frederic Jameson, in his critiques of postmodernism, attacks what he calls 'the nostalgia film' for presenting a pastiche of past representational modes that is essentially detached from history.[28] According to Jameson, films like *American Graffiti*, *Chinatown* and *Body Heat* are not about a real historical past, but instead merely recreate the look and feel of existing representations of the past. By depending on an intertextual pastiche of other cultural productions, postmodernism has become divorced from history and from the real, 'as though we have become incapable of achieving aesthetic representations of our own current experience'.[29] *William Shakespeare's 'Romeo + Juliet'* seems in many ways to be susceptible to this critique. Not only does it exploit a whole range of cultural styles and *clichés*, but its use of teen film archetypes suggests a strong connection to the era Jameson most condemns as an artificial past, the Eisenhower 1950s of *Rebel Without a Cause*. Yet the intertextuality of *William Shakespeare's 'Romeo + Juliet'* goes beyond being a mere self-referential hodgepodge; Luhrmann confronts the social realities as well as the media modes of the new millennium. As Barbara Hodgdon has pointed out in a compelling paper, *William Shakespeare's 'Romeo + Juliet'* points to how 'there seem to be no answers, fictional or real, religious or legal, to gender, ethnic and class differences and conflicts, to generational strife, or boys with guns'.[30] The film's unresolved ending, with the lovers' timeless idyll reduced to a grim TV news item, is an honest response to the culture of the new millennium. The nostalgia with which Luhrmann enshrouds his Romeo and Juliet inevitably gives way to the violent and media-crazed culture of which they are, necessarily, already a part.

Notes

1   *William Shakespeare's 'Romeo + Juliet'*, directed by Baz Luhrmann, Twentieth-Century Fox, 1996. The film's title is noteworthy, not only for its claims to literary legitimacy in invoking the author's name, but for the use of the cross in place of 'and': both the standard formula for youthful love inscriptions ('Romeo + Juliet = Love 4 Ever') and an allusion to the Catholic iconography that dominates the production design. The cross thus functions as a small emblem of the film's juxtaposition of contemporary and historical sign-systems.

2   John Lewis, *The Road to Romance and Ruin: Teen Films and Youth Culture* (New York: Routledge, 1992), p. 3.

3   The story of doomed young lovers battling parental or societal opposition has been repeatedly reinvented by Hollywood in fascinating ways, from melodramas like *Splendour in the Grass* or Zeffirelli's *Endless Love* to crime odysseys like Terence Malick's classic *Badlands* or the Tarantino-scripted *True Romance*. (The archetype is also frequently recast in the comic mode, as in *Pretty in Pink*, *Say Anything* and their ilk, or the much darker *Heathers*.) The staggering success of Jim Cameron's *Titanic* must be blamed, in part, on the popularity of the *Romeo and Juliet* archetype, as well as on Leonardo DiCaprio's appeal as a teen tragic hero.

4 The treatment of the play as a contemporary socio-economic parable, in which the young lovers reject the materialist values of their parents' generation, became fairly common on the stage, most notably in Michael Bogdanov's 1986 modern-dress production for the Royal Shakespeare Company, which in many ways anticipated Luhrmann's film.

5 Michael Barson and Steven Heller, *Teenage Confidential: An Illustrated History of the American Teen* (San Francisco: Chronicle Books, 1998), pp. 88–9.

6 Baz Luhrmann, quoted in Twentieth-Century Fox promotional material, http//www.clairedanes.com/rjintro.html.

7 *Romeo and Juliet*, ed. Brian Gibbons (London and New York: Methuen, 1980), V.i.24. All further references appear in the text.

8 Race functions in the film in a somewhat ambiguous way. The Montagues and Capulets are plainly represented as Anglo and Latino, but Gloria Capulet (Diane Venora) and Juliet (Claire Danes) have fair hair and skin and do not use the Hispanic accents adopted by the other Capulet actors, including the Italian-American Paul Sorvino (Fulgencio Capulet) and the English Miriam Margolyes (Nurse). The character of Escalus, who mediates between the two households, is represented as an African-American police chief, Captain Prince; his kinsman, Mercutio (Harold Perrineau), is also African-American, but his other kinsman, the Governor's son, Dave Paris, is white (Paul Rudd). The other African-Americans in the film are not involved in the feud, and may be viewed as sympathetic to the lovers: they include the newscaster who frames the story (Edwina Moore), the diva who sings Romeo and Juliet's love ballad (Des'ree) and the boy chorister who sings at their wedding (Quindon Tarver). I am indebted here to the comments of Margo Hendricks and Barbara Hodgdon (in Hodgdon's 'Totally DiCaptivated: Shakespeare's Boys Meet the Chick Flick', a paper first presented at the International Shakespeare Conference, Stratford-upon-Avon, August 1998).

9 See Steven Conner, *Postmodernist Culture: An Introduction to Theories of the Contemporary* (Oxford: Basil Blackwell, 1989), pp. 73–81.

10 See Jay Carr, *Boston Globe*; Roger Ebert, *Chicago Sun-Times*; and Janet Maslin, *New York Times*: all 1 November 1996.

11 Luhrmann is explicit about his use of cinematic conventions: 'In fact, what we've done was set the film in the world of the movies. You will notice that the film changes in style very dramatically, echoing very recognizable film genres, from Busby Berkeley to 70s' naturalism to even European expressionism. These severe changes of style refer to cinematic worlds or looks or ideas that audiences are familiar with on some level; using them to construct this "created world" will hopefully produce an environment that can accommodate a stylized language and make it easier for the audience to receive this heightened language'. Baz Luhrmann, quoted in Twentieth-Century Fox promotional material, http://www.clairedanes.com/rjintro.html.

12 See Susan Hayward, 'Postmodernism', in *Key Concepts in Cinema Studies* (London: Routledge, 1996), pp. 259–72.

13 Baz Luhrmann, quoted in Twentieth-Century Fox promotional material, http://www.clairedanes.com/rjintro.html.

14   Martin sought to imitate 'the heightened reality of a Fellini film; the way
      that Fellini can have this incredible dream sequence in a particular situation
      that has an exceptional reality about it. They are always extraordinarily
      well observed'. Quoted in Twentieth-Century Fox promotional material,
      http://www.clairedanes.com/rjintro.html. The numerous helicopter shots of the
      monumental Christ statue overlooking the city may be a homage to the opening
      of Fellini's *La Dolce Vita*.
15   One such allusion – a building-site hoarding reading 'retail'd to posterity by
      Montague construction' – deserves special mention. It derives from a scene in
      Richard III (ed. Antony Hammond [London and New York: Routledge, 1990])
      where young Prince Edward, about to be sent to the Tower and his death, inno-
      cently discusses the history of the building with his treacherous uncles, Richard
      and Buckingham. Assured by Buckingham that the Tower's foundation by Julius
      Caesar is 'upon record', Edward goes on to moralize upon the importance of truth
      having an existence independent of historical evidence:

> PRINCE.   But say, my gracious lord, it were not register'd,
>   Methinks the truth should live from age to age,
>   As 'twere retail'd to all posterity,
>   Even to the general all-ending day.
> RICH.   [*Aside*] So wise so young, they say, do never live long.
> PRINCE.   What say you, uncle?
> RICH.   I say, without characters fame lives long.
>
>   (III.i.75–81)

By using 'retail'd' in its modern capitalist sense, and applying the doomed
prince's words to one of Montague's hastily erected skyscrapers rather
than the Tower of London, Luhrmann's film neatly pinpoints a postmodern world of transience and consumption, where truth lives not from
age to age, nor even from minute to minute, but only in a Jamesonian
perpetual present.

16   In the introduction to the published screenplay, Luhrmann performs the common
      directorial strategy of enlisting Shakespeare to justify his approach: 'Shakespeare's
      plays touched everyone, from the street sweeper to the Queen of England. He
      was a rambunctious, sexy, violent, entertaining storyteller. We're trying to make
      this movie rambunctious, sexy, violent, and entertaining the way Shakespeare
      might have if he had been a filmmaker.' Baz Luhrmann, 'A Note from Baz
      Luhrmann', in *William Shakespeare's 'Romeo & Juliet': The Contemporary Film, the
      Classic Play* (New York: Bantam Doubleday, 1996), p. i.
17   Luhrmann, *William Shakespeare's 'Romeo & Juliet': The Contemporary Film, the
      Classic Play*, p. 32.
18   Kenneth Rothwell, 'The Luhrmann *Romeo and Juliet*: Yesterday and Today, from
      Nickelodeon to Megaplex', p. 8, a paper prepared for the Shakespeare and
      Film Seminar, annual meeting of the Shakespeare Association of America,
      Washington D.C., March 1997.

19 Rothwell, 'The Luhrmann *Romeo and Juliet*', p. 8.

20 Richard Wagner, *Tristan und Isolde*, 1965. The film uses a recording by Leontyne Price.

21 http://www.romeoandjuliet.com.

22 http://www.geocities.com/Hollywood/Lot/1767/links.html.

23 http://www.geocities.com/Hollywood/9251/signs.html.

24 Quoted in Lynda E. Boose and Richard Burt, 'Totally Clueless?: Shakespeare Goes Hollywood in the 1990s', in Lynda E. Boose and Richard Burt (eds), *Shakespeare, the Movie: Popularizing the Plays on Film, TV, and Video* (London and New York: Routledge, 1997), p. 18.

25 Peter Newman, 'Luhrmann's Young Lovers as Seen by Their Peers', *Shakespeare Bulletin*, 15:3 (1997), pp. 36–7. The four comments quoted came respectively from L. A. and C. L., both aged 15, and M.S., aged 14.

26 Quoted in Judy Brennan, 'Where Art Thou? In First Place', *Los Angeles Times*, 4 November 1996.

27 See also James N. Loehlin, ' "Top of the World, Ma": *Richard III* and Cinematic Convention', in Boose and Burt (eds), *Shakespeare, the Movie*, pp. 67–79.

28 Frederic Jameson, 'Postmodernism and Consumer Society', in E. Ann Kaplan (ed.) *Postmodernism and Its Discontents* (London: Verso, 1988), pp. 18–20 and *Postmodernism: The Cultural Logic of Late Capitalism* (Durham, NC: Duke University Press, 1991), pp. 19–20.

29 Jameson, 'Postmodernism and Consumer Society', p. 20.

30 Hodgdon, 'Totally DiCaptivated'.

Index

366 *Index*